PENELOPE LEACH

BABYHOOD

INFANT DEVELOPMENT FROM BIRTH TO TWO YEARS

KU-247-580

PENGUIN BOOKS

Penguin Books Ltd, Harmondsworth, Middlesex, England
Penguin Books Australia Ltd, Ringwood, Victoria, Australia
Penguin Books Canada Ltd, 41 Steelcase Road West, Markham, Ontario, Canada
Penguin Books (N.Z.) Ltd, 182–190 Wairau Road, Auckland 10, New Zealand

—

First published 1975
Copyright © Penelope Leach, 1975

—

Made and printed in Great Britain by
Cox & Wyman Ltd, London, Reading and Fakenham
Set in Monotype Baskerville

For Melissa and Matthew:
The two babyhoods I know best

CONTENTS

LISTS OF
TABLES AND FIGURES

TABLES

FIGURES

ACKNOWLEDGEMENTS

A book of this kind relies on knowledge accumulated from so many sources that to thank each individual is impossible. The research work actually reported and therefore listed in the bibliography is only a small part of the whole. I gratefully acknowledge my debt to all the others.

Friends and colleagues have given most generously of their time and expertise in reading and criticizing drafts of the manuscript. In particular I should like to thank Drs Jane and Anthony Costello, Dr Corinne Hutt and Dr Richard Bell for their comments.

Without my husband Gerald Leach and Mrs Anne Hurry, the book really would not have been written. With her long experience of helping troubled children, Mrs Hurry helped me to sharpen my ideas about normal development. With his long experience of shaping research data, Gerald helped me to make the results into a book – and made sure that I did not get all my sums wrong! Neither of them has ever failed in their infectious enthusiasm for what I have tried to do.

Audrey Segal and Jennifer Kane strove to teach an amateur to index; I hope they succeeded. If they did not the fault is mine.

Alison Forbes was immensely helpful in tidying up the final draft.

Finally a very special thank you to Peter Wright of Penguin Books for all his help as friend, publisher and perceptive editor.

Despite all this help, the facts selected and the opinions expressed throughout the book remain my responsibility alone.

Penelope Leach
1974

INTRODUCTION

This book is about being a baby and becoming a toddler. It traces the rapid, varied, but always orderly sequence of changes which take any infant from a helpless parcelled newborn to a roving chattering child.

Babies have parents. They, or their substitutes, have to care for the child, do for him the myriad things he cannot do for himself, anticipate wishes which he can barely recognize let alone formulate, and keep the environment they provide and the demands they make in step with his growing maturity. This book is intended for them. But it is meant to provide them with something different from a handbook of advice on child rearing. It does not tell parents how to toilet train their baby; rather it sets out what is known about children's acquisition of control and hence the choices of timing and method which parents can make. It does not tell parents whether to give their baby a dummy; it discusses what sucking seems to mean to infants, and why dummies 'work' if they do. It does not only tell parents when their baby should sit up; it describes the sequence in which infants gain control of their wobbly necks and weak shoulders, until they reach a point where sitting alone is the next development to be expected.

The book is not only intended for parents. Many groups of people deal with babies or with the parents of babies, in their professional lives. Student doctors, nurses, social workers will all have to cope with families; playgroup leaders and primary-school teachers will devote themselves to people who have only just stopped being toddlers; even housing managers and park-keepers will find that the nature and needs of young children are relevant to their jobs. Such people already undergo lengthy and rigorous training in their own specialities. They cannot be expected to trace the complex literature on child development from technical journal to obscure book. This book tries to give them a comparatively easy overview of what is known about how infants develop; a feel for what it is like to be a parent in charge of a developing child and enough acquaintance with research studies to show them how we know what we know, why we do not know more, and where to look for further information on topics that particularly interest them.

Most people take it for granted that infants are mainly the parents', and particularly the mother's, business. Those who are not immediately involved in rearing children do not think about them very much. And when they do, they assume, with a sort of woolly emotionalism, that 'motherhood' is instinctive, and that the close emotional tie which they assume to exist between every mother and her child automatically makes the whole thing easy for her. When a father says smugly, 'I don't know how she does it,' he usually means that he does not propose to think about it too much, but is very sure he would not like to be in her place.

Being a mother is probably the most exhausting job which exists in Western society. Hours on duty and on call add up to 24 per day. There are no overtime payments, time off in lieu or money for unsocial hours. No week-end or holiday breaks are provided, and you only get a tea break if you make the tea yourself. The pay is usually atrocious. No union would stand for it. It has to be done and it is more worthwhile than any other job, because without new people nothing is meaningful. But it would be very much easier to do the job well and happily if the rest of the population would recognize it as interesting, difficult and valuable. At present, mothers themselves are scarcely allowed to acknowledge the value or the skill of what they do. If they meet a problem with their baby and devote time and effort to solving it, they are only doing what is expected of them. In any other job they would be looked on with respect.

Of course mothers do love their babies. Of course love does make much of the business of mothering possible and enjoyable. But interest in a baby and loving mothering of that baby go together. Interest in the processes of his development makes one look and listen closely, and it is by watching and listening that one sees the signs of his dawning attachment, *his* love, which reinforce one's own. Interest makes one wonder what will happen if one does this rather than that with the baby. That means thinking oneself into his non-existent shoes, and that is close to love. Interest makes one wonder why he cries and what will make him stop. When that wondering is put into action, it is the same, from the baby's point of view, as love. And when everything goes wrong, the baby's behaviour seems almost intolerable, motherhood a hideous burden, interest in that same behaviour can tide the mother through. Why does he behave like that? Do many babies? What will have to happen in other areas of his development before he is likely to stop? Just as information about childbirth can make it less frightening, so information about infant development can make it less maddening.

Because the book is written from the point of view of the developing child, the impression of parenthood which it gives is an unrealistically dedicated one. The book takes for granted the parents' wish to give their child any kind of care, contact or communication which he seems to need. But while most parents want to do their best for their children, this is not the whole story. They can be unaware of a child's need. Or they can be aware of the need but decide not to meet it, feeling that in this instance their own or their other children's needs must come first. Or they may be unable to meet known needs. Money, patience, time can all be thinly spread in a family. None of us is an ideal parent any more than we are ideal husbands or wives, children or friends. No child will ever have all his needs met all the time.

But unrealistic though this view of dedicated parenthood may be I make no apology for it. In these days of good contraception and world overpopulation there is a moral obligation to rear as well as we can the children we choose to have. And there is a strong, practical, self-interested obligation too. As this book will hopefully illustrate, handling of a baby which is sensitively tuned to his developing needs carries a double payoff. All babies demand, but the babies whose needs are met or anticipated do not demand more than the others, they demand less. Unlike a spoiled 4-year-old who can think of a million things he wants and may ask for them by the thousand if the limits are not made clear, a baby wants only what he needs. If he gets it he is content. If he is content he demands no more until he needs more. To double the benefit of sensitive handling, the more the mother meets or anticipates those needs, the more the baby will reward her with smiles, coos, all the special signs of his passionate devotion which she earns by tuning in to him. She not only gets fewer demands made, she also gets emotional payment for what she does. The mother who gets up cheerfully in the night to feed her baby may spend half an hour awake, and go to bed warmed by his toothless grin. The mother who fights his demands for food, staying in bed while he howls, getting up crossly to offer boiled water, will end up feeding him. But she will probably have been awake for two hours, and go to bed feeling that motherhood is hell.

So even though this book is not designed to tell mothers how to rear their babies, but rather how their babies develop, and therefore what they need, I hope it will help mothers to find ways of doing the job so that life is as satisfactory as possible for the infant and therefore as easy as possible for themselves. Bringing up a baby is a tough job. As with any other tough job, interest and job satisfaction go together.

ON USING THIS BOOK

Apologies to all parents of girls. In the interests of clarity a book of this kind has to reserve 'she' and 'her' to refer to the mother, and this means calling all babies 'he'.

The book is arranged to cover five age periods, represented by Sections I–V in the contents list.

Within each section, except the first, similar topics are covered chapter by chapter.

Any reader who wishes to follow a single topic right through from birth to 2 years will find that he or she can do so, simply by picking one relevant chapter from each section. Hence learning to walk would be followed through by starting with Chapter 4 and reading the section called 'Postures'. Chapter 7 'Beginning to Manage His Body' will be found to follow logically. Chapter 15 'Getting Control of His Body' would come next, followed by Chapter 21 'Becoming a Biped' and finishing up with Chapter 28 'Mobility'.

Pounds and ounces, feet and inches have been used throughout the book as the basic units of measurement. Metric equivalents are, in all cases, given in brackets.

On graphs and charts it will be found that either form of measurement can be read off.

The small numerals in the text refer to source material and research studies listed in numerical order of occurrence in the bibliography at the back of the book. Casual readers can ignore them. Others will find the bibliography full enough to give them a starting point for further reading on specialist topics.

SECTION I

THE FIRST SIX WEEKS: SETTLING INTO LIFE

CHAPTER ONE

OPENING THE PARCEL

Many parents remember the first few weeks after a baby's birth – especially a first baby's – as a unique period. They face a total upheaval in the pattern of their lives, their relationship with each other, the kind of marriage they have established, their expectations of each other and their social group. And all this when both of them are still churned up by the actual birth: the mother physically and hormonally, the father by fatigue and empathy. However carefully, lovingly, dedicatedly a birth is prepared for, it is a startling, overwhelming event.

Once the birth is over both parents tend to feel that they need time to recover their equilibrium, to think and talk about it, and to rest. But the birth resulted in a baby. And the presence of that baby usually means no recovery period for either parent. They must somehow struggle straight from giving birth to caring for the baby. There is no time to think about the amazing business of *becoming* a parent because *being* one starts straight away.

So these first weeks tend to be remembered as a peculiarly atmospheric mixture of worry and exhaustion, tenderness and concern. Everything seems to be felt too much: the stitches and the pleasure, the responsibility and the pride, selfishness and selflessness. The mother may have moments when she wonders why on earth she ever had the baby, how she will ever again feel like a fully autonomous person, how she will stand the constant demands of this small creature. She may wallow in private agonizing guilt because she does not feel love for the baby; then again she may have times when she is so overwhelmed by the miracle of minute fingernails, or the helplessness of a heavy downy head that she finds the weight of her love for the infant almost too great to bear. The father too is liable to violent swings of feeling. He has a difficult and delicate path to walk. He has to concede the prime role to his wife: she, after all, is the one who laboured, the one whose breasts begin to hurt. Yet he must make her feel that this is the child of them both, that he is deeply involved too. He must allow his wife to wrap herself in a symbiotic relationship with the new infant, yet he must reserve enough of their adult relationship to carry his wife through those moments when she feels the infant is eating her alive. Many husbands remark wryly that you cannot get it right during these weeks. If you come in and inquire after the infant's well-being, your wife moans that you only care about the baby now, not about her; if you come in and tell her something interesting, she wails that you don't care about the baby.

Much of the anguish of looking after a very new baby arises from the fact that the mother inevitably lacks the first essential for watchful care. She lacks any baseline of appearance and behaviour for *this* infant. He is brand new. She knows nothing about him. She does not know how he looks and behaves when he is content and well, and therefore she cannot easily know when he is discontented or unwell. She does not know how much he 'usually' cries, so she cannot know whether today's crying suggests something amiss. She has to make judgements as to the baby's well-being, and she cannot feel secure in those judgements until he has been around for long enough for those baselines to be established.

The baby has no baselines himself. He has no established patterns of behaviour. He is adapting himself – easily or with difficulty – to life in the outside world; he is recovering from the birth experience, getting himself moving into life. So in these first weeks the mother cannot 'know' him. He has not yet got himself into predictable, knowable shape. Only as he settles down and begins to pattern his sucking and his crying, his sleeping and waking, his kicking and wriggling, his looking and listening, can the mother begin to feel that he is a person whom she knows and understands.

Some babies take longer than others to reach this stage, and indeed the stage itself is a subjective judgement by the mother. But most mothers begin to feel that their infants are predictable, knowable, at somewhere between a fortnight and six weeks after birth.

In the meantime, an infant needs what it is hardest for parents to give him. Calm. His physiological needs are few, simple and repetitive. He needs food, warmth, tactile comfort and a modicum of cleanliness. But the fulfilment of every single one of these needs constitutes a novel experience for a brand new nervous system. The mother may tremble because she has never bathed a newborn before; but this newborn has never known water since he started to breathe for himself. Everything needs to be done for him as gently, as calmly and as slowly as possible. He needs no extra stimulation from adults, he has all he can cope with in the myriad new sensations of being outside the womb. He will feel changes of temperature on his skin, detect light and darkness; feel fullness and emptiness, wetness, dryness; feel himself moved through the air, held, put down, moved around. He will hear noises; he must suck for food and water; he will feel his own limbs move, experience different textures against his skin, different tastes in his mouth. He is very busy, in these first weeks, just being alive and staying that way.

Once upon a time most Western mothers received their new babies almost literally as parcels. Clean and wrapped, the baby was brought to the mother by a midwife and taken away again to the nursery. The mother discovered the contents of that parcel gradually over a 10-day hospital stay.

A few mothers still learn their way around their infants under medical care. But more and more mothers, even if they have given birth in hospital, are handed the parcel after 48 hours and told, so to speak, to unwrap it at home. Of course they have met their babies during that brief hospital stay. Of course they will be visited daily by midwives. And of course they would not have been allowed to go home so soon if the contents of the parcel was not basically a sound baby. Worry is therefore irrational, panic is shameful, yet both are so common in the first couple of weeks that we might as well allow for them.

BIRTHWEIGHT

One of the first things a new mother is told about her infant is his birthweight. Figures 1 and 2 show the weights and lengths of average, large and small babies, by their sex. Girls tend to be lighter at birth than boys, and first children tend to be lighter than subsequent ones.

If the new infant is of roughly average birthweight, his mother is unlikely to be concerned and, as we shall see, she will be fortunate in that her calculations of weight gain and required food will be comparatively simple. Mothers who have very large babies may be surprised to find that medical staff are not entirely congratulatory: heavy babies are more prone to difficulties in the newborn period than babies of average birthweight, and an 11-pounder may be kept in hospital longer than the planned 48 hours, so that medical staff can satisfy themselves that all is well with him. This does not necessarily mean that they have noticed anything untoward about the baby. They may well simply be taking precautions on the basis of the statistical evidence that such large babies are at greater risk than smaller ones.

Small infants are very seldom allowed home from hospital until they weigh at least 5½ lb. (2·5kg). Mothers whose babies weigh in at around or below this weight sometimes get confused and worried by the terms 'premature' and 'small for dates'.

Sometimes the term 'premature' is used of any infant who weighs less than 5½ lb. (2·5kg) at birth. But usually the term is reserved for babies who are born before they have spent their allotted forty weeks in the womb. Used in this sense, an infant weighing 6 lb. (2·7kg), born after 37 weeks' gestation, is premature, but because he is well grown may need little special care. A 37-week baby weighing 5 lb. (2·3kg) may start his life in an incubator, but may be able to suck and to breathe without assistance from the beginning. With a lighter birthweight and/or a shorter gestational time, the infant is likely to need very special care, with a controlled addition of

oxygen to the air in the incubator, and perhaps assisted respiration, and tube-feeding, with accurate monitoring of his
body's biochemistry.

'Small-for-dates' infants are those who have spent the full
40 weeks in the womb, but who nevertheless are born weighing less than 5½ lb., or those whose time in the womb was curtailed, but who weigh even less than would be expected after
their gestational period. Sometimes medical staff make careful inquiries of the mother after the birth, in an attempt to
establish whether or not her infant is truly 'small for dates'.
If the mother is doubtful about when the pregnancy began
the infant may be simply premature.

Both premature and small-for-dates babies start life with
a degree of handicap. Both groups are more prone than
babies of average birthweight to neonatal difficulties. Both
must be expected to take some time to catch up, developmentally, with babies of similar *birth* date, but greater
maturity.

We cannot yet duplicate a uterus in order to give babies
born prematurely, or before they have reached an average
birthweight, the extra time they need before they face the
world. Care in a specialist unit, in an incubator, with assisted
breathing and tube-feeding, gives the infant the nearest
possible equivalent. For the mother, a tiny frail-looking baby
whom she can only see through glass, and who may have a
tube down his nose, and various other gadgets attached to his
body, is at best a disappointment, at worst a ghastly shock.
Both from her point of view and the infant's, it is important
that this period is regarded as a hiatus; a sort of interim between the delivery and the 'real' birth, when the infant is
mature enough to come out of the incubator into his mother's
arms. For some months afterwards the infant should be
thought of as being the age he would be if he had been born
at the normal time, or at the ordinary sort of weight. If he was
born at 35 weeks' gestation, he should not be expected to
measure up to other 3-month infants 13 weeks later. He will
probably need at least 18 weeks to reach that developmental
point.

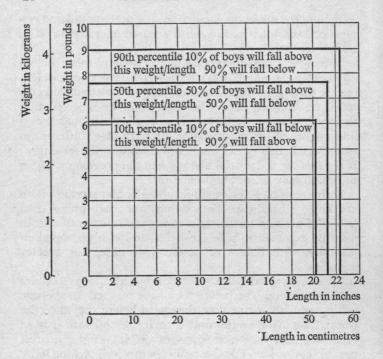

Figure 1. Birthweight and length for average, large and small boys

Percentiles are a means of dividing up the population in such a way that 50 per cent fall either side of the 50th percentile point, while 10 per cent fall above the 90th and 10 per cent below the 10th percentile points. Any birthweight or length which falls between the 10th and 90th percentiles is usually regarded as 'normal', since that range comprises the weights and lengths of 80 per cent of all newborns. Weights and lengths above the 90th percentile would be regarded as high; those below the 10th percentile would be regarded as low.

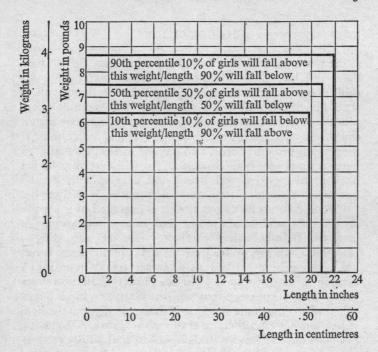

Figure 2. Birthweight and length for average, large and small girls

At birth boys are usually both heavier and longer than girls.

In the absence of prematurity or disease, the most usual reason for exceptional size is the size of the parents. Small parents tend to have small babies and large parents large babies.

Size at birth is significantly related to size throughout childhood. Small babies tend to remain small children, and large babies to be large children, at least until the growth spurt at puberty.

(Adapted from Tanner, Whitehouse and Takaishi.[67])

CIRCUMCISION

If the newborn baby is a boy, his parents may decide that
they wish him to be circumcised. Ideally parents should
think about this before the birth, for if it is to be done at all, it
should be done in the first three days of life. And many hospitals and doctors refuse to circumcise babies simply because
the parents wish it, in the absence of medical indications. If
the baby is brought home, and days or weeks pass while his
parents arrange his circumcision, he will certainly be set
back in his general well-being and development by the
operation. The older he is, the more upset his is likely to be.

Circumcision is a curious rite. It is practised over a wide
area of the world by about one sixth of the population. We
know that it dates back at least 6,000 years and, according to
Herodotus, the Egyptians were the first practitioners. It has
been variously described as a secret tribal marking, a
method of marking slaves, part of puberty initiation ceremonies and, of course, a religious rite. Gairdner, in his paper
called 'The Fate of the Foreskin',[1] shows clearly that medical
indications for circumcision are extremely rare. Among 100
newborn boys whom he studied, only 4 had a fully retractable prepuce, while in 42 the foreskin could not be pulled
back far enough to expose even the tip of the glans penis. In a
further 200 boys, four fifths had prepuces that could not be
retracted at 6 months, half were still not retractable at 1 year,
and one fifth were still not retractable at 2 years. It is therefore normal for the prepuce to be non-retractable in infancy.

Parents who accept that an adherent prepuce in infancy is
not a reason for circumcision sometimes put forward other
reasons for it. They may have read that cancer of the penis is
more usual in uncircumcised males, and cancer of the cervix
in their wives. These findings are now very much open to
doubt. Recent work suggests that findings of circumcision
and low cancer figures among certain populations are a
chance combination rather than a cause-and-effect correlation. The argument that circumcision makes it easier to keep

the penis clean is a curious one. No doubt it would be easier to clean away the normal secretions of the little girl's vulva if we removed the labia, or of all our noses if we split the nostrils. On the whole bodies look after themselves remarkably well if we let them alone, giving them ordinary external hygiene.

In a national study of 2,428 children,[2] 24 per cent were found to have been circumcised. There are probably at least 100,000 of these operations carried out every year in the United Kingdom and perhaps 200,000 in the United States. The Registrar General's returns show about 16 deaths every year as a result of circumcision, while around 22 per cent of baby boys suffer some complications from the operation – usually haemorrhage or sepsis.

If the operation is to be carried out, even on a newborn, parents should not allow themselves to be persuaded that the infant is not old enough to feel pain. Circumcision without anaesthetic is cruel.

An unusually low or high birthweight, prematurity whatever the birthweight, or circumcision, together with any neo-natal complication, will mean that the new infant is kept in hospital at least during his first week. Other mothers may find themselves in full charge of an infant merely 48 hours old. While the midwives provide day-to-day assurance that all is well, worried parents have to get through many hours between their visits. Many things can worry parents. Newborns are physiologically very different from babies even a few weeks old, and dramatically different from older children or adults. They are prone to all sorts of conditions and appearances which are perfectly normal for *them* but unheard of, or a genuine reason for anxiety, in any other age-group. If the mother's own feet suddenly turned bright blue she would be right to feel concerned; how is she to know that the feet of newborn babies often turn blue from time to time while the circulation is adapting to life outside the womb?

The following list of things which parents may notice and worry about during the infant's first week or two is not intended to prevent them consulting their midwife or doctor about anything that concerns them; rather it is intended to help them get a night's sleep, or pass a reasonably calm day while waiting to consult. The list covers only phenomena which appear alarming but are in fact normal or insignificant.

NORMAL PECULIARITIES

1. *Peculiarities of Colour*

BLUISH HANDS AND/OR FEET A bluish tinge to the extremities is perfectly normal. It may be continuous or intermittent. If intermittent, it is more likely to be noticed when the infant has been asleep and still for a long period. It does not mean that he is cyanosed (failing to get enough oxygen), it is merely a sign of the immaturity of his circulation. In true cyanosis the tongue is also blue and there are blue-grey shadows to either side of the nose.

HALF RED, HALF PALE Occasionally the side on which the infant is lying becomes suffused a bright red, while his upper half remains pale. There is a definite line right down his body, marking the junction of red with pale areas. This phenomenon is called the 'harlequin colour change'. It is thought to be due simply to gravity causing the blood to collect in the lower half of the body. It passes as soon as the infant is picked up or turned over, and it has no significance at all.

MONGOLIAN BLUE SPOTS These are accumulations of pigment, forming spots or patches of a bluish colour. They form principally on the buttocks, and are most often seen in infants of African or Mongolian descent. They may also occur in infants of Greek or Italian origin, or in any baby who is going to have a fairly dark skin. They become far less noticeable as the overall skin colour darkens.

Mothers are sometimes alarmed by the name, thinking it relates to Mongolism. It does not. They are also sometimes afraid that the blue patches may be bruises, suggesting either ill-treatment or a blood disease. They can be reassured.

2. *Other Skin Peculiarities*

SPOTS   New babies' skins are liable to a variety of eruptions. The kind that usually cause anxiety are raised red spots with yellow–white centres, which look as if they might be infected. They are called 'neonatal urticaria'. They usually appear in the first 24 hours and vanish during the first week. They are completely insignificant and require no treatment.

BIRTHMARKS   There are innumerable varieties of these, some of which fade and others of which do not. If there is a mark on the infant's skin which causes anxiety, the doctor will be able to say whether it is a birthmark, and what type it is.

Red marks on the skin, or tiny broken blood vessels in the skin or in the eyes, can arise from pressure during birth – even if the delivery was unassisted. These are quite insignificant, and vanish within a few days.

SKIN PEELING   Most infants' skin peels a little in the first few days. It is usually most noticeable on the hands and the soles of the feet.

SCURF ON THE SCALP   Known as 'cradle-cap', this is just as normal as peeling of the skin elsewhere. It suggests neither disease nor lack of hygiene. If the scurf really covers the scalp, in a cap-shaped thick layer, and the appearance of it is distressing, a doctor can suggest alternatives to simple soap-and-water washing. But from the infant's point of view it is probably best left alone. He is likely to be quite un-distressed by his cradle-cap, and thoroughly irritated by having his head cleaned with oil.

3. *Hair*

Babies vary in the amount and the type of hair they are born with. Most have very little, very fine hair; a few have a luxuriant growth, and some – especially those born after their expected date of delivery – have coarse, wiry hair. Whatever the hair is like at birth, most of it will fall out during the subsequent few weeks. Some infants will have a period of semi-baldness, while in others the new hair grows in as the newborn hair falls out. Neither the texture nor the colour of the newborn hair bears much relation to later hair.

BODY HAIR   In the womb, infants are covered with a fine fuzz of hair. At birth some are still thus covered; others have traces left, usually across the shoulder blades and down the spine; others have no body hair at all. None of it has the least significance. Any excess hair will be rapidly shed in the first week or two.

4. *Swellings*

HERNIA   While an umbilical hernia – a small swelling near the navel, which usually becomes more protuberant when the infant cries – cannot be classified as 'normal', it is very common. Such hernias are caused by a slight weakness of the muscle wall in the abdomen, or by a failure of the muscle wall to close completely. Most umbilical hernias right themselves by 1 year. Many authorities now believe that they heal more quickly if they are not strapped up. Very few ever require operation.

SWOLLEN BREASTS   Both male and female babies sometimes develop quite definite breast swelling in the first three days. The condition is known as 'mastitis neonatorum'. It is caused by the pituitary hormone which floods through the mother just before the birth, to stimulate *her* milk secretion. Some passes across the placenta and stimulates the infant's breasts too. There may even be droplets of milk coming from the infant's nipples.

Mastitis neonatorum does not suggest any abnormality, nor require treatment. The breasts should be left strictly alone, as any attempt to squeeze out the milk could lead to infection. The swelling subsides over a few days as the infant's body rids itself of the hormone intended to stimulate his mother and not him.

SWOLLEN GENITALS Swelling of the genitals in both sexes is equally usual, transient and insignificant. This too is caused by the mother's hormones reaching the baby across the placenta just before birth.

5. *The Head*

MIS-SHAPEN HEAD No baby with a significant skull problem will be allowed home from hospital, or left at home if he was delivered there. So the mother can assume that all is well with her infant's skull, however peculiar it may look.

Even without the use of forceps or vacuum extraction at delivery, the infant's skull may appear lop-sided or elongated after birth. The areas of the skull where the bones are not rigid or fully fused allow a considerable degree of this 'moulding'. Without them there would be many more difficult deliveries, as a rigid head tried to get through a narrow birth canal.

Marked degrees of 'moulding' may take several weeks to right themselves, although they will become less noticeable as the infant grows more hair. Some infants continue to have lop-sided skulls for many months, especially if they develop a marked preference for lying on one particular side. The pressure of the skull on the cot mattress can be sufficient to flatten one side of the head slightly. This does not matter in the least, but it can be avoided in most infants by ensuring that he is put down to sleep on alternating sides or on his tummy, at least for as long as he will accept it.

THE FONTANELLES The most noticeable of these soft areas on a baby's head lies towards the top of the back of his skull, roughly at the crown. This fontanelle does not close up and become hard for months. With normal handling there is absolutely no danger of damaging it, for it is covered by an extremely tough membrane. Often, especially in a baby with little hair, a pulse can be seen beating under the fontanelle. This is perfectly normal. If the infant becomes dehydrated, during illness, fever, starvation or even extremely hot weather, the fontanelle may appear sunken. This is a useful sign that the infant needs more fluids immediately. If the fontanelle should ever appear tense and bulging, a doctor should see the infant.

6. *Elimination and Secretions*

STOOLS   The first substance passed by the new infant is usually the greyish-white 'meconium plug'. Over the next two or three days, he passes meconium stools, which are greenish-black and very sticky – very *unlike* a normal stool. These must be passed before ordinary digestion can commence. About 70 per cent of newborns pass their first meconium stool in the first 12 hours after birth. About 95 per cent do so in the first 24 hours. Failure to pass meconium in the first day or two needs investigation, and may be a reason for the infant being kept in hospital for longer than was planned.

Once the intestine has cleared itself of the meconium with which it was filled in the womb, the infant passes what are known as 'changing stools'. As their name suggests they are simply the stools produced as the infant adapts to milk feeding from the transfusion feeding of his time in the womb. These stools are greenish-brown. After this the stools settle into the normal 'milk stools' which are described on page 64.

BLOOD IN STOOLS   Occasionally this is noticed in the first day or two. It is usually due to maternal blood swallowed during delivery.

URINE   Most infants pass urine in the first hours after birth.

About 10 per cent do not pass any for the first 36 hours due, it is thought, to passing urine during delivery.

In both boys and girls very early urine may contain a substance called 'urates'. This appears red on the nappy and may resemble blood.

Once the urine flow is established the infant may urinate as often as 20–30 times in the 24 hours. This is entirely normal; indeed few mothers will actually know how often the baby urinates – all they will know is that his nappy is always wet, however often he is picked up.

A newborn infant who is *dry* for as long as 6 hours should be seen by a doctor or midwife. There is a possibility of some obstruction causing retention of the urine.

VAGINAL BLEEDING A small amount of bleeding from the vagina is common in girls at any time from birth to about 7 days. It is due to the rapid excretion of maternal or placental oestrogens transmitted to the infant before birth.

A clear discharge, which may become thicker and whiter in appearance, is also common. It ceases in a couple of days. There is no significance in such vaginal secretions.

NASAL DISCHARGE Many infants accumulate enough mucus in the nose to cause snuffles and sneezing. This need not imply a cold or other infection, and has no significance unless the infant is otherwise unwell.

TEARS Most newborn babies cry without tears until they are 3–6 weeks old. About 10 per cent produce tears within the first week. This is of no importance either way.

SWEATING OF THE HEAD Many infants sweat copiously around the head, so that the sparse hair appears soaking. This is quite normal and unimportant unless the infant gives other indications of being feverish or unwell. It is, however, a good reason for frequent rinsing of the hair and scalp, as the salt in the sweat can cause skin irritation (especially around the back of the neck) if it is allowed to accumulate.

VOMITING   When infants suck, they take in air as well as milk. Once the milk reaches the stomach gravity ensures that it settles to the bottom, leaving the air at a higher level. The infant then brings up his 'wind' in a series of burps and belches. Very often he brings up some of the milk with the wind. This 'spitting up' has no real relation to vomiting in the sense this word is used in older people. Mothers often believe that the quantity of milk brought up is much larger than it really is. They worry that the infant is keeping down too little for adequate nourishment. Even a dessertspoonful of milk, mixed with a little saliva, looks a great deal if it is spilt all over somebody's shoulder.

A very few infants do suffer from projectile vomiting, in which the milk is literally shot back, as if from a water pistol, sometimes hitting a wall some feet from the infant's mouth. Such infants should see a doctor, who will probably want to see a feed, and therefore the vomiting, for himself.

Vomiting partially digested milk, an hour or more after a feed, does count as true vomiting, and may indicate anything from maldigestion to the beginnings of a cold or other feverish illness.

7. The Mouth

TEETH   About 1 in 2,000 infants is born with a tooth already through. Julius Caesar, Hannibal, Louis XIV and Napoleon are supposed to have been among them.

The roots of such a tooth are not firmly fixed, so the tooth bends out of the way when the infant sucks and there is little danger of him hurting the mother's breast or puncturing the teat. If left alone such teeth become firmly fixed and part of the normal dentition. Some authorities prefer to remove them. There is a very small risk of bleeding attached to such an extraction, but later dentition will replace the tooth in the normal way.

TONGUE TIE   Mothers often worry unnecessarily about this. The young infant's tongue is normally attached over a proportionately greater length than are the tongues of older children or adults. True tongue tie is extremely unusual and never requires any action before the infant is about a year old, so there is no point in looking for it.

WHITE TONGUE A tongue which is uniformly white all over is perfectly normal in a purely milk-fed infant. It clears in a few weeks. Infection does not give a uniform whiteness, but produces patches of white on an otherwise pinky-red tongue.

BLISTERS ON THE UPPER LIP These are produced by sucking and are therefore known as 'sucking blisters'. They can occur at any time while the infant is purely milk-fed. They may recede between feeds and re-occur. They are of no significance.

8. *The Eyes*

SWOLLEN OR PUFFY EYES Often occur soon after birth as a result of pressure during delivery. The puffiness resolves over two or three days.

BROKEN VEINS IN THE EYES Broken veins may make tiny streaks or patches of red on the white of the eye. Again these arise during delivery and rapidly resolve afterwards.

'STICKY EYE' A slight yellowish discharge, or collection of yellow matter in the corners of the eyes, suggests this very common neonatal infection. The infant should be seen by the doctor or midwife, who may prescribe drops or a solution for bathing the eyes.

'WANDERING EYE' Many newborns appear to squint. Often this is because of the fold at the inner corner of the eyes which can give them a squinting appearance when in fact they are entirely normal.

An eye which 'wanders' away from the focus of the other

eye usually rights itself without treatment by 6 months. But a fixed squint, in one or both eyes, should be referred to a doctor as soon as it is noticed. If it is a true squint early treatment is important and highly successful.

9. *The Ears*

DISCHARGE Discharge from the ears is not normal and should always be referred to a doctor whether or not the infant appears ill. It is very unusual in the neonatal period.

STICKING-OUT EARS Opinions differ as to whether the mother can usefully do anything about ears which stick out. The ears of a new infant are very soft, and some authorities suggest that they can be persuaded to grow flatter to the head if they are strapped back with adhesive tape. Most authorities would agree, however, that there is little point in this procedure which, to do any good, would have to be continuous over months and might well lead to sore skin from the tape. It is worth making sure that when the infant is put to lie on his side his ear is not bent forward under his head.

Ears which appear to stick out to the point of deformity often cease to be noticeable as the infant grows and acquires more hair.

Even the calmest parents, with the least worrying infants, need medical advisers whom they really trust. They need them at this early stage because they can advise the parents on the basis of their experience of hundreds of infants, while the parents are finding their way around this one particular one. However healthy the child turns out, they will continue to need that medical help, because there are immunizations to be carried out, childhood infections to be got through, developmental checks to be made. Furthermore the kind of relationship with a doctor which parents need tends to be very different from the relationship they may have found perfectly satisfactory during several years of healthy adulthood.

When they consult a doctor about a child, they want to know how worried they *should* be; when they consult him for themselves, they already know how worried they are. When they consult for a child, they are often discussing behaviour as well as physical symptoms, their child's psychology as well as his physiology, his misery as well as his fevered throat. When they consult for themselves, they already know how much of their bad temper is flu and how much is boredom.

In the United States it is usual to register new babies with a pediatrician, but in the United Kingdom general practitioners look after all members of the family. The one who was right for a childless couple may not be ideal once they have a baby. Like every other professional, doctors like some parts of their job better than other parts. Some very much enjoy pediatrics; others have little interest in babies, little tolerance for maternal anxiety and a marked dislike for making home visits. It is worth finding the right one in advance. If other mothers with young children are not unanimous in their praise for one particular local practice, a search for a G.P. who runs his own child-welfare clinic and/or does his own antenatal work and perhaps even some obstetrics will usually be fruitful. G.P.s do not have to do these things, so those who choose to do them usually turn out to enjoy doing it. The vital point is that the mother should not be too shy to ask advice, should not be afraid of 'looking silly' to the doctor. It is most unlikely that anything disastrous will happen to the new infant, but any doctor would rather the mother asked unnecessarily than took the slightest risk. The kind of doctor she needs would also rather she asked than worried herself into a depression, which is quite an easy thing to do immediately after giving birth.

Even with some possible causes for worry explained, and advice that the parents trust available, there are still going to be times in these early weeks when they wonder whether the infant is all right or not. Later on they will go by whether his behaviour and appearance are different from usual. But at this stage there is no usual.

Rule-of-thumb methods can give some guidance as to

whether or not any infant is in trouble; they all concern his
basic behaviours. The baby must eat, sleep and eliminate.
Inability to do any of these things is a signal; it means something. How much it means depends on how it relates to the
baby's general appearance and behaviour. So to begin with,
whatever a baby's symptoms, he is unlikely to be very ill if he
is eating well, sleeping peacefully and eliminating. He can
wait to see the doctor at the next surgery. Equally, if he has
no appetite, cries continuously so that he does not sleep and
has diarrhoea he should probably see a doctor at the first
possible opportunity. In between these extremes the infant
may refuse his feeds, but sleep neither too little nor too much,
cry no more than usual and have no digestive disturbance.
In circumstances like these the mother has to decide whether
he *seems* ill. This 'seeming ill' is a very unscientific, subjective
matter – one which becomes second nature to mothers with
practice. Largely it is a matter of whether the baby seems
floppy, whether he *feels* wrong in her arms, whether his head
seems heavier than usual, his crying sounds peculiar, his
interest seems less than the day before. If the mother finds
herself worried about the infant in some way, even if she
cannot exactly specify to herself what she thinks is wrong, she
should probably take him to the doctor. After all, she chose
the doctor because he did not make her feel she was a bother.

CHAPTER TWO

FEEDING

METHOD

Remarkably few babies in the Western world are breast-fed. In the United States it is reckoned that since 1969 less than 25 per cent of babies are ever put to the breast at all. In the United Kingdom, where the National Survey of 1946[3] showed 60 per cent of infants as being breast-fed to 1 month, 42 per cent to 3 months and 30 per cent to 6 months, two studies carried out in 1970–71[4, 5] showed only 14 per cent and 8 per cent respectively of babies breast-fed even for 1 month.

The fewer the babies who are breast-fed, the fewer new mothers will take breast-feeding for granted. The majority of children and of young women today have probably never even *seen* a baby put to the breast. The more recent methods of milk suppression, which prevent the milk from ever coming in, rather than drying it up afterwards, destroy the connection between hungry baby and breast full of milk, for mothers who may not have thought about it much either way.

Some mothers like breast-feeding and find it easy and obvious. Others do not like it and find it difficult. To maintain that it is a natural function, and therefore easily possible for all mothers, is as idiotic as it would be to maintain that there is no such thing as constipation. Partisan supporters of breast-feeding make much of the fact that in past times babies were always fed on the breast and that in many parts of the world they still are. They ignore the unknown numbers who did, and still do, die because breast-feeding fails; the numbers who are and always have been undernourished because the mother's diet or health were poor; the numbers of mothers who suffer, and always have suffered, from sore nipples and breast abscesses. The difficulties of breast-feeding in so-called 'natural societies' are not much written about simply because there is no viable alternative. People only begin to debate the pros and cons of different methods of doing anything when they have a choice as to how they should do it.

From the baby's point of view, despite hotly partisan writings on the subject, there is probably little difference between *satisfactory* breast-feeding, and *careful* bottle-feeding. The mother who breast-feeds easily and with pleasure probably offers her baby the ultimate in warmth and physical comfort; and she will probably keep him waiting less often than the bottle-feeding mother who can be caught out with no feed ready if the baby wakes unexpectedly, or the car breaks down in mid journey. On the other hand the mother who is breast-feeding because she feels she ought to, or is in a state because she is overtired or her milk is scanty or her breasts sore, probably offers the baby a less satisfactory feed than he could get from a calmly and cheerfully given bottle. Ideal feeding requires of the mother the right food, hygiene, the right rate of flow, ready availability, a comfortable object to suck the food from, contact and comfort while the sucking goes on, and calm affection. A contentedly breast-feeding mother does not have to work to provide any of these things; they automatically come with comfortable breast-feeding. But a bottle-feeding mother can provide them perfectly well if she tries.

Some of the factual differences between the two methods are listed in Table 1. Only the individual mother can decide which point of difference tips the balance in favour of one method or the other. For example, the easy, casual, feed-anywhere-anytime quality of breast-feeding might be a boon to the relaxed mother who wanted to travel with her husband and did not mind baring her breast in a café or car park as need arose; it might mean nothing to a mother who intended to stay at home for the first 6 months and devote herself to nursery routine; it might horrify the mother who blushed to imagine undoing her bra outside her own bedroom.

TABLE I.   BREAST-FEEDING AND
BOTTLE-FEEDING COMPARED

Breast	*Bottle*
Colostrum, the clear fluid which precedes milk in the 3–4 days after birth, conveys some useful antibodies to the baby.	No artificial equivalent to colostrum.
Food is always suitable (except in very rare biochemical disorders). Remains suitable throughout suckling period.	May need trial and error to find most suitable food. Food formula may need adjusting as baby gets older, or in illness.
Food always available, clean (virtually sterile) and at correct temperature.	Food must be prepared; food and utensils must be sterilized. Food will usually be warmed, although experiments show infants neither object to, nor fail to thrive on formula from the refrigerator.
Infant is far less likely to get gastro-enteritis. He probably also gets some protection, via the mother's antibodies, against other diseases.	Gastro-enteritis need not occur if sterilization procedures are carefully carried out, and formula is not kept in bottle warmers, carried in a thermos, etc. But it does occur in many bottle-fed infants and can be serious.
Infant is less likely to get too fat and less likely to suffer from nappy rash.	Bottle-fed babies need not get fat and sore, but often do if formula is not correctly made up.
Stools will be looser and of varying frequency.	Stools will be firmer and normally more regular.

Breast	Bottle
No equipment for feeding need be carried when travelling.	A surprising amount of equipment, such as powdered milk, bottles, teats, sterilizing chemical, sterilizing utensil, bottle brushes, etc. must be carried whenever even overnight travel is undertaken.
Night feeding is less of a chore.	Night feeding is more of a chore.
Milk supply will adjust itself to infant's demands, but varying quantities which are available at different times of day may cause problems if the infant is fed on a strict schedule, and is not permitted to slip in extra feeds when the breast needs extra stimulation to produce more milk.	Milk supply is in the mother's hands; infant can always be offered as much as he needs, whether fed on schedule or on demand.
Mother cannot tell, without test weighing, how much food the infant has had.	Mother can tell exactly what the infant has taken.
Mother's own health and well-being affect milk supply; tiredness, illness, menstruation may reduce it.	Milk supply independent of mother's state.
Some chemicals pass into the milk and affect the infant. Among them are some sedatives and tranquillizers, some antibiotics, most laxatives, alcohol, caffeine, some antihistamines and some contraceptive pills.	Infant is unaffected by medication taken by the mother.

Breast	Bottle
Breast milk is comparatively expensive, as humans are less efficient at turning food into milk than cows are. Mother must eat more than the calories the infant needs, in order to provide those calories in milk form. Mother's diet must be adequate in protein and vitamins if milk is to be adequate.	Expense may not *seem* less, as actual money has to be found to buy the milk, where the breast-feeding mother simply spends a little more on overall house-keeping.
Mother cannot delegate feeds, unless she can persuade infant to accept a bottle.	Babysitters or husbands can stand in for the mother.
Nipples can get cracked and sore. Milk can leak if a feed is delayed, or in the early morning.	Mother is physically unaffected by feeding the infant.
Feeding involves baring breasts. Embarrassing to some mothers; unacceptable in some public places.	Baby can be fed without embarrassment anywhere where his very presence is acceptable.

TECHNIQUE

So much has been written about the vital pleasure infants get from sucking food that people sometimes forget that the *newborn* has no experience of sucking his food, and therefore no expectations of pleasure. All he has is an instinctive reaction to being touched on the cheek – turning his head towards the touch – and an instinctive sucking response to the nipple or a similarly shaped object. At the very beginning these instinctive reactions have no backing in experience. The baby does not know that he is crying because he is hungry, that the preliminaries of a feed mean food, and that food will stop the hunger-pain. Some babies, crying for food, will indeed go through the approved reflex actions, and take a hearty suck, only to continue bawling. Even the first gush of milk does not tell them that the sooner they stop crying and suck the sooner they will feel better. How could it? Other babies seem to have approved reflexes only to a very limited extent. It is difficult to persuade them to latch on to the breast or bottle, and difficult to persuade them to suck once they have. But there are others who seem to be born suckers; there is even some evidence that these may be the ones who have practised sucking their fingers in the womb. They learn the lesson that sucking = food = cessation of hunger-pain so rapidly that it is difficult to realize it ever was a learning process.

The infant has got to have food, and he has got to have it by sucking. He has got to learn the relation between sucking his food and being comfortable. His instincts are there; relating them to satisfactory experience is up to the mother.

The infant's very first feeds are usually closely supervised by a midwife. But often feeding is not fully established before the mother is left to manage mostly on her own. And often supervised feeds are not very helpful. The midwife would undoubtedly feed the baby expertly *herself*; but she may be far less good at helping the mother to do so. Especially in breast-feeding, it is as difficult to help somebody get an infant comfortably sucking as it is to help somebody tie their tie. You can do it for them, or let them do it, but the two of you doing it together tend to get in a muddle. Feeding a baby is a very one–one procedure. There is really no room for a third party except as demonstrator or admiring audience.

Whether he is easy or difficult to teach about sucking milk, the baby will learn fastest if all concerned keep a clear picture in their minds of the instinctive reactions he already has, and which they must use in the early feeds.

The baby turns his head *towards* a gentle touch on the cheek. It follows that if both cheeks are held, however gently, in an attempt to steer him to breast or bottle, he is confused and angry. In breast-feeding this gentle touch usually happens automatically. The breast brushes against the baby's cheek as the mother gathers him towards her. He then turns inwards, towards the breast, and if the nipple then touches his mouth, the mouth purses ready to suck. Timing is therefore important; if he turns inwards towards the breast and the mother is not ready to present the nipple the optimum moment for him to latch on may have been lost.

In bottle-feeding, there is often no preliminary touch to the cheek. The bottle may be presented straight on, so that the first the baby knows of it is the mother's attempt to put the teat in his mouth. He may accept it, but his natural head-turning and mouth-pursing reflexes have been by-passed, and he may not. In summary, the best chance of a successful feed, in the early days, lies in giving the baby cues to turn towards the food and purse his lips to receive it before giving it to him.

Unfortunately both mothers and attendants tend to be so concerned over the new infant's need for milk, and so frustrated by his apparent inefficiency in taking it, that they often create difficulties. A very new baby who is distressed and crying will seldom settle easily to a feed, yet because the adults know he is crying because he is hungry, they try to force him to accept the teat or nipple. The angrier and more desperate he gets, the harder they may try to force him to suck. A situation which should never have arisen in the first place is made worse. If tactful attempts to slip the nipple or teat into the baby's mouth fail, some other way of calming him – such as wrapping him tightly and rocking him – ought to be tried first, and then the whole cheek-stroking, head-turning, mouth-pursing routine tried again when he is calmer.

Often, too, they have a distorted picture of what the very new infant *ought* to take, and when he ought to take it. Very sleepy babies, who suck $\frac{1}{4}$ oz. (7ml) and fall asleep again, and wake half an hour later to repeat the process, are wearing for the mother, but they will grow out of this pattern in a few days as they become more awake. In the meantime they are probably not getting less food from those minuscule bottle-feeds than they would be getting if they were taking colostrum from the breast. It is arguable that they do not in fact *need* food at all during the first 3–5 days, but only some liquid. Certainly the continual jouncing, flicking and general shaking around that goes on in an attempt to wake the baby enough to suck some more has nothing to recommend it.

Bottle-fed babies are often wildly frustrated in their early feeds by the hole in the teat being too small. Tests show that once the breast milk is established breast-fed babies take at least three quarters of their total feed in the first 4–5 minutes; any further time is spent sucking far more slowly. To equal this rate, the milk should drip out of an inverted bottle at several drops per *second* without any shaking. It is no use test-ing the teat with water, which, being thinner, comes out faster.

QUANTITY

Breast milk has an average calorific value of 20 per fluid ounce (70 per 100ml). Proprietary infant milks, whether liquid or dried, are manufactured so that when made up exactly as instructed they provide a feed of this strength. As long as breast milk, or a full-cream infant milk, is being used, all calculations as to the infant's needs can be made on the basis of the same figures, irrespective of the particular brand of milk.

Up to about 5 months infants need about 55 calories for each pound of their weight per day (about 110 calories per kilogram per day). They therefore need about 2¾ oz. of made-up milk per lb. per day (about 165ml/kg per day).

Both in order to simplify the arithmetic and in order to ensure that the infant's needs are more than adequately met, it is reasonable to call that 2¾ oz., 3 oz. and that 165ml, 180ml. This slight over-allowance also makes it legitimate to simplify weight calculations by taking them only to the nearest ½ lb. or 250g.

In calculating the requirements of any individual infant it is essential to calculate according to his *ideal* weight (usually called his 'expected weight') rather than on what he actually weighs at any given moment in time. If his actual weight is used as the basis, there is a real risk of underfeeding the infant who lost a great deal of weight after birth, regained his birth-weight very slowly, or has since gained slowly due to illness or underfeeding. Clearly there could be a vicious circle such that the infant was half-starved during his first fortnight, and continued to be half-starved because he continued to be fed as if that starved weight were his natural weight.

Calculating the expected weight is very simple.

(a) *If the infant is less than 10 days old*
Start with his birthweight.
Subtract 1 oz. or 30g for each day up to and including day 5.
Then add 1 oz. or 30g for each further day of his age up to and including day 10.
The infant is thus expected to weigh at 10 days what he weighed at birth.

(b) *If the infant is more than 10 days old*
Start from his birthweight, which is also his expected weight for 10 days.
Add 1 oz. or 30g for each day up to 3 months.

e.g., a baby born weighing 6 lb 14 oz. (3·1 kg.) now aged 15 days. Because he is over 10 days old, we do not need the arithmetic of his weight loss and regain in the first 10 days. We assume he weighed 6 lb. 14 oz. (3·1 kg.) at 10 days.

We have to add 1 oz. (30g) for each of the 5 days between 10 and 15. So we now expect him to weigh, say, 7 lb. 3 oz. (3·3kg).

To calculate this same infant's needs per 24 hours, we need only multiply his weight in lb. by 3 oz. (his weight in kg by 180ml). We ignore the 3 oz. as we are working to the nearest ½ lb. (we call the 3·3kg, 3·25kg for the same reason). He therefore needs 21 oz. (around 600ml) of milk per 24 hours. The actual milk consumption and weight gain of an average birthweight baby, breast-fed 'on demand', is shown in Figure 3.

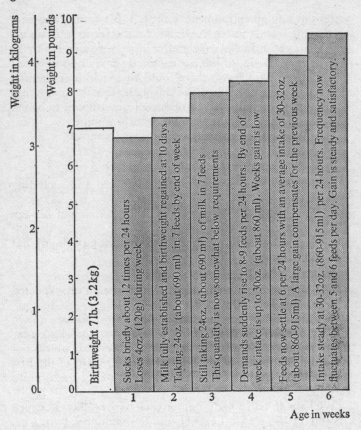

Figure 3. Milk intake and weight gain of one infant breast-fed 'on demand'

This particular infant was test-weighed at each feed during his first six weeks, giving an unusual opportunity to demonstrate the 'fit' between a breast-fed baby's demands and the milk supply which those demands evoke.

During the first week he demands frequent 'feeds' which get the milk supply established. He loses some weight while the milk

Having said all this, it is only when it is doubtful whether the baby is getting enough milk that calculations of this sort are necessary. If feeding is going smoothly and the baby is contented, active and gaining weight at a reasonable rate, then he need only be offered the breast at the compromise intervals arrived at by him and his mother, or the quantity of bottle feed which he willingly takes, and all will be well. There are, however, some pitfalls.

Underfed Breast-Fed Babies

Breast-fed babies can be underfed, continually but to a small extent, without their mothers realizing it until the scales give them a shock because the baby is failing to gain weight, or is doing so very slowly.

If the breast milk is marginally inadequate over the 24 hours, this can be enough to reduce the weight gain, without the infant's behaviour alerting the mother. Often, for example, the milk is scantiest in the evening. The baby may indeed be more restless during the evening than he is during the day when supplies are better. But because he seems content by day the mother may put his evening restlessness down to colic or simply to this being his chosen period of wakeful-

---

comes in, but regains it rapidly, and goes on to make a positive gain in his second week.

In his fourth week, the supply which he has established, and kept flowing by taking $3\frac{1}{2}$ oz. (100ml) seven times in the 24 hours, becomes inadequate for his increasing size. He demands far more frequent feeding, and, by the end of the week, has increased his intake by 6 oz. (170ml). His weight gain for this week is low, reflecting the days early in the week when he was not getting quite enough.

By the fifth week he is getting plenty of milk, and he therefore settles down to six feeds in the 24 hours. He makes a large weight gain, reflecting the large increase in daily intake, and compensating for the low gain of the week before.

During the sixth week the milk supply is abundant for his needs, and he makes a good weight gain while beginning to move from six towards five feeds in the 24 hours.

ness. Similarly if the baby continues for some weeks to demand two feeds during the night the mother may assume that this is simply his pattern – that it is a question of maturation rather than chronic underfeeding. She may be confirmed in this view by the very copiousness of her milk supply in the early morning. It is hard for a mother who wakes each day soaked in milk, with hard swollen breasts, which positively spurt as the baby starts to suck, to realize that later in the day her milk may be inadequate.

If a baby is to be fully breast-fed it is very convenient to hire baby scales, at least for three months. Test weighing is simple if there are scales in the home, and it is the only way to be sure that the baby is getting sufficient for his needs, once his behaviour or his weight gain have given any cause for wondering.

Test weighing must be done over 24 hours to be of any value at all. The breast-milk supply can vary so widely from feed to feed that knowledge of what the infant took at a single feed is useless.

The baby is weighed, in his clothes, before the feed. Once weighed, his clothing must be left as it is until he has been weighed after the feed. If he soils or wets his nappy, this will not alter the test weight as long as the nappy is still on the baby.

The before-feed weight is written down, and then the baby is fed as usual and weighed again immediately afterwards. The second weight is written down, and the difference between the two weights is the quantity of milk taken at that feed.

Each feed of the 24 hours is recorded similarly and the 'feed values' are summed to give the infant's intake for that day. If the sum is less than his calculated daily requirements for his expected weight, then he needs more food. Some mothers may make intensive efforts to increase their milk supply, by resting more, putting the baby to the breast more often, remembering to notice and drink when they are thirsty, and expressing any milk which remains in the breasts after the feeds which are superabundant. Others will prefer to offer the baby a complementary bottle feed; simply topping him up with as much as he wants once the breast feeding is over. If the discrepancy between what the baby needs and is getting is very great, or the mother feels that any further effort on her part is too much trouble, she may decide to switch from breast to bottle altogether.

One course of action must be adopted cautiously. If the baby is 6 weeks old or more, the mother who wants to continue breast-feeding may decide that she can make up the difference by starting solid foods. In calorie terms of course she can, provided the baby will take it. But in *fluid* terms the baby still needs his requisite ounces. If he is to have two thirds of his calories as breast milk and the remaining third in solid foods, he must have extra water. Not a whole third, of course, as his 'solid food' will have a lot of liquid content, but some water or juice. And since he will almost certainly need to take this from a bottle, a complementary milk feed might be easier in the end.

Underfed Bottle-Fed Babies

These are usually the unfortunates whose mothers take advice from books like this one too literally. Such a mother painstakingly works out her baby's requirements, and then makes up 21 oz. (600ml) of formula, divides it into 6 feeds of $3\frac{1}{2}$ oz. (100ml) each, and feeds that to the baby. Then she congratulates herself because he always drains his bottle. Finishing a bottle is not a virtue in small babies. It is a reproof to mothers. If he drains every drop, there is no way of knowing whether he would have liked more. Just because his body requires 21 oz. (600ml) in 24 hours, it does not follow that he will want the same amount at each feed, nor that he may not have extra hungry days and less hungry days. For bottle-fed babies, calculated requirements should only serve as data for mothers to think about if the baby fails to gain weight or seems discontented. If the mother knows what he needs and knows he is taking what he needs, then she can exclude hunger as a cause of discontent, and can seek advice if lack of hunger is leading to low weight gain. Knowing what he

needs, she should see to it that each bottle contains at least
2 oz. (about 55ml) more. If he drinks it, fine; if he does not,
equally fine.

As much care needs to be taken about the fluid-intake of
bottle- as of breast-fed babies. In hot weather, or in illness, a
baby is likely to be less hungry and more thirsty than usual.
If he is offered nothing but formula he is in a real dilemma.
He wants the water content but not the food content. Either
he must go thirsty or he must take food he does not want. In
an extreme case he may get dehydrated. It seems common
sense to offer a baby a drink of water or diluted fruit juice
once or twice in any day. It is urgent to do so whenever he
reduces his milk intake.

His extra drinks, although they must be made with boiled
water, need not be warmed. In fact his feeds need not be
warmed either. Several studies have now shown that babies
accept and thrive on feeds taken straight from a refrigerator.
Roller-dried milks may, however, cause problems if fed
cold, for the fat globules tend to congeal and block the teat.

FREQUENCY AND TIMING

A baby's digestion is such that a full feed, taken calmly over a
reasonable period – in 25 minutes, say, rather than in sips
over an hour – will probably last him for between three and
four hours. But that is once he is settled, once his digestion has
begun to have a pattern. It has, after all, to learn to accept
comfortable fullness and near emptiness, rather than the
constant 'topping up' of nutritional needs which went on in
the womb. Furthermore it has to accept our diurnal rhythm,
to accept a long period unfed during the night. All this takes
time. Because it takes time, the much disputed questions
about whether babies should be fed 'on demand' or 'on
schedule' make very little sense. If a pre-calculated rhythm
is imposed on the baby's feeding, he will eventually accept
that rhythm, and be ready for food at roughly the pre-set
hours. But during the intervening weeks he will have had

periods of acute distress, when his new digestion told him different from the clock. If, on the other hand, his mother tries, in the early weeks, to follow the demands of his digestion, she will end up similarly placed. He will only want food at the 3–4-hour interval. The only difference is that the mother will have suffered some inconvenience in the intervening weeks, instead of the infant suffering hunger and frustration. The advantages of pre-set feeding times do not outweigh the advantages of a more contented baby for many mothers. The hunger cry of a very young child is extremely difficult to resist. Many who reared their children during Truby King's era can tell horror stories of sitting weeping in nursery doorways, listening to their baby, watching the clock, uterus and breasts aching with empathy as the crying got more desperate and the minute-hand slower. The actual feeding, sleeping and crying times of one baby girl, breast fed 'on demand', are shown in Figures 4 and 5. The irregularity of her demands at 5 days contrasts with the spontaneous pattern which she had adopted by one month.

There is no doubt that some infants accept scheduling far more easily than others. If the infant always has to be woken for his feeds anyway, then there is obviously no reason why he should not be woken to suit the mother's wishes. She is having to tell his digestive system that it needs food, rather than it telling her; so she might as well tell it that it needs food at the 'right' time. If, when he wakes, the baby stops crying when he is picked up, and waits calmly, then again there is no reason why his feed should not be delayed if the mother prefers. But if, as is more usual, the hunger cry is urgent, the calming on being lifted transitory, then nothing is gained by waiting. With some babies something may actually be lost. In the early weeks, a baby whose experience and expectations are so limited can quickly cry himself into such a state that when he is finally fed he cannot or will not calm down enough to suck properly. He may suck a little and fall into exhausted sleep before he has had enough. The whole dilemma then has to be faced again when he wakes an hour or so later.

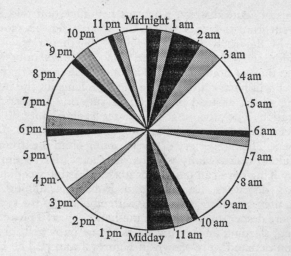

Figure 4. Feeding, sleeping and crying times of one demand-fed infant aged 5 days

This baby shows very clearly the random quality of basic behaviours in the newborn period as compared with even a few weeks later.

At day 5 the time interval between feeds varies from nearly 5 hours (after the 10.15 a.m. feed) right down to 1½ hours (after 11 p.m.). On day 28 the intervals are much more regular.

On day 5, while there is generally crying before a feed – this being the mother's cue to feed the baby – there is also crying after feeds on several occasions. Indeed it looks as though the feed given

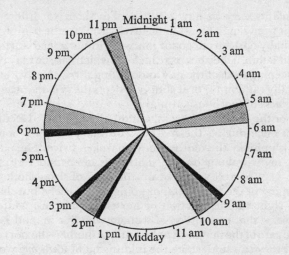

Figure 5. Feeding, sleeping and crying times of the same infant now
aged 28 days

at half past midnight was ineffective in ending a long crying
session. On day 28 there is still brief crying before feeds, but only
on one occasion is there crying after feeding.

On day 5 feeding – which includes sociable time awake – is
usually only half an hour at a time. By day 28 feeds and their social
accompaniments are taking nearly an hour on each occasion.

On day 5 the infant spends *less* time asleep than he does on day
28. By this fourth week, sleeping time and social time have both
increased at the expense of crying time.

Infants vary in how long it takes them to differentiate night from day, at least in terms of sleep. At the beginning, if the baby happens to go for longest without a feed during the night hours, it is either pure luck (in which case he may return to sleeping most of the day and waking three-hourly at night, equally randomly) or it simply reflects the greater peace and darkness of the house at night.

For the first 4 or 5 weeks, almost all babies need feeding at least once during the mother's ordinary sleeping hours. If she is unlucky the mother may be woken twice. The effect of this night-waking on the mother is often underestimated. She may be able to make up the *hours* of sleep she loses by napping in the afternoon, or going to bed early, but she cannot right the destruction of her sleep patterns. Maternity nurses – that rare breed of women who live in, and help to take care of the newborn baby and the mother – do not reckon that they can undertake the infant's night feeds *and* work an ordinary eight-hour day as well. Agencies supplying them will not send them to houses where this will be expected. Yet mothers have to undertake the night feeds and work what often amounts to a twelve-hour day as well, *and* they are the ones who have recently given birth.

Unfortunately, before about 6 weeks little can be done to increase the mother's chance of a long sleep at night. If the baby is woken for a feed just before the mother goes to bed, he *may* give her four or five hours. But equally, waking him may simply break what would have been a long sleep period. He may wake three hours later all the same. Persuading him to take every drop he can hold *may* keep him asleep for an extra half hour – or it may give him wind and indigestion.

But like everything else in the settling period, night feeding does eventually rationalize itself. Around 4–6 weeks the infant's pattern of night hunger becomes clear. Perhaps he is woken for a feed at around 11 p.m. and then wakes around 5 a.m. Once this is regular it is worth seeing whether if he is fed at midnight he will last until a more civilized 6 a.m. Equally if he always wakes at 9 p.m. and then again at around both 1 and 5 a.m. it is worth seeing whether waking him at midnight will enable him to skip the small hours' feed altogether.

But at this age inconsistency is the order of things. One good night does not predict another. Nor is there the least purpose in leaving the baby to cry. He may cry himself back to sleep because he was not urgently hungry, and crying tires him. But what is the point? His crying has already woken the mother, and he will certainly wake again within the hour with the hunger really intense. Water and other milk substitutes are similarly useless. Sucking may put him back to sleep, but if what he sucked was not food it will not satisfy his hunger, and he will wake again, probably just as the mother has got into deep sleep. She would have saved precious sleeping time if she had fed him in the first place.

CHAPTER THREE

OTHER PHYSICAL FUNDAMENTALS

SLEEP

Very few reliable statistics exist to tell us how many hours in the 24 babies actually sleep. This apparently simple question is very difficult to research: workers must either observe infants themselves, continuously, over several days and nights, or they must ask the mothers. The first procedure is enormously time-consuming and therefore expensive, as well as imposing a great burden on the family being studied. The second method is usually very unreliable. Most mothers do not *know* whether or not their small infants are actually asleep. They only know whether or not they are quiet and undemanding.

Books of advice on child-rearing tend to imply that new infants sleep practically the whole time except when being fed or handled. By implication they suggest that there may be something wrong with the infant who wakes up before he is hungry, or who refuses to go to sleep after a feed.

The few small-scale observational studies which have been carried out give a quite different picture. Kleitman and Engelmann,[6] for example, studied 10 infants at home. At the age of 3 weeks their average sleeping time was 15 hours, and the variation around that average was enormous. If 6 hours in the 24 are allowed for feeding, changing, cuddling, bathing and generally caring for the infant, that average of 15 hours' sleep still leaves 3 hours in the 24 when the infant can be expected to be awake just because he is not asleep.

At one extreme, there really are babies who sleep almost continually in the first few weeks. Their mothers rightly assume that they will settle as soon as they are put in their cots after a feed; they expect to have to wake them up for at least one or two feeds in the day, and they take an 8-hour sleep-span at night for granted from very early on. At the other extreme, there are perfectly healthy, normal babies who never sleep for more than 10–12 hours in the 24.

A new baby cannot have 'sleep problems' himself, unless he is ill, or being maltreated. Provided he is reasonably fed and moderately comfortable he will sleep when he needs to. Any problem is his mother's, not his. Often new mothers find it very difficult to relax and get on with what they want to do if they know their baby is not peacefully asleep. Obviously relaxation is, and should be, impossible if the baby is sending out distress signals. But if he is simply awake, because he is an awake kind of baby in an awake kind of mood, there is nothing the mother can do to put him to sleep. Somehow she has to re-adapt her expectations, stop feeling that the baby *ought* to be asleep, and find a companionable *modus vivendi* with him. In this respect he is behaving more like a 3–4-month infant than a newborn; reference to Chapter 14 may therefore be useful.

Many mothers find it useful to help their newborns towards a complete differentiation between sleep and waking. At this stage many infants spend long periods in between the two states, as if they neither knew how to be quite awake nor how to be quite asleep. Later on, the mother's life will be much easier if she knows that the infant is either sleeping, and therefore needing nothing, or awake and therefore likely to need company. Most infants can be moved towards this state of affairs if, from the beginning, they are helped to associate certain places and situations with sleep, and other places and situations with being awake. If the infant is always put either into his pram in the garden, or in a special corner of the living room, or into his cot, when he is expected to sleep, he will eventually come to associate those places with sleep. If, on the other hand, he is left to drop off on his mother's lap in the middle of a cuddle, he is far more likely to drift vaguely from wakefulness to dozing to wakefulness again.

Putting the infant into special regular places to sleep does not mean that the house must be hushed, or other people's activities curtailed for him. New infants are woken up far more easily by internal stimuli, such as hunger, or passing a stool, than they are by external ones. Most will sleep in the middle of a family row, or with the television set on, or three toddlers playing soldiers around the pram. What disturbs them is any violent *change* in the level of outside stimuli. When the row ceases, the television set is turned off, the room lights are turned on, or the telephone rings, the baby may wake.

Having to feed the infant in the night is disturbing enough for the mother; additional night waking can turn her life into a somnambulistic nightmare. Most infants in this age group only wake at night when they are hungry, but some wake very frequently indeed. Often the trouble comes from the infant sharing his parents' bedroom. Studies have shown that all babies 'surface' several times during each sleep period. They open their eyes, perhaps lift their heads and move their limbs. If nothing stimulates them, they drop straight back into sleep again. They do not 'want' anything; they are not hungry, or cold or uncomfortable, so they do not cry. If the baby is in a separate room, the mother knows nothing about these small awakenings. But if the baby's cot is beside her, *she* is probably woken by his small rustlings. She gets out of bed and looks into the cot. The baby sees her, or hears her, and that moment of consciousness at once turns into a demand.

While the mother may get more sleep if she does not know about her infant's momentary surfacings during the night, the evidence shows that she gains nothing at all by ignoring his real awakenings. Moore and Ucko[7] found that the infants who woke most often in the night in their early months were the ones whose parents were most afraid of 'spoiling' them, and therefore most reluctant to pick them up when they cried.

ELIMINATION

The stools of fully breast-fed and bottle-fed babies are very different. Breast-fed babies pass from the 'changing stool' described on page 36 to a stool which is an orangey-yellow liquid paste, with a slight 'sour milk' smell, entirely different from the smell of the stool of those on a mixed diet.

While this is often called the 'normal' stool for a breast-fed baby, there are quite alarming variations on the theme which are also entirely normal.

Many infants take as much as 3 to 4 weeks to arrive at the 'normal' stool. During this period the baby may pass as many as 12 motions a day. They may be violently expelled; they are often bright green in colour, and contain obvious mucus and lumps of curd. Taught about the dangers of gastro-enteritis in small babies, many mothers assume that their newborns have violent diarrhoea.

Diarrhoea *can* occur in a breast-fed baby, but it is extremely uncommon. If the baby is under 3 to 4 weeks, and is otherwise well and thriving, his extraordinary stools are no cause for alarm. If he really did have diarrhoea at this age he would have other signs of illness, such as lack of appetite, listlessness and dehydration – with eyes that looked sunken, a depressed fontanelle and very low weight gain.

By about 3 weeks the colour and consistency of the stools will probably have changed to the mustard-like substance described above. The frequency may remain. Perfectly normal breast-fed babies sometimes have more motions in a day than their mothers know about; they are always soiled whenever the nappy is changed. Research workers have followed babies who were passing 20 motions in the 24 hours, and babies have been mistakenly admitted to hospital on this account alone. If the baby is well the mother can reassure herself by checking with the doctor and then stop counting.

Just to complicate matters further, this same breast-fed baby who has been worrying his mother with his frequent stools may, over a period of a few days, slow right down to a point where she begins to worry about constipation. Many babies on the breast have periods when they only pass a motion every 2 to 5 days. Occasionally it may be as infrequent as every 10 days. No treatment is needed, and all home treatments, such as soap sticks and enemas, are wrong. It is not known why these periods of extreme infrequency occur, but it is thought that the loose and unbulky stools of the breast-fed baby simply do not provide enough stimulus to the bowel to lead to emptying. Such phases seldom last long. Over a few weeks the baby is likely gradually to revert to having 2, 3 or more motions per day.

Often it is difficult to distinguish between the loose green stools of the breast-fed baby under a month old and the so-called 'starvation stools'. These are usually small, frequent and dark. They are semi-fluid, often contain mucus and usually are semi-transparent. If a baby who has been passing the yellow mustard-like stools described above *begins* to pass stools of this description, then it may well be a sign of under-feeding. If the baby is still having the explosive green stools of the changing period it may be difficult to tell the difference, and the mother will probably have to rely on other signs of underfeeding to give her the cue. The importance of the starvation stools is that they are sometimes taken for diarrhoea. This can be tragic for the baby, since the treatment for diarrhoea will almost certainly include semi-starvation, and that was what he was suffering from in the first place. It cannot be too strongly stressed that if the baby is still fully breast-fed, underfeeding is a far more likely cause for loose, frequent, dark stools than is diarrhoea. Certainly test weighing should be carried out to exclude underfeeding before the diagnosis is made.

Babies fed on cow's milk have stools whose exact colour and consistency depends on the type of milk preparation they are receiving. In general their stools are, from the beginning, much more formed and solid than those of the breast-fed baby, with a colour which is a pale brown rather than mustard yellow. The smell is more like that of a child on a mixed diet.

Bottle-fed babies tend to produce fewer motions than breast-fed ones. Because of the different chemical composition of cow's milk, particularly its relatively high casein content, the bowel contents move much more slowly through the intestines. This effect is increased if the baby is not receiving much carbohydrate, since the fermentation of carbohydrate in the intestine hurries the passage of the contents.

Unlike breast-fed babies, bottle-fed babies may become genuinely constipated. Instead of a day or two without a motion being followed by a perfectly normal, soft one, it is followed by a hard dry motion which causes discomfort. The remedy is simple, but involves trial and error: the carbohydrate content of the feed needs adjusting. Sometimes it is enough simply to add a little extra sugar to the feed. Brown sugar is slightly more laxative than white and, in extreme cases, maltose, the most laxative of all sugars, can be used. It is probably better to use a normal quantity of maltose than a very large amount of white sugar, for if the infant becomes accustomed to a feed which tastes very sweet, he may later find it more difficult to accept unsweetened foods.

Since adding sugar rights the occasional constipation of bottle-fed babies, it is logical that adding too much sugar is a frequent cause of non-infective diarrhoea. Mothers sometimes routinely add sugar to a product which already contains sufficient carbohydrate. Others rely heavily on glucose water or other highly sweetened drinks between feeds. Infants vary widely in their carbohydrate tolerance, but many cannot tolerate much extra.

Intolerance for fat may also give a bottle-fed baby loose offensive stools. Such babies may do better on a half-cream product during their early weeks.

Milk with a high protein content, or insufficiently diluted liquid cow's milk, produces bulky, greyish, greasy motions with an unpleasant smell.

Diarrhoea due either to fat intolerance or too much carbohydrate usually begins slowly, developing only over several days. It can easily be differentiated from infective diarrhoea, or gastro-enteritis, which usually begins suddenly. Such disorders can be of any severity from mild to extreme, but in babies of this age group they should always be taken seriously. An infant who is vomiting and passing frequent liquid motions will become dehydrated very rapidly indeed. Even diarrhoea without vomiting can cause a degree of fluid loss which is serious, especially if it is associated with a rise in temperature.

As a rough guide, bottle-fed babies who suddenly develop diarrhoea with or without vomiting and fever should be seen by a doctor on that same day. It will help the doctor to decide what treatment, if any, is needed if, while waiting, the mother keeps all soiled nappies and makes a note of how much fluid the baby has drunk. If he is in the least reluctant to take his feed he should be offered plain boiled water – as much as he will drink.

Even before the beginning of mixed feeding certain substances can produce very marked colour changes in an infant's stools which sometimes alarm parents. For example if the baby is given rosehip syrup his stools may be red or purple; if for any reason he is prescribed iron the stools may be black.

Blood in, or on, the stools (after the first day or two, when it may be due to swallowed maternal blood) must always be referred to a doctor. But if it is in the form of streaks or flecks on the outside of the motion it is likely to be due either to an anal fissure – especially in a bottle-fed baby who has been constipated – or to the careless placement of a rectal thermometer.

Unlike the stools, a baby's urine seldom concerns a mother very much. Very young infants do not concentrate their urine as much as older people, nor do they wait until the bladder is 'full' before passing it. Wet nappies are therefore the rule rather than an event; some studies have shown urination to occur as often as every half an hour in the early weeks.

The only cause for concern which is at all common is sudden *infrequency* of urination. A baby at this age, if he is taking enough fluid, and is not dehydrated due to fever or diarrhoea or vomiting, is most unlikely to remain dry between feeds. If he is found to be dry after one 3–4-hour interval, he should be watched. If he is still dry at the end of the next couple of hours advice should be sought, in case some obstruction has occurred.

Occasionally the urine suddenly becomes extra strong smelling. It may be so concentrated that it stains the nappy yellow and reddens the baby's skin. Again, lack of fluid on a hot day, or when the baby is feverish, is the most usual cause, but if the smell is actually foul or 'fishy', there is just a possibility of urinary infection, and a doctor's advice should be sought. In this case a urine specimen will almost certainly be wanted, and the mother will save everybody time and effort if she can catch one in a clean container and take it with her.

Blood in the urine obviously means medical consultation; but a short pause for thought often leads to the realization that the red urine follows the baby's first drink of black-currant juice! If this is the case the mother can wait for 2 or 3 hours and another wet nappy before declaring an emergency.

TEMPERATURE CONTROL

Newborn infants can regulate their own temperatures, so as to remain comfortable in environments of differing warmths, but the mechanism by which they do this is not nearly so efficient as in older people. If an infant is placed in circumstances which force him to use the most extreme temperature-regulating mechanisms of which he is capable, keeping his temperature stable takes so much of his 'physiological energy' that he functions less than perfectly in other respects. If he is forced to keep himself warm when the outside temperature is too cool for him, he will have little energy to spare for anything else.

There is, for any infant, at any particular stage of his development, what is termed a 'neutral thermal environment'. This simply means the outside environmental temperature at which the infant remains at a constant temperature without expending any energy in doing so. This temperature can be established, for the individual baby, by measuring his metabolic rate in terms of his oxygen con-

sumption. The question being asked is: 'At what temperature
is this infant consuming no extra oxygen – not increasing his
metabolic rate – simply in order to maintain his normal
temperature?'

The lower limit of the neutral temperature range is usually
referred to as the 'critical temperature', because cold is a far
more frequent enemy to young infants than heat. An extensive study of the 'critical temperature' for babies of
normal birthweight was made by J. W. Scopes.[8] At birth it
was found to be 88–92°F (31–4°C). It remained well over
80°F (27°C) for at least 2 weeks after birth.

Scopes's experiments were carried out with naked babies
in the controlled environment of an incubator. At home,
babies are usually dressed, and clothes steady the infant's
temperature, helping him to stay both warm and cool by
reducing conduction, convection, radiation and evaporation. Scopes himself found that the temperature inside an
infant's wrapping shawl may be 89°F (32°C) when the air
temperature is only 77°F (25°C). Such a combination of air
temperature and clothing would be ideal for a newborn, but
rather too hot for a 6-week baby, who is better able to regulate his heat, and uses less energy in doing so.

Clearly, if infants are to use a minimum amount of energy
on keeping warm they need higher environmental temperatures than are usually provided. The normal advice
given to new parents is to keep any room used by the baby at
a temperature of 68–70°F (20–21°C). Such a temperature is
perfectly adequate while the baby, who was already warm, is
well wrapped up, but it becomes woefully inadequate when
he is undressed for a change of nappy, or – worse still – put in
a bath. After such an event, the infant may have to work
extremely hard to get himself warm again.

Of course it does not harm a healthy baby to have to expend a little energy on creating heat. But the baby who is
exposed to actual chilling is in a very different situation. If he
is mature and awake, he will respond to actual cold as
efficiently as a full-grown man: his metabolic rate will shoot
up; he may actually treble his oxygen consumption. But fast

as he *makes* heat, he cannot conserve it; the metabolic effort must go on and on and on, until outside warmth relieves his body of the necessity.

The immature baby – usually the premature one – may be in even worse case. He tends to lack the deposits of 'brown fat' which are an important site of heat production, and are only laid down in the last weeks before birth. Such a baby may be quite incapable of the increase in heat production the cold demands of him.

Babies who are deeply asleep when the environmental temperature begins to drop are at risk too. Infants do not appear to begin the metabolic adjustment that results in increased heat production until they are on the verge of waking up. If the temperature in the baby's room drops rapidly while he is deeply asleep, he may have lost so much body heat before he surfaces that the battle to maintain his temperature is lost before it begins. Bedrooms which cool rapidly at night are an obvious danger here. A thermostatically controlled central heating system may switch itself off at midnight, and the infant's room temperature may drop 15 degrees in an hour, especially if it is not well insulated. If a thermostat is used for the rest of the house the infant's room must be separately heated. Covers which can easily be dislodged are also a danger, especially if plastic pants are not used, so that the infant's wet nappy cools him by evaporation. There is a good deal to be said for swaddling the infant at night, or for using a baby bag.

If an infant is having to work hard to regain lost heat, parents – thinking he seems a little chilly – often make the tragic mistake of putting extra wrappings round him. More clothing will only insulate the cold *in* and make it infinitely more difficult for the baby to regain his heat. If he has got cold, he needs to be warmed *first* and then wrapped up so that warmth is insulated in.

Babies who are allowed to become really chilled may develop the 'neonatal cold syndrome'. The infant gives up the battle to make heat. His respiration and pulse (which were rapid while his metabolic rate and level of oxygen con-

sumption were high because he was trying to make heat)
drop very low. He lies still. When handled, he is lethargic
and cannot muster the energy to suck properly. As the syndrome develops, he may refuse to suck altogether; his hands
and feet become swollen and pink and his skin feels cold to
the touch. It is vital that medical help should be sought
urgently if this happens. The baby may have succumbed to
the cold syndrome because he was predisposed to it by illness.
Even if this is not the case, his re-warming has to be extremely
slow and careful, and must be carried out with medical help.

High temperatures are far less of a problem for young
babies. The upper limits of the 'neutral thermal range' have
proved difficult to measure experimentally, because infants
tend to wake up and cry and kick as the temperature goes up,
thus raising their metabolic rate and their oxygen consumption in crying, so that it is impossible to tell whether
they are also doing so to cool themselves. But it is clear that
the vast majority of very young babies are extremely content
with an environmental temperature as high as 90°F (32–3°C),
provided they are not swaddled so that natural evaporation
from the skin is prevented. Many parents have discovered,
almost by accident, that their restless infants sleep more
peacefully, and are more active when awake, if their rooms
are allowed to get very warm indeed.

Radiant heat can, however, be unexpectedly dangerous to
young babies. Most mothers are aware of the danger of sun-
burn. But even a 60-watt light bulb can burn a new baby's
skin if it is too close to him, and many mothers have been
horrified to find red marks on a baby who has been put on a
cosy rug by the fire.

CRYING

Crying is the young infant's only sure method of communicating with his caretakers on whom his very life depends.
Later, the baby's mother will recognize all kinds of other
cues, which will help her to interpret cries, or may them-

selves be sufficiently communicative. But in the very first weeks the baby's facial expressions, physical movements and non-crying noises are often unfocused, and therefore difficult for either mothers or research workers to interpret. The baby must cry. It is the only absolutely reliable signal for assistance or care in his repertory. Many mothers feel that they would prefer it if their new infant never cried. In fact if he never cried, they would never know, certainly, that he was content. Because he cries when he is *not* all right, his not crying can be taken to mean that he is all right.

Some research workers have attempted to add up the total minutes per day that new babies cry and to give an average figure. This is not a very helpful way of looking at crying. If crying is regarded as signalling, then its duration becomes an index of the sensitivity of the receiver of the signals. In other words how long an infant cries reflects the length of time it takes his mother to attend to him and to find out what he needs. Such a measure may tell us something about the mother, but nothing about the baby. A more useful index might be the number of *times* in 24 hours that the infant uses the crying signal. As far as I know there are no figures on this.

The causes of crying have been extensively studied. One of the most straightforward reports is that by Peter H. Wolff.[9] He studied a series of newborn babies in a hospital nursery, and followed them up in their homes to several months of age. Many of the following comments are based on his fascinating paper.

1. *Hunger*

Hardly surprisingly, hunger is the most usual reason for crying in the first weeks of life. At any visit to the nursery, many more babies were found to be crying in the half hour before they were due to be fed than in the half hour after they had been fed.

When a baby feeds, many different things are happening simultaneously. They include sucking, swallowing, filling of the stomach and absorption of food. Furthermore feeding tends rapidly to become associated by the baby with being picked up and held. Wolff was able to separate and examine these different elements, by studying a series of babies who had incompletely separated tracheas and oesophaguses. Otherwise healthy, the babies were at first fed by a tube into the stomach. Later they were fed by mouth in the normal way, but with the tube left in place in case it was needed.

Wolff found that if the babies were allowed to suck a dummy for the 20 minutes a feed would have taken, but were given no food through the stomach tube, none of them settled; sucking alone, without food, was not enough to stop them crying.

If they were fed through the stomach tube, but were given nothing to suck, all settled happily. The lack of sucking did not appear to bother them.

If they were fed normally, by mouth, but the milk was removed from the stomach through the gastrostomy tube, they did not settle. Even sucking real food was not enough if the food did not remain in the stomach.

If that same milk was returned to the stomach through the tube they did settle.

If they were fed normally by mouth, but were propped with their bottles rather than being held, they settled; being picked up and held did not seem to be relevant.

2. Cold

As we have seen on page 70 very young babies function best, physiologically, if high ambient temperatures are maintained. This study also showed that they cry more and sleep less if their cots are kept at around 78°F (25–6°C) (which would be a high temperature for an ordinary home) than if they are kept at 88–90°F (31–2°C). It seems that while the lower temperature may not in itself be enough to make the baby cry, it predisposes him to cry about other things. Mild discomfort, mild hunger and noise are more likely to penetrate his sleep and disturb him if he is less warm.

3. *Wet or Soiled Nappies*

Many mothers and nurses believe that a baby will cry if his nappy is wet or soiled. Wolff tested this among babies who were crying shortly after a feed. Nurses picked all the babies up and changed them, but in half the babies they put back the wet nappy, and in the other half they put on a dry one. All the babies settled down happily. The actual wetness made no difference at all. Presumably it is being lifted and having the position changed which stops crying in these circumstances.

4. *Spontaneous Jerks and Twitches*

Almost all new babies jerk and twitch in their sleep. Very few find this disturbing when they are deeply asleep, but in the drowsy period before deep sleep takes over, some babies jerk awake and cry over and over again; they find it difficult to get *past* the jerky drowsing state *into* deep sleep.

5. *Being Undressed*

A mother often assumes that a baby's crying when he is undressed reflects her own clumsiness or inexperience. Indeed if a baby is roughly handled or feels loss of support while clothes are pulled off him, he is likely to cry. But some cry literally for the loss of their clothes. In Wolff's sample one third of the babies objected increasingly vigorously to being undressed from their first to their third weeks. Babies who react in this way convey great pathos. They remain calm while outer garments are removed, and become increasingly tense, usually finally dissolving into crying when the mother attempts to remove the last garment next to the skin – usually the vest. I have seen a 3-week-old girl literally hang on to her vest with her fingers.

This reaction is not related to cold, as it occurs whatever the temperature. It appears rather to reflect the loss of restraint, and the loss of skin contact. It is as if the baby fears the unrestricted movement and air on his skin which will give so much pleasure in a few weeks' time.

Such babies invariably stop crying when they are re-dressed, and can always be pacified for the moment by being covered with a blanket or towel. It has been shown experimentally that this covering must be of textured material – plastic or silk is ineffective – and that it must cover the chest and stomach. Covering the arms and legs does not stop the crying.

6. *Pain*

From the moment of birth, babies cry if they are hurt. Their reactions to various procedures, such as heel prick to obtain blood for study, or to circumcision, make this quite clear.

Their reactions to internal pain, from wind and so forth, are more difficult to gauge. It seems likely that a great deal of crying is put down to wind when it is really of another source. Nevertheless a baby who is crying for no other reason that can be discovered does sometimes stop once he has got rid of wind from one end or the other. Fortunately a baby who does need to belch will normally do so in the course of the handling which his mother gives him while looking for other sources of discomfort.

7. *Over-Stimulation*

Too much, or too intense, stimulation of any of a baby's senses is liable to make him cry. Very loud sudden noises, sudden very bright lights, too sudden or violent a movement, too sharp or bitter a taste, too hot or cold or tickling a touch can all overstep the limits and cause distress.

Interestingly, almost any of these acute stimuli will momentarily silence a baby who is already crying. But this is merely a pause while he focuses on the sound or sight or feeling; once it is registered the crying is redoubled.

OTHER PHYSICAL FUNDAMENTALS

8. *Mistiming*

Stimuli which a baby appears to enjoy when he is alert and
happy often cause distress if he is grumbly or tired. Talking to
him, rocking him, swinging him, tickling him will all give
him pleasure by the end of his first month. But all of these have
been shown to work in reverse if they are used to 'jolly him
along' when he is impatient for a feed, or to 'cheer him up'
when he is grizzling. It seems likely that stimulations of this
kind are at the upper limits of acceptability for very small
infants. He can cope with and enjoy them when he is at his
best and calmest; at other times they are just too much. It is like
the older person who can enjoy being frightened by a ghost
story when he is feeling well companioned and protected,
but cannot cope with his own fear if he is alone in a dark house.

Other kinds of mistiming also often cause crying. They
vary widely with individual infants and individual kinds of
mothering, but some are fairly general.

i. The most obvious: mistiming feeds and keeping the
   infant waiting.
ii. Offering food at the wrong rate – almost always too
    slowly – so that the distress of hunger breaks through the
    relief of feeding, thus creating a vicious circle with the
    infant crying because he is hungry and staying hungry
    because he is crying too much to suck.
iii. Bathing or changing or otherwise manipulating a hungry
     baby who would enjoy these ministrations once fed.
iv. Altering the surroundings – light, or sound, or movement
    – when the baby is half into sleep. If he must be pushed in
    the pram, let the ride start before he settles, or once he is
    soundly off.

9. *Lack of Kinaesthetic or Contact Comfort*

Most of the causes for crying discussed so far are simple to
remedy once they have been discovered. But most parents
bitterly discover that their infants sometimes cry without ob-

vious reason. It is this apparently causeless crying which tends to drive mothers frantic. The sadness in the noise churns them up emotionally; their inability to stop it makes them feel woefully inadequate as mothers.

Some authorities take such crying lightly. They may attribute it vaguely to 'wind' or to 'colic'; some even suggest that infants must cry to 'exercise their lungs'. The mother is advised to do everything she can to make the infant comfortable and then to leave him to cry himself out.

Working from the simple and universal observation that such infants always stop crying when they are picked up, other people suggest that they cry to *be* picked up. While close to the truth this is a risky way of looking at the problem. It suggests that the infant is capable of a kind of reasoning and planning which will be impossible for him for months to come. He cannot say to himself, 'If I cry and go on crying she will come and pick me up.' If the mother is encouraged to believe that he can think in this way she may be tempted to feel that she should not give in to the infant.

In these early weeks it is more likely that the infant cries simply because he feels uncomfortable. In the absence of any other obvious cause for discomfort he may be missing physical contact with his mother. He does not cry to be picked up; he cries because he has been put down.

Western civilizations are unique in the amount of physical separateness which they impose on infants. We have invented innumerable gadgets – from prams and cots to babychairs and bouncers – which make it safe for mothers to put their infants down. In other times and other parts of the world it would be dangerous to put them down for more than a moment. So infants spend their days carried by the mother or another female relative, their nights cuddled against the mother or in a huddle of bodies. Such a child seldom meets the situation of physical aloneness until he is mobile enough to travel voluntarily away from his mother.

It seems that in our preoccupation with sucking and feeding as a psychological need for infants we may have come to neglect the whole area of contact comfort. Our infants are usually cuddled while they feed, so both needs are met together during feeding times. But an increasing body of evidence (largely from animal studies) suggests that if the two are sorted out, experimentally, the infant's need for contact comfort often exceeds his psychological need for sucking. A selection of such studies is well reviewed by Scott.[10] For example, Brodbeck bottle-fed half of a batch of newborn puppies by hand. The other half sucked their milk from a machine. But Brodbeck gave all the puppies identical amounts of handling and petting. All became equally and intensely attached to him. The puppies loved the hand that petted whether it also fed or not. Harlow,[11] in his famous study of baby rhesus monkeys, provided two 'substitute mothers'. One was a cold uncomfortable structure made of wire, which held the infants' feeding bottles. The other was a warm comfortable padded structure which provided no food or sucking. The infant monkeys would feed from the wire mother, but it was to the cloth mother that they went when they were tired or afraid.

If crying does not stop when the baby is held on the mother's lap, walking with the baby often produces miraculous silence. The actual position in which the baby is held can make a difference too. Just as the baby who hates to be naked can be comforted by having his chest and stomach covered, so the baby who is being held will usually relax most if he is held against his mother, so that he is looking over her shoulder with his chest and stomach pressed against her.

Mothers in our culture cannot carry their babies constantly. Too much else is expected of them, and too much that they do is impossible with a baby on the back. Often contact comfort of a similar kind can be given by wrapping the baby up. Again there is a way that works and a way that does not. The idea is to provide a constant, unchanging contact between the infant's body and the wrapping material. If the infant is too loosely wrapped the contact varies every time he moves, and this changing stimulation, in combination with a slight restriction of his limb movements, may have exactly the opposite of the desired effect. He becomes increasingly restless and cross. If the wrapping is sufficiently firm, the shawl or cot sheet remains in contact even as he moves, so that he moves *within* the swaddling, rather than moving *it*. Wrapped like this he is quite likely to drop off to sleep in mid cry.

Plastic makes life very uncomfortable for babies who yearn for contact comfort. Plastic-covered mattresses, changing tables and floor mats are desperately unwelcoming surfaces for a creature who, if he was a few million years less evolved, would be clinging to his mother's fur. He will be happier on warm, textured materials.

10. *Other Methods of Dealing with Crying*

Crying can almost always be halted by picking up and cuddling, or at least by cuddling while walking. The problem for desperate parents is where to go from there.

In the very early weeks of life a large variety of continuous, regular rhythmical stimuli predispose infants to sleep. It seems that they act by blocking out the changing, minor, internal or external stimuli which were preventing the baby relaxing into sleep. The principle is much the same as the counter irritant whereby you forget your headache when you stub your toe. Wolff[9] has demonstrated the efficacy of 'white noise'. Ambrose has shown that rocking is universally effective, if carried out at the correct rate. He found that rocking, through a travel of about 3 in. at a rate of 60 rocks per minute or above, stopped all babies he studied from crying, and that most babies became relaxed and went to sleep within short periods.[12] Some mothers habitually rock their infants, others have found the method useless, or do not use a rockable cot for the baby. It may be that those who do not find rocking useful do not rock fast enough; it is quite difficult to keep up a rate of 60 rocks per minute by hand. The parallel with walking the baby is, however, inescapable. Sixty steps per minute is a very slow walk for an adult. A baby carried on the hip or on the back by a walking adult would almost certainly be rocked at a higher rate.

Many workers, including Wolff, have demonstrated that non-nutritive sucking stops crying, *provided* the baby is not hungry. Sucking a dummy did nothing to quieten the hungry babies in Wolff's study, unless they were simultaneously fed by tube. But slipping a dummy into the mouth of a crying baby who is *not* hungry is very often effective. Dummies also seem to protect sleep, so that stimuli which disturb the non-sucking infant, making him move restlessly and eventually cry, merely make him suck vigorously if there is a dummy in his mouth. It is as if the activity engendered by the stimulus was channelled into sucking, and the infant thus lulled back into peace.

CHAPTER FOUR

STARTING TO BE A PERSON

In the very earliest weeks of a baby's life it is easy to write about him, and indeed to handle him, as if he were a precious object rather than a person. There is so much to learn about his physical appearance, his feeding, his elimination, his crying and his general physiological reactions to the world, and he is so unpredictable, that his mother can easily find herself caught up in his physical care to the exclusion of everything else.

Yet with every day that passes, the infant is developing all those qualities and capacities which mean that he is indeed a human being, and not just an especially precious little animal for whom the mother is uniquely responsible. At this stage, the infant does not react to people as one person reacts to another. But a detailed study of his reactions to the world around him show that he is *predisposed* to interact with people in quite a different way than with any other object. If a study is made of the sights which interest the infant most, the sounds which get his attention, the sensations he enjoys most and seeks to repeat, they all turn out to be most readily available in the form of an adult care-taking human.

Bowlby[12] puts it like this: 'Newborns do not respond to people as people, nevertheless (as we have seen) their perceptual equipment is well designed to pick up and process stimuli emanating from people and their reactive equipment is biased to respond to such stimuli in certain typical ways.'

PHYSICAL CONTACT

As we have already seen in the previous chapter, infants are usually at their most contented when they are held by the mother in one of the positions which simulates clinging. Unlike infant monkeys and apes, human babies cannot cling until they are several months old. Indeed the 4–5-month infant may be very much easier for his mother to carry than is the lighter newborn, just because he holds on so efficiently by this later stage.

There is some evidence of an instinctive tendency to cling, left over from earlier evolution. In 1918, Moro, a German pediatrician, described a reflex by which newborns reacted to any sudden change of position, and especially to any change which made them feel they were about to be dropped, and which caused their overheavy heads to fall back on their unsteady necks. Put down carelessly in his cot, so that he does not feel the security of the firm mattress before his mother's hands start to release him, the infant throws out and then bends both his arms and his legs, he gives the impression of being violently startled, and he usually cries. This reflex – called the 'Moro response' – puzzled research workers, who could not see what function it could serve in evolutionary or survival terms. In 1965 Prechtl[13] showed that the Moro response takes a very different and far more comprehensible form if it is evoked while the infant's hands are being gently pulled. In these circumstances his palmar grasp reflex is also brought into play, and the Moro response takes a form which clearly suggests a sudden gripping, with hands, arms and legs. It is now thought that this response is, in fact, a leftover from a time when the infant habitually clung to his furry mother, and that it would have been evoked by any sudden movement on her part that made the infant feel he was going to be dislodged.

The instinctive desire to cling probably explains the discomfort which infants display when they are held in positions which prevent them from making full body contact with the mother. Few, for example, are happy if they are carried in a cradled position, with the mother's hands under their heads and shoulders, thighs and knees. Few like to be laid across the mother's lap, or to be held with their backs to her.

As we have already seen, being firmly wrapped in soft textured material often comforts distressed infants who cannot be carried. Similarly, physical exposure in open space usually alarms this age group. Even if the infant's clothes are not removed, he is likely to appear worried and tense if he is put down on a hard flat surface, or if he is held in space. He needs, all the time, to feel the kind of contact which he would feel if he were clinging to warm fur. Modern baby-aids are a great help to *mothers*, but many of them directly contradict the needs of infants. Weighing a baby provides a composite example. He is undressed – which he may well find frightening – he is then placed in a hard plastic or wicker basket, suspended in space. The basket descends suddenly under his weight, and makes a sharp sudden sound as it reaches the bottom of its travel. To weigh a baby without tears takes real understanding, foresight and skill.

SEEING

If the infant is predisposed to remain in close physical contact with human beings, so he is innately predisposed to look at their faces rather than at anything else. From birth an infant will focus his gaze for about two seconds on any new sight which is brought before his eyes. This brief focus shows that he has 'noticed' the object. The length of his gaze thereafter can be taken as a measure of his actual interest in it, and some very interesting research has been carried out into the kind of object which newborns look at for longest.

Fantz[14] found that at 48 hours of age infants looked for longer at a coloured pattern than at a plain block of colour, and for longer at a circle with eyes, nose and mouth sketched in than at a plain circle. Most interest of all was always elicited by a face-pattern which also moved. These very new infants were therefore selecting for visual inspection objects which had the qualities of a human face.

Studying 4-week-old infants, Wolff[15] found that infants would look for much longer at an actual human face than at any other object, however garish the alternative objects were. This scientific finding is regularly confirmed in ordinary homes. A mother, striving to get her infant to look at a new toy, finds that the infant continually disregards it and returns his gaze to her own face.

HEARING

The human voice also seems to be innately attractive to new babies. Infants are almost always startled by loud sudden sounds, and usually seem soothed and pleased by music or by gentle rhythmic continuous noise. But a human voice elicits a special response from the baby. If he is crying, he is likely to stop when his mother talks to him, remain quietly alert as long as she goes on talking and cry again as soon as she stops. If he is content when she starts talking, her voice may elicit a very brief, fleeting smile, even as early as the third week of life. By the time the baby is 5 weeks old he may always smile when his mother talks to him. From this time on, he may also babble in response to her voice, although he does not yet babble in reaction to any other sound.

LANGUAGE

At the beginning a new infant has no language other than crying. Various types of cry can be distinguished, by means of sound spectrographs. These do form a 'language' in the sense that all infants' hunger cries have one typical pattern, all pain cries another and so on. Mothers have to learn to interpret their infant's cries by experience. Most maintain that they would not recognize their own child's cry from those of other babies of similar age, but various experiments have shown that in fact mothers are extremely good at recognizing the cries of their own newborns. Formby[16] showed that of 23 mothers in one maternity ward, 12 successfully recognized the tape-recorded cry of their own child at 48 hours old, and all were successful during the next few days. Furthermore in the first three nights after they had given birth, 15 mothers woke only when their own babies cried; on subsequent nights only one mother ever woke to the cry of another woman's baby. Wolff[9] found that mothers' reactions to different cries in their babies were extremely variable: they might, or might not, go at once in answer to the basic, hunger cry. But the mothers in his experiment all reacted with extreme speed to their babies' pain cries – and were both furious and relieved when they found that these were tape-recorded rather than immediate.

Until about 3 weeks old, babies usually have a repertory of cries consisting of the basic or hunger cry, the distinctive pain cry and what is often described as an 'anger' cry, which mothers often call 'trying it on'. It is a grumbly, grizzly cry which often lasts for some minutes, and which turns into the basic hunger cry if the mother does not intervene first.

By about 4 weeks old, the first non-crying sounds usually appear. Not distinct separate sounds at this stage, but gurgly googly noises. Often they occur first of all when the infant is just beginning to feel fretful. They may give way to grumbling and thence to basic crying, in a regular sequence.

By 6 weeks there will probably be some phonetic syllables among the gurgles. Sound-making tends to become differentiated from feeling fretful at this point. The infant probably now 'talks' most when he is talked to. Some babies will even 'talk back' by this age, making a sound, listening to the mother make the sound back, and then making it again themselves.

SMILING

Smiling is a vital social accomplishment. It is the means whereby infants ensure that adults will interact socially with them, will pay them the personal attention they must have for full human development. Such a bald statement is justifiable because for any normal adult a new baby's smile is irresistible. The bored visitor may bend dutifully over the cot, and make some trite remark to the mother about the occupant's beauty. But if that occupant smiles at him, he will almost certainly drop his guard and smile and talk directly and spontaneously to the baby.

However much mothers know, intellectually, about the early development of infants, and the importance of treating them personally, looking at them directly, talking to them by name from the beginning, all these things cease to be intellectually governed once the infants respond and reward them with smiles. Of 120 mothers whom the author saw over two years, all but one made some spontaneous remark during the week when her child began to smile, along the lines of 'Now he really knows me' or 'Now she's really getting to be fun.'

The actual dating of smiling varies wildly according to different authorities. No doubt this is partly because it varies wildly according to different babies. Most smile fleetingly, in response to a variety of stimuli, almost from birth. These fleeting pseudo-smiles used to be put down to wind. It is now thought that they are actual practice smiles.

By about 4 weeks these pseudo-smiles tend to occur most often in response to the human voice, and they begin to have some social effect – they *look* more smiley. A little after this, the baby seems transfixed by the human face. He gazes at it, often for a minute at a time, slowly exploring its contour from hairline to chin; returning always to the eyes. By 6 weeks, about 50 per cent of babies complete their detailed examination of the face by returning their gaze to the eyes, and smiling. The other half of any given group of babies will reach this stage in a diminishing scatter over the next $2\frac{1}{2}$ months. Only a very few – probably including those who were born prematurely – will fail to smile by four months.

In a way an infant's smiling, gurgling responses are the mother's reward for her devoted care while he got himself settled into life. Earlier on, the baby could give his parents pleasure by his very existence, by his contentment, his growth, his obvious 'all rightness'. But once he begins to react to being handled in this brilliantly social, enchanting way, he gives them pleasure of quite a different sort. His smiles and his 'talk' are an immediate reward to the mother who has torn herself out of deep sleep to feed him in the night, an irresistible compensation for yet another nappy needing changing in the middle of her favourite television programme. Even from these very early weeks, the infant whose social responses start early and are frequent and easily evoked is likely to get more attention than the one whose social development is slower. All human beings like to be liked. The mother whose baby smiles at her has no doubt of his affection or of his humanness.

New babies have typical postures associated with their physical immaturity. To some extent these mediate *against* their displaying the dawning humanity of their reactions to things and to people.

Placed on his back, when he is relaxed, the middle of the back of the infant's head will seldom touch the mattress. Characteristically he turns his head towards one preferred side, extends the arm on that side, and flexes the opposite arm in towards the chest. This means that while he remains relaxed, there will be no symmetrical movements of the limbs, but merely a movement of the free ones. If his head does turn to the midline, and all four limbs thrash symmetrically, then he is either highly startled, extremely hungry or very angry about something.

The flexed posture is important because it limits the baby's range of vision and of movement. If the mother hangs something interesting, be it a mobile, a rattle, or even her own face, directly above the cot, the infant is unlikely to see it because his head is turned. If the object is deliberately brought within his field of vision, he will, by 2 weeks of age, follow it through a very small arc by a combination of head and eye movements. By 4 weeks old he will probably follow it through a horizontal arc up to 90 degrees, and a little way vertically also. By 6 weeks he may actually search his surroundings for things to look at, turning his head to look for new objects of interest, but his visual field is still limited by his posture.

If the baby is placed on his stomach, he will turn his head towards a preferred side, and probably adopt a character-istic posture with his arms and legs flexed under him and his bottom in the air. Unwary mothers have allowed this position to convince them that they had given birth to a genius who would crawl at a month old. The posture vanishes in a few weeks. Meantime in active babies, unwarily placed on in-adequately covered plastic mattresses, it can lead to sore elbows and knees, as the infant 'scrabbles' on a slippery surface.

All the postures of the newborn when he is not lying down are dominated by his gradually acquired ability to manage his own head. At the beginning his head is quite literally too heavy for the muscles of his neck and back. If his mother does not support it with a hand at his back and fingers spread be-tween shoulder blades and neck, it simply flops, uncontrol-lably. The baby's own drive to acquire control is very obvious. By 1 week old, if he is comfortably held against the mother's shoulder, he will lift his head away in little inter-mittent jerks, so that it feels as if he were deliberately bump-ing his head. By 3 weeks he will be able to hold his head clear of the shoulder for several seconds at a time. By 6 weeks most will be able to support their heads for a minute or two while the mother is still; a few will be able to remain in control while they are being carried about.

Throughout this age period mothers who want their infants to prove the truth of what we have said about their interest in human faces, their preference for patterned, mov-ing objects and so on, must allow for the typical position of their heads. Only very gradually does the infant begin to be able to turn his head at will. In these early weeks he cannot show that he is interested in looking at something unless he is put in a position from which he can see it. And that means directly in front of his eye line, and remarkably close to the bridge of his nose (see page 120).

USING HIS HANDS

From the earliest days, a finger inserted into the loosely closed fist of a baby will be grasped. Indeed experiments have shown that in the first two days of life this grasp reflex is so strong that the baby can in fact hang all his weight by his grasping hands. This ability passes quickly though, so it is not an experiment recommended for home trial.

This kind of reflex grasping has to be distinguished both from deliberately holding *on* to an object and from the very earliest signs of reaching out for an object.

By 3 to 4 weeks, many babies will hold on to a rattle or similar object once it has been put in their hands. They may indeed get some pleasure out of the movements *it* makes as their own arms randomly move. It goes without saying that the object should be light, as the baby's arm is as likely as not to land the rattle in his own eye.

By 4 to 5 weeks, although the infant still cannot voluntarily grasp an object but must have it placed in his hand, merely touching his hand with it may lead to movements of the arm, and unclenching of the hand. It is as if the infant knows that he has to use that arm and hand to get the object, but simply lacks the coordination needed to take it.

An infant's most successful holding on and early taking hold usually occur in the context of being held by the mother or some other adult. If the baby is held in a clinging posture, the adult's body supports him so that his head does not flop, and his limbs do not take up the characteristic asymmetry which they display when he is lying in his cot. Held thus he is more free to move than he is when he is lying down. Even while he must still have a rattle put into his fist before he can hold on to it, he will manage to get and to hold a handful of his mother's hair or the neckline of her sweater. Before he has ever managed to reach out and take a toy, he will have managed to get hold of his mother's nose or chin as she feeds him.

CHAPTER FIVE

DIFFICULTIES IN GETTING SETTLED

Earlier chapters have assumed that while the first 4–6 weeks of a baby's life may, in many ways, be hell for his parents, they are a settling period, during which one by one problems will resolve. The unpredictable waking hours that made it impossible for the mother to plan her day gradually give way to more regular intervals. The extraordinary stools give way to something more reasonable. The circulation, the skin, the hair all become more like those of an 'ordinary baby', and with the advent of different types of crying, some smiling and some non-crying sounds, the mother begins to feel she is dealing with a person. And we can all manage those.

But babies vary. There are satisfactory models and less satisfactory ones; ones that are easy to operate and others that are tricky. The genetic lottery produces some mother–infant pairs which are better matched than others.

The physical care and the emotional sensitivity given to a baby interact with what he has already brought into life. As well as his genetic characteristics, including his sex, he brings a vast range of experiences in the womb and at birth. Many of these are still incompletely understood, but it is clear that factors such as the efficiency of the placenta and some aspects of the mother's health in pregnancy, together with the timing and nature of the actual birth, can all affect the 'kind' of baby who emerges. It is even thought that quite a lot of babies may be born with a very minute degree of damage to the brain or the central nervous system; handled well, such a baby adapts and matures to a point where the very slight disadvantage with which he was born is completely lost in the advantages he gets after birth.

Obviously all parents want to give their particular infant every possible advantage, whether or not he appears to have any problems. But it is less obvious that some 'types' of baby are very much easier for some mothers to handle than for others. If a mother gets the kind of baby she was expecting, the kind who needs the sort of handling which comes most naturally to her, she will have an easier job than if she gets a baby who needs handling in a way which takes positive thought and effort from her. The very wakeful baby, for example, is likely to be much more of a problem to a woman who likes her life extremely organized, with the housework completed in the morning, leisure in the afternoon, and the place spotless when her husband comes home from work, than he is to a more casual easy-going woman who does things as they need doing, and finds it easy to drop the ironing to play with the baby and to vacuum the sitting room at 9 p.m.

MISERABLE BABIES

Some babies are born inclined to the miseries. It is impossible to say how many, because the definition is subjective, and in any case many babies who seem this way inclined are being made so by the way they are handled. Often their discontent, their sad fretfulness, appears to centre around digestive troubles. But this may be because when a very young baby is miserable, more food, or different food, is the first solution people tend to turn to. These babies do not seem to settle happily into patterns of being definitely, soundly and comfortably asleep; awake and ravenous; full, awake and happy and then asleep again. It is as if little bits of all these states remained jumbled up with each other. The baby is tired and fretful but he cannot relax fully into sleep. Having grizzled his way through a period, he is crossly hungry, but not joyous in his sucking. He may be slow and difficult to feed. Finished, he is awake but not very sociable; he quickly tires of being held but is not pleased to be put in his pram or cot. He probably wakes often in the night. Some, but not all, of these babies gain weight slowly. They may actually look unhappy. They are the opposite of that stereo-type the 'bonny baby'.

Anything or nothing may help, except the kind of despair which too easily strikes parents who are overtired, and who feel constantly criticized by this infant who *will not* reward their care with happiness. Food is certainly a starting point. Is he getting enough if he is breast-fed? Test weighing will answer that. If he is not on the breast, it is sometimes worth changing the formula. He might, for instance, do better on a humanized milk; or he might actually *like* another milk better.

Temperature is another possibility. Like the small mammals who blossom, and double their eating and their activity when they are made warm after getting too cold, some babies are kept constantly below their optimal temperature (see p. 74). It is worth trying keeping the infant's room at 75°F (24°C) and *not* putting him out in his pram for a few days.

Sometimes physical contact produces a private minor miracle. The late Dr Doyne Bell, a consultant pediatrician at the Charing Cross Hospital, once said that if he was faced with a very sick baby under three months, the first thing he did was to institute necessary treatment. The second was to assign that baby a nurse who would carry him, wherever she went, all day, every day, awake and asleep, until he started to be better. Since then I have seen mothers do the same thing with sad babies. A simple sling on the mother's back, made out of a small cot sheet, makes it possible for her to do simple household jobs. It is not a scientific method and nobody can say why it works when it does. But it could be that the baby is not ready to adapt and settle to extra-uterine life, that he misses the constant jolting and movement of life in the womb, or the warmth or some other aspect of the symbiotic tie with his mother.

JUMPY BABIES

Another group of babies, less worrying, less all-engulfing, but nevertheless more difficult than most to handle, are the very jumpy ones. Most small babies startle to loud noises, turn away from bright lights, throw up their arms and cry if they feel loss of balance when they are picked up or put down. But there are some who startle and cry, tremble and pale at quite minor stimuli. These babies seem happiest if outside stimulation is reduced even below the level suggested for all newborns. They may relax and sleep more calmly if they are securely wrapped up, literally rolled into a cot blanket so that they make a loose parcel. Obviously they need to be lifted with due notice, never unexpectedly, never from behind, and always very gently and slowly so that their muscles have time to adapt to each change of position as it is made. In extreme cases mothers may find that they are easiest to handle if they are carried and fed still wrapped up. Most of them will be among those who hate being naked, seeming to lose security with every garment, every touch of the air on bare skin. Baths are not, of course, strictly necessary. Every bit of a baby can be adequately washed and dried without ever fully undressing him. Pram riding may be a mistake too. The outside air moves; the baby sees a blur of movement, and every curbstone may make him jump and cry.

Nothing will finally right this situation except the baby's maturation. There is no way in which this can be hurried. In the meantime, caring for him can be even enjoyable if it is seen as a challenge. The challenge is simply whether each day can be got through without him ever being frightened or made to jump. It takes constant thought. It means never being distracted so that the overhead light is suddenly switched on in a dark room, never sitting down to feed him just where the telephone is going to ring in his face, never hurrying downstairs with him under your arm to answer the door, never pulling his vest over his head because the strings are in a knot.

SLEEPY BABIES

At the other end of the spectrum are the babies who sleep and sleep, and who go on being sleepy and lethargic past the 4–6 weeks point. Very occasionally babies have been known to succumb to malnutrition because they did not demand food, and could not wake up enough to suck properly. This is extremely rare, but nevertheless a salutary warning. The danger of a sleepy baby is that he is such bliss for the parents. He is 'no trouble'; he makes almost no demands. The mother can pick him up and play with him if she feels like it, knowing that she can dump him back in his cot without him protesting, if she thinks of something else to do. He may never demand a night feed, being happy to sleep for a 12-hour stretch from the beginning. The mother who decides to feed such a baby 'on demand' can easily underfeed him.

The quantities of food which are suggested as necessary for babies of different weights (see page 50) are a rough guide only, but they *are* a guide. However contented the baby appears to be, however little trouble, the mother must check that he is taking something near his calculated needs. If he is breast-fed, then either she must check his weekly weight gain or carry out a test weighing.

If he is eating enough, and gaining weight, and seems cheerful and normal on the rare occasions when he is really awake, then probably he is only reacting to extra-uterine life as the sad baby did, but dealing with it more comfortably. He also is unready for it, and is going to be dozy until he is. All the same, it is important that his willingness to be shut away for hours in his cot should not lead the mother to *expect* him to behave like this. It is vital that he be offered social contact: people, things to look at, conversation. If the mother feeds him and then tries to play with him and he goes to sleep in her arms, it is fair enough to put him back in his bed, but it is a mistake to assume his sleepiness without giving him the chance to behave differently.

Mothers often act as if broad differences of these kinds between babies had some bearing on the personality of the child later on. They may do and they may not. Many studies have produced results in both directions. It may be that it is impossible to prove the matter one way or the other without taking a great deal more than the usual account of the *mother's* reactions to the baby's behaviour, rather than merely concentrating on how he behaves. If a sleepy no-trouble baby comes to be taken for granted, during his first 6 months, as an easy-going placid type, his mother is likely to treat him as such. He may get, for example, a great deal of social attention, because the mother is not afraid of him getting too demanding, or getting into bad habits. She may be happy to bring him out of his cot at night to show off to visitors and so on. At the same time she may assume that he will not mind if she leaves him with a neighbour for a few hours, or loses his dummy. In all sorts of ways he may be steered towards growing up in a way which represents some sort of continuum with his infancy.

On the other hand a different mother may resent the new-born sleepiness. She may work at stimulating the infant, do everything she can think of to jog him into awareness. She may expect him to be upset by things which she believes ought to upset a baby. She may subtly steer him along quite a different path.

While it is certainly not true that mothers can decide what kind of person they want their infant to become, and bring him up in such a way as to produce the required model, the way she does bring him up affects his behaviour from the beginning. And the way she brings him up is at least par-tially dictated *by* his behaviour. The infant's environment and handling are therefore something which he and his parents together provide: a given type of baby and a given type of mother may interact in different ways to produce quite different results.

With all babies who have difficulty in settling into life and who have been passed as healthy and normal by their doctors, a policy of wait and see is by far the most sensible. As the infant gets a little older, most of these early problems will re-solve. And as he becomes more consistent in his behaviour it will get easier for the parents to see what handling he needs. In the meantime it is best if no labels are attached to him. It is a pity if a newborn jumpiness, which was actually merely associated with immaturity of the nervous system and a stressful delivery, leads to him being known as a 'nervous child', a 'highly strung type', so that he has to fight his way out of over-protection when he reaches robust toddlerhood.

SECTION II

FROM SIX WEEKS TO THREE MONTHS:
MAKING PATTERNS

CHAPTER SIX

FUNDAMENTAL PHYSICAL PATTERNS

The first section of this book was called 'Settling into Life'. An infant is 'settled' once his behaviours begin to make sense. It is likely still to be extremely idiosyncratic sense, but nevertheless sufficiently clear for his mother to feel she can understand him.

Predictability is the essence of this 'making sense'. By around 6 weeks most infants have reached a point where their behaviour on a Monday to some extent predicts their behaviour on Tuesday. In earlier weeks the infant might cry himself into a lather over his bath one day, and barely bother to wake up for it on the next. Once he is settled, he is likely either to enjoy his bath or hate it; either way his feelings about the matter are likely to be consistent.

This predictability gives most mothers an enormous upsurge of confidence, even where the infant is predictably difficult! Once the mother knows what to expect of the baby – even if it is the worst – she can begin to plan her own activities round him and to make reasoned assessments about whether she is handling him in the way he needs. It is the very randomness of newborn behaviour which makes it so depressingly difficult for mothers to know whether or not they are doing a good job.

Between about 6 weeks and about 3 months, all the infant's physical functions tend to become patterned along with his emotional reactions, his likes and dislikes. These patterns make up norms for that particular baby. Deviations from them therefore become cues for the mother that there may be something amiss. The more accustomed she becomes to her particular infant's patterns, the more automatically she will tend to adjust her behaviour to fit in with them. If, for example, this particular infant always sleeps well and soundly between the first two feeds of the day and, equally, always

remains wakeful during the afternoon, the mother will probably find herself reacting quite differently to crying during
these times. If the baby cries between the first two feeds, she
will pick him up, perhaps change him, but put him straight
down again, assuming he will go back to sleep 'because he
always does'. If, on the other hand, he cries during the afternoon, she will probably go to him, pick him up and begin to
play: she does not expect him to return to sleep.

FEEDING

Most of the problems of feeding, whether from breast or
bottle, should be over by 6 weeks. The baby now has clear expectations at feed times. He does not yet visually recognize his
bottle as it is prepared, but it takes no tactful evocation of
reflexes to get him sucking once the nipple or teat is presented.
His sucking is more rapid and efficient than before. Sleepy
babies may still tend to suck themselves to sleep after only a
couple of ounces, and having done so they may be unwake-
able. If this means that they wake again, hungry, in a couple
of hours, it is extremely tiresome for the mother. But there is
nothing that can be done except to ensure that the baby is
fully awake before the feed starts, to concentrate on him, trying to get him to watch the mother's face while he sucks, and
to wait for him to mature.

An appetite spurt is usual at around 8–10 weeks. The baby,
who if he was born weighing 7 lb. (3·2kg), will by 8 weeks
weigh roughly 10 lb. (4·5kg), demolishes his 'required'
30 oz. (860ml) of milk and looks around for more. At some
feeds he may drink a complete 8-oz. (230ml) bottle. His
nutritional needs are, of course, still adequately met by milk
alone, but such an appetite spurt is often used as a cue to start
some mixed feeding. Certainly if his milk intake goes up to
40 oz. (1140ml), or 5 8-oz. (230ml) bottles in the 24 hours,
some additional food should be given. More than 2 pints of
milk a day is too great a bulk for the baby's stomach. He
needs more concentrated calories. Unfortunately the com-
mencement of mixed feeding, even if it is begun because the

infant genuinely needs more food, often means that he begins to get too fat. Figure 6 contrasts the weight gains of two infants of identical birthweight, one of whom was exclusively breast-fed, the other being bottle-fed with early solids.

There is a growing weight of evidence to suggest that overfeeding in the first half year alters the actual chemistry of the body, increasing the number of fat cells, and programming an increase in the production of insulin (which metabolizes sugars) and growth hormones. One such study by Eid[17] showed a very strong relationship between rapid weight gain even as early as 8 weeks, and real obesity at 6–8 years. Fatness in early infancy can therefore mean fatness throughout childhood, and a tendency to obesity for the rest of life.

Bottle-fed babies having an appetite spurt are the ones most at risk of obesity, as a recent study by Taitz shows.[5] He found that mothers tended to make two errors when their infants started to be extra hungry. Firstly they often increased the ratio of milk powder to water, thus giving their infants extra-concentrated feeds. Secondly they tended to add extra sugar, or baby cereals, to the bottles.

The danger with these practices is that an infant's bottles are his drink as well as his food. He is accustomed to drinking, say, 7 oz. (200ml) of formula. If his mother has packed extra calories into that 7 oz. (200ml) of formula, his habitual drink may give him far more food than usual, without his *appetite* being given a chance to refuse it. Furthermore a vicious circle can be set up, especially if bottles are made extra-concentrated, for this means that the infant gets a heavy extra dose of sodium in his milk. His kidneys have to work hard to get rid of the excess, and he may therefore be very thirsty. Thirst makes him cry, and if his mother is unwary she may assume he is hungry and give him yet another over-concentrated bottle.

A fat baby is not necessarily a healthy nor a contented one. It is a pity that fat babies are so adored in our society when fat children are mocked, and fat adults feel unattractive and are at increased risk for many diseases.

A baby who is hungry, who is drinking almost 2 pints

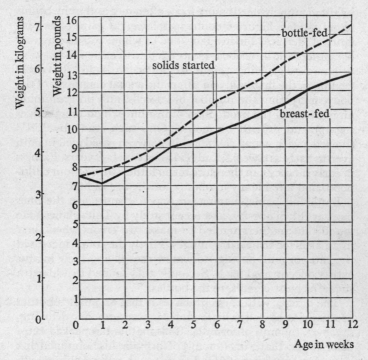

Figure 6. Comparison of the weight gains of one purely breast-fed
infant with another bottle-fed with early additional solids

The difference in the weights of these two babies begins in the first
week of life, although they weighed the same at birth. The bottle-
fed baby does not lose any weight during this first week, while the
breast-fed baby does lose, while waiting for the breast-milk supply
to be established, and does not regain his birthweight until he is
ten days old.

Both babies gain weight steadily, and at the same rate, during
the first month. Their weights begin to diverge between weeks 4
and 6, with the bottle-fed baby beginning to average 12 oz. (350g)
gain per week as compared with the breast-fed baby's 8 oz. (230g)
per week.

(1140ml) of properly made formula per day and is not gaining weight at more than about 6 oz. (170g) per week, may do very well if one feed of the day is thickened with a teaspoonful of baby cereal. If he needs more than this, or is already gaining weight fast, he will do better if he is started on proper mixed feeding in addition to his formula.

Conventionally, baby cereal is still the first 'solid' food offered to infants. But many, in fact, prefer puréed fruit.

Taking food without sucking is extremely difficult for young babies. If food is placed on the tongue, the baby cannot get it far enough back in his mouth to swallow; it simply trickles out of the corners of his mouth. The trick is to use a tiny spoon, and to hold it to the baby's lips so that he can suck off the contents. If he likes the taste positive enthusiasm will develop quite quickly. The more usual technique of waiting until his mouth is open and then dumping the spoonful right at the back of his mouth often leads to gagging, and even more often to a complete rejection of spoon feeding – sometimes for weeks.

Once the child will accept a familiar food from a spoon, his need for extra nourishment can be met without giving him too much carbohydrate, by offering finely puréed vegetables and fruits – always of semi-liquid texture. There is much argument about whether or not babies naturally prefer sweet foods. Unfortunately most do appear to accept fruit more easily than vegetables, sweet cereals more easily than creamed fish. This apparent preference may be partly due to the extensive use of tinned baby foods of which the fruits and puddings tend to be extremely sweet, while the savouries tend to be bland and tasteless. Many mothers who have been willing and able to prepare their own baby foods – perhaps because they owned a freezer and could prepare large quantities at a time – have found that savoury foods were accepted

---

The divergence becomes even more marked after solid foods have been added to the bottle-fed baby's diet during week 6.

By three months, the bottle-fed baby has more than doubled his birthweight. If he follows a consistent curve, the breast-fed baby will not have doubled his birthweight until around 20 weeks.

with pleasure if they were salted and flavoured to ordinary adult taste.

A certain amount of tact is often needed in the timing of the 'solid' part of a meal. A very hungry baby of 8 to 10 weeks expects to suck either breast or bottle. If he is offered solid food first, he may reject it with fury. Equally if it is offered at the end of his milk feed he will probably not be hungry enough to bother with it. A sandwich system seems to work best, with a good suck to assuage the first hunger pangs, followed by spoon feeding, and finishing up with whatever further quantity of milk the baby wants.

Whatever system is used, it is important to remember that the solid food is an extra. It will be some weeks before the solids become the infant's principal food and the milk becomes a beverage. Unless the infant is extra hungry, he does not *need* any solid food at all at this age, and many authorities would argue that he is better off without it. Solid food should be used simply to bridge the gap between his hunger and the amount of milk his stomach can comfortably hold. There should be no question of trying to persuade the infant to take more solids, and then cutting down his milk.

SLEEPING

At this age sleeping is usually intimately bound up with eating, the baby being inclined to go to sleep immediately after a feed. But even if he was one of the newborns who slept for 20 hours out of the 24, he is likely, by now, only to be sleeping for about 16 hours, and he will probably begin to have wakeful periods which are not entirely dependent on food.

Most babies fall into one of two groups. The first 'type' tends to fall asleep after each feed, and to wake in about three hours, ready to be sociable for a period before hunger overtakes him and the eating–sleeping cycle repeats. The second 'type' of baby tends to have one period of the day during which he is wakeful, often the second half of the afternoon. During the morning he wakes to be fed, goes to sleep again, and wakes again ravenous. But after his lunchtime feed he naps, perhaps for an hour only, and then is awake for most of the afternoon.

By 6 weeks, almost all babies will be prepared to spend one period of about 6 hours asleep. Hopefully, this is the parents' 'night'. But often the baby's *preferred* long sleep-period is from, say, 7 p.m. to 1 a.m., rather than the midnight to 6 a.m. which his parents would prefer.

Whatever the individual baby's pattern, once it exists, it can be tactfully manipulated. Such manipulation usually works best if it is done on the basis of feeding the baby a little *before* he demands food, rather than on the basis of making him wait a little time *after* he demands it. Adjusting the baby's long sleep-period towards the parents' night, for example, can usually be accomplished painlessly by waking the baby for a feed at midnight, rather than waiting for him to wake the parents at 1 a.m. For a few nights he may wake in the small hours all the same, but eventually he will adapt, and may even begin to wake himself for that late-night feed, pushing his long sleep forward.

Adjustments of this kind are often bedevilled by the fact that mothers regard 'giving up a feed' as a sign of progress in their infants, and are therefore extremely loath to give an extra one. They would rather he went for five hours without feeding than slip in the extra feed that will give them more sleep. This rigid view can often make a great deal of trouble. If the mother can make herself feel better about it by calling such extra feeds 'snacks', so much the better. The need for them will occur whenever efforts are made to change the baby's eating pattern, particularly when attempts are being made to persuade him that he does not need breakfast at 6 a.m. and again when he is being persuaded to accept three family mealtimes per day rather than specially timed 'feeds'.

Whatever the baby's timings, he will, at 6 weeks, probably still demand 6 feeds in the 24 hours, though some babies may already be down to 5.

Over the next few weeks, feeds will be elided together rather than abandoned. Taking the old standard timings of

6 a.m., 10 a.m., 2 p.m., 6 p.m., 10 p.m., 2 a.m. as a pattern, the 2 a.m. feed will be the first mothers will want to abandon, and this will be accomplished by pushing the 10 p.m. feed forward towards midnight, and pulling the 6 a.m. back probably nearer to 5 a.m. Most babies – except those who were premature or who are gaining weight very slowly – will be ready to do without that sixth small-hours feed by the time they are 10–12 weeks old. In the meantime there is no other way, apart from adjusting the timings of the feeds either side, of hurrying the process. Left to cry it out, the baby will, in the end, go back to sleep. But not for long. He will wake again, probably just as his mother relaxes back into sleep. He is hungry, and there is nothing to be gained by pretending that he is not.

Once he has accepted 5 feeds in the 24 hours, the 'night' can be very gradually stretched, even though 5 feeds will remain necessary for some months. If, fed at midnight, the baby begins to sleep on until 7 a.m., the mother may prefer to start waking him earlier in the evening, so that she herself can go to bed earlier. If the baby does not wake himself for that late-evening feed, the mother can suit herself whether she prefers an early night and an early start to the day, or a later bedtime and a more leisurely start to her day.

ELIMINATION

By 6 weeks, a mother will recognize her baby's stools as normal for him, and can therefore use a marked *change* in those stools as her only cue for concern. The variation between very frequent and very infrequent stools may continue in breast-fed babies; bottle-fed ones are likely to produce a more regular 1–4 stools per day, and these are likely to be more formed than those of the breast-fed baby.

As in the very first weeks, a *sudden* attack of diarrhoea, whether or not there is vomiting, is reason to seek medical advice quickly, while a gradual loosening of the stools over several days is more likely to reflect an excess of sugar or other carbohydrate in the milk.

Constipation is not constipation if, when the stool is finally produced, it is of normal consistency. Many infants produce their motions with much scarlet-faced straining, giving every appearance of constipation. But only if it is hard or dry, or difficult for the baby to expel, does it require dietary adjustment. As in the earlier weeks, a change to a more laxative type of sugar – such as maltose – is probably all that will be needed.

As mixed feeding is introduced, undigested particles are likely to appear in the nappies, together with quite dramatic colour changes associated with various vegetables and fruits. The baby's digestion has to adjust to these new substances, and they should therefore be started in tiny amounts, such as half a teaspoon of any new food.

Some babies, as they adopt more regular feeding times, also adopt more regular elimination times, the two functions often being linked, so that the baby passes a motion while he feeds. Some mothers try to make use of this eating–elimination connection, by holding the baby on the pot in the middle of a feed, or immediately after it. Some motions can be caught in this way, but it is very doubtful whether the time the mother saves on washing those nappies equals the time she spends in potting the baby. Furthermore, if she attempts to catch the motion, she will inevitably often fail and may well be irritated. It seems a pity to introduce frustration into the feeding situation.

Authorities differ as to whether a baby who is regularly held on a pot from this very early age is being 'trained'. Some believe that babies develop a reflex response to the feeling of their buttocks on the pot so that they pass a motion when they are held on it. For a few months the mother may believe she has him trained. Almost invariably a few weeks later the baby's elimination pattern changes, or his developing independence and mobility leads him to fight being held on the pot, and a totally unnecessary toilet-training battle may have begun before the baby is even 6 months old.

Newson and Newson,[18] who studied the child-care practices

of mothers in Nottingham, found that 20 per cent of mothers had in fact 'held out' their babies in this way from the first 2 weeks of life. 63 per cent had started potting the child before he was 8 months, yet only a minute proportion had actually succeeded in training their babies by 1 year. The sum of wasted hours of mother and baby time represented by these figures is enormous.

CRYING AND COLIC

As in the earliest weeks of life, some babies between 6 weeks and 3 months cry more than others. Those who were miserable as newborns may still tend to the miseries at this age. Some, who were very jumpy as newborns, may still find a lot of causes for fear and unhappiness in the stimulation of a normal family environment. Yet others may cry for comparatively long periods in the day because their mothers deliberately delay fulfilling their expressed needs for fear of spoiling them. On the other hand there are babies who by 6 weeks are so readily consoled by adult handling that they rarely cry more than momentarily. Whatever the cause of the original distress, the baby stops crying when his mother picks him up, and is then easily made comfortable.

As the patterning typical of this age period takes place, some unfortunate parents recognize in their babies a particular syndrome of distress which is usually known as 'three-months colic' although 'evening colic' describes it better.

A baby with evening colic typically refuses to settle after his late-afternoon or early-evening feed. If he falls asleep, he quickly wakes again with spasmodic attacks of screaming. During these attacks, he draws his knees up to his stomach, screws up his face, and gives every appearance of being in acute abdominal pain.

Evening colic, if it is going to occur at all, usually begins in the first fortnight after birth, but it is often not recognized as distinct from the disorganized behaviour of the rest of the newborn baby's day, until his behaviour at other times has settled down and become predictable. Only when he is feeding and sleeping with some regularity do the parents realize that this particular trouble *always* occurs after this particular feed of the day.

The facts available about evening colic are both inadequate and contradictory. Its frequency, cause, palliation and cure are all matters of hot professional dispute. What cannot be disputed is that a baby with the true evening-colic syndrome presents a trial to his parents' marriage, their self-confidence as parents and their sheer physical stamina.

Illingworth[19] made a detailed study of 50 cases. He found that the average time which the trouble lasted for an individual baby was 9 weeks. Half the affected babies had stopped having colic by 2 months of age; more than three quarters by 3 months of age, and all by 4 months of age.

The numbers of babies affected can hardly be guessed at. Some authorities put babies who tend to suffer from flatulence or other colicky pains in with those who have true evening colic. Others include all babies who show a tendency to cry in the evening, and many of these are breast-fed babies who are hungry in the evening because the mother's milk supply tends to be scantiest at this time of day.

Rather than trying to assess how many babies *do* have evening colic, it is probably more useful to describe those who do *not* have it, whatever the appearances may suggest.

A baby who cries in the evening, but in the same way and to the same extent as he does at other times of day, has not got the evening-colic syndrome. His evening crying is simply part of his normal crying pattern.

A baby who cries in the evening and will take a feed and be comforted by it has not got colic either. He is hungry.

A baby who cries in the evening, brings up wind and then sleeps as usual has not got evening colic. He has wind.

A baby who cries in the evening until he is picked up, and is then happy until he is put to bed again has not got colic. He has probably decided to have the early evening as his wakeful period, and is simply not ready to be alone and asleep.

The baby with true evening colic cries in a different way

from at any other time of day. His screams are piercing. They leave him shaky and sobbing between attacks. Everything comforts him momentarily; nothing comforts him for more than a few minutes. The trouble appears to be abdominal, and passing wind may relieve him for long enough for him almost to drop off to sleep on his mother's shoulder, but the screaming begins again. Putting him on his tummy, rubbing his tummy, wrapping him tightly, all bring temporary relief, but just as the parents dare to hope it is over, the screaming starts again. The baby may suck ravenously, but he does so only for a minute or two, then he rejects the nipple or teat and screams again. If the baby is left alone, with no help offered, the pattern is little different. Listening parents will live through minutes of screaming, blessed minutes of silence and then screams again. Most parents feel that they have to do what they can to alleviate the attack; at the same time they have to accept that they cannot give real aid. Tired at the end of the day, needing to talk to each other and to relax, it is little wonder that evening colic is remembered with real horror by parents whose infants suffered from it.

A list of some of the causes suggested by eminent authorities may at least save some parents from shopping round from doctor to doctor, unable to believe that such an acute phenomenon can be transitory and, in the end, unimportant. Various authorities have suggested all the following causes, and more: overfeeding, underfeeding, too rich, strong or weak feeds, food given too hot or too cold, too often or too seldom, too fast or too slowly. Allergies to certain foodstuffs, hernias, intestinal deformities, ulcers, appendicitis, gall bladder trouble. Pediatricians have tended to blame the mother for faulty feeding techniques, suggesting that the basic trouble is wind, and failing to explain why the mother should feed the baby wrongly at one, and only one, feed in the day. Illingworth has demonstrated that however thoroughly a baby is winded after his early evening feed, if he is subject to evening colic he will have it all the same.

From the psychiatric angle, explanations have tended to centre around the mother. Maternal fatigue and irritation at the end of the day has often been suggested, since it neatly explains the regular timing of colic attacks. Such attacks, however, do not tend to cease when the mother is temporarily assisted by her husband, or put to bed for the day by her own mother. Lakin[20] described the mothers of babies with colic as being less confident in their maternal role, less loving towards their infants, and having more marital conflict than the mothers of non-colicky babies. These findings could well be the *result* of having a baby with colic, rather than a cause. They are, in any case, completely contradicted by Paradise.[21] He found no psychiatric factors whatsoever in the mothers of the babies with colic. The only difference of note between these mothers and the mothers of non-colicky babies was that the mothers of the evening-colic babies tended to be highly intelligent. Paradise thought that this difference probably only reflected the fact that intelligent mothers would tend to take notice of, and seek advice about, colic in their infants.

While it is clear that ordinary gastric flatulence (wind) is not the cause of colic, and while X-ray studies have shown that there is no excess of gas in the bowels of colicky babies, Jorup[22] did find unusually strong contractions of the colon while the baby was having attacks of pain. He believes, and Illingworth[19] agrees with him, that the probable cause is normal gas being trapped in loops of a highly mobile colon. Overall, Paradise believes that the colic attacks reflect an immaturity of the central nervous system. These two suggestions may logically go together, so that one is left with immaturity of the infant's physiology leading to painful but insignificant and temporary malfunction of the colon.

Illingworth[23] highly recommends a drug with an anti-colonic-spasm action. He believes that if this drug, given half an hour before the feed which colic normally follows, does *not* relieve the colic, then the diagnosis of evening colic cannot have been correct. Many doctors would dispute this, however, and some – however desperately mothers consult them – simply recommend waiting it out; they do not believe that any drug will much shorten this self-limiting syndrome.

During this age period, babies will, of course, continue to cry from pain, or hunger, or from shock or fear or any over-stimulation, just as they did when they were newly born. But now they are infinitely easier to comfort. Apart from exceptional circumstances, such as evening colic or illness or continuing pain, babies of this age can *always* be stopped from crying by being picked up and talked to. They can often be prevented from starting full-fledged crying by social distraction at the right moment. For the vast majority of mothers, the era of being faced by a baby who cried and cried, while she tried every remedy she could think of in turn, and all to no avail, should be over.

The nature of the infant's crying alters too. The basic hunger cry remains, as does the distinctive pain cry. But the 'angry cry' and the 'grumbly cry' which began at around 3 weeks both become much more frequent. Indeed a baby who is being fed when he is hungry, and kept pleasurable company when he is awake, may seldom produce any other cries than anger and grumbles. He is angry – or so his cry indicates – when his mother terminates a conversation he was enjoying, by turning away out of sight. He grumbles when he begins to be hungry or tired. But his crying may seldom build up to full-fledged yells.

Once the individual baby's crying behaviour has settled into a pattern in this way, changes in the pattern become valuable cues for the mother. If the baby always quiets when he is picked up, and never does more than grumble while his feed is brought to him, then a sudden refusal to be comforted, continuing to yell while the mother cuddles him, or crying himself into such a lather that he cannot suck, may indicate illness. Of course any baby can have a particularly grumbly day. But this usually takes the form of *beginning* to cry more often than usual. It does not usually take the form of refusing to be comforted.

For breast-fed babies, a sudden excess of crying should cue a period of test weighing. The appetite spurt of the infant of this age group has already been described. Often, a mother whose breast-milk supply was only just adequate in the first

6 weeks finds that it becomes inadequate during this period, because the baby's increase in appetite coincides with an increase in her activities as she returns to her normal life fully recovered from the birth.

CHAPTER SEVEN

BEGINNING TO MANAGE HIS BODY

When a baby becomes settled, in the sense of making predictable patterns in his eating, sleeping, crying and his reactions
to motherly comfort, he also tends to be sufficiently settled into his own body to start doing things with it. Of course physical and motor development are progressing daily from birth,
but a sudden spurt in the beginnings of bodily control and
coordination usually becomes noticeable at around 6 weeks.

POSTURE AND HEAD CONTROL

The factor which dominates an infant's physical abilities in
the early weeks is the weight of his head relative to the rest of
his body. At birth an infant can lift his hand, or his foot, but
he cannot lift his head; his neck and shoulder muscles are not
strong or controlled enough. The development of this muscular control starts at the top and moves downward. First he
must get his neck muscles under control. At 4–5 weeks, he
holds his head momentarily clear of his mother's shoulder,
and practises doing so, so that it feels as if he is deliberately
'bumping'. By 6–8 weeks, the neck muscles have strength-
ened to a point where the infant can hold his head clear of the
shoulder for minutes at a time; he may even be able to balance
his head while his mother carries him gently about. But his
control is still so precarious that any sudden movement on
the mother's part makes his head flop again; fatigue makes
him unable to hold it up at all, and he must still have his
mother's hand under his neck when he is lifted or put down.
By around 10 weeks his head control has developed still
further; his neck is fairly steady when he is carried about.
Now it is his shoulders which require support and in another
2–3 weeks they too will be steady.

The baby's posture when lying down will at least roughly parallel his development of head control. In the early weeks the infant is a scrunched-up creature. Whether the mother lies him down on his back, his side, or his tummy, he will curl inwards (see page 88).

As his head control increases, so this constantly flexed position gradually diminishes. Its departure is vitally important to what the infant can do. If, when he lies on his back, he still takes up the typical newborn flexed position, head turned to one side, the arm on that side outflung and the upper arm curled inwards, he cannot use all four limbs at the same time. Only the upper arm and the upper leg are free to move. Furthermore he cannot see very much except his own mattress and underneath arm. But once he uncurls, and lies, at least when he is awake, with the back of his head on the mattress, and all four limbs free, he becomes able to do and to see all kinds of interesting things. Much the same applies to the flexed position taken up by newborns lying on their tummies. From the beginning they will turn their heads to one side to avoid smothering. But as long as their knees are pulled up beneath them and their bottoms are in the air there is not much else they *can* do. At about the same time that they uncurl when lying on their backs, they will begin to lie on their tummies with their legs straight out behind them. And as soon as they do this, new possibilities for physical activity are opened up.

By around 12 weeks, the baby kicks when he lies on his back. There is a new rhythm to his movements. He waves his arms, he bicycles with his legs. When he is awake, he is hardly ever still, and his movements flow into one another, without the jerkiness, the apparent lack of control of earlier weeks. When he lies flat on his tummy, he practises his new head control. At first he lifts his head only with extreme effort. He 'bobs' up, rather as he bumped his head against his mother's shoulder 6 weeks before. Very soon he becomes able to hold this head-up position, and may even push hard enough with his forearms to lift his lower chest off the mattress too.

As early as 9 weeks most infants will have learned to roll

themselves from the comparative instability of their sides
on to the broader base of their backs. By 12 weeks or so, at
around the same time that he learns to lift his head control-
ledly when lying on his tummy, the baby will accomplish the
far more difficult manoeuvre of rolling from his back on to
his side.

All these developments between about 6 and 12 weeks are
vital clues to the handling the infant needs. In the newborn
period his own helplessness, his obvious fear of quick movement, nakedness or any loss of balance, made it clear that he
was happiest and felt safest when he was securely wrapped,
softly cushioned, totally protected. In this period his increasing physical activity, his stretching out, the smoothing
out of his movements, his own control of his head, all make it
clear that he no longer needs or benefits from *constant* physical
padding. Once he can kick, he will kick and therefore should
kick. Once he can roll, he will and should do so. Once he can
move his head he must move it, and needs some payment for
effort in terms of interesting things to see.

Where a hard smooth surface distressed the infant when he
was younger, it now thrills him. Where earlier he would have
cried if he were undressed and put on a rug on the floor, or on
the centre of a double bed, or on a groundsheet on the grass,
now he glories in the freedom. His whole demeanour makes it
clear that he is playing. It takes very little to frustrate his play,
to spoil it. A ruckled up rug will prevent him rolling on to his
side. Too soft a mattress will prevent him getting the purchase to raise himself on his forearms. Restrictive clothing
will stop him moving his arms and legs freely.

Very soon after the infant becomes able to balance his head
while he is carried around, and to lift it when he is lying on his
tummy, his muscular control will move on downwards from
neck and shoulders to upper back. If he is gently pulled into
sitting position he will no longer droop pathetically forward
so that his head almost touches his knees, his whole back bent
over. Rather he will support his head and shoulders, so that
he sags only at lower back and hip level. At this stage he is
ready to spend some of his waking time propped up. But

propping him takes some care and thought: supported by pillows or cushions, in his pram or in a corner of the sofa, he quickly begins to slip downwards – his back bends increasingly, his head is forced forward. He does not yet have an adult's ability to wriggle himself back into a comfortable position. For this reason the kind of baby chair which can be adjusted from a semi-reclined to an almost upright position is ideal. Using one of these, the infant will himself cue the mother as he becomes ready for more upright postures. As he sits in the chair, he will practise lifting his head and shoulders forward from the back support, leaving that still uncontrolled lower back supported. When he can sit for a minute at a time without touching the head–shoulders support, he is ready for one more notch of uprightness.

PHYSICAL AND MANUAL PLAY

Just as the infant who still lies in scrunched-up positions is not ready for physical play, so the baby whose hands are scrunched into loose fists is not yet ready for play with objects. The hands open at just about the same time as the posture changes, so that by around 8 weeks they are open most of the time the baby is awake. And when they open, they are ready for the very beginnings of manipulative play.

The first 'toy' an infant manipulates is usually his own hands. He finds one with the other, by touch alone, at around 6 weeks. He clasps them together, pulls at the fingers, opens and shuts them. But even at the 8-weeks stage the infant is probably not aware that these hands are part of himself. He uses one to play with the other as if that other was an object. At this stage he does not relate them to himself visually; he plays by touch alone, not bringing the hands up to his own eye-line.

The infant can still not reach out for a toy, nor take it if it is held out to him, but if a rattle or similar object is put into his hand, he holds on more deliberately than at 6 weeks, and he is far more likely to make it sound, because his arm movements are so much larger and freer than they were. Often it is the sound a toy makes which first leads the infant to *see* his own hands and what they are holding. His eye follows the sound and makes the discovery which marks the beginning of hand and eye coordination.

By about 3 months, most babies have truly discovered their hands, by eye as well as by touch. For several weeks the infant may be happy to spend minutes on end simply watching his own hands, bringing them together, spreading his arms apart until they go out of sight, bringing them back within view, pulling the fingers, opposing the thumb, as concentrated as a 5-year-old watching television.

Once the infant has got his hands under this much control, so that he can 'find' them whenever he wants them, he explores them with his mouth as well as with his eyes and the other hand. He will put a finger in his mouth, take it out, look at it, put it back again. He will try putting his whole fist in his mouth, take that out for visual inspection and then replace it with both his thumbs.

Just as whole-body development gives the mother cues as to the kind of handling the infant is ready for, so this manual development gives cues too. As soon as the infant's hands are usually open, he is ready to be given light objects to hold, both for practice and against the day when he makes the connection between holding and seeing. Once he plays with his hands, watching them as he does so, he is ready for real toys as well. And once his hands go in his mouth, so will everything else. For some months the infant's mouth will be an organ of exploration. He cannot fully comprehend an object at this stage if he does *not* put it in his mouth. Mothers who are concerned over hygiene must find objects which are suitable for sucking as well as for looking and holding. Trying to stop him putting things in his mouth is wasted and misguided effort, which would be better spent on washing the toys from time to time.

Babies who have become attached to dummies by this point in their development are unwittingly deprived of the mouth as an organ of exploration. Very sad or fretful babies, who really need the comfort of almost constant sucking, are probably not ready for much manual play and will not there-fore be missing anything. But most babies can, by this age, have their comfort sucking confined to sleep periods or times of stress, so that when they are awake and playing both their mouths and their hands are free. The close wrapping of ear-lier weeks is obviously inappropriate at playtimes now, too. But many babies will still settle to sleep best if they are securely wrapped, especially if they are now wrapped from the armpits down, so that they can still get at those precious hands. As soon as they wake up from a sleep, they are likely to fight to rid themselves of all coverings, in order to kick; indeed by 3 months a sleeping-bag may be the only way of ensuring that the baby stays warm throughout the night.

All these new characteristic behaviours help to finalize the differentiation between sleep and waking. When the infant wants to sleep, he wants to be wrapped and warm and may need to suck. When he is awake he wants to be free and occu-pied. When he sleeps, it will be in cot or pram; when he plays it may be on the floor, on a bed, in a baby chair or on an adult's lap. There is a pattern to his daily activities now, just as there is patterning in his physical demands.

CHAPTER EIGHT

MAKING SENSE OF WHAT HE SEES

Until about a generation ago the visual perception of young infants was almost totally misunderstood. Visual perception can loosely be defined as 'meaningful seeing'; it is different, therefore, from simple sight, in that what is seen must convey some message, some kind of understanding to the person who is looking.

It used to be thought that very young infants saw little and understood less. They were thought to be visually attracted to lights, to large expanses of brilliant colour, and to moving objects, and not to be much interested in looking at anything else. An upsurge of research in recent years has altered that view completely. The outstanding, beautifully simple explanation for the misunderstanding of earlier workers is that young infants are *extremely* short-sighted, and at least until about 2 months can make almost no visual accommodation to distance. Under this age, an infant sees an object most clearly if it is about 8 inches (20cm) from the bridge of his nose. This was not discovered earlier because the equipment necessary to test the visual acuity of infants had not been developed. Perhaps, also, it had not been developed because it had not occurred to many people that it would produce interesting results.

We now know that the apparent interest which infants have in bright lights, bright colours and movement simply reflects the fact that in normal family handling these are the only things which the infant can actually *see* during most of his waking hours. Left in a cot or pram, in an ordinary room, the nearest object which is within the infant's eye-line will probably be a ceiling light fitment some 7–10 feet (2·10–3·05m) above him. It will be nothing but a blur. If the light is lit, its brightness may catch his eye, as may the bright window or a blowing curtain, even though they are too distant for him to see their shapes or contours. It is easy to see how the myth grew up that these were the things babies preferred to look at. It was all they were given, except human faces, and their passion for those was assumed to be purely social.

Infants are capable of fine visual discriminations from birth. Workers such as Robert Fantz[14] have studied both what they can see, and what they choose to look at, using a variety of techniques.

Fantz, for example, found that within 12 hours of birth infants could differentiate between a plain grey disc and an identical disc striped in black and white. But at this age they could only tell the difference if the disc was placed less than 9 inches (23cm) from the bridge of the nose, and the stripes were at least 1/8 inch (0·32cm) across. Given that these brand-new infants *could* see the stripes, they all preferred them to the plain grey. The actual visual acuity of the infants in this sample increased very rapidly between 2 and 4 months, so that by 3 months they could discriminate the striped disc from the grey at 15 inches' distance (38cm) and with stripes only 1/64 inch (0·04cm) wide. But this would still be a very marked degree of visual handicap in an adult.

If due allowance is made for their short sight and their lack of distance accommodation, infants look more readily, and for longer, at any complex pattern or interesting shape than they do at simple objects even if they are bright or highly coloured. If movement is added to the complex, interesting object, they like it even better. In Fantz's study, for example, all the babies from 5 days old to 6 months 'preferred' black and white schematic face sketches to identical ovals of brightly lit brilliant colours. Furthermore the more complex the schematic face, the better they liked it; faces with shading and expression were preferred to simple eyes–nose–mouth sketches.

This kind of research work has given rise to a great deal of controversy, not over the facts of infant visual perception, but over their interpretation and the theoretical framework into which they best fit.

Some workers believe that infants see, without understanding what they see, until such time as they are able to touch and handle objects. Supporters of this view would argue that when, and only when, the infant begins to handle things, he puts together the feeling of the object and his experiences of its behaviour, with the sight of it, and then understands it. Other workers believe that the purely visual perceptions of the very young infant, not yet old enough to handle objects, are more important than that. They believe that infants see, and understand a good deal about what they see, so that by the time they *can* reach out and handle things, they do so with a certain store of knowledge about those things.

On the whole the weight of the evidence in a very fast-moving and difficult field does tend towards the second view. The infant is not only capable of seeing the difference between one thing and another (provided they are brought close enough to his eyes), he actually chooses to look at just those things, and just those aspects of things, which are likely to be most useful to him if he is visually learning about the world. He likes to look at complicated, patterned, contoured objects, and movement increases his interest. Thus he is sure to study human faces – which fit that prescription so well. And it is vital that he *should* look at people, in order to interact socially with them. He is less interested in colours and in outline shapes than he is in patterning, texture, detail and complex contours. These are just the visual cues which make for recognition of objects. If the infant were to concentrate on colour and outline-shape and, using these cues, learn to recognize a brown dog seen sideways on, he would be markedly confused by a Dalmatian met face to face. It is *not* colour and outline shape which remain constant under different lighting conditions, and viewing positions, but just those patterning, detail, complex contour variables which interest him so much.

At 6–8 weeks, infants look equally readily and for equal lengths of time at familiar things and at new ones. But by 2–3 months the infant much prefers to study things he has not seen before. By looking less at things he has already 'visually learned', he gives himself more time to look at new things, still choosing the most complex and the most patterned new things available for him to see.

Until about 2 months most infants will choose to look at a pictorial representation of an object, rather than at the real thing. But just at the developmental point when the baby's hands begin to be open while he is awake, and he becomes ready to start handling things (see page 117) he transfers his interest, and will study a doll rather than a picture, a ball rather than a disc.

At about this time, too, he makes it clear that he has visually learned about human faces. As we have seen, the infant has been interested in looking at people's faces since very early on. By 6 weeks he may have smiled at his mother or some other adult. And he will smile too at schematic face representations, or pictures of faces. At around 2 months his mother will get a smile most easily if she smiles and talks and moves her head all at the same time. Her talking may be more important even than her smiling. Each time the baby does smile at her, he first makes a visual examination of her whole face, going from her hairline down her face to the chinline, and then returning his gaze to her eyes. Then, and only then, will he smile if he is going to.

At this same 2-month point, the infant becomes remark-ably fussy about the 'correctness' of any pictorial representa-tions of human faces. Offered a simple but correctly arranged eyes–nose–mouth diagram, he will look at it in preference to a more interesting, well shaded but wrongly put together face. While he may smile at a correct sketch, he will not smile if the drawn eyes and mouth have their positions reversed, or if he cannot see the nose.

During the infant's third month, the talking which made it easier for his mother to get him to smile earlier on becomes less and less important. Her face and her smile become enough to elicit his response. But the features and the feature-order that he has learned in all that careful visual scanning of faces remain vital. His mother will not get a smile if she is in profile or wearing sunglasses which hide her eyes. By 3 months, the infant has moved on yet another stage: he may still smile at pictures of faces, but real people now elicit his smiles more quickly, and when the smiles come they are bigger and smilier. He now not only knows what a face ought to look like, in terms of those vital hairline, eyes, nose and mouth features, he also clearly knows the real from the phoney.

Very shortly afterwards, his visual sophistication about faces is such that he knows familiar people from unfamiliar ones by sight alone. He may still be prepared to smile at any-one who smiles directly at him. But whereas a stranger in a bathing cap, which hides the hairline and alters the con-figuration of the whole head, may be accepted and smiled at, his mother in the same cap will be greeted with a sober stare. She is not looking as he knows she ought to look. And he does not like it.

This kind of research implies that even while infants can-not manipulate objects, handle them, experiment with them, they can learn a good deal about them by vision alone. Sup-portive evidence comes from some animal studies, par-ticularly those which have been carried out with infant monkeys. If infants did *not* learn about objects just from look-ing at them, infants who are prevented from looking until they are ready to handle objects should be no less efficient in their object handling than infants reared normally. But infant monkeys reared in total darkness throughout the first 8 weeks of their lives, when normal monkeys would be clinging to their mother's fur and looking, remain extremely bad both at visual discrimination and at using vision to direct their own activities. They are clumsy in their first forays off their mothers' bodies, seeming unable to judge distances. They are clumsy in manipulating food, and find it difficult to pick things up accurately. They behave as if they had missed out on a whole stage of learning about the world.

If we accept that human infants do a lot of learning by looking, it seems a pity not to give them the things they are interested in to look at, in a position from which they can actually see them.

We know, for example, that infants cannot see detail across

the width of even the smallest room. We know, too, that they choose to give their attention to what they have not seen before. So it seems a pity to waste nursery mobiles, pictures, brilliant wallpapers and all the other accoutrements of a really interesting room on a baby who will not see the interesting features, but will probably see just enough to get bored with it all before his distance accommodation catches up. It would seem that such a room, organized when the infant was around 4–6 months, would give infinitely greater pleasure.

We know that babies like pictures of things; that they actually choose to give them their attention. Yet many a mother would feel it ridiculous to sit a 2-month baby on her lap and show him a big, bold picture book.

We know that infants focus best on objects between 8 and 15 inches away from them, yet we seldom make use of this knowledge. Interesting things hung from the hood of a pram, for example, are usually too high up for close inspection; mothers may even be afraid that putting them closer will make the baby squint. Even grandmothers, desperate for some sign of recognition from the baby, are more likely to get him to smile if they will put their faces up to the baby's own.

CHAPTER NINE

RELATING HAND TO EYE

As we have seen in the last two chapters, infants make enormous strides in their second and third months in controlling and beginning to *use* their bodies, and in learning about things by looking at them. At the beginning, the infant's 'play' with objects is separate from his looking at them. He fingers his own hands or a rattle, or he looks at his own hands or the rattle: he does not, at first, relate his touching and his looking. His manual play and his visual exploration must eventually come together so that he can handle what he looks at – look at what he is handling. Only then can the information given him by his eyes and by his hands be put together.

As long as the baby can only look at things, he remains comparatively passive within his environment. Once he can reach out and take up things he can see, he can become an active participant.

Getting hold of things is an extremely complex procedure, involving not only visual abilities, but also physical abilities: voluntary movements of the body, arm and hand. Furthermore it involves putting all these things together into smooth, coordinated movements. The development of 'hand–eye' coordination is as dramatic and as important in this first half year as is the development of locomotion – the ability to get around unaided – in the second half year.

Earlier research workers tended to see the development of hand–eye coordination as being almost entirely dependent on the infant's own maturation. He would reach out for things, grab at them, pick them up, when, and only when, his neurology and his muscle control were sufficiently mature to allow him to do so. Gesell was perhaps the supreme exponent of this point of view in his early pre-war work, and he was followed by workers like H. M. Halverson,[24] whose study did not even commence until infants were 16 weeks old and – as we now see it – well advanced in the development of reaching out for objects.

While it is true that infants cannot be taught to coordinate hand and eye until their physiological equipment is capable of the necessary movements and adaptations, it is equally true that without the stimuli and the experiences which come from even the most restricted environment these abilities would develop very slowly, if at all. Their development is therefore an interaction between what the baby can physiologically do, and what he is stimulated into doing.

Because infants vary in their capacities at any given point in time, and because their environments vary too, it is extremely difficult to design research projects which can give us norms for development in this field. The normal baby will accomplish, at a given stage in his development, exactly what his development and his environment combine to teach him.

It is hardly surprising then that the norms for the development of hand–eye coordination are the subject of hot professional dispute. Thomas Bower,[25] for example, has reported on infants in whom he has observed postures, movements and early reaching out behaviour during the first fortnight. What he observed would usually be described as typical of infants 2–3 *months* of age, rather than 14 *days*. Bower believes that infants are in fact born with various motor and visual abilities which atrophy during the first month after birth because they are not stimulated, and then have to be relearned. He believes, for example, that if a baby a fortnight old is fully awake, and is supported in a semi-upright position, and is then offered an object within reach of his hand, he will swipe at it in a coordinated fashion. He believes that this behaviour is seldom seen in such young babies only because we do not expect it of them and do not therefore facilitate it. Such infants are seldom fully awake and alert; and in our culture they are nursed lying down, and are seldom held in the right position for reaching out. It is to be hoped that some research worker will investigate this fascinating proposition in the near future – perhaps by studying infants in cultures which use cradleboards, in which infants are slung upright almost all the time.

In the meanwhile, Bower's findings are unlikely to bring about overnight a radical change in the way Western cultures treat their infants. The most detailed, large-scale study of the normal sequence of the development of hand–eye coordination as most workers would see it, and of the extent to which the sequence can be modified or speeded up by extra stimulation, was made by Burton, White, Castle and Held.[26,27]

They carried out a careful study of infants being raised in an institution. The babies were receiving good physical care, but they were given a minimum of handling or attention by adults. They were kept in a visually boring environment, with very little to see within their short-sighted range. In this setting, White and his collaborators were able to study both the normal development of coordinated hand–eye behaviour, and the extent to which it could be speeded up if more and/or different stimuli were offered to different groups of infants.

Where newborn infants spent much time in gazing unfocusedly into space, it was found that by 6 weeks most of them spent some of their waking time in voluntary visual exploration. Their visual range was, of course, still limited by their flexed posture and their inability to move themselves around. But they would focus on the hand towards which their heads were flexed, or on the edge of the cot blanket, or the cot bars.

Offered a bright, complicated party favour to look at, all the infants would focus readily on it, provided it was shown to them within their best visual range – 8–9 inches (20–22cm) – and provided it was offered on the side to which the infant preferred to keep his head turned. The infant's interest in this object was usually shown not only by his ready focusing on it, but also by a marked change in the level of his physical activity. If he had been moving his free arm and leg when he caught sight of the object, he would typically 'freeze to attention'. If he had been still when he first saw it he was likely to become physically excited, and begin to wriggle.

At this age the infants would try to keep the object in view, by 'tracking it' with their eyes if it was moved in a small arc. But they lost interest immediately if the arc took it beyond their best focusing distance. They had not yet got any visual distance accommodation to enable them to keep it in sharp focus as it moved away.

By 2 to 2½ months, the infant's typical posture had changed, so that much of the time he lay with the back of his head on the mattress, and his head, arms and legs all free to move. Some of the infants in White's sample already had their hands open for some of their waking time.

At this stage the babies were usually looking at *something* when they were awake, and there was far more visual searching than before, with the infants swivelling both their heads and their eyes to find something to look at. Often they chose to watch their own hands waving in the air. But they appeared to have little idea that those hands were within their own control; they would simply look at a waving hand if it happened to appear in their view.

The experimenter came in for a good deal of interest at this stage, and the infant's attention was even more easily caught by the party favour, which he would track visually by moving his head as well as his eyes. Changes in level of activity were more marked than at the earlier age. For the first time this whole-body change in level of activity was sometimes translated into action directed *at* the object, so that if it was presented in exactly the right place, exactly within the ideal focusing distance, and towards the infant's favoured side, he would occasionally swipe at it with his hand, instead of just wriggling with excitement at the sight of it.

By around 3 months the infant's range of visual adaptation had increased to a point where he could keep the party favour in focus when it was as close as 3 inches (8cm) to the bridge of the nose, or as far away as 20 inches (51cm). Visual tracking through quite a wide arc was efficient, and the infants would follow the object through a vertical movement as well as horizontally. By this age the infants were watching their hands *as* they played with them. Offered the party favour, they might swipe at it as they did earlier, or they might display a very clear stage in learning how to get hold of it. If the object was presented to the baby's preferred side, he might focus on it, raise the hand on that side towards it, and then glance repeatedly from hand to object, as if measuring, visually, the distance between the two. If the stimulus was presented centrally, so that it was equidistant between the child's hands, he might raise both arms towards it, and then clasp them together across his chest.

By this stage the infants were clearly aware of a connection between what they could see, and their own arms and hands; they had grasped the idea of looking and reaching, but could not yet carry the look–reach sequence to a coordinated conclusion.

These age norms, which will be carried through into the stage of fully efficient reaching out for objects, in Chapter 16, were found to be surprisingly open to environmental adaptation. As we have seen, these infants were being reared in an environment which can best be described as 'bland', containing the minimum of visual, physical or emotional stimulation for any baby. Various changes were made, by the experimenters, to the environment experienced by different groups of infants. An increase in the daily 'ration' of handling by the nurses, with all the stimulation that such handling provides, was found to produce a dramatic increase in the babies' visual interest in the world around them. The more they were taken out of their cots, moved around, talked to, handled, allowed to see different things from different angles, the more interested they became and the more they looked around for something to look at when they were returned to their cots.

The provision of numbers of suitable things to look at, within the infant's visual range, and designed to suit his interest in complex pattern and contour, appeared to *delay* the infants' discovery of their own hands. Infants with very little else to look at typically began to finger their hands at

6–8 weeks, while the experimental group, whose cots were festooned with mobiles, stabiles and pictures, did not start concentrated hand play until around 9 weeks.

But the experimental group of infants used the stabiles and hanging objects around their cots. And they learned from them. On average the babies in this group were reaching out and grasping for objects efficiently by 14 weeks, nearly 5 weeks earlier than the control group (see page 225).

Such an acceleration is remarkable. But at present there is no evidence to suggest that it is of lasting benefit to the baby. In our society, we tend to be so achievement-oriented that we feel that it must be good for a baby to learn anything ahead of time. It must be a sign that he is extra bright, or extra well-handled or extra something-desirable.

But faint notes of warning can be detected in this research, and in other work within the same area. The extremes of stimulation offered to the experimental group did not produce *any* acceleration of hand–eye coordination before 2 months of age. Until that time, the experimental infants lay in their jazzy cots, covered with bright patterned sheets, hung around with carefully chosen toys, and they cried. They cried more and were generally less contented than the control group, who lay peacefully in their white institution cots, playing with their fingers.

The difference between the two groups, with the stimulated babies forging ahead in their learning, came at or after 2 months. It came, therefore, at just the time when the infants were uncurling their bodies; opening their hands; getting control of their necks; beginning to kick, and starting to look around to see what they could see.

It may be that these developments are signals of the infant's readiness for stimulation; that they herald the beginning of what is often called a 'critical period' for manual–visual learning. If so, infants may actually be better off if they are allowed to come to terms with their own bodies, find their own hands in peace, before they are bombarded with outside stimuli. After all, we know that in these early weeks extremes of noise and light and movement are obnoxious to infants; perhaps extremes of visual stimulation are disturbing too.

If the third month is indeed a critical period for this kind of stimulation, it is probably worthwhile to offer it in full measure once the infant *has* shown that he is ready to make use of it. Learning to get hold of objects early does not mean the infant is a genius, but it will serve both infant and mother well when they reach the stage where boredom becomes a problem (see Chapter 18). Once the infant can hold and manipulate objects, he can play. And once he can play, he becomes very much easier to entertain. Besides, once he is *ready* for lots of things to look at, and swipe at, and reach for, he will enjoy having them. It seems that he may not enjoy them if they are forced on him too soon.

CHAPTER TEN

HEARING AND MAKING SOUNDS

Infants discriminate between different levels of sound from birth. Sudden, loud noises will almost always make a new baby jump, and will make many of them cry. Equally, sudden *changes* in the level of sound tend to have the same effect, so that if the infant has become used to the noise of the vacuum cleaner working around his cot, he may cry when it is turned off. 'White noise' seems to soothe many infants (see page 80) and many mothers use a radio to provide the nearest home-equivalent to white noise, an endless stream of 'light music' playing quietly in the background of the child's room.

It is obvious that babies react differently to different kinds of sound. But it is not obvious, nor easy to discover, to what extent they discriminate in detail between one sound and the next. Crying when an ultrasonic boom occurs, and relaxing to sweet music only suggest a very coarse degree of discrimination. We need to know all we can possibly find out about the detailed auditory discriminations of young infants, because those discriminations between sounds must at least partly explain how, and indeed why, human infants as opposed to the young of any other species eventually learn to speak.

Various workers have examined the actual hearing apparatus of the human infant and compared it with that of higher animals. Very few important differences in the structure of the ear or inner hearing mechanism have been found. Békésy and Rosenblith[28] said: 'Our measurements demonstrate that the auditory systems of man and higher animals function in many respects as if they were governed by the same principles . . .', but these, and other, workers have found differences in the way in which the auditory apparatus is *used* in man and in animals. It looks as if the human animal is not born with unique equipment which will enable him to

understand and use speech, but is unique in the use to which
he puts that equipment.

Although far more research is needed, it does seem as if
human infants' auditory perception may be innately programmed to distinguish between human speech and other
sounds from a very early age. As we saw in Chapter 8, a
baby's visual preferences lead him inescapably towards looking at human faces. In the same way it seems that his auditory preferences lead him towards listening to human voices.
In a long and careful series of studies of 700 very young babies,
Rita Eisenberg[29-32] exposed infants to a variety of sounds
of varied frequency. Their reactions to each sound were
assessed in terms of their motor movements, their eye
movements, the extent to which they were generally aroused
or quieted, changes in their respiration and heart rate and
in their vocalizations. Eisenberg found that any individual
infant's response to a particular sound was largely dependent
on his own state at the time he was exposed to it. Hence the
same sound might excite a baby who was already happily
awake but produce crying in one who was already fretful. It
might awake a baby who had been dozing, but merely
interest one who was quietly alert.

Eisenberg's findings about the nature of the sound, as opposed to the state of the baby, are less obvious. Sounds within
the same frequency range as the normal human voice were
usually reacted to positively. Such sounds led calm infants to
exhibit interest, and distressed infants to stop crying. Sounds
at higher frequencies than the human voice had quite a
different effect. Calm infants tended to 'freeze' in apparent
alarm or displeasure. Many cried, and any who were already
fretful or distressed became much more so.

The clearest and most favourable responses of all were seen
when infants were exposed to sound within the human-voice
frequency range, *and* intonated to follow roughly the patterns
of rise and fall in ordinary adult speech. They reacted far more
positively to this intonated sound than they did to sound
in the same frequency range presented flat and uninflected.

Some infants even turned their heads in apparent search
for the source of sound.

No wonder mothers find that their own voices are among
the best of all calming devices for infants who are upset. No
wonder, either, that very young infants, incapable of seeing
the picture, nevertheless often take an interest in television
programmes.

Further research will undoubtedly reveal other detailed
auditory discriminations which infants can make. But the
reason for their particular reactions to different sounds cannot
be seen on a sound spectrograph; such reasons have to be
deduced. For example Marvin Simner[33] has already shown
that, even in the newborn period, infants are far more likely
to begin to cry if they are exposed to the sound of another
baby crying than if they are exposed to a band of 'white
noise' of exactly the same frequency range and volume. Nurses
in hospital nurseries amply confirm this finding, dreading the
infant who cries a lot because 'he sets the others off'. Mothers
of twins complain that they are seldom given the chance to
deal with *one* crying infant, because as soon as one starts to
cry, the other joins him. It really does seem as though from
the very beginning of life the infant recognizes some social
dimension to sounds, and reacts to that dimension emotionally.

The infant's own sounds before 3 months are not entirely
dependent on his own hearing of them. Research workers
interested in deaf babies have found that even the totally
deaf, who cannot hear the sounds they make at all, make the
same sounds and the same number of different sounds as
normally hearing babies at this age. If it is arranged that a
normally hearing baby does not hear the sounds he makes
until after a delay of several seconds, he continues to make
them. An adult finds it almost impossible to continue to
speak if he cannot hear what he is saying.

Many of these very early sounds may be the direct result of
physiological states rather than 'deliberate' sounds. For
example, the contented gurgling sound of the well-fed baby

who is half asleep results directly from the combination of his total relaxation, half-open mouth and relaxed vocal organs. Similarly the tiny whimpery sounds which often precede crying result from the combination of faster respiration and tension in the vocal organs. Such sounds may, therefore, have nothing to do with the feedback of hearing. Yet that cannot be the whole story. As we shall see in Chapter 17, normal sound-making continues in totally deaf babies well into the period of deliberate sound-making; infants must, to some extent, be programmed to produce sounds, even without the stimulus of hearing.

Nevertheless by 2 months in some babies, and by 3 months in almost all, hearing spoken sounds becomes a very definite stimulus to the infant to make sounds of his own. When he is spoken to, he looks for the source of the sound, watches the face of the talking adult, changes his level of activity (either 'freezing to attention' or beginning to kick excitedly) and he usually smiles. As he smiles, he 'talks back', producing small explosions of liquid sound. Every bit of the baby seems, to an observer, to go into this delightful social exchange, and every bit of him exudes dejection if his mother terminates it by turning away.

This voluntary talking usually begins in close association with social smiling. The infant smiles and talks when his mother smiles and talks to him. By 3 months the specific stimuli and responses have sorted themselves out. The infant smiles when his mother smiles at him – whether she also talks or not – and he talks when she talks to him, even if she is not also smiling.

Almost all infants under about 3 months do most of their talking when they are being talked to, but there is very wide variation in the amount which individual babies also talk when they are alone. Nakazima,[34] whose work in comparing American and Japanese infants will be referred to at length in Chapters 17 and 23, felt that his subjects could be divided into two quite distinct groups during this age period: those who talked most when they were being talked to, and those who talked most when they were alone. While some babies certainly do vocalize extensively to themselves when they are in their cots or prams, it seems surprising that Nakazima's sample babies were not also willing to talk extensively to adults. Further research might show that if they had been talked to more, or differently, they might in fact have done so. In which case the two groupings would comprise highly vocal and less vocal infants, rather than vocal and socially vocal ones.

Most workers in this field have demonstrated a very clear relationship between the amount an infant is spoken to, directly, face to face, rather than casually as the mother moves around, and the amount he talks himself. Rheingold's studies[35] demonstrated clearly that mothers who did talk a great deal in this direct face-to-face way with their infants, tended to be able to carry on 'conversations' with them, even as early as 6 weeks. The mother would talk to the baby; the baby would make a sound back, and then pause; the mother would reply, and the child would make a further sound. Conversations of this kind have been recorded lasting as much as 15 minutes, and containing a wide range of inflexion and tone from the infant.

The baby who will 'converse' in this way will also probably 'practise' his sound-making when he is alone. Instead of a burble of sound, the listening adult hears the baby make a noise, pause, as if listening to that noise, and then make it again. This sound-practising, together with playing with his own hands, is often the infant's best method of self-entertainment. Babies who do it are more likely than others to remain happily in their cots after waking, or to be content if put down for a nap before they are quite ready for sleep.

But some mothers find it more difficult than others to talk to a very young baby. Where some instinctively chat whenever they are handling the infant, others feel self-conscious, and find it more natural to handle the baby silently. There is no alternative to the genuine human voice for stimulating the baby's speech. Various workers have experimented to see whether arranging for some other sound to follow closely on the infant's own noises would stimulate him to go on and 'converse'. Weisberg,[36] for example, arranged for a pleasant-sounding bell to ring every time his sample infants uttered. This response did not stimulate further sound from the babies. The infant 'talks' because he is being talked to, not just because he hears a sound. He talks when he is talked to because he is in some way innately programmed to respond to human speech.

THREE MONTHS' SUMMARY

By 3 months babies are already complex human beings; the more complex they become, the more difficult it is to generalize about what they will (or 'should') be doing at a given age. The range of ages at which they do certain things is enormous, without the babies at either end of the range being in any way abnormal. Furthermore there is no convincing evidence that a baby who is slow in certain areas of development will continue to be slow, or conversely, that the advanced 3-month infant will go on being ahead of his peers.

Generalizations of the kind given in this summary are therefore of interest in respect of the individual baby only if they are read with full knowledge of that particular baby's past development. The *rate* at which he moves from stage to stage may vary, but the *sequence* in which he does so is almost invariable. A specific example may clarify this. Later in this section will be found the statement that by 3 months most babies will be able to roll themselves from their backs to their sides. To say that an individual baby is slow to accomplish this, without knowledge of his prior development, is meaningless, because he will not learn to roll from his back to his side until after he has learned to roll from his side to his back. The latter will always precede the former. On the other hand if the baby begins to roll from side to back just around three months, he may learn the opposite manoeuvre almost immediately afterwards, so that he ends up equal in 'rolling ability' with the baby who learned the first direction at 8 weeks.

Summaries such as this one serve two purposes. They give a rough guide to what 'most' babies do at a given age, and they tell people who are involved with individual babies roughly what to expect the next development to be. They do not enable anyone to make spot checks on the advanced or retarded behaviour of the infant.

One further note of caution is necessary. At this age, babie who were in any way disadvantaged at birth, due to pre maturity, low birthweight, illness, acute feeding difficulties, changes of caretaker, or just to being very miserable or sleepy babies, have not had nearly enough time to catch up with infants who had a better start. Such babies are likely to be well behind. It may take them several months more to catch up to the norms.

BEHAVIOUR	LIKELY STAGE REACHED AT 3 MONTHS	COMMENTS
Feeding	Five feeds per 24 hours from breast or bottle.	Sixth feed will not be dropped until baby can go for one period of 6–7 hours without feeding.
Quantity of food	6–8 oz. (170–230ml) milk per feed. Possibly some solids.	Not as much if birth-weight was low; solids certainly not needed if milk intake is still below about 35 oz. (1000ml) per 24 hours.
Weight	Is likely to have gained about 7 oz. (200g) per week from birthweight except for first week, i.e. baby born weighing 7 lb. will now weigh roughly 7 lb. + 12 × 7 oz. = 12 lb. 4 oz. (3.2kg now 3.2kg + 12 × 200g = 5.6kg).	Low birthweight babies will gain at similar rates, and will therefore be roughly the same amount lighter than their peers at this age as they were at birth.

BEHAVIOUR	LIKELY STAGE REACHED AT 3 MONTHS	COMMENTS
Sleeping	Very approximately 16 hours out of 24.	Actual hours of sleep will depend on how much the baby has slept in earlier weeks: the total hours will have dropped, but to what level depends on the individual starting point.
Crying	Probably no frequent, 'purposeless' crying. Causes of crying are usually clear and comprehensible.	Babies who have always been 'miserable' may still appear to be so. They will not become readily comfortable until their social development reaches the norm for their age group (see below).
Colic	Over. Continued evening screaming is now much more likely to be due to hunger or frustration of social inclinations.	Colic, once established, usually lasts 9 weeks. Babies who started it late may continue to about 4 months. Colic after 4 months is extremely rare.
Posture	On the back, the baby now usually lies straight, with back of head on mattress and all limbs free. On face, he raises upper chest on fore-arms; legs straight out behind him.	All these developments go together. Baby who still lies in 'scrunched-up' neonatal position on back will only turn head when placed on face.

BEHAVIOUR	LIKELY STAGE REACHED AT 3 MONTHS	COMMENTS
Posture	Held sitting, he supports his own head and upper back, sagging only from the hips. Carried, he supports his head unless mother bends down or moves very suddenly.	Similarly baby who cannot support own head when carried will not support it when held sitting.
Motor activities	Provided he has reached the postural stage described above, he will now wave arms and legs smoothly, rhythmically and almost constantly when awake.	None of these developments will take place until head control is almost perfect. Until this stage, arm and leg movements remain jerky and unplayful.
	Will be able to roll from his side on to his back. Once having done this, will learn about now to roll from back to side.	Rolling over is unlikely and being rocked and swung may actually distress him.
	Will enjoy being gently rocked, swung, held sitting or standing.	Will *not* enjoy these things until he *has* begun playful motor activity himself.
Grasping	Hands will now be open most of the time when awake.	Baby whose hands are still habitually loosely fisted is unlikely to be ready for manual play. Hands will open when baby is ready to use them.
	Will grasp an object put in the hand.	

BEHAVIOUR	LIKELY STAGE REACHED AT 3 MONTHS	COMMENTS
Grasping	Will clasp one hand with the other, finger and play with clothing at chest level. Put fingers or objects in the mouth. May finger breast or bottle.	
Seeing	Can now adapt focus to objects as close as 3 inches (9cm), as far as 20 inches (50cm). Clarity of distance vision is much improved; adult acuity will be reached by about 4 months. Visual interest is now great. Looks at something whenever awake; swivels head and eyes to follow object. Watches mother as she moves around room.	Baby who still lies in the neonatal posture is not free to move his head in the same way, and will therefore see and follow objects very much less. Just as postural growing up is needed to free limbs for motor activity, so it is needed to free head and eyes for increased visual activity.
Coordinating seeing and grasping	By 3 months, the baby has 'found' his own hands with his eyes as well as by touch. He spends much time looking at his hands, watching them as they move; putting them to his mouth and then bringing them back into his line of vision.	Baby will not 'find' his hands with his eyes, until he has begun to play with them by touch.

BEHAVIOUR	LIKELY STAGE REACHED AT 3 MONTHS	COMMENTS
Coordinating seeing and grasping	Presented with an object within range he will swipe at it, and often hit it. A hanging ball will be swiped, watched as it swings, swiped again. Once swiping is accurate, the baby may raise his hand towards an object, glancing from hand to object to hand, as if visually measuring the distance between.	He is unlikely to 'swipe' at other objects until he *has* begun to watch his own hands moving.
Social responses	Now smiles readily at a smiling face, even if it is not also talking. Will still smile at masks or drawings of faces, but smiles to real people come faster and look 'smilier'.	*Early* social smiles are slow in coming, and usually are a response to the adult smiling *and* talking. Smiling to a *silently* smiling face follows this phase.
Smiling	Still needs to see all features, full face. Will not smile to profile. While smiling strangers still get a smiling response, familiar adults who look strange – with new hairdo, sun-glasses or hats–may get an adverse reaction.	

BEHAVIOUR	LIKELY STAGE REACHED AT 3 MONTHS	COMMENTS
Talking	Baby will 'talk back' when he is talked to. Practises sounds when alone – often in the early morning.	Will not 'talk back' until he has started to smile to a silent smiling face. This marks the separation of smiling and talking responses.
Pleasure and anticipation	When extremely pleased, the baby tends to put all his new abilities together, so that he smiles, burbles, kicks and waves simultaneously.	
	Such behaviour is often seen as a 'greeting' to the mother when she comes in to the baby in the morning. It may also be seen when the baby is presented with his bottle, or put in his pram for an outing. At this stage, the baby may also react with this sort of pleasure to his own motor play.	'Greeting' behaviour and other spontaneous expressions of delight will not be seen until the baby smiles readily to people and talks back.

FROM THREE TO SIX MONTHS:
DISCOVERING PEOPLE

CHAPTER ELEVEN

SINGLING OUT MOTHER

In most families, the period from 3 to 6 months marks the change from the infant being 'the baby' to his being a very noticeable, noticing person. He becomes a full family member, with clear-cut likes and dislikes, able to signal his demands and likely to raise Cain if these are not met. People, together with the total environment, become highly important to him. All his functions now become inextricably bound up both with each other and with that total family environment.

For ease of reference, a book of this kind has to try to separate out the infant's different accomplishments, the changes that take place in different areas. But in truth such separation is false. The baby is all of a piece. His eating is not separate from his mood; his 'talking' is not separate from his relationships; his physical play is not separate from either of these things.

The foundation of these shifts towards becoming a whole complex person is the infant's growing ability to discriminate between one person and another, and his strengthening attachment to one or two people. He is increasingly sociable, and increasingly fussy about who he socializes with. Basic to most of the other types of discrimination which the baby will make during this age period appears to be his singling out of his mother from all other people.

The infant does not know who gave birth to him. There is no suggestion here of magic in the blood tie between mother and baby. But there is the suggestion that the baby chooses to make a very special relationship with whoever *mothers* him. In our culture that person is likely to be his natural mother and it makes for less convoluted writing to refer to her as such, but the arguments apply equally to substitute-mothers.

While it can be conclusively demonstrated that infants will make an intense exclusive relationship with their mothers if they get the opportunity, millions of words of hot controversy have been expended on the question of whether or not this special relationship is necessary to their optimal development in all fields. It is a question which has attracted attention from many people who are not developmentalists. All those who must deal with orphaned, abandoned or in any way institutionalized babies have a stake in this. Indeed it was to them that John Bowlby's first impassioned work on the subject was addressed. [37] The many groups all over the world, from the established kibbutzim of Israel to the mushrooming communes of the United States, who are experimenting with different forms of group living, have to examine the proposition carefully. Such a mother–child tie is difficult to arrange in most forms of communal life, and against the principles of many such groups. Meanwhile, mothers who devote themselves exclusively to their infants seek assurance that they are right to do so; mothers who divide their attention between their infants and a career want to be reassured that they do their children no harm; and mothers who feel they must work for money want to be told that they have their priorities right. Many husbands resent, at least a little, the implication that they are less important to their infants than are their wives. Finally there are increasing numbers of people who believe that the nuclear family, as an institution, is no longer appropriate to modern life – if indeed it ever was appropriate. They believe that marriage and family patterns need radical rethinking. Many believe that if child-rearing was undertaken as a professional activity by trained personnel, rather than as a direct responsibility by the parents, many of the bitter family conflicts and neuroses of later years could be avoided.

It may be that the present-day Western view of the emotional needs of infants is blinkered and biased by generations of monogamous nuclear-family child rearing. It may be that in the future our views of what infants need, of how they actually develop and of what is important in their development will radically change. All we can do now is to consider the evidence, ignore the partisan arguments, decide what facts there are, and institute new research to find the facts that are at present only theories.

John Bowlby's report to the World Health Organization[37] was designed to suggest ways of improving the care given to motherless children. It stimulated an enormous and timely amount of discussion, and has probably done more than any other single work to improve the lot of children who must, for whatever reason, temporarily or permanently, live in institutions. But due to the amount of popular interest it evoked, that report, together with many of Bowlby's subsequent papers, has been widely misinterpreted. It has been suggested that nothing less than the 24-hours-a-day, 7-days-a-week, 52-weeks-a-year care of a baby by its own mother would suffice to fulfil its emotional needs. Bowlby did not say this. He said that it was essential for a baby to experience a warm, intimate and continuous relationship with its mother or permanent mother-figure. But he also said, even in this first early report, that it was important to accustom the baby, from the beginning, to being cared for occasionally and for short periods by other familiar figures. He has never suggested maternal chains.

The attitudes of research workers to the question of the infant's need for a close exclusive tie with his mother inevitably depend on their attitudes to infant development as a whole. In the past, students of infant development tended to subscribe to one of two radically opposed points of view.

Watson,[38] often described as the father of behaviourism, saw the new infant as a blank slate on which parents could draw almost at will. For him, psychological development was a one-sided process; something that arose from what was done *to* the child. The characteristics found in that child as he grew up were seen therefore as almost entirely the result of parental handling.

Gesell[39, 40] took an equally one-sided although opposite view. He believed that development was primarily a matter of maturation, of the child unfolding as he got older along largely predetermined lines. He believed that the child's environment could make only minimal differences to his development.

In more recent years, a Skinnerian model, suggesting that infant learning and development takes place almost entirely through conditioning effects, has gained many advocates. This approach, perhaps epitomized by the work of Gewirtz,[41] suggests that for learning to take place, the environment must provide stimuli which the child can discriminate, and reinforcers for his behaviour in reaction to those stimuli. While this is undoubtedly true, it is inadequate as a theory. The fact that the infant smiles more if his smiles are pleasantly responded to is a statement of fact; it is not an explanation. Why does the infant react in this way? Why can he discriminate a smile? Why does he smile? Why does an answering smile make him smile again?

All these theories stay outside the baby's skin. More recent work has concentrated on looking not merely at what is done to the baby from the outside, nor at his inherent rate of maturation, nor even at the cause-and-effect links which are forged between the two. Rather it concentrates on looking at the cognitive structures within the baby, which mediate between information coming in to him and his own behaviour. Something within the baby makes him likely to smile when his mother smiles, and *unlikely* to cry when she smiles. The baby takes an active part in shaping his own environment, in dictating what stimuli he will receive. And he takes a particularly active part in shaping the way in which his mother – and other caretakers – behave towards him. The organism which is the baby interacts with his environment; the results of that interaction change his behaviour, but they also change the environment. The two are totally intermixed.

This point of view has been most cogently put forward by Piaget.[42, 43] He sees the infant, from birth, as being possessed of certain 'schemata', which are initially organized round innate reflexes such as sucking and visual orientation. These schemata dictate the newborn baby's first interactions with the environment. The sucking schema, for example, ensures that the infant will attempt to suck any object which his mouth encounters. But experience of the variable 'suck-ability' of objects leads to changes in the original schema – for instance a thumb requires a different type of sucking from a nipple; the baby therefore accommodates his original schema by adapting it to different stimuli.

Adaptation to the environment is a constant balancing by the baby of assimilation and accommodation. Where a stimulus fits into an existing schema it is assimilated. Where it does not fit, the schema is adapted to accommodate it. Events are always selected, interpreted, and fitted into the existing pattern of cognitive structures. The flexibility of the human being is such that the inborn schemata can become adapted to an ever-increasing range of external circumstances. Finally such a complex and diversified cognitive structure is reached that the child can handle not only all external events, but their internal representations, in terms of symbols and abstractions.

This view of development finds a parallel in systems engineering with its principles of self-organization and feed-back. Frank[44] discusses this parallel, and sees the infant as 'a self-organizing, self-stabilizing, self-directing, largely self-repairing open system which becomes progressively pat-terned, oriented and coupled to the culturally established dimensions of his environment, natural and human'. This creature is no blank slate for parents to draw on, nor Pavlovian dog who will automatically respond to a pre-determined stimulus.

As we have seen in earlier chapters, infants appear to have schemata towards other human beings. They are visually interested in the human face (see page 122), they are interested in the human voice (see page 134) and they re-spond soothedly to being held and cuddled. But at the begin-ning, these responses are not specifically social. When he starts to smile, the infant will do so as readily to a mask face as to his mother. When he cries, he is comforted as readily by being swaddled in a soft blanket as by being held in his mother's arms. Often mothers assume an importance for themselves that, in the *early* weeks, they do not really have. In the early weeks, when a baby cries, his mother is likely to pick him up and cuddle him and be gratified when he is comforted. Why should she experiment with putting him, instead, into a gently moving, warm, soft, vocalizing gadget? She assumes that she is the comforter, whereas at this stage she is merely a readily available sum of comforting elements. But gradually a narrowing down takes place. The baby learns social preferences; soon only real people, real voices, real faces, real bodies, will do.

For many years it was assumed that the baby learned to associate people with being fed; that it was the hunger drive which acted as a stimulus, and feeding as the reward, and that a child's attachment to his caretaker could therefore be simply explained. Freud placed heavy emphasis on the feeding relationship as the context within which the baby learned dependence on his mother. Dollard and Miller[45] made the theory even more explicit:

In general there is a correlation between the absence of people and the prolongation of suffering from hunger, cold, pain and other drives; the appearance of a person is associated with a reinforcing reduction in the drive. Therefore the proper conditions are present for the infant to learn to attach strong reinforcement value to a variety of cues from the nearness of the mother and other adults ...

This is a tempting idea, and one which a superficial look at real life tends to confirm. The mother is usually the person who deals with an infant's hunger or cold, fear or pain. And it is usually the mother to whom the baby becomes most attached. It all seems simple and 'natural'. But the theory does not fit the facts.

Mothering behaviour does not appear to be necessary in any species before attachment can take place. Mothering behaviour *takes place* in human infants before attachment manifests itself, because human infants are relatively so slow in their development. But in other species attachment often precedes any form of mother care. In birds, for example, chicks emerge from the shell with an inbuilt and determined desire to follow the mother bird. No contact need be made at all between mother bird and chick before this following behaviour (known as 'imprinting') occurs. Furthermore chicks can be experimentally 'imprinted' on to almost any other moving object, if that object (even a human being) is the first thing the chick sees on hatching. The imprinted following is an instinctive attachment behaviour in no way dependent on prior satisfaction of any infant need.

Moving closer to the human species, extensive research with rhesus monkeys[11] has shown that feeding is by no means the strongest drive in the development of attachment behaviour. Harlow has shown that if infant monkeys are deprived of their real mothers at birth, and are offered two 'surrogates', one made of wire and holding the feeding bottle, and the other made of comfortably padded cloth, they develop a passionate attachment to the 'cloth mother', clinging to it, sleeping on it, returning to it in times of stress. They use the 'wire mother' purely as a bottle holder.

In human infants there is a considerable amount of evidence, touched upon in Chapter 3 and discussed more fully later (see page 240), that not even feeding, together with all other aspects of infant care, necessarily dictate the direction of an infant's attachments. In the Israeli kibbutzim, for example, the complete physical care of infants used to be taken over by nurses from the earliest weeks of life. Contact with the natural mother was confined to a couple of hours in the day. But it was nevertheless with the mother, who offered emotional gratification but no physical care, that the infants formed their close attachments. Schaffer and Emerson[46] similarly found that infants often formed close attachments to fathers, siblings or other relatives, even when they took no part in routine physical care or feeding.

The infant does not need reduction of hunger or other unpleasant sensations to provide him with motivation for becoming attached to people. His motivation is inbuilt; part of his cognitive structure. He has certain schemata, in Piaget's phrase, and these direct his attention to certain aspects of his environment. People are uniquely able to provide all that interests the baby, rolled into one stimulus. They are interesting to look at, to listen to, to touch and feel, to be held and moved around by. They are warm, soft, brightly coloured and so forth. The infant is made so that people will interest him more than anything else around him. The more he sees of them, the more he wants. The more he sees, the more he becomes able to tell one from another. And the more he discriminates *between* people the more he comes to want particular people, not just any people.

In what our culture regards as 'normal families', the object of the baby's first real attachment is likely to be the mother, but research has made it abundantly clear that this is a matter of environmental chance. If the mother is mothering her own baby, more or less full time, she is the obvious, the most available candidate for his first intense attachment. But it is availability not magic. If someone else is mothering the baby, that someone else will get his attachment, provided that their interaction began *before* the baby began to differentiate his natural mother from other people. Allowing for the wide age variation within which such discrimination can begin to occur, 6 weeks is probably late for an ideal adoption; and the baby's formation of attachments will almost certainly be disturbed if he is moved from one caretaker to another later than about 3 months.

Bowlby[37] believed that whether or not the infant had his natural mother to attach himself to, this first or primary attachment would be to one person only – that the infant had, as it were, an inbuilt monotropy. Other workers have shed some doubt on this proposition. Schaffer and Emerson[46] made repeated studies of the same babies over several months, in what is termed a longitudinal investigation. They found that 29 per cent of their sample of 58 babies formed their first attachments to several people at the same time. Schaffer refers to various animal studies, which showed similar findings. For example, dogs often form primary attachments to littermates as well as to their mothers, because the mother tends to begin to leave the nest just at the time the puppies are ready to attach. Similarly, Bonnet macaque monkeys have a polymatric rearing system, which leads to the formation of multiple attachments. It seems likely that the number of attachments made by the infant does vary with the number of relationships offered to him. But it is possible that the relationship with the mother-figure is always primary, and that the formation of the additional relationships is contingent upon the maternal one, even if their formation is separated only by a few days. Measures of attachment are not yet sophisticated enough for anyone to be sure exactly who, in this situation, the infant attached to first, nor which attachment is the most meaningful for the child.

Unfortunately it is difficult to find naturally occurring situations in which it would be possible to study an infant's attachment behaviour if he was offered two adults, both equally available to him all the time. It is not known whether the infant would select one of them as his primary person, or whether he would interact equally with them both. There are plenty of highly participant fathers, but few of them are at home with the baby as much as their wives. There are plenty of mothers who share their babies with nannies – but few families where both women hold themselves constantly available to the child. The essence of such a situation is that when one is 'on duty' the other is not.

So for practical purposes it is reasonable to assume that the baby will attach himself primarily to his mother or her substitute. But her central role does not remain for long unless she earns it, and she cannot earn it simply by feeding and physically caring for the baby. In Schaffer and Emerson's sample nearly one third of the babies had shifted their primary allegiance by the age of 18 months, usually in favour of the father, even if he participated little in baby care, and could spend comparatively little time with the infant. As age increases, the choice of person to whom the baby is attached seems to be dictated firstly by the object-person's responsiveness to the infant's cues and social advances, and secondly by the amount of interaction which he is prepared to *initiate* with the infant. As Schaffer and Emerson put it,

When . . . the most available person (generally the mother) does not show a great deal of responsiveness and is not prepared to interact much with the infant, the latter is more likely to search for another object towards whom he can direct his most intense attachment behaviour . . . Thus when a relatively unstimulating mother is found in conjunction with, say, an extremely attentive father, the latter is more likely to head the infant's hierarchy of attachment objects, despite the mother's greater availability.

But that is in the future. At 3 months infants have not reached the point where they will abandon one attachment because it seems less satisfactory than another. They are only just beginning to make that first, primary one. Yarrow[47] studied a large sample of infants to see how many showed definite pleasure and excitement at seeing their mothers rather than the unknown experimenter, and at what ages they reached this stage. At 1 month, only 20 per cent of the infants showed any behaviour which even might have demonstrated a discrimination of mother from stranger. By 3 months 80 per cent clearly differentiated between the two, while by 5 months every single infant not only clearly knew mother from stranger, but infinitely preferred her.

The development of the infant's attachment to his mother can be seen in subtle behaviours, which are not always clear unless the infant is watched when he is with mother *and* somebody else. Alone with mother, he behaves as infants behave when they are in pleasant social contact with an adult; when another person is added into the situation it can be seen that he increasingly treats his mother differently. Ainsworth[48] found, for example, that where most babies would smile at a mask or photograph of a face at 14 weeks, they already smiled faster and more fully to a human face. By 16 weeks the mother's face got the widest and fastest smiles of all, and being picked up by mother when he was distressed always stopped a baby's crying, where being picked up by a stranger might not. By around 4 months the babies in this sample showed quite different behaviours when they were happily seated on their mother's or the stranger's lap. On the mother's knee, they behaved as if the mother's body belonged to them, exploring her face, her clothes, her hair with their hands and mouths. But on the stranger's knee they were far more restrained, often barely touching her. By 5–6 months, most of the infants would bury their faces in the mother's shoulder or lap if they were shy or upset; they never did this to the stranger.

So the signs of an infant's discrimination of and attachment to his mother are, during this age period, positive ones. It is not that he is calm with his mother and distressed with strangers, but rather than he is free, confident and joyous with his mother and more restrained with strangers. Few mothers can fail to be pleased when their infant, having sat calmly in a visitor's arms, comes to hers with grins and crows of delight. The more the baby singles his mother out for these charming attentions, the more she is likely to respond to them in kind. He makes her feel marvellous; mother and baby reinforce each other.

But this picture of mutual reinforcement by mother and baby is an idealized one. The pair of them do not live in isolation. At about the same time that the infant is making his primary attachment to his mother, he is usually also making his debut into family life. During the first 3 months babies tend to be very much sheltered from the rest of the family. They sleep long hours; they do not eat food, in the family sense, and mothers often select times of day when they can be alone with the baby for procedures such as baths and play. But at around 3 months the infant's horizons are widening, and he is forcing himself on the attention of his family. He is awake for long enough periods that at least some of his waking time will coincide with the presence of others, and his demands for sociability will bring him increasingly into the family circle. The infant's basic attachment is with his mother. Under ideal circumstances, he can get from her all the stimulation which he needs to develop his growing abilities in all fields. She can offer him social contact, objects, experiences, physical play, as well as the physical care which he needs. But in practice very few mother–infant pairs experience such an intense relationship, even during these early months. The mother must share herself among many people. She needs private time to be herself – rather than one half of a symbiosis with the baby – time to spend with her husband, other children, her own parents, friends. The baby takes his place in the family, and gets much of his stimulation from other people.

A simple listing of the possible combinations and per-mutations of 'family' which the baby may meet would take a whole book in itself. The baby may be a first child, and within that position, he may be male or female. Whichever he is, he may be closely, distantly, or never followed by a sibling either of the same or of the opposite sex. Again he may be a second, third or fourth child of either sex, in which case he may have one, two or three siblings older than himself, each of which may be a girl or a boy, and each of which may be anything from 10 months to 20 years older than he is; other siblings may, or may not, be born after him. When one adds to this all the possibilities of grandparents living in the house, of cousins next door, of aunts in residence, not to mention step- or half-siblings, it becomes clear that it is impossible to define the possible people in a baby's immediate environ-ment.

Yet from this age period onwards all such relationships are important to the baby: all can be expected to affect his de-velopment to some degree. The baby is busy learning to dis-criminate people. Therefore he is learning to relate to people. The experience of the baby who has many people of all ages and both sexes to relate to will obviously be different from the experience of the baby who spends most of his time alone with his mother, sees his father at week-ends, and smiles at the milkman.

CHAPTER TWELVE

STIMULATION AND ATTENTION

As we saw in the last chapter, between 3 and 6 months people become the most vital factor in an infant's environment and therefore in his development as a person. He learns to know one person from another; he chooses the person or people to whom he becomes most closely attached, and he learns about the world through them. He needs them to mediate the world for him, to show him things, to help him to do what he cannot yet do alone and to comfort and reassure him when things are strange or difficult.

We still know very little about the differences which various kinds of family structure and family experience make to an infant's development. But we know a little about some extreme situations, about infants who are isolated with their mothers in high apartment blocks, for example, or the relative progress of infants in large families as compared with only children. It appears that the critical factor which differentiates one family environment from another, for a young baby, is the amount of social stimulation which he receives. Later chapters will touch on the evidence that such stimulation tends to speed up, or at least to optimize, development in many areas, especially in speech and in manual abilities. But our knowledge is still scattered and scanty. Social stimulation is not a clearly definable *thing*. It is partly to do with how much time adults spend in direct inter-action with the baby – and this can be measured. But it is also to do with how much they *enjoy* being with the baby – the whole atmosphere of their interactions – and that is not measurable. Research workers repeatedly try to define these 'atmospheric variables', trying to find ways of measuring 'warmth' or 'love' or 'pleasure in the child'. But often the definitions arrived at by one group of workers are slightly different from the definitions of another group, and we rarely have the knowledge to judge whether those slight differences are likely to be important.

It is impossible to lay down the amount of 'social stimulation' which an infant needs. In some areas it can be shown that particular kinds of stimulation improve his performance in specific ways. We have already seen that being talked to a great deal improves his vocal performance (see page 137). But even this does not mean that the more the infant is talked to the better off he will be. If he were talked to *all* the time, he might, in theory, lack the peaceful times he needs for practising his new motor skills, or learning about his hands with his eyes.

In Western societies, under-stimulation is more usual than over-stimulation. Most mothers have to ration the time they spend interacting with their infants; the babies tend to be left alone whenever they will tolerate solitude, and a high premium is placed on their ability to 'amuse themselves'. It is a rare mother who would actually like to play with her baby more than that baby appears to want to play with her.

As a result most research work in this area has concentrated on demonstrating the beneficial effects of extra stimulation to infants. One group of studies such as those by Burton, Castle, White and Held[26, 27] and Yarrow[47] has been conducted in institutions. In studies such as these, the level of overall stimulation offered to the infants has tended to be extremely low: the infants' lives have been so bland, uninteresting and lonely that the extra individual attention provided by the experimenters still did not bring their experiences up to any kind of 'norm' for children in families. In circumstances like these it is hardly surprising that the experimental groups showed a great increase in happiness, in interest in the world, and in performance.

Another group of studies has tended to use infants in ordinary families, and to manipulate the amount of stimulation they received in very specific areas, so as to demonstrate accelerated progress in those areas. For example, studies have been carried out to show that concentrated walking practice may lead to earlier independent walking, or that concentrated and regular periods of story-telling may lead to earlier speech. In studies of this kind the interpretation of the results tends to be confused by an almost unanswerable question: is the extra *specific* stimulation responsible for the infant's improved performance, or is it the extra general stimulation of attention from the mother? From the infant's point of view, his mother's attempts to give him daily practice in using his limbs means that at least once a day she plays an intensive physical game with him. The stimulation of the game, of her attention, her physical handling, may be as important, or more important, to his development than what she is trying to teach him.

In the present state of knowledge, it is probably most valuable to look at stimulation for infants in a more general way. To avoid talking of stimulation as if it were a clearly definable thing, which can be measured, divided into 'kinds', and whose effects can be separated out in the baby, but rather to consider what stimulation is, in terms of how it can be *used by* the individual baby.

Many of the things which are done for babies, with the intention of stimulating, amusing or interesting them, are often done with so little understanding of the baby himself that they fail completely. Just as food on a plate does not nourish a child until it has been eaten, so stimulation offered to a child does not stimulate him until he has noticed and *used* it. Often parents will buy and lovingly hang a complicated colourful mobile in their infant's room – and then continue to lie him on his tummy. A stimulating sight cannot stimulate unless it is seen. Often, too, an adult will begin a stimulating interaction with a baby, smiling and speaking to him and then not have the patience to wait for his slow response. By the time the baby has begun to smile back, the adult has turned away to do something else. An interaction that is merely one-sided is not interactive nor truly stimulating.

The child has to be ready to receive the stimulus if it is to mean anything to him. At the simplest level it is no use trying to play with a baby who is trying to be asleep, nor trying to love and cuddle one who is furious with hunger. At a slightly more subtle level, new and exciting experiences will mean most to the baby when their degree of novelty is just exactly right for his particular developmental stage. Between 3 and 6 months, apart from known faces which, as we have seen, retain their fascination for the baby, the objects and events which will interest him most will be those which are just slightly different from what he has met before. Totally new events or objects, which he cannot relate at all to his existing schemata, are likely to be ignored. He will *not* enjoy a pantomime. On the other hand things he has seen many times before are boringly familiar. In between these extremes, a ball just like his old one except that it has a different coloured pattern, a piece of paper which is like yesterday's but more crumply, a music box which works like the old one but plays a different tune will all fascinate him. And then of course there are all the infinite variations in people: his father, whose hands are bigger than his mother's, whose voice is deeper, whose chin is bristly, but who stills baths the baby in his usual bath; the aunt who pushes him in the same pram, but not in the same way; the new food that comes in the same bowl, from the same hand, but has a different taste. Kagan[49] put it neatly when he said that the baby is likely to be most genuinely stimulated by those things or events which 'require tiny, quiet, cognitive discoveries – a miniaturized version of Archimedes' Eureka'.

Even when careful thought is given to the kind of stimulus which is being offered to the baby, and to the use which he can make of it at one particular stage in his development or moment in his day, each baby has many individual characteristics which will affect the way *any* offered stimulus strikes him.

There is abundant evidence that some infants are born with a greater degree of perceptual and tactile sensitivity than others, and that some are innately more physically active than others. Some of these characteristics have been described in earlier chapters as newborn phenomena. But while the extremes of sleepiness, irritability or jumpiness have

usually passed by 3 months, milder versions of them remain –
certainly throughout infancy and perhaps throughout life.

Overall sensitivity to stimulation has been well discussed
by Escalona.[50] She believes that there are discernible differences between infants in their sensitivity to all kinds of stimulation. She points out that infants of differing sensitivity
receive quite different experiences from identical handling.
For example, a highly sensitive infant may receive the same
amount of stimulation from a relatively quiet unstimulating
mother as the insensitive infant receives from a relatively
boisterous highly stimulating one. The handling the two
infants receive is quite different, but the effect may be the
same. Equally, if those two infants were swopped over the
sensitive infant might be overwhelmed by the highly stimulating mother, while the less sensitive infant was bored and
understimulated by the quiet one. In recent years there has
been a resurgence of interest in the idea that too high a level
of stimulation tends to lead the infant to withdraw, where a
milder stimulation makes him want to explore.[51]

Sometimes parents have to learn this lesson the hard way, if
they have two children who vary along this dimension. The
rough-and-tumble games which delighted the first baby on
father's nightly return from work may drive the second into a
frenzy of fear. Or the gentle lullabies which mother sang to
the first baby may quite fail to catch the attention of the
second.

Just as the novelty of a stimulus has to be adjusted to suit
the baby – the familiar being boring and the totally new incomprehensible – so the intensity has to be adjusted too. The
infant likes objects which are just slightly novel. He likes
other stimulation to be strong enough to be noticeable, but
not too strong.

Differences in levels of physical activity from birth have
been demonstrated by many workers, and they have also
been shown to remain consistent over long periods of
time.[52, 53] The newborn who is always on the move and
sleeps little tends to be the wakeful 6-week baby who acquires
a powerful kick very early on. Later in his first year he may

crawl and walk early; even if he does not, he is likely to need endless exercise and to be furious if he is physically restricted. On the other hand, the sleepy newborn, who moves very little, may be content to be rolled in a bundle for much longer; he may never take the extreme delight in motor play that the active baby has, and he may be content to be a 'sitter' until much later in the first year.

These differences appear to be innate, and independent either of the mother's behaviour, or of any other factors in the child's environment.[54] And they are important. A baby's own physical activity provides him with entertainment, but it also provides him with other kinds of stimulation. As he kicks, he brings his feet into view and out again; he alters the feeling of the blankets over him; he makes a draught which tickles his nose. When he learns to roll over, earlier than most babies, he can provide himself with a new view of the world as well as with a change of physical position. A very active baby may therefore provide himself with so much stimulation that he needs less from the adults around him than does the inactive baby who depends on them for every new experience. Schaffer[55] put this point of view to experimental test. He measured the 'developmental quotient' (see page 425) of active and inactive babies before they underwent similar brief periods in an institution. At the end of the period, the developmental quotients of the inactive babies had dropped far more than the quotients of the active babies. It seemed that, even when they were deprived of much of their accustomed stimulation from handling and play, the active babies were able to make the very most of any stimulation which *was* offered to them, and to keep themselves alert by the feedback, and the changes of position and view which came from their own physical activities. The inactive babies, on the other hand, suffered far more from not being given much stimulation, because they were not able to compensate by providing it for themselves.

The infant's sex may also affect the amount and the kind of stimulation he receives within his family. Of course parents are aware, from the moment of birth, whether they have pro-

duced a boy or a girl. In some families the awareness may be
overwhelming: a boy may end a one-sex run of three girls,
thus delighting his parents; or he may make yet another boy
to add to the other three boys, and make his parents painfully
aware that they did not actually *want* a fourth child if it was
not to be a girl. But where the parents were comparatively
neutral about the baby's sex before his birth, the actual sex
tends to impinge increasingly after 3 months, as the infant
ceases to be 'our new baby' and becomes 'Johnny' or 'Jane'.

Everybody who has handled children knows that boys and
girls are different. But whether they are genetically different,
or whether we make them different in their behaviour by
expecting differences and therefore handling them differently, remains a matter of hot dispute. There is some evidence of inherent sex differences in sensitivity to some forms
of stimulation, from a fascinating longitudinal study by
Bell.[56] There is also evidence of differences in behaviour
between the sexes in the early months from an observational
study by Moss.[57] The boys in Moss's sample were more likely
to be irritable than the girls, they tended to cry more, and
their mothers found the causes of their crying more obscure.
The boys also responded less readily, and less rewardingly,
to their mothers' attempts to comfort and cheer them.

If the boys and girls in this study behaved differently from
each other, they also received very different handling from
their mothers. The mothers of girls tended to pick them up
whenever they cried, and to be willing to pick them up and
cuddle them more than usual if they had an extra fussy day.
The mothers of boys on the other hand rapidly stopped adjusting their handling to fit in with their sons crying. They
picked the boys up as much as they thought proper and no
more. When the boys cried at other times the mothers labelled
them 'fussy', and left them to get on with it.

Few studies produce such clear-cut differences in behaviour between the sexes in the early months, nor such
clear-cut differences in maternal handling, but other studies
do suggest such differences. For example, a body of further
work by Moss[58–60] suggests that at three months boys get

more cuddling and rough-and-tumble, physical, play from their mothers than do girls of the same age. The girls tend to get more direct talking, smiling and looking contact from their mothers instead. We do not know how general these differences in handling the two sexes are. But they are certainly not general or intense enough to override wider cultural differences in infant handling. In a comparison of Japanese and American families, for example, Caudill and Weinstein[61] showed that Japanese mothers concentrated more on quieting and soothing 3-month babies of both sexes than on stimulating them. The babies appeared extremely quiet and passive beside their American counterparts. The differences between the nationalities far outweighed differences between the sexes within the national groups.

Very preliminary results do, however, indicate that there may be neurological differences between the sexes. For example, two highly technical papers[62, 63] suggest that the left hemisphere of the brain, which is normally the speech-processing area, develops more slowly in boys than in girls. The right hemisphere, normally the area concerned with visio-spatial functioning, would therefore be preponderant in boys at this age as compared with girls. If further results confirm findings of this kind, then differences in maternal handling of the kind discussed above may turn out to be appropriate to the sex of the child in neuro-physiological rather than only in socio-cultural terms. It may be that in these early months girls are more able to use stimulation directed towards their looking and their listening, when boys are more able to use motor play.

Yet even if these structural differences between the brains of boys and girls at different ages and stages of development are eventually confirmed by further research, we shall still not be able to state a simple common-sense relationship between sex differences and differences in early handling. It will be tempting to say, 'Their brains develop differently and therefore it is only sensible to handle them differently.' But there is other work, with animals, which suggests that handling in infancy may actually be able to create neuro-physiological changes in brain structure. For the past ten years a group of psychologists and biologists have been work-ing together in California on the effects of various kinds and degrees of stimulation on the brains of rats.[64, 65] Over the years they have discovered a very wide range of neurological, physiological and structural effects arising from enriching the experiences of their experimental rats. They are rightly cautious about extrapolating their findings to human beings. But it is by no means impossible that we shall eventually find that stimulation affects not only performance but the very size and structure of the parts of the brain that control per-formance. So we may come full circle. Boys and girls behave differently. We handle them differently. If their brains do indeed develop differently, this may still be due to our differential handling.

Clearly a large number of each baby's characteristics, as well as his particular moment in development, affect the amount and the kind of stimulation he receives and can use. But this baby-oriented view of stimulation cannot be accepted alone, any more than the old views which saw the infant as a blank slate on which the parents wrote.

A sensitive response by the parents to cues from the baby is vital if they are to provide the 'right' kinds and levels of stimulation for him. Maternal sensitivity is often described, in research literature, as if it were a supreme virtue. But it is made up of innumerable factors, only a few of which are under the mother's control. Much 'maternal sensitivity' is the result of fortunate chance. The mother finds herself with an infant whose personal characteristics meld with her own, to provide a smoothly functioning unit. The baby is somewhat jumpy; she is characteristically calm and gentle: they do well together. The baby is very active – so is she. She asks nothing better than to have a reason for lots of walks, lots of physical play. The baby is very active in seeking social contact; she is a highly vocal, sociable person, who is delighted to find that a young baby can be 'good company'.

In all these circumstances, and hundreds more, the mother's ability to take her cues from the baby, and provide him with the kind of stimulation he needs, comes at least as much from his demanding what comes naturally to her as from her skill.

Less fortunate mothers can be faced with an infant who demands from them a kind of handling and of stimulation which they actually find it difficult to provide. For example, some babies are more 'cuddly' than others.[66] Some definitely resist being held, cuddled, tucked up or restrained for dressing. Such a baby may be soothed by being talked to, may delight in looking at his mother and in smiling at her, but may very definitely reject her if she tries to pick him up and hold him. Yet many mothers have a permanent baby-shaped space at their left hip and shoulder; many instinctively pick up a baby if he cries, cuddle and rock him to convey their love and carry him about when he is miserable. Handling a non-cuddly baby in the way he needs to be handled may require such a mother to make a real intellectual effort and to tolerate what she feels as emotional rejection.

Practical circumstances, too, may vitally affect that 'maternal sensitivity'. A mother with her first baby is often alone with him for much of the time, able to expend as much attention on him as she wishes, free to interact with him just as she pleases. Such a mother may watch the baby, be alert for his cues and respond to them freely. That same mother with a new baby and a furiously jealous 2-year-old is quite differently placed. She has to steer constantly between the two children, making an unending series of choices, compromises and diversions. If she is happy, and well-supported by her husband, and the new baby is a 'good fit' with her, she may manage. But if her other circumstances are depressing, her husband makes it clear that he is getting fed up with his child-oriented household and the baby is difficult for her, she is likely to go quietly frantic. In these circumstances even the most 'sensitive mother' is likely to take a 'let quiet babies lie' attitude and ignore the newcomer unless he insists on her attention.

Fortunately those who are concerned with individual

babies never know what their infant *might* have been like had he been differently handled. There is no temptation to expend hours and agony on adjusting his daily life in infancy, because there is no prescription for infant handling that will produce a given kind of child or adult. We do not have to know that we did not stimulate our infants in exactly the right way, at exactly the right time. On the whole, stimulation or handling which gives the baby pleasure is right for him. And contrariwise very few kinds of handling or stimulation which distress him are right. If he is happy and contented, his handling is good enough. If he is happier still with more of it, then he can use more if his parents feel able to give it to him. In the end the only guide to the right amount and kind of stimulation is the baby himself.

CHAPTER THIRTEEN

FEEDING AND GROWING

Food for infants is not a rational subject in the Western world. Everybody is taught that correct feeding is vital to optimal development, so every mother worries – often endlessly and frantically – about what her infant does or does not eat. Yet because the vast majority of infants in our culture are more than adequately fed, the subject of their eating is seldom discussed, outside textbooks of biochemistry or dietetics, in the kind of detail which would show mothers that their worries are unnecessary and destructive. The few infants who are not adequately fed would benefit from detailed discussion too. If their mothers cannot afford to feed them lavishly, or they will not eat the wide choice of foods available to them, their restricted diet is often inadequate simply because the mother does not have the information which she needs, or worse, has misinformation.

Unfortunately feeding is tied up in our society with socialization. Eating is linked with meals; getting adequate nourishment is linked with acceptable behaviour, with table manners, with emptying the plate, not being greedy, not wasting good food and so on. Nutritional and social–moral statements are mixed together. For example, many mothers would agree that an infant should eat green vegetables. But often the mother herself does not know whether she means that it is *nutritionally* important that he should eat them, or socially and morally right that he should eat them. Is making a child eat cabbage a way of giving him sufficient vitamin C or a way of disciplining him? It is vital that issues of this kind should be sorted out. In terms of the child's development they are totally different matters. Both issues are important, but neither can be sensibly handled while they are muddled together.

The kind of general dietary advice which is given in most

books on child-rearing tends to reinforce this kind of muddle. After detailed advice about breast-feeding, about choosing a formula for bottle-feeding and about introducing the first solids, they tend to leap to the stock phrase 'a good mixed diet'. This diet, at which everybody is supposed to aim, is an ideal. If any human being is given three good meals a day, with a variety of meats, fish, eggs, cheese, vegetables, fruits and so forth, he will, without doubt, get everything he needs to eat. The trouble is that few infants will really eat that diet and few mothers have the money or the time to prepare it. It is an ideal far removed from the realities of mother and infant at home.

This chapter, and Chapter 20 which covers feeding in the second half of this first year, attempt to show what infants actually do eat, and to consider what they need to eat and why. It is about food, not about socialization – about food for health, not food for virtue.

Finding out what infants actually eat is more difficult than it sounds. We know (see Chapter 2) that only a tiny proportion of infants are being breast-fed by the time they are 3 months, and we know that those who are will probably be receiving other foods as well as breast milk. But there our certain knowledge almost stops. The only way to find out what infants are being fed is to ask their mothers, and their replies are likely to be inaccurate. Food is an emotionally laden subject and mothers will therefore tend to answer research workers in what they think of as a socially acceptable way. In Nottingham the Newsons[18] found that mothers interviewed by a health visitor reported far more breast-feeding, giving of vitamin drops and attendances at welfare clinics than did mothers interviewed by a university worker, who was not a representative of the health authorities.

Even where mothers truly strive to be accurate they may not be able to be. Some personal experiments carried out in an ordinary kitchen may illustrate this difficulty. A tin of a famous brand of strained baby food, available all over the U.K., contains $3\frac{1}{2}$ oz. (100g) of food. This statement, printed on the tin, is accurate if that tin is scraped out so thoroughly that it is left almost clean. But the scraping process takes at least 25 seconds. Emptied more carelessly, as a busy mother might empty the tin when getting an infant's lunch, it yields nearly ½ oz. (15g) less. Such a difference probably does not matter to the well-fed baby; but it makes a great deal of difference to the poor research worker who is trying to find out exactly what the baby ate.

Feeding the same food to a 3-month baby, wearing the type of bib which catches the drips in a pocket at the bottom, I have given meals which yielded ¼ oz. or 1½ oz. (7g or 45g) of what would technically be called 'plate waste'. Mothers are unlikely to *know* how much food dribbled down the infant's chin.

Similar problems apply to baby cereals and instant powdered meals. Different brands require different quantities of added fluid to arrive at the same texture. If the added fluid is water, the addition does not affect the food value and need not bother the researcher. But usually it is milk. Does the mother know how many ounces of milk went into that cereal? Usually she will simply have gone on stirring in more milk until the food reached the baby's preferred texture.

Even bottles of formula do not escape these problems. Mothers will know how many bottles the baby has had. Usually they will know how much was in each bottle and whether the baby finished it. But the food value of those bottles is a vexing question – and one we shall return to when we discuss what babies ought to eat. The dangers of mixing formulae too strong have long been recognized. Some mothers do seem to work on a sort of 'one for the pot' principle as they add the scoops of milk powder. But leaving aside those mothers who make the bottles extra-concentrated on purpose, there is still wide variation in the concentration arrived at by mothers who are trying to follow the instructions on the tin. Using full-cream Cow & Gate, I found that 8 of the manufacturer's scoops, gently filled, and accurately levelled off with a palette knife, weighed just over 1 oz. (30g). Exactly what the manufacturer intended. But putting a little pressure on the palette knife during levelling, so that the scoops were very slightly packed, led to a yield of $1\frac{1}{4}$ oz. (37g). Worse still, hurrying, and using the edge of the tin as a leveller instead of a palette knife, I ended up with slightly rounded scoops, 8 of which yielded $1\frac{1}{2}$ oz. (45g). A bottle made up with my last method would have given the infant 50 per cent more nourishment than his mother would report to the poor researcher.

So we know that only a few infants of this age are receiving breast milk. We know that most are receiving bottles of formula made more or less to the manufacturer's specification. We also know that with rare exceptions they will be receiving solid foods in addition, but we do not really know exactly how much of what.

A recent study carried out in Worcestershire[4] asked mothers of 300 normal babies under 1 year, making routine visits to a welfare clinic, to recall the food intake of the previous 24 hours. 40 per cent of these infants had had some solid food – usually a baby cereal – in the first month of life. 93 per cent were having solids at 3 months. A similar early start with solid feeding was found by Taitz,[5] who studied 260 normal Sheffield babies, and found that almost all began solid feeding in the first month, and most in the first *week* of life.

In the Worcestershire study 498 different types of food had been given to the 300 infants. The variation in the nutritional value of the reported diets was enormous. The first solids fed to the infants were usually proprietary baby cereals. By 3 months, 'strained' dinners from tins, or instant powdered dinners had been added. Very few mothers used any home-cooked foods at all except eggs.

This picture, scanty though it is, is very different from a picture of what an infant between 3 and 6 months actually needs to eat. Any discussion of 'requirements' or 'recommended' intakes must, of course, be extremely generalized. The authorities who compile nutritional tables are careful to warn readers that they are averages worked out for large groups of people of a given age, not for individuals. Infants vary, as do all people, in their food needs, their hunger, their general enthusiasm for the business of eating, and in the speed and completeness with which they use up, or metabolize, food. Therefore to feed a baby strictly according to any table setting out his 'requirements' would be idiotic. Nevertheless it does seem that mothers have a very different view of an infant's needs from nutritionists, and that this may be partly due to some misconceptions which only a familiarity with the nutritional facts can correct.

People are made up primarily of water, and they lose water continually through the skin, the breath and the urine. Infants therefore need water, and will die far more quickly for lack of it than for lack of food in general or any one food in particular. A curious reluctance to give infants plain water to drink can be responsible for many feeding difficulties (see page 56).

People also have to have the foods which are incorporated into the body, the proteins. Proteins are made up of 20 amino-acids which are strung together in varying orders and numbers in different foods. All 20 amino-acids are needed by human bodies, but all but 8 in adults and 10 in growing children can be made by the body out of the others.

Protein foods are usually described as either 'first class' or 'second class'. First-class protein is so named simply because it already contains the vital amino-acids in complete form, as well as all the others. Eating meat, fish, eggs and dairy produce therefore ensures that the body receives the amino-acids it needs. But second-class proteins can do an equally good job by human bodies if they are eaten in a mixture. They are proteins which are eaten in plant form, rather than in the form of plants which have already been converted by an animal. They usually contain large proportions of the commoner amino-acids, and have some of the rarer ones missing. A mixture of these proteins will almost always compensate for the deficiencies of any one of them, thus giving the body all the amino-acids it needs.

First-class proteins tend to be expensive; indeed the eating of meat is, in many societies, regarded as an index of rising prosperity. The Western world reads of the developing nations suffering for lack of protein and, perhaps as a result, increasingly glorifies protein foods. It is often the protein foods which mothers press upon their children and the possibility of too little protein which worries them when they face a fussy eater. Anything which has liver, or egg, beef or cheese in it is 'bound to be good for him'. And of course the baby-food manufacturers play up to this myth: 'High-protein cereal with egg,' 'Full of the protein your baby needs,' 'Full of beef for extra bounce,' they say.

A certain quantity of complete (or completed) protein is an absolute requirement for growth and for continuing good health. Because of the horrors of protein-deficiency diseases, and the work which is being done on their prevention and cure in other parts of the world, we do know approximately the minimum quantities which are required by people of differing ages and weights. To people accustomed to eating the privileged meals of the Western world, these quantities are remarkably small. We do not know whether there is any benefit in a much *higher* intake. The '*recommended* intakes' given by the Ministry of Health, and referred to in more detail below, already make a substantial extra allowance to cover the possibility of some infants needing more than others. And they are already set at higher levels than the *minimum* requirement figures used by organizations such as the Food and Agriculture Organization. So while controversy rages as to how much is *just* enough it can be assumed that these recommendations are generous ones.

Once proteins have entered the digestive process they are used by the body immediately, if the body requires protein for tissue repair or for growth. But if it already has enough protein, it cannot store the extra nor can it 'hold' surplus incomplete proteins against their completion at a later meal. The surplus amino-acids are taken to the liver, where they are converted into glycogen and thence into glucose, and re-leased to the bloodstream for energy. Some authorities believe that feeding an infant too much protein may be actually harmful. If protein is thus converted into glucose, there is a heavy load of nitrogen left, which may stress the kidneys which have to excrete it. But whether it is actually harmful or not, overfeeding of proteins is certainly inefficient. The conversion of the surplus to glucose actually uses more energy than it releases to the body. Since protein foods are vastly more expensive than the carbohydrates which the body can easily turn into glucose, using roast beef for energy instead of bread is roughly equivalent to fuelling a car with cognac instead of petrol.

Energy, for keeping the infant alive, and for his physical activities, comes from carbohydrates and from fats, both of which are converted by the body into sugars. If the protein foods have come to be overvalued in our society, the carbohydrate foods are undervalued. Efficient feeding requires some carbohydrates. An infant's need for energy takes biological precedence over his growth. Energy is the first demand which will be fulfilled out of the nutrients available to the body. Therefore if the infant is fed too little carbohydrate, those precious proteins will be inefficiently burned to give him energy, instead of being used for his growth. Carbohydrates therefore act as 'protein conservers', ensuring that the infant has all the fuel he needs, so that his body can retain all the protein it needs for optimum growth. Unfortunately for a fat society, *surplus* carbohydrates are not burned and excreted as surplus proteins are. They are stored in the form of body fat.

Fats are made up of fatty acids, just as proteins are made up of amino-acids. Like the carbohydrates they are used by the body for energy, and they are useful in that weight for weight they provide far more concentrated calories than do carbohydrates. Some special groups, such as Eskimos, who require high-calorie intakes because of intense cold, or athletes, who expend large amounts of energy, would be hard put to it to eat enough calories if a proportion were not in the concentrated form of fats. But in less extreme circumstances there seems to be no absolute dietary requirement for fat, other than a need for minute quantities of certain specific fatty acids. Since these fatty acids are widely distributed in both animal fats and vegetable oils, deficiencies are extremely rare.

In addition to these main food groups, which give the body its growth, repair and energy needs, minute quantities of vitamins and of mineral substances are an absolute requirement. Many of these are so widely distributed that it would be impossible to eat at all without getting enough of them. But the more important ones, and those which an infant could lack, are set out in Table 2.

TABLE 2. VITAMINS AND MINERALS KNOWN
TO BE ESSENTIAL TO THE BODY

	Technical details	Required for	Comment
Vitamin A	Technical name = retinol. Measured in retinol equivalents because body can use a substance called carotene to make retinol, but absorbs the result less well than pure retinol. Our vitamin A is roughly $\frac{2}{3}$ retinol / $\frac{1}{3}$ carotene, and the measure is therefore μg (micrograms) of 'retinol equivalents'.	Growth. Perception of light. Protection of surface tissue and mucous membranes.	Not soluble in water. Can be stored in the liver. Excess can be harmful.
Vitamin B group	A group usually, but not always, found together in same foods. Most important = thiamine (B_1), riboflavine (B_2), nicotinic acid or niacin	Control and facilitate the process by which the body gets a smooth continuous release of energy from carbohydrates.	Soluble in water. Unstable at high temperatures. Body cannot store.

	Technical details	*Required for*	*Comment*
Vitamin B group	also known = folic acid (B_{12}), pyridoxine (B_6), pantothenic acid, biotin Measured in mg (milligrams).	Part of enzyme system protects nerve cells prevents certain anaemias.	
Vitamin C	Technical name = ascorbic acid. Measured in mg (milligrams).	Concerned with the structure of connective tissue. Wound healing.	Soluble in water. Unstable at high temperatures and in sunlight. Body cannot store.
Vitamin D	Dietary requirement variable, as can be manufactured by the body following exposure of skin to sunlight. Measured in μg (micrograms).	Absorption and laying down of calcium and phosphorus in bones and teeth.	Not soluble in water. Body can store. In extreme cases storage leads to hyper-calcaemia.
Calcium	The calcium in certain foods is more easily absorbed than that found in other foods.	Development of bones and teeth. Blood clotting. Muscle function.	Stored in the bones and released into the blood by the parathoroid gland.

	Technical details	*Required for*	*Comment*
Calcium	Furthermore it can only be absorbed in the presence of adequate vitamin D. Much more is present in hard water than in soft. Exact dietary requirements are therefore difficult to assess. Measured in mg (milligrams).		
Phosphorus	Found with calcium. Needs for phosphorus can therefore be ignored in normal dietetics.		
Iron	Individual ability to absorb iron is very variable, and different forms of iron are differently available to the body. Varying quantities are derived from water; from the use of iron cooking pots, and from such culturally variable adjuncts to food preparation as curry powder and red wine. Measured in mg (milligrams).	Vital component of the haemoglobin which transports oxygen all over the body in the blood.	Once absorbed, iron is used and re-used, as well as being stored in the liver. A little is lost in general wear of the body, some in the digestive juices in the faeces, a great deal in bleeding.

Before this kind of information can be related to real live babies eating real kitchen-type food, a hard look at the question of growth is needed. Traditionally an infant is said to be 'growing well' if his weight gain is adequate. But a baby who gains weight without gaining height to match would be getting fat rather than growing big. It is essential that the infant should gain both weight and length; it is highly desirable that he should gain them in strict relationship to each other. Figure 7 illustrates this. Both the boys charted in this figure were born at average birthweights. Both grew in length along the 50th percentile line (see Figure 10). The difference in their weights speaks for itself. One gained weight

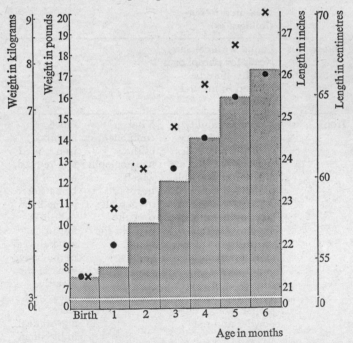

Figure 7. Comparison of appropriate and inappropriate weight gain in two boys of average length

to suit his length, along the 50th percentile. The other gained weight at a rate which would have been suitable had he been of a length to put him on the 90th percentile (see Figure 8). He was an extremely fat baby.

Infant growth is remarkably steady. It is rare to find a child who puts on either weight or height by fits and starts, except where acute or long-drawn-out illness, or extreme emotional upset, has temporarily retarded his growth. After such a period of deprivation infants commonly have a period of 'catch-up growth', during which they put on weight and height at a much faster *rate* than before the illness until they are back on their old trajectory. Then, almost magically, the accelerated growth slows down again, and the child settles into his old pattern.

His own pattern is the vital point. If he starts below or above the average for height or weight, he is likely to remain at a similar position relative to that average throughout infancy; like a rocket, he has a pre-selected growth trajectory, fuelled by his environment. Given normally adequate feeding and other care, he will grow his predetermined amount, and at his predetermined rate. While we commonly talk of the first year as being the most rapid period of growth, he will, in fact, never grow as fast or as much as he did in the womb. In 9 months he grew from microscopic to around 7 lb. and 20 inches (3·2kg and 51cm) (see page 28); if he continued to grow that much, or that fast, he would be a giant indeed. Figures 8 and 9 give the average gains in weight for boys and for girls from birth to 2 years. Figures 10 and 11 give comparable height gains.

These figures (adapted from Tanner *et al.*[67]) each give 3 'growth curves' which are labelled as being the values for the 10th, 50th and 90th percentiles respectively. The 10th percentile curve is that which 10 per cent or 10 out of every 100 infants will fall below. The 50th and 90th percentile curves are similarly those below which 50 in 100 or 90 in 100 infants will fall. The middle line, in each case, therefore represents not the average or mean, but the line which will have 50 per cent of U.K. babies above it, and 50 per cent below.

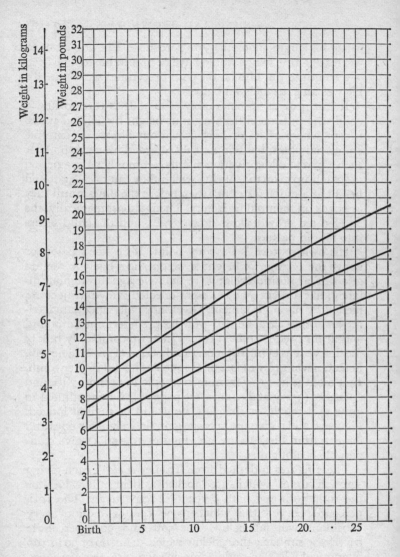

Figure 8. Weight gains, from birth to two

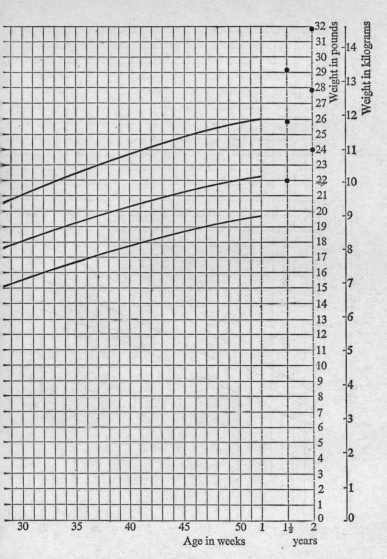

Weight in pounds

Weight in kilograms

Age in weeks

years

years, for average, large and small boys

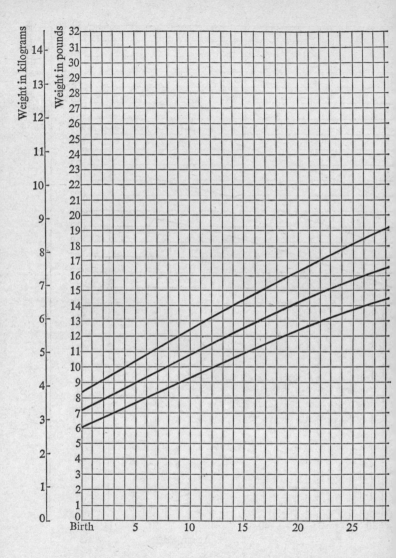

Figure 9. Weight gains, from birth to two

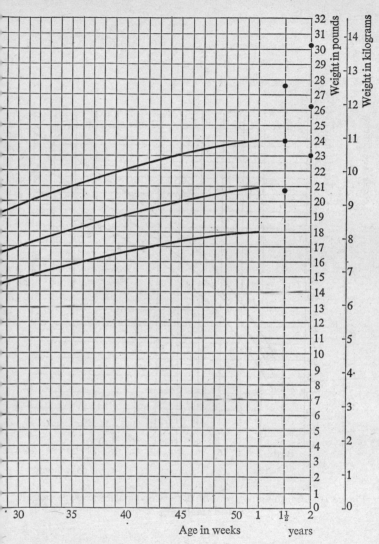

Weight in pounds

Weight in kilograms

Age in weeks · years

years, for average, large and small girls

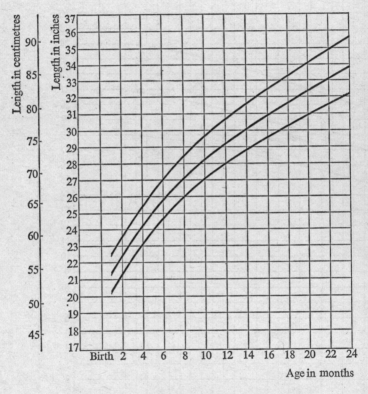

Figure 10. Length gains, from birth to two years, for average, large and small boys

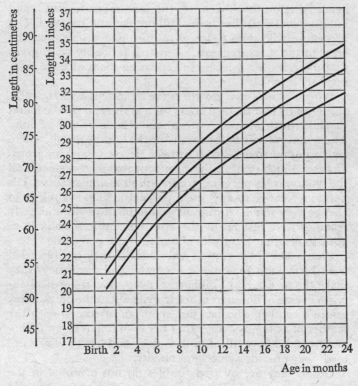

Figure 11. Length gains, from birth to two years, for average, large and small girls

The weight chart is simple to use. It only requires the weigher to find the infant's age in weeks along the bottom, and his measured weight up the side, and make a mark where the two lines intersect. The length chart is more difficult. Infants are measured from their heels to the crowns of their heads lying on their backs on the tape measure. But many infants intensely dislike being laid out flat and kept still. The procedure will almost always require two people, and the error in the measurements taken will probably be so great that there is little purpose in repeating them at more than monthly intervals.

When a child's own growth curve is plotted, week by week, or month by month, on a chart such as these, it will be found that his growth follows a pattern similar in shape to these lines. There may, of course, be small 'jiggles' in the graph, where he has put on 10 oz. (290g) instead of 8 oz. (230g), or grown an extra $\frac{1}{4}$ inch (6mm). But over repeated measurements all the points on his personal graph will fit a similar curve. His position, relative to any given percentile line, is unlikely to change very much. An infant whose birthweight and early readings were just below the 10th percentile is unlikely to grow so fast that he crosses above the 50th percentile.

Charts like these can be valuable. If they are recorded from birth with reasonable accuracy and frequency, they make the best of all possible records to show to medical advisers in case of illness or other worries about the child. They assure a mother who has just spent an afternoon with the mother of a 'bonny baby' that her own infant is not fading away. And, above all, if both weight and length charts are used, they provide a check on obesity.

Unless they are overfed, babies do not continue in the second 3 months of life to gain weight at the rate they did earlier. The gain of roughly 7 oz. (200g) per week expected then slows up to around 5 oz. (150g) per week in this quarter, as can be seen from Figures 8–9. Bearing this in mind, and looking at these figures, it can be seen that any attempt to relate an actual baby to a fictitious 'norm' is likely to be misleading. Norms are based on averages. An infant's growth depends on his starting point, his birthweight. If his birthweight was around that 50th percentile, then so will his growth be. But if it was not, it will not be. Rules of thumb about 'normal babies' can be positively dangerous. In child-welfare clinics all over the U.K. one such rubric is quoted over and over again: 'A baby should double his birthweight by 6 months and treble it by 1 year.' A premature baby who followed this rubric would be half starved; an average birthweight baby will probably follow it more or less; a heavy baby who followed it would be obese.

TABLE 3. RELATIONSHIP OF BIRTHWEIGHT TO ABSOLUTE AND PROPORTIONAL WEIGHT GAINS

Expected gain in first 13 weeks	= 7 oz. (200g) per week after the first fortnight
	= 77 oz. or 4 lb. 13 oz. (2·2kg)
Expected gain in second 13 weeks	= 5 oz. (150g) per week
	= 65 oz or 4 lb. 1 oz. (1·95kg)

Birthweight	Weight at 3 months	Weight at 6 months	Comment
5 lb./2·3kg	9 lb. 13 oz./ 4·5kg	13 lb. 14 oz./ 5·45kg	Weight virtually doubled at 3 months; approaching *treble* at 6 months.
8 lb./3·6kg	12 lb. 13 oz./ 5·8kg	16 lb. 14 oz./ 7·75kg	Closely follows the rubric.
11 lb./5·0kg	15 lb. 13 oz./ 7·2kg	19 lb. 14 oz./ 9·15kg	Weight not nearly double at 6 months.

All babies tend to gain the same *amount* of weight whatever their birthweight. That gained weight is a very different *proportion* of the bodyweight in heavy and light infants.

Drillien,[68] who followed up a large group of Scottish babies from birth into school, illustrated this dramatically. She showed that premature babies followed the *rate* of growth of average- and above-average-weight infants so closely that at 5 years the *actual* difference in their weights had remained constant, although its significance had diminished. Thus the baby who was born weighing 5 lb. (2·3kg) tended at 5 years still to weigh 4 lb. (1·8kg) less than the child who was born weighing 9 lb. (4·1kg). The low birthweight babies did, however, grow in length at a rather faster rate than the others, although they never grew quite as tall. They were therefore always rather taller for their weight than the heavier babies, and tended therefore to be thinner.

Infants need to be fed according to their expected weight (see page 51). This means the weight to be expected of the individual baby, if he was gaining at the expected rate. It does not mean feeding the premature baby, who at 3 months weighs less than 10 lb. (4·54kg), as if he were the average baby who at the same age weighs 3 lb. (1·3kg) more.

Turning now to the daily food requirements in this quarter, we have to return to the very average figures just disparaged. Any reader attempting to use the figures to assist in the management of an individual infant must work out just how 'average' the infant is, and make adjustments accordingly. The basic figures are the recommended intakes of nutrients given by the Ministry of Agriculture, Fisheries and Food[69] and the Department of Health and Social Security.[70]

Postulating an average baby for the period between 3 and 6 months, these authorities expect his weight to be around 14½ lb. (6·6kg). As can be seen from Table 3 a baby of heavy birthweight may be around this weight at 3 months; a baby born at around 7 lb. (3·2kg) will reach this weight between 4 and 5 months, while a low birthweight baby is unlikely to reach it until after 6 months. The recommended intakes are therefore only approximately applicable to any individual child. They are given here to convey an *idea* of what is needed, and of how those needs can best be met. Any mother who is tempted to take them literally, to weigh everything she gives the infant in an attempt to construct an 'ideal diet', would be well advised to think how foolish it would be to try to buy clothes for an older child on the basis of his age without his measurements.

In the following table, the infant's requirements are given in terms of calories, protein and the essential minerals and vitamins already discussed (see Table 2). The calorie count is the sum total of the energy value of all the food taken, irrespective of the source (protein, fats or carbohydrates) of that energy. Within that total, carbohydrate and fat are not specified. Calories not coming from proteins must come from one of these two sources, and in terms of the body's fuel requirements it does not matter which. Protein is always specified separately, as a requirement *within* the total energy of the food, because, as we have seen, the protein is an essential for its building, rather than its energy-giving qualities.

The scientific measures for nutrients are somewhat confusing. Readers who do not wish to labour with them will find that they can be accepted simply as 'measures' and that in all subsequent food tables, one food can be compared with another on the basis of its *relative* richness in the given substance. But for those who are interested, the basic measures can be very approximately defined as follows:

kilocalorie (kcal)   often loosely abbreviated to 'calorie' in nutritional discussion = the amount of energy required to heat 1 pint of water 3°F (1 litre of water 1°C). Theoretically (making no allowance for cooling) 47 kcal would heat 1 pint of water to boiling point from a room temperature of 70°F.

gram (g)   = 1/28 oz.

milligram (mg)   = 1/1000 gram.

microgram (μg)   = 1/1000 milligram.

T–B–G

TABLE 4. RECOMMENDED DAILY INTAKE OF
NUTRIENTS FOR INFANTS AGED 3–6 MONTHS

TOTAL CALORIES	PROTEIN	MINERALS		VITAMINS					
		Calcium	Iron	A	D	Thiamine	Riboflavine	Nicotinic acid	C
kcal	g	mg	mg	μg	μg	mg	mg	mg	mg
760	20	600	6	450	10	0·3	0·4	5	15

Notes:
Infants will require approximately:
1. 52 kcal per day for every 1 lb. of their weight; and 1·5g of protein.
    115 kcal per day for every 1kg of their weight; and 3·0g of protein.
2. *Minimum* protein levels, i.e. those below which there is a chance of protein deficiency, are approximately two thirds of the above figures.

The major part of the infant's diet at the beginning of this quarter will still be milk. Most infants will be bottle-fed. The few who are breast-fed can be assumed to be as well (if not better) off in all dietary respects, as long as the quantity of milk they are getting is adequate.

The bottle-fed infant should, at least until he is 6 months old, be fed on one of the specially prepared infant formulae. Most of the dried milks which are marketed for general consumption are totally unsuitable for babies. They tend to lack fat – which makes them low in calories – and they almost always lack vitamins and minerals. Most tinned evaporated milks are also unsuitable, especially those which contain a lot of sugar. Fresh cow's milk is, of course, the basis of infant formulae. But fed to the infant fresh, it tends to make heavy casein curds in the stomach. The protein which it contains is suitable for calves, not for infants. The roller- or spray-drying processes which are used in the preparation of formulae modify these curds, making them far more digestible. Furthermore the fat, vitamin and mineral content of fresh cow's milk is variable. Different cows, different cattle feeds, different seasons and different methods of storage all affect milk. And a mother cannot hope to know about these variables, let alone control them. The actual difference between similar quantities of good fresh cow's milk and the same quantity of formula can be seen in Table 5 (page 196).

Given that an infant formula is used, it is arguable that it does not much matter which one is chosen. Some people recommend a 'humanized milk' in which the protein has been modified to approximate more closely to breast milk. Such milks are comparatively expensive. Most babies do very well on ordinary formulae, but if a search is being made for a different milk for a baby who is not thriving, and if money is not a problem, a humanized milk may be worth trying.

A few infant milks are prepared in liquid form. They are comparatively easy to mix, and to measure, but they are also heavy to carry home, and expensive.

At 3 months, most bottle-fed babies will be taking five feeds in the 24 hours – one at his parents' bedtime, one in the very early morning, and three during the day. Most will drink somewhere around 6–7 oz. (170–200ml) per feed. So we look first at what the infant gets from 32 oz. (915ml) of formula, made up exactly according to the manufacturer's instructions, without added sugar or cereal. In order to give exact figures, one particular formula – full-cream Cow & Gate – has been chosen. Other full-cream infant formulae will be found to yield similar values, although there may be small variations in sugar content or vitamin additives from one brand to another.

Table 5 sets out what the infant gets from 32 oz. (915ml) of Cow & Gate; what he gets from the same amount of liquid cow's milk, and the difference between these yields and his needs, according to Table 4.

In both cases the infant lacks calories. On the formula, his only other lack is a little iron – and since his iron stores from birth may not be used up by 3 months, his immediate need for that is arguable. But on the liquid cow's milk he does not get *any* iron, and he also lacks vitamins A and D. For safety's

TABLE 5.   NUTRIENTS FROM 32 OZ. (915ML)
OF FULL-CREAM COW & GATE
COMPARED WITH LIQUID COW'S MILK

| Nutrients | Cow & Gate | | Liquid Cow's Milk | |
	Infant gets	Infant lacks	Infant gets	Infant lacks
Kcalories	556	204	576	184
Protein (g)	28	0	29	0
Calcium (mg)	1,000	0	1,000	0
Iron (mg)	4	2	0	6
Vitamin A (μg)	900	0	350	100
Vitamin D (μg)	10	0	trace	10
Thiamine (mg)	0·3	0	0·3	0
Riboflavine (mg)	1·2	0	1·2	0
Nicotinic acid (mg)	9·6	0	9·6	0
Vitamin C (mg)	32	0	0	15

sake it must be assumed that the cow's milk contains no vitamin C either. In fact, it may contain large quantities *if* it is high summer, the cow is eating good rich grass and the conditions under which the milk is pasteurized, transported and stored are ideal. One can count on none of these things.

The infant's need for additional calories can, of course, be met in a variety of ways. He does not lack protein, so there is no purpose in giving him his extra food in a high-protein form – indeed it may be better for his kidneys if he is *not* given extra protein at this age. Many mothers are unwittingly already supplying the infant's full calorie needs, simply by adding sugar to the bottles of formula. Every teaspoonful (British measure) of sugar adds 25 calories to the energy value of the milk. 8 teaspoonfuls divided among the bottles would therefore fill the calorie gap, but they might be inadvisable. They would add sufficient sweetness to the milk so that the infant would definitely notice the difference in taste if it was withdrawn later. Some authorities believe that an unfortunate taste for sweet things can become a habit in these early months. Furthermore such additional sugar would do nothing to increase his iron intake which, while it is unlikely to be critical now, becomes important as this quarter year passes.

Baby cereals are usually the first solids added to an infant's diet, and looked at in these terms they are ideal. A typical infant cereal (not necessarily one advertised as 'high-protein') yields around 110 calories, if one heaped table-spoon of the dry powder is mixed with 3 oz. (90ml) of milk to yield 3 tablespoons the texture of thick cream. Most of them will contain around 3mg of iron. The addition of 2 teaspoons of sugar will add another 50 calories to the meal. Two feeds of this kind in the 24 hours will more than meet the infant's requirements. Alternatively, one feed of cereal may well be enough, if at another meal the infant receives an egg yolk, which gives him 50 calories and 1mg of iron, and if he is also receiving orange juice whose sugar content is high.

At this age, many mothers are using tinned infant 'din-ners'. As a source of calories there is nothing against these, except that the labels give no clue to the high variation in food value from one variety to the next. For example, while one might expect a strained-fruit variety to be lower in calories than a cheese variety, one would not expect to find Heinz strained 'cheese and egg supper' yielding 75 calories, when their 'cheese savoury' yields 136. Furthermore the manufacturers do not guarantee the iron content of their foods, as do the manufacturers of infant cereals.

It should be clear that while there is no need or purpose in counting the calories one feeds to a baby, there is a very marked tendency to overfeed, and to feed a great deal of un-necessary protein. Many babies of 3 months regularly drink the quantity of formula we have discussed, *and* receive egg yolk, perhaps with infant cereal, at breakfast time, a tin of a baby 'dinner' in the middle of the day, and more cereal per-haps with a tin of baby fruit at supper time. It is not surprising that some of these babies become obese.

Obesity in infants is too often regarded as a matter for congratulation. People tend to think that fat babies look sweet. The dimples in the plump knees make other mothers coo. The baby's 'adequate' weight gain is on display for all to see. Unfairly, we react quite differently to fat *children*. Adults assume them to be greedy; their mothers are thought to ply them with sweets and other 'unsuitable foods'; their school-mates deride them. And of course the Western world is full of adults who are dieting to try and lose weight.

There is increasing evidence that making a baby fat in this age period may predispose it to fatness in later life. Brook, Lloyd and Wolf[71] have developed a technique for assessing the total number of fat cells in the body, by counting those present in a tiny specimen of body fat. They have found that the number of adipose (fat) cells in the body becomes fixed by the end of the first year, and that infants with a higher than normal number of adipose cells are more likely than others to get fat, and to stay fat. In one group of fat children studied, about half had normal numbers of adipose cells, the other half had more. The main difference between these two groups of fat children was in the length of time the fatness had lasted. The children with high numbers of fat cells had become fat as infants, and had remained fat. The others had become fat later in childhood.

Dieting can, of course, get rid of the fat *content* of the adipose cells. But it cannot reduce their number. By not making infants manufacture a high number of these cells in the first place it looks as though we can ensure that, if they later become fat from over-eating, their fatness is easier to control.

We do not know how general is over-feeding in this age quarter, but all the available evidence points towards it being very general indeed. Shukla *et al.* showed that the average weekly weight gains for the 300 babies in their study were way above the expected weight gains used here, and by most authorities. In the first 3 months, for example, where one would expect a weekly gain of around 7 oz. (200g), following initial weight loss, they found gains of 8·4 oz. (240g) for boys and 6·7 oz. (190g) for girls – and this without any loss during the days after birth. For the second quarter, where gains of around 5 oz. (150g) would be expected, the average weekly gain for boys was 7·5 oz. (214g) and for girls was 6·6 oz.

(190g). To make the picture blacker, these infants were not particularly tall. Their ratio of weight to height was higher than would be expected. The proportion of babies who were frankly obese in this sample fell as the year progressed. But if even a short period of obesity, at a critical time, is enough to lead to increased multiplication of adipose cells, the infants may already have been predisposed to obesity.

Taitz[5] studied the birthweights and weights at 6 weeks of 260 normal babies born in the Sheffield area. More than 50 per cent of them became overweight even in this short period.

There seems little doubt that early mixed feeding is partly responsible for this situation. But it also seems likely that the decline in breast-feeding has a bearing too. Breast-fed babies may be given solid foods early as an alternative to sup-plementary bottle feeds when the milk supply is only just adequate. But often a mother who is successfully breast-feeding finds it easier to accept that the food she is giving her baby is perfect than does the mother who is bottle-feeding, and is therefore less anxious to start 'real' food. And whether the breast-feeding mother gives solid foods or not, she can-not tamper with the quality of the breast milk. The baby's appetite regulates the quantity she supplies, and the com-position is out of her hands. If she therefore decides to intro-duce extra food, early, she has to introduce a spoon and a cup. She cannot turn to the 'thickened feeds' so beloved of bottle feeding mothers, who feel that a bit extra in the late-night bottle may give them an hour of extra sleep.

Bottle-feeding may predispose to obesity in other ways too. The question of making up formulae was touched upon earlier (see page 174). If the formula is made up carelessly, so that each scoop is slightly rounded instead of perfectly flat, the resulting 32 oz. (915ml) of formula will compare with the manufacturer's intentions as shown in Table 6.

If the mother also adds sugar to each bottle, the total calorie intake may go up by another 100 or even by 200 calories if she puts 2 teaspoons into each bottle. It is clear therefore that the infant will be getting more than he needs

TABLE 6. COMPARISON BETWEEN FOOD VALUES
OF 32 OZ. (915ML) OF CORRECTLY MADE
AND OVER-CONCENTRATED FULL-CREAM
COW & GATE

	CORRECT	CONCENTRATED
TOTAL CALORIES:		
	556 kcal	834 kcal
PROTEIN:		
	28 g	42 g
MINERALS:		
Calcium	1000 mg	1500 mg
Iron	4 mg	6 mg
VITAMINS:		
A	900 μg	1350 μg
D	10 μg	15 μg
Thiamine	0·3 mg	0·45 mg
Riboflavine	1·2 mg	1·8 mg
Nicotinic acid	9·6 mg	14·2 mg
C	32 mg	48 mg

of *all* nutrients from his bottles alone. The excess may, in itself, be quite enough to make him fat.

But the hazards of making formulae wrongly do not stop there. Such a concentrated formula contains a heavy load of protein and a very high concentration of sodium. The resulting load on the infant's kidneys is likely to lead to thirst and to crying. All too often the crying is taken for hunger. The infant is given more formula, which he drinks because he is thirsty. A vicious circle is thus set up. Unless water is frequently offered, the 'natural' appetite on which mothers can, and should, normally rely when feeding infants can give false information.

Natural appetite is still the best guide to the quantity of milk to give an infant, provided that care is taken to distinguish thirst from hunger, but it is difficult to see how natural appetite at this age can be much of a guide when an infant is being fed either thickened bottle feeds or solids from a spoon. If the baby's normal bottle has a spoonful of cereal added to it, it is being made more concentrated in food value without being made much more bulky. The infant is most unlikely to notice the difference. He will drink it if he wants the milk, even if that extra carbohydrate is going straight to his fat cells. Fed with a spoon, very young babies take quite a long time to associate the spoon with food: their instinctive way to satisfy hunger is by sucking, and they have to learn that it can also be quelled by spoonfuls. If you watch a hungry baby during his first spoon-feeds, spoonfuls of food are often dumped into his mouth between angry yells of hunger, the yells only gradually diminishing as the infant finds himself less urgently hungry. Furthermore such young infants are extremely inefficient with a spoon. Food which is placed in the front of the mouth is usually pushed out again with the questing tongue. It is extremely difficult to tell whether the infant has spat out the mouthful because he did not want it, or because he failed to get it far enough back in his mouth to swallow.

All in all it does seem that infants might be better off if solid foods were left alone entirely until around 3 months, and were then introduced in *minute* quantities as learning experiences rather than as foods. As we shall see in a later chapter, that 'good mixed diet' is not even appropriate as a goal until the second half of the first year.

CHAPTER FOURTEEN

PHYSICAL FUNDAMENTALS AGAIN

EATING AND SLEEPING PATTERNS

Three to six months marks, in many babies, a changeover from 'feeds' to meals, and from automatically sleeping between meals to discrete 'naps'.

At 3 months, eating is still intimately tied up with sleeping, so that the infant tends to wake up when he is hungry, and go to sleep when he is full. But already there is likely to be one particular period in the day when he is usually wakeful, even though well fed. For the majority of babies this seems to be the mid afternoon. The baby goes to sleep after his dinner, and wakes again an hour or two later, staying awake until his 5 p.m. or 6 p.m. meal. Whether this pattern is a genuinely inbuilt one, or whether it merely reflects the comparative willingness of most mothers to play in the afternoon, and their reluctance to play during the morning – the conventional time for household chores – we do not know. Certainly one can find babies of this age whose chosen period for wakefulness is the morning, or the evening.

While eating and sleeping are still so closely related, the amount of manipulation of the infant's day which the mother can easily carry out is very limited. He wakes ferociously hungry, and almost all mothers, willingly or unwillingly, will feed him within a few minutes. Having eaten, he needs to sleep, and may, if the mother tries to keep him up, drop off to sleep on her lap or on the floor.

But gradually eating and sleeping become disassociated. The infant eats, and probably sleeps soon afterwards. But gradually he begins to wake up because he has had a long enough nap, not because he is hungry again. A little later still, a full stomach does not necessarily send him to sleep. If interesting things are going on around him, he may eat and

then play. He still needs his meals, and he will still take a
rough average of five hours' sleep between 6 a.m. and 6 p.m.,
but both the meals and the naps become more adjustable.

During these months the infant becomes able to suck his
fingers whenever he likes, and to get some fun – and increasing amounts of nutrition – out of mouthing hard foods
clutched in his hand. Both these abilities help in disassocia-
ting eating from sleeping. When the infant wakes, the mother
can feed him if it suits her – he has no objection to eating
before he is acutely hungry – but if it does not suit her, his
fingers or a rusk may keep him happy for anything from two
minutes to half an hour.

During this same period the frequency with which the baby
demands to be fed drops. At 3 months a few will still be demanding a night feed, between say 10 p.m. and 6 a.m. These
will probably be having a variable five *or* six feeds in the 24
hours. They do not quite need six and cannot quite manage
with five. But most are already only having five feeds by 3
months; and by 4 or 5 months many will only be having four.
Once four feeds are the infant's settled pattern, his food ceases
to be a matter of 'feeds' and becomes instead a matter of
three meals a day and an additional bottle of milk.

How these meals are organized depends partly upon the
infant's sleep pattern and partly on the mother's convenience,
and the routine of the rest of the household. The infant is
probably going to have breakfast, lunch and tea/supper.
In addition he is going to need a bottle *either* last thing at
night, before the mother goes to bed, *or* first thing in the
morning. Three common eating/sleeping patterns are out-
lined below:

Wakes at 5–6 a.m.   Cannot wait for family's normal break-
                          fast time. Given bottle feed; sleeps
                          again until 9–10 a.m. when given
                          breakfast. Sleeps again until around
                          1 p.m., but after lunch takes only a dis-
                          crete nap, being otherwise awake until
                          after his tea/supper at around 6 p.m.

Wakes at 8–9 a.m.   Has breakfast, and stays awake until around midday, when he is given lunch, and then sleeps at once for most of the afternoon. May not wake until around 5 p.m. Probably then wishes to be sociable, so that bedtime becomes later – around 7–7·30 p.m. He may wake, or be woken for his late-night bottle.

Wakes around 7 a.m.   Can wait until breakfast time, then takes a nap of one to two hours between breakfast and lunch, and a similar nap between lunch and tea. His day is more evenly divided than either of the other two between sleep and wakefulness.

Obviously any combination or permutation of these patterns is possible. Their interest lies in how they can be adapted to the household. The first pattern might suit the mother who has a husband and other children to get off to work and school, and who is therefore pleased to have the infant out of the way over their breakfast time. She may be happy to play with him, or take him out during the afternoon, and glad to have him in bed early, leaving her free to give her attention to the others during the evening. She can therefore encourage him to go on with the early-morning bottle, giving it to him even on mornings when he happens to wake a little later.

The second pattern might suit a mother whose husband wanted to see as much as possible of the baby, and who, perhaps because it is a first child, does not find herself too loaded with work to cope with a baby who is wakeful all morning. She can continue to wake him for his late-night bottle.

The third pattern is, perhaps, the easiest of all, because it shows a more complete separation between eating and sleeping than either of the other two, and spaces the hours of sleep more evenly through the day. Such a baby is not likely to be as tired and cross at 6 p.m. as babies in the first group, nor as determinedly wakeful as babies in the second group. His final bedtime can therefore be adjusted, even from day to day. And the mother can choose whether she continues his early-morning or his late-night bottle; with this pattern he may soon make it clear that he needs neither.

The actual hours of sleep and the pattern of 'naps' is not likely to change very much during these 3 months. As he gets older the infant may sleep slightly less at each nap, but since he is also likely to be happy for somewhat longer periods in his pram or cot alone, the mother is unlikely to notice, or even to know this.

Sleep difficulties are unusual during this age period. Where they do exist, the problem is still the mother's, not the infant's. As we have seen (see page 63), dropping off to sleep cannot be voluntarily inhibited at this age. Given reasonable conditions the baby will go to sleep when he needs to. Problems only arise if he does not need to sleep when the mother thinks he should. Sometimes she is unable to fathom the infant's preferred pattern of sleep and wakefulness; she may fail to follow his cues and try to put him to sleep when he is wakeful and perhaps to play with him when he is sleepy. Probably the most common error is to allow the infant to nap through most of the afternoon, and then expect him to be ready to sleep again by 6 p.m., as soon as he has been washed and fed.

Occasionally the pattern of concerned care which evening colic (see page 110) has set up leads to difficulties. The baby's sleep rhythm may have become adjusted to a long period of evening wakefulness and its attendant social attention. When the cause of the wakefulness (the colic pain) ceases, the baby still wakes every evening. Unless the parents allow themselves to be trapped into taking an angry and moralistic attitude to this behaviour it is usually easy to deal with. The baby wakes and is given the attention he is accustomed to, but because the pain is no longer there to keep him awake, he rapidly drops off to sleep again. A shorter and shorter period of cuddling each evening will usually suffice, so that within two or three weeks of the colic's end the baby no longer wakes at all.

TEETHING

Many sleep difficulties are put down to teething. Often an acute concern with teething will follow directly on from parents' worrying about colic, or much incomprehensible crying in the early weeks. Many parents prefer to have something positive to which they can attribute their baby's misery. It is easier to remain patient with a constantly crying baby if you can believe he has a physical reason for his misery. Teething is an accepted cause, and far easier for most people to understand than more probable but nebulous causes such as loneliness.

Authorities have been concerned with teething since Hippocrates, who said: 'Teething children suffer from itching of the gums, fever, convulsions, diarrhoea . . .'. All the early authorities are well reviewed by Guthrie,[72] and some of the more hair-raising suggested cures such as gum-lancing, leeches behind the jaw or wolves-teeth necklaces are described by Illingworth.[73] He has reviewed the modern evidence on the symptoms of teething and believes that while it is not quite true that 'teething produces nothing but teeth', it certainly does not produce more than a little irritability from time to time, a lot of dribble, and occasional frantic sucking or biting.

A baby of 3 months or more who cries excessively, or frequently wakes in the night, is most unlikely to be behaving in this way because he is teething. In the first place he probably is not teething, since most children do not cut their first tooth before 5–6 months (see Table 7). In the second place, if he is teething, the process is most unlikely to be uncomfortable enough to cause more than very occasional misery. If such a baby also has diarrhoea, fever, convulsions, vomiting or loss of appetite, he may or may not be teething. But if he is, it is totally irrelevant. He needs to see a doctor as his symptoms are those of *illness*, not of *teething*. In 1839, the Registrar General's report on mortality in the first year of life attributed more than 5,000 infant deaths in England and Wales directly to teething. We now know that these deaths must have been due to illnesses which were missed because parents, nurses and doctors were prepared to believe that teething could cause almost any physical symptom.

TABLE 7.   ORDER AND AVERAGE AGES FOR THE ERUPTION OF FIRST TEETH

Teeth	Average age for first appearance
Lower incisors – i.e. the two middle teeth of the lower jaw	First at 6 months Second at 7 months
Upper incisors – i.e. the two middle teeth of the upper jaw	First at 7½ months Second at 9 months
Lower first molars – i.e. the grinding teeth furthest forward in the lower jaw	12 months
Upper first molars – i.e. the grinding teeth furthest forward in the upper jaw	14 months
Lower canines, or cuspids, – i.e. the pointed teeth between incisors and molars in the lower jaw	16 months
Upper canines, or cuspids, – i.e. the pointed teeth between incisors and molars in the upper jaw	18 months
Lower second molars – i.e. the grinding teeth at the back of the bottom jaw	20 months
Upper second molars – i.e. the grinding teeth at the back of the top jaw	24 months

CRYING

The prime causes of crying at 3 months are still similar to those of earlier weeks (see page 73). Crying is likely whenever the baby is physically uncomfortable; his discomforts may range from hunger through cold to physical pain. On the other hand, most babies by this age give other cues to their discomfort, before they begin to cry. The attentive mother can tell, from her baby's expression, from restless movements, from the little noises which presage full-throated crying, that something is wrong. Very often she can abort what would have been an episode of crying before it really gets under way. David and Appell[74] have described some mother–infant pairs where the mother is so attuned to the distress signals of her baby that crying-point is very seldom reached. They have observed others where the mother, albeit with the best intentions, cannot spot the baby's distress until it is voiced in a full-throated roar. It may be that some of these infants do not, in fact, give the full range of subtle distress signals; or it may be that they move through the stages of growing distress very rapidly, so that the mother has barely time to see the downcast face before it crumples into howls.

Causes and cures for crying that are nothing to do with physical discomfort or its alleviation appear with increasing frequency during these months. Both are directly related to the attachment to people, and especially to the mother, which was discussed in Chapter 11.

As soon as the infant's social development has advanced far enough for him to discriminate between friends and strangers, mother and others, it becomes extremely rare for his crying, whatever its cause, not to be halted by being held and talked to by familiar people. At the same time much of his crying can be seen to be caused by his need for social interaction with people.

Whatever the infant is crying about, he is likely to stop when his mother picks him up, unless he is in severe pain, or sedated, or ill. If the original cause of his distress was some form of mild discomfort, he will probably put up with it as long as his mother holds him, remaining calm and cheerful while she fetches his bottle or sorts out his ruckled bed. If the original discomfort was severe, and is ongoing, he may start to cry again even as his mother holds him. But even then it is likely to be a different kind of crying, much calmer and gentler than when he was alone.

Very often, the mother can discover no cause for the crying. If she then returns him to his cot or pram, alone, away from company, he is likely to begin to cry again immediately. He was crying for people, crying for her.

Many mothers, health visitors and doctors believe that such crying for company is in some way illegitimate. They believe that infants have a right to cry if there is 'something wrong'; and that it is the mother's job to find out what is wrong and put it right. But 'something wrong' means hunger, or a chafing nappy, or sun in the eyes; it does not mean loneliness or boredom. If there is nothing *physically* wrong, mothers are advised to put the baby down again, and let him cry it out. It is a curious attitude. Without his desire for human company, without his need for his mother, the baby could not develop as a normal human being. Furthermore we do not treat social demands in this way in any of our other relationships. We do not reckon that a husband who has been given his supper 'should not' require anything more of us until morning. Nor do we greet friends on the telephone by saying, 'Do you actually need me to do anything for you? Because if not I am going to ring off.' A chat is a valid reason for the telephone call.

Usually it is the spectre of spoiling which leads to this irrational behaviour towards infants. Many mothers fear, perhaps only partly consciously, that if the baby is allowed to make all the emotional demands he wishes on them, they will be engulfed, drained, left with no individuality, nothing to offer husbands, friends or older children. The relationship which the infant wants with the mother is so intense that mothers tend to want to keep it under their own control; ration it, in case it gets out of hand.

Yet only Western cultures tend to take this attitude towards young babies. It is only we to whom it ever occurs to leave a baby alone for long periods. Elsewhere the baby is automatically with the mother or grandmother or older sister all the time; carried by her during the day, cuddled up with her during the night. In many cultures the implicit recognition of this need is so strong that it is embodied in sexual taboos on the relationship between husband and wife. It is the baby who shares the mother's bed, not the husband.

The fear of spoiling a baby of this age is a tragic one. Implicit in it is the view that babies are demanding monsters who given an inch will take an ell. But why should they? They only want as much as they need. Given what they need, they will not demand more and more. Indeed given what they need when they show they need it, they will tend to demand less and less. It is the baby who is firmly left alone in his pram, awake and crying for an hour at a time, who tends to become demanding and difficult. He is the one who begins to fear his pram or cot, because they spell isolation. The baby who is always picked up, talked to, played with, included in the household, whenever he indicates his need, has no reason to cry when he has not the need. He is confident.

Fear of spoiling often leads to a different but related kind of crying. As the baby develops new accomplishments, he has a very strong desire to exercise and practise them. Most of them, as we shall see in later chapters, directly involve the mother, either as a partner, or as a facilitator. The baby who is determinedly left alone for long periods when he is awake may be not only lonely, but also frustrated and bored. He is being prevented from doing all the things he wants to do, needs to do, is developmentally programmed to do. Play is not an indulgence, it is a developmental necessity; the child's job. It may not earn him money, but it earns him growth.

CHAPTER FIFTEEN

GETTING CONTROL OF HIS BODY

Where the first 3 months of the infant's life saw him fighting and winning a battle for control over his own heavy head, these 3 months see him getting to know his own body, and finding out what he can do with it.

In the early weeks of life, it is thought that infants do not 'know' their own bodies even in the sense of being aware that they are all of one piece, and a separate piece from anything else. Their awareness of where they stop and other things begin is probably extremely blurred. Their pleasure when their own waving hands move across their field of vision is just the same as their pleasure when the mother's hand is seen. When they catch sight of their own hand lying on the blanket, they do not at once move it; rather they consider it, interestedly, as if it were an object. The mother's body is often used by the infant as if it was his own – without apparent awareness that she may react for example to having *his* fingers in *her* mouth. The infant's own body can often be offered him in place of the mother's – by gently disengaging his clutching hand, for example, and giving him his own other hand to hold instead. So the infant makes an exceedingly exciting discovery during these 3 months: he discovers that all the bits of his body are attached and part of *him*, and as a corollary, he discovers that they are all more or less under his own control. A great deal of his drive, his energy, his concentration during this period goes into making his body obey him.

In gross terms, the motor developments which take place are very small. The infant does not learn to walk during this period; he does not learn to crawl, or even properly to sit up. To a casual observer he still seems very immobile, very incompetent physically at 6 months. And compared with the young of any other species he is indeed incompetent. Never-

theless the consequences of each small development are immense, if they are considered in scale with the small scope of
the infant's world.

For several weeks he was totally dependent on his mother
for the very position in which he lay. Once she had put him
down, apart from turning his head, he could do nothing to
change his position. Now, soon after 3 months, he learns to
roll himself over. First from his side to his back (see Chapter
7) and then from his back to his side. A small achievement,
perhaps, but one with far-reaching consequences for the infant. By rolling over, he may make himself more physically
comfortable, or less so. He may hurt himself, by banging his
head on the cot bars or rolling off the sofa; he can change his
view of the world, see new things, perhaps even catch sight of
his mother. He may increase his own freedom to move
around, by releasing his legs from a blanket; he may trap
himself into immobility by catching his arm underneath his
body. The list of possibilities is endless. The important point
is that the baby is greatly increasing the stimulation he gets
throughout his waking hours by providing stimulation for
himself. And the stimulation is giving him innumerable
lessons in cause and effect, in what is him and what is outside
him, and in visual accommodation to different objects at
different distances. The change in his environment which
being able to roll brings about is equivalent to the change
which uncurling from the neonatal position brought about
at the 6-weeks stage.

As with most aspects of development, once a baby *can* roll,
he *will* roll. His ability to do so will increase by fits and starts
so sharp that they may catch his mother out. It takes only
one extra-frenzied effort on the baby's part to turn the nappy-
changing table from an acceptable convenience to a hazard
that is banned too late. The baby's efforts are dedicated to
rolling right over, from his back to his stomach. The earlier he
has managed to roll from side to back the earlier he will roll
from back to side. And the earlier he accomplishes both these
manoeuvres, the earlier he can be expected to manage to get
all the way over. In the meantime he will try and try, and he

needs to be helped over, placed on his tummy so that he can practise the preliminaries to crawling which will become so important soon after 6 months (see page 299).

By 3 months (see page 115) most infants placed on their tummies lie with their legs straight out behind them, and can take the weight of their upper bodies on their forearms so as to lift their heads well clear of the floor. By around 15 weeks, the infant will probably be able to lift his whole chest clear of the floor as well as his head, and he may hold this position for several minutes at a time. A few infants, by 4 months, even learn to transfer their weight from forearms to hands, thus raising themselves even higher.

At around 4 months, while he is lying flat on the floor, resting from the head-up posture, the infant begins to pull his legs under him, rather as he did when he was newborn, so that his bottom is in the air. As with forearms and hands, some infants quickly learn that they can get even more purchase if they push up with their feet rather than with their knees.

By 5 months many babies have both the head-up and the bottom-up position perfected, but cannot put the two together so as to be on hands and knees. They therefore alternate the two, and look rather as if they were see-sawing – first one end up and the other down, then the first end down and the other up. By this stage, while a true crawl with the tummy clear of the floor, is very unusual, quite a lot of babies will make some progress across the floor, as they see-saw. It is not deliberate locomotion, but it is quite enough movement to take them over the top of a flight of stairs, or into an unguarded fire.

Some babies do not progress in their pre-crawling manoeuvres as fast as this, because they strenuously object to being put to lie on their tummies at all. Often these are the babies who seem to be most alert to people, and to things around them. It may well be that they object to the reduction in their field of vision which being put face down brings with it. There is no evidence to suggest that such a baby is likely to be late in crawling. He may, however, be early in learning

to sit up. Probably he will simply cut out some of the preliminaries of learning to crawl, refusing to be put on his
tummy until he is very nearly ready to move off.

As we saw in Chapter 7, most infants take a great
pleasure in free kicking and other physical play by the time
they are 3 months. From 3 to 6 months such play becomes
much more obviously purposeful. Where at 3 months the
infant enjoyed having his hands held while he was gently
pulled up to sitting position, by 4 months the mother has only
to take his hands for him to try and pull *himself* to sitting. By
6 months he may indeed provide all the power for this manoeuvre himself, using the adult's hands purely as balancing
handles. Even without adult hands the baby will try to sit up.
By 4 months, lying flat on his back, often during a short rest-
pause following an energetic bout of kicking, the infant will
lift his head clear of the floor. A month later he will be able to
lift both his head and shoulders clear, and may get an amazing glimpse of his own feet as he does so. Propped up in sitting
position, he cranes his head forward from the backrest, as if
he yearned for a more and more upright posture. By 6 months
the infant's control of his back has moved downward, so that
only the base of his spine, at hip level, still tends to sag when
he sits. He can sit in his pram with only a single pillow
wedged behind his bottom; and he may be able to sit alone
for a few seconds, often leaning forward to put his hands on
the floor for extra balance. But even the best 6-month sitters
cannot really *use* the independent sitting position. Even if
they can balance while their full concentration is on the
sheer business of sitting, distraction by a person, or the sight
of a toy, or any attempt to turn their heads or use their hands,
will still topple them.

A 3-month infant held in standing position tends to sag
pathetically at the knees. But over the next few weeks, most
babies begin to take a fractional amount of their own bodyweight on their feet, pushing down with their toes while they
intermittently straighten their knees. By 4 to 5 months, the
knee-straightening has become rhythmical, so that the infant
feels as if he was 'jumping' on the mother's lap. At this stage

some babies acquire such a passion for the standing position that it is exceedingly difficult to persuade them to *sit* on a lap at all. They turn themselves inwards, fasten their fists in the nearest portion of their mother's body or hair, and fight to get themselves upright against her shoulder. Once in position they have a delightful view of the world over her shoulder, and a view, moreover, which moves around as they 'jump'; they are in warm contact with the mother's body, face to face, and they can exercise their legs to their heart's content. By the time the infant reaches 6 months, the mother may feel that she is nothing but a convenient trampoline for a budding gymnast!

Most of these physical activities require the mother's participation, or at least her preliminary help. The infant cannot practise his rolling over unless she puts him on a suitable firm surface, and frees him from hampering wrappings. He cannot sit himself up unless she helps him, nor stay sitting unless she arranges a suitable seat. He cannot practise taking his weight standing up unless she will enter the game. Babies who are left, alone and awake, for long periods therefore have good reason to be bored as well as lonely. They need their mothers to play, not only for emotional reasons, but also as partners who provide the muscle power and the balance for these new physical adventures.

Yet placed on a mat on the floor, or even in his pram with the blankets removed, a baby of this age period can make some entertainment for himself. Many mothers accept the healthy exercise which goes with what is usually called 'kicking'; but few realize the extent of the learning which goes on at the same time. We have seen that by 3 months most infants have coordinated their limbs to a point where their legs move in a smooth, rhythmical bicycling motion, and the waving of their arms is fluid, without the jerkiness which characterized the early weeks.

Soon after, the infant learns that he can alter this motion; change the rhythm; start and stop his legs at will. He learns, for example, to kick both legs together instead of alternating them. He finds that that motion is the quickest way to get his covers off, or a good way to make his pram bounce. Certainly he is taking exercise, but he is also learning that those limbs are part of him; that he can control them.

As he waves his arms around, apparently aimlessly, he is also practising all the skills which go into reaching out for things and grasping them (see Chapters 7 and 9). At 3 months most infants have discovered their hands by touch and by eye simultaneously. They watch their hands playing together. But the infant's notions of his own *control* over his hands are probably still very primitive. If he is watched carefully, it can be seen that he greets his own hand with pleasure when it moves into his view; plays with it dedicatedly for a while, but then, when it falls out of view, he accepts that it has gone; he makes no attempt to turn his head and look for it, nor to raise it into view again. He has not yet learned that objects still exist when they are out of sight, nor that his hand is not an object, but part of himself.

Over a few weeks of concentrated hand play, the infant gradually learns that he himself can make his hands come and go. Again if he is carefully watched, this stage can often be spotted. The infant plays with his hands for a while, and then stops, with both hands held in the air where he can see them. He drops both arms to his sides, so that both hands vanish; and then he lifts them again, and looks from one to another. A lucky observer may even see the next stage: this time the baby does not just bring about the miracle of the re-appearing hands, he drops the arms to his sides, turns his head to find one of them, and then watches it all the way back to the centre again. By about 5 months, it is usually clear that the infant has got his hands thoroughly under control, in the sense that he knows where they are even when he cannot see them, and can bring them back into sight at will. But for some weeks more he will continue to look as if he 'checks up' on them, taking the fist he is sucking out of his mouth for visual inspection, or glancing at the hand that is supporting him as he lies on his tummy on the floor.

Once his hands are under this much control the baby uses them to explore other parts of his body. He may pull and twist his ears or his hair, finger his navel, grab his own nose, but it is play with the genitals that is most often noticed by the parents. The penis is an obvious 'handle' for a little boy at the grasping stage to get hold of. The vulva makes interesting folds for a little girl to explore. This kind of play is no different at this stage from play with other parts of the body. Yet even at this early age parental attitudes often make it different. The genitals are normally closely covered by nappies and plastic pants, so that play with them is concentrated into moments when the baby is naked. Many parents misinterpret the baby's renewed discovery of his genitals each bathtime, and see him as waiting for a chance to get at himself. Furthermore what the baby does with those organs is often alarming to parents accustomed to adult sexual parts. An infant penis is extraordinarily elastic: the little boy may pull it out, twist it around his fingers, in a way which makes his father shudder. Furthermore, that infant penis becomes spontaneously erect from time to time. Genital play when the penis is erect may look to the parents like true masturbation, and be treated as a moral, or at least a modesty issue. The Newsons[18] reported a widespread incidence of smacking for genital play, even at this age, and many mothers reported that by one year babies were aware of parental disapproval and looked to see if the mother was watching before touching themselves.

At around 5–6 months, babies who are given plenty of physical freedom often transfer their fascination from their hands to their feet. As we have said, the infant often catches a first glimpse of his feet when he begins to lift his head and shoulders off the floor while lying on his back. At other times he catches entrancing sight of them as they wave about on the end of his kicking legs. For about 3 weeks, the infant's free kicking time may seem dedicated to getting hold of those feet. And it is a problem. If he lifts his head and shoulders to get his hands nearer his feet, those feet go down out of reach; if he lifts his legs to bring the feet closer, his shoulders go down. Getting hold of his feet challenges everything he has been learning during this 3-month period: his muscle power, his coordination of one bit of his body with another, and his ability to judge distances and accommodate his vision to things which are moving about. Success often comes at round about the half-birthday, with the feet captured, and put in the mouth for thorough examination. A passion for feet is seldom popular with mothers – there are few things more difficult than changing the nappy of a baby who *will* suck his toes.

CHAPTER SIXTEEN

USING HAND AND EYE TOGETHER

At 3 months, babies still behave most of the time as though their looking and their touching systems were entirely separate. The baby will often look at an object within his reach without attempting to reach out for it. And he will often manipulate an object put into his hand without lifting it up so that he can look at it. Yet, as we saw in a previous chapter (see page 122) the baby is learning about things while he looks at them, even without handling them. And he is rapidly learning how to get hold of them too. By the end of this 3-month period he will be able to reach out swiftly and accurately for anything which is within his reach, and pick it up. Only tiny objects, which require the fine juxtaposition of finger and thumb, will still defeat him for a few further weeks.

We have already seen how extremely selective babies are in their choice of *what* to look at, what to expend their attention on. In recent years new research has also radically altered our views about how much infants who cannot yet handle objects actually understand about them. Where common sense, and older research, leads to the supposition that a baby cannot understand such things as the shape, solidity or size of objects, until he can both look at and handle them, this new work suggests that the infant has an inbuilt understanding of many of these things, and that when he does come to handle a particular object for the first time its properties do not come as a complete surprise to him.

One piece of research, for example, has made it clear that infants have some understanding of the significance of size. Bruner and Koslowski[75] studied infants aged from 10 weeks to 22 weeks. They were shown two balls within easy reach. The balls were identical, except that one was so small that the infant could have grasped it in one hand, had he been capable of getting hold of it, while the other was much larger, so that the infant would have needed to clasp it in both arms. Even the youngest infants tended to react to the small ball either by clasping one hand tightly with the other, or by holding one hand hovering in mid-air. Their reaction to the large ball was quite different. They tended either to open their arms wide, or to make wide-sweeping swipes towards it. Clearly, even without tactile experience, the babies had some ideas of relative size, by eye alone, and some idea of the grasping methods suitable to objects of different sizes.

Thomas Bower[76] found that infants also 'know' about the solidity of objects, before they have had much chance to discover solidity by touch. He showed infants a projected shadow object which, viewed through polarized goggles, looked exactly like a solid three-dimensional one. When babies swiped at this, even before 3 months of age, they were obviously both surprised and distressed when their swiping hands encountered thin air. It was clear that they *expected* to touch something solid, and the contradiction of this expectation was definitely unpleasant. When the same infants were shown a real object which looked exactly the same as the 'fake' one, they swiped it with pleasure.

Many other aspects of the infant's understanding of the nature of objects are currently being explored. Much of the work is highly technical; almost all of it is preliminary. These studies involve the continual invention and refining of *methods* of studying young babies, of ways of measuring cognitive processes which a few years ago would have been regarded as immeasurable. Therefore it is often difficult to know whether the earliest age at which infants demonstrate a given ability – such as adjusting their rudimentary grasp to size – reflects the earliest age at which they can actually *do* it, or the earliest age at which the experimenters have been able to *measure* it. In this situation it is hardly surprising that research results often contradict each other. Workers are finding out how to find out, just as much as they are discovering the facts. So all findings in this field are interesting, and none can be regarded as final.

Bruner, and many other workers in this field, believe that

there is already enough evidence to show that the whole question of whether the infant's eye teaches his hand, or his hand teaches his eye, is irrelevant (see Chapter 8). He believes that the information infants get from looking at things and the information they eventually get from touching things are already genetically mapped upon each other. The infant 'knows' what to grasp, and he 'knows' how to grasp. His principal task in this area is to learn how to *order* his grasping actions, how to get the sequence right, and how to allow for his own length of reach. Bruner makes the excellent point that it is likely that infants would be genetically programmed to know some of the qualities of objects that they see, and some of the appropriate ways of handling those objects, but it is most *unlikely* that they would be born knowing the length of their own arms. Babies after all come in a large variety of shapes and sizes, and they grow extremely rapidly. Any genetic programming about their own arm-reach would therefore be highly inefficient; the infant would have to unlearn the length of his own arms as he grew.

Observation certainly suggests that both order and reach are vital factors during these months. Often infants will reach out towards an object, make careful, painstaking adjustments of the position of their hands in space until they actually touch the object, but be unable to grasp it because they have already closed their hands. They have got the order wrong. Similarly infants will often look at an object, bring their hands together directly beneath it, and then grasp one hand with the other at chest level. They have carried out the whole process of grasping, and in the correct order this time, but they have not extended their arms enough to reach the object.

The concentrated hand play which is typical of these months probably serves a valuable purpose in giving the infant information about his own length of arm, his grip, his reach. By $3\frac{1}{2}$ to 4 months, infants almost always watch their own hand play. The purely tactile manipulation of one hand by the other gives way to very deliberate, visually guided play, with the hands being brought together, taken to the mouth, returned to within eye sight and so on.

While all this work suggests that young infants know far more about objects than used to be thought, one series of preliminary experiments by Bower[76] suggests a confusion about the actual identity of objects. This research has not yet been repeated, and cannot therefore be taken as confirmed, but it is interesting and thought-provoking.

Most people, while they assume that a baby cannot know that a bottle of milk is hard, heavy and solid, without touching it (which in fact, as we have just seen, they *do* know), take it for granted that the infant will realize that the same bottle taken from the table, and placed on a stool, remains the same object. Bower on the contrary believes that, until about 4 months, babies identify objects largely *by* their position in space, or their position relative to other objects, and that when they are moved out of this spatial context the baby sees them afresh as new objects.

Bower ran a small brilliantly lighted train along a table in front of the infants. In the course of its journey, the train vanished momentarily behind a screen, reappearing on the other side a second later. After one or two trials the babies expected the reappearance of the train, and looked, in anticipation, to the other side of the screen as soon as it vanished from sight. After a few trials, the train was changed, during its moment behind the screen, for a plain white figurine. This reappearead, instead of the expected train. Infants under 4 months were quite unsurprised by this. They had seen a still train, a moving train, and a moving figurine. All, Bower believes, quite separate objects to them. But the babies who were over 4 months were most disconcerted. They clearly expected the reappearance of the same object they had watched vanish and they were surprised and distressed when this expectation was not fulfilled.

This extraordinary finding does seem to be confirmed by a further experiment in which Bower used an arrangement of mirrors so that infants saw their mother and several reflected images of her, all at the same time. Once again the babies who were less than 4 months old remained quite calm and unsurprised. They smiled and cooed at each 'mother' in turn.

But the older babies were again bewildered and distressed. They looked from image to image and responded to none.

Taken together, these findings suggest that until he is around 4 months old, the infant may live in a very fragmented and over-populated world. A world where the mother who leans over the cot is one mother, the one who walks across the room is another mother, and the one who finally sits down in the chair is yet another. A world full of objects too, and objects that vanish. Not one pram that may be in any one of six positions in the room, but six prams, each of which vanishes as it moves, in favour of the appearance of another.

We do not yet know whether further work will confirm these extraordinary findings. But they could lend a new dimension to what we already know about the 3–5-month infant's reactions to people and to daily life. We know (see page 149) that during this age period infants make the fine discriminations between people that lead to high degrees of attachment to the mother. It may be that this is a perceptual as well as an emotional development. The infant may learn not only to know the mother from all others, but also to know that there is only one of her, that she is unique. Her exit through the door is much more final to the baby once he knows there is only one of her, that another mother will not suddenly materialize beside the pram. The sorting out of this perceptual confusion about the nature of objects may contribute both to the development of attachment and to its typical behaviours, such as crying when the mother leaves.

But all this is still speculation. Whatever the infant 'knows' about objects, or whatever misapprehensions he may have about their nature and behaviour, he will certainly become comparatively adept at handling them during this 3-month period. By the time he is 6 months, all questions about whether he learns to understand what he sees by touching it, or to understand what he touches by seeing it, or about whether he learns both together or merely practises what is genetically inbuilt in him, become academic. By that age interest will focus on what he *does* with what he touches (see Chapter 22).

As we saw in Chapter 9, the sequence of the development of reaching out and getting hold of objects is less rigid than are most developmental sequences. In this sense the development of hand–eye coordination is unlike the development of motor abilities. The child must learn to control his head before he can sit up; he must roll from his back to his side before he can roll from his back to his tummy. But he may learn to swipe at objects before he learns visually guided play with his hands, or he may leave out one of the stages of reaching altogether. Furthermore, while all developmental sequences are to some extent open to environmental speeding up, it seems that hand–eye coordination can be speeded up more by appropriate stimulation than motor abilities can be. But this may be because in our society babies are usually given as much motor stimulation as they can use and therefore develop their physical abilities as fast as they can, while they are often not given the optimum amount of visual–manual play, and can therefore develop hand–eye coordination faster if they are offered more.

Returning to the normative studies of Burton, White, Castle and Held, described on page 128, the stages which most babies will pass through in learning to get hold of objects can be summarized as in Table 8. The 'age at first appearance' is the earliest age at which any baby in the sample was seen to accomplish the manoeuvre. The 'age range' encompasses both that first and the latest age at which a baby first performed the manoeuvre. The age range is as wide as it is because both highly stimulated 'experimental babies' and the under-stimulated 'control babies' are included. But this does not mean that it can be assumed that ordinary family babies will come midway between the two extremes. As we saw in Chapters 11 and 12 both the stimulation offered by homes, and the stimulation taken by infants, vary widely.

Any individual infant may miss out one of these stages, or pass through it so rapidly that his mother never notices it. Indeed the middle stages of glancing between hand and

TABLE 8. SUMMARY OF REACHING-OUT
BEHAVIOUR

Behaviour	Age at first appearance	Age range
Swiping at objects with occasional hit	6 weeks	6 weeks–3 months
Raising one hand towards seen object	8 weeks	8 weeks–3½ months
Raising both hands towards seen object	8 weeks	8 weeks–4½ months
Glancing between raised hand and seen object as if measuring the gap visually	8 weeks	8 weeks–4½ months
Turning body towards seen object presented to one side	2½ months	2½–5½ months
'Piaget-type reach': glancing between raised hand and object, with progressive correction of gap, finally achieving touch	3½ months	3½–5½ months
'Top-level reaching': lifting hand directly to object without intervening visual corrections	4 months	4–6½ months

wanted object, measuring the distance, adjusting the reach, seldom are noticed except by those who observe babies with some care.

For practical purposes, then, all that matters is that at the beginning of this age period the baby will swipe at objects, occasionally hitting them. Somewhere around the middle of the period, he will slowly, painstakingly, succeed in touching things. Towards the end of the period he will reach out efficiently and swiftly for what he wants.

As we have seen, research suggests that the provision of appropriate stimuli can accelerate the infant's acquisition of these skills (see page 130). While we have no reason to suppose that this acceleration is of long-lasting benefit to the baby, it can be of immediate benefit to the mother, and *therefore* to the baby. Infants in this age group definitely suffer from boredom. The provision of the kind of toys which allow them to practise these vital skills can go a long way towards keeping them entertained at a stage of life when the possibilities of physical play without the mother's help are still limited (see Chapter 18).

Swiping at objects can provide happy entertainment for 10 or even 20 minutes at a time, several times a day, while the infant is at the swiping stage. Unfortunately few homes and even fewer institutions provide suitable objects. A soft, light object, which cannot break however hard it is bashed, needs to be hung within 1 foot (30cm) of the bridge of the infant's nose. This goes against many people's instincts. They feel that hanging something so close to the baby's face may encourage squinting. Some also feel, perhaps, that 'hitting' should not be encouraged. In one day nursery, all the infants of this age group were put in the garden in prams for the afternoon. We hung woollen balls on long cords from trees above their prams. Every time a swipe connected, the ball swung, and the tree twigs moved gently. Staff had their most peaceful afternoon in the nursery's history. Occasional exclamatory gurgles were all that could be heard, instead of the usual cacophony of fury from babies put down when they were not ready for sleep.

In the middle stage, when the baby may occasionally succeed in touching an object, if he is given time, his problem is usually adult impatience rather than lack of suitable objects. The mother may offer him a rattle or other toy. He advances his hand, looks at it, looks at the toy, moves the hand fractionally and repeats the process. His longing for the object is clear in his whole demeanour. All too often the mother does not wait for him to achieve success. She either shoves the object into his hand because she wants to do something else, or she gives it to him because she does not like to see the fearful (and, to her, frustrating) effort he is making. Either way she aborts the incident. Very often the baby's successes at first will come when the mother is not actually *offering* him anything and therefore does not notice that he is trying to get something. Perhaps she is sitting with him on her lap, talking to someone else. The baby may have the two minutes he needs to succeed in getting hold of the beads around her neck.

If the mother can be patient when she offers something, the right timing for help is when the baby has succeeded in making his hand and the object connect. Often, at this stage, he will have closed his questing hand before it reached its target. Then he does need it put into his hand. Otherwise the success in getting *there* is lost because he still has not got *it*.

Once the infant can reach out and get hold of things, he will reach out and get hold of anything which is within his reach. And his reach is often surprisingly long, with all his new rolling over and craning up abilities. Some of the hazards of this stage are obvious. If the mother has not quite taken in the extent to which his abilities have suddenly developed, it may be her hot cup of coffee he reaches out for, or the iron, or his father's chisel. And, of course, anything he does get hold of will go into his mouth. His mouth, just as much as his hands and eyes, is an organ of exploration. But babies should not eat cigarettes, forks, kittens, buttons, money. . .

On the other hand babies need to be allowed to put more than bottles, dummies and teething rings in their mouths. All too many mothers limit the objects their infants are allowed to handle because they feel it is unhygienic for the baby to mouth everything. Such an attitude leads to extreme tedium for the baby, who wants new and different things to feel and handle. Nor is it a logical attitude. Once the baby is spending some time on the floor, his own hands – which he will suck whatever his mother feels about it – are just as likely to be grubby as the saucepan lids, pieces of paper and wooden spoons which he so longs to be allowed to play with.

At this early stage, the infant's approach to objects is almost always two-handed. He traps things between his two palms, and scoops them up. It follows that his most active play with

objects will take place while he is securely supported in a
sitting position so that both his arms are free. A baby chair
with its own tray is ideal.

All through this age period the infant can cope with only
one object at a time. Even at 6 months, if he takes one small
cube, and is then offered another, he will drop the first in
order to take the second. The first cube falls because his attention transfers to the second. He cannot yet deliberately
let go, or hand back an object. When the mother wants something back she must take it – offering another in its place if
she wants to avoid a commotion. At this age, the main interest
for the baby is in *getting* objects, and holding them and sucking them. He needs to see and feel and hold as many different
things as possible. He is not much concerned, yet, with what
he can do with an object once he has got it. Very few 6-month
babies are tool-users.

CHAPTER SEVENTEEN

LISTENING AND BABBLING

While babies begin to 'practise' making sounds and may begin to react to being talked to by 'talking' back towards the end of the first 3 months, the second 3 months typically produces a positive spate of sound. Just as the 4- or 5-month baby is seldom still when he is awake, so he is seldom silent. All the new social, physical and hand–eye adventures of the 3- to 6-month period tend to be increasingly accompanied by the infant's own sounds.

Yet pitifully little research has so far been done into the nature, the development and the function of what is technically referred to as 'babble'. Clearly it is a vital stage in the eventual development of actual speech, but it is unclear exactly what role it plays in this development.

The study of infant babble is more difficult than it might first appear. If the babbling sounds of many infants are recorded on tape, the listener tends to analyse the sounds in terms of his own language, or at least in terms of 'language' as a whole. The bits of the babble which he tends to note will, inevitably, be those bits which most closely approximate to words. If babble is analysed by methods which avoid this kind of obvious bias – by sound-spectrograph, for example, which reproduces the sound waves in a visual graph form – the researcher is still left with information whose significance it is remarkably difficult to assess. He records what the infant utters. He can compare that with the utterances of many other infants. But it is still extremely difficult to find out whether the *baby* could hear the difference between one of his own sounds and the next. And it is even more difficult to guess whether the baby *intended* to make one sound rather than another.

At 3–4 months, most of an infant's babble consists of open vowel sounds. He says 'aaaa' and 'ooo'. Often he is de-

scribed as 'cooing', and indeed he may sound very dove-like.
The researcher notes the first occurrence of consonants being
added to these vowel sounds. He hears the infant begin to say
'Paaa' or 'Baa' or 'Maa'. The addition of consonants makes
the cooing sound much more like words, in any language.
But does the infant hear the difference between 'ooo' and
'mooo'? If he does, does he intend to say 'moo' rather than
'ooo'? Usually it is impossible to know. But we do know that
the open-vowel cooing comes before consonants are added,
and that the consonants P, B and M are almost invariably the
first ones added to them.

As we saw in an earlier chapter (see Chapter 10) the mechanisms necessary for hearing and for producing non-cry
sounds are present in the infant from birth. They mature
rapidly during the early months, and the infant's ability to
control his own sound-making therefore parallels the
maturity of his vocal apparatus. Just as he seems to be
genetically programmed to attend and respond to human
speech-like noises, so he appears to be genetically programmed to practise his own. While, as we shall see, social
stimulation works even more markedly in these months to
increase his sound-making than it did earlier, his noises will
increase and become more complex even in the absence of
any such stimulation. Total deafness is often not recognized
in babies under 6 months just because such infants develop
their babble almost as normal babies do. Recognizing that
they are deaf therefore depends on the parents noticing that
they do not react to sounds made outside their eye-line; they
do not, for example, turn their heads to look for the mother
when she speaks from behind them.[77]

While all infants increase and diversify their babbling
during these months, careful analysis by sound-spectrograph
has shown marked differences in the number of different
sounds made, and the richness of their use. Highly stimulated
infants are far more vocal than less stimulated ones. Irwin,[78]
for example, found that infants in this age group from higher-
social-class families produced more and richer babble than
did infants from families of lower social class. Kagan[79] con-

firmed this curious finding, but only for girl babies. Boys babbled the amount they babbled irrespective of the mother's social class, while girls babbled more, the higher her social class.

The relationship between social class, sex and early babbling has been carefully reviewed by Kagan. It seems that middle-class mothers tend to talk more, directly to their infants, than do working-class mothers, and that (as we saw in Chapter 12) all mothers tend to differentiate in their handling of the two sexes, giving their sons much rough-and-tumble play, and their daughters more talking and looking play. A highly talkative mother who concentrates on talking and looking interaction is likely to produce a highly vocal baby – while a less talkative mother who concentrates on rough-and-tumble play is likely to produce a less vocal one. So the sons of working-class mothers are likely to be the least vocal babies, the daughters of middle-class mothers the most vocal babies.

But these are generalizations. There are plenty of working-class mothers who talk a great deal to their infants, and plenty of middle-class mothers who do not. The interest of the work lies in the inescapable conclusion that the talkativeness of the baby is directly related to the nature of the mother's typical interactions with him.

As we saw in Chapter 10, even by 3 months infants exhibit a clear tendency to 'talk' most to a talking adult. We saw, for example, that ringing a bell in response to the baby's utterances did not stimulate him to go on talking, but talking back to him did (see page 138). In this second 3 months, the infant becomes even more selective. Just as he learns to distinguish visually first between human faces and other objects, and then between actual human faces, so he learns auditorily to distinguish first between human voices and other sounds and then between actual human voices.

Kagan and Lewis[80] conducted a series of experiments with infants of 6 months. They played them a random intermittent tone, some jazz music and a prose passage read by an unfamiliar male voice, an unfamiliar female voice and the mother. Careful measurements were taken of the infants' heart-rate changes, motor activity, crying, fretting and vocalization in response to these different sounds.

The infants responded quite differently to each one. They saved their most positive responses for the female and the mother's voices reading the prose passage. They vocalized extensively during these readings, and tended to vocalize also during the pauses, as if they were answering what had been said. The experimenters definitely felt that, by this age, talking had a social content for the babies which was absent from mere noise or from music, that their own responses also had social intent, and that they 'preferred' the unfamiliar female or mother's voice to the voice of the unfamiliar male. The same authors have even found significant differences in the way infants responded to the sound of the greeting 'Hello' from a strange male, a strange female and the mother.

But while it is clear that infants of this age group recognize and respond to the social intent behind talking, and that they begin to reply to this social intent with a socially intended response, there is no direct imitation of the *content* of adult speech. Babble contains syllables which sound like words, and parents are therefore inclined to pick out these word-like noises and assume that the infant is trying to imitate the actual words he hears around him. This is a clear case of the listener imposing his own knowledge of a language on his interpretation of the child's sounds. The English parent recognizes babble which sounds like an approximation to an English word; the Italian parent recognizes the sounds which are close to an Italian word. Each ignores, as 'mere babble', the sounds which approximate to words in the other language. In fact babble is universal. Babies do not make every sound known to man in the course of their babbling, because there are still many sounds which they are physiologically incapable of making. But they do make equal numbers of sounds typical of every known language. Nakazima,[34] for example, studied groups of Japanese and American babies. The two languages, Japanese and American–English, are extremely different from any linguistic point of view. Yet even using spectrographic analysis, Nakazima could find no differences whatsoever in the babble sounds produced by the two groups of children. The sounds made by the two groups remained identical right up to the time when the first words were being produced at around 1 year. There was no Japanese babble, no American babble, just babble.

So it seems that being talked to by adults does not influence the infant's talking by teaching the child, nor by offering him sounds to copy. The effect comes from increasing the infant's motivation, his pleasure in practising what he was genetically programmed to do anyway: babble.

CHAPTER EIGHTEEN

BOREDOM AND THE NEED FOR PLAY

The period from 3 to 6 months is often a comparatively easy one for mothers. The alarms and tribulations of caring for a newborn are over; the baby is socially rewarding, often turning a routine nappy-change into a joyous social occasion by his brilliant smiles and persuasive babble, and yet he is still not mobile. The mother can still put him out of danger and expect him to stay put. And she can still expect at least some periods of peace during the day while he sleeps.

Two related spectres can ruin this period for both mother and child. The first is the infant's boredom. The second is the mother's fear of spoiling him.

Whatever a baby *can* do, he is going to want to do. His drive to practise new skills is enormously strong, and it has to be. Without that drive he could never overcome the fearsome difficulties of his own immaturity, and become competent. So during these months he needs and wants to practise his motor skills: lifting his head, trying to sit up, trying to balance when someone else sits him up, trying to roll over, experimenting with near-crawling positions and so on. He needs and wants new things to look at and new things to reach out for. He needs and wants to handle objects, mouth them, get to know them. Above all, he needs and wants more and more social contact with adults, especially the mother: he wants to smile and talk and play.

The baby has, then, a full programme of activities mapped out for these months. But very few of them are activities which he can start alone, or conduct without help for more than a couple of minutes at a time. His abilities are too new, his incompetence is too great for him to be able to entertain himself.

Placed on a rug on the floor, the infant may occupy himself with kicking, playing with his hands, looking at his toes, and exclaiming over the joys of life for several minutes. If so, the mother is lucky. She can get on with her own affairs. But it is just as likely that as soon as the infant is put on his rug, he will try to roll over, trap the underneath arm so that he can neither complete the manoeuvre nor go back, and then cry for help. And he is likely to repeat the whole process as soon as he *has* been helped. If trying to roll over is his chosen activity at that moment, he is not going to abandon his efforts just because it irritates his mother to have to keep rescuing him.

Put in a baby chair, with objects he has not seen a thousand times already on the tray before him, he may occupy himself for some time, looking and touching and eventually mouthing them. But he is just as likely to knock the one that interests him most off the tray, and then cry.

Placed in his pram with objects hung above him, he may hit and swing them delightedly for 20 minutes. Or he may try to get hold of one, discover that he cannot because it swings, and cry.

Almost everything the baby of this age wants most to do requires help from the mother. He has very little control yet over himself or his world.

Often social play is the only thing the baby wants. He does not want to play with objects, to look at things, to kick and play physically. He wants to interact with his mother. Where giving him a toy will sometimes pacify and please him and sometimes not, giving him mother will always succeed. Where he may or may not enjoy himself on a rug on the floor, he will unfailingly enjoy himself on his mother's lap. Where his own activities may make him smile and talk or may not, pleasure in his mother's activities will always do so. Without fairly constant help and attention and plenty of freely given social play, he gets bored; when he is bored, he gets cross.

It is difficult to imagine what it must feel like to be so totally dependent on someone else for almost every activity. Difficult to conceive of having no autonomy, no independence, of being utterly in someone else's hands for day-to-day happiness. Of course there is no real parallel with any adult experience, because an infant's expectations are not the same as an older person's. Nevertheless, an experienced infants' nurse had her view of an infant's life radically altered when she had a stroke, and lay for some weeks more or less helpless in bed. She could not speak and, for a while, she could barely move. When she recovered, she picked out as supremely irritating the very things which adults do to infants without thinking about them. She mentioned her desperate efforts to communicate with people, by facial expression and the few sounds she could make. All too often the people turned away, unaware that she was trying to communicate, or too impatient to work out what she was trying to 'say'. She mentioned, too, the fury which she felt when people looked after her physical needs as if her body was an object, swiping a flannel across her face before she had had time to see that a wash was imminent, or chatting with somebody else while they dealt with her incontinence. She likened people's attempts to provide her with entertainment to her own previous behaviour with infants, too. Saying: 'They would switch on the television, and say to themselves, "There, that should keep her happy," but it would be a programme I had seen before – it was just like handing a baby a rattle every time it grumbled, without stopping to think whether it could possibly have any further interest in that same old toy.'

Some mothers find it very rewarding to be so necessary to their infants socially as well as physically. They take pride and pleasure in the baby's pleasure in *them*, and pride and pleasure also in keeping the baby interested and 'busy' whenever he is awake. Other mothers react quite differently: they feel that the social demands of these months are not legitimate in the way that the demands of the neonatal weeks are. They can accept ravenous hunger or discomfort as a valid reason for demanding attention, but they cannot accept boredom or loneliness in a similar way. They feel that if he is comfortable in his pram, and has a rattle to play with, the baby *ought* to be content, that he has no right to demand more of them.

In extreme cases a really vicious circle begins. The baby fusses because he is bored, and the mother decides he is getting spoiled. So instead of offering him more company and

fun, thus dealing with the boredom, she offers him less because he has 'got to learn'. Offered less, left to fuss and then to
cry alone, the baby eventually goes to sleep. But next day he
is even quicker to fuss. His needs are not being met, and he
begins to anticipate boredom and loneliness whenever he is
put in his cot or pram or playpen. As he gets more difficult, so
the mother's attitude hardens. She will not give in to him. He
becomes, in her mind, a demanding monster whom she has to
defeat.

Sometimes such a pattern of sadness lasts between mother
and child until, with mobility, the baby becomes more able
to *take* what he needs; able to crawl after mother; to find
things to handle and explore. Then, at last, he may calm
down, and the mother may feel she won the battle with her
spoiled infant. The tragedy is that it was a totally one-sided
battle in the first place.

A baby in this age group does not know how to demand
more than he actually needs. His needs and his wants are still
the same thing. If he wants company, it is because he needs it.
If he needs a new plaything he will also want it. He has not
the sophistication to 'try it on'. You cannot 'spoil' a child so
young that he has no idea of other people's feelings, no idea
of right and wrong, appropriate and inappropriate, no idea
of other people's rights. If such a child is given the attention
and the help which he shows he can use, he will demand less
because he is busy and happy, not more and more.

Of course the family's practical circumstances make an
enormous difference to the ease with which this stage (and all
other stages) can be handled. Ideally, the baby needs several
complete changes of scene during his waking day, whether
these are from house to garden to street, or simply from room
to room within the house. And he needs many changes of
physical position and type of activity, as well as lots of different objects or 'toys'. When he tires of lying quietly in his
pram watching the trees, he will welcome a sit in his baby-
chair with objects to mouth. When he tires of those objects, he
will probably be happier with a complete change, to kicking
on the floor. When that becomes boring he may be happy

sitting in his cot with objects in his lap. And all the while, the changing scene – his mother doing interesting things, friends coming in, other children playing – entertains him as a cinema entertains adults. When everything else is boring, mother, interacting directly and exclusively with him, is riveting. An infant only gets bored on his mother's lap if she ignores him and talks to someone else while he sits there.

Space, money, friends and not too many other demands make it easy for the mother to give her infant this sort of day. Poor accommodation, other young children, demanding and inconvenient domestic responsibilities make it infinitely more difficult.

Simply in terms of time, the mother who can do a week's shopping in the family car and store it in a large fridge, pop the day's washing in an automatic machine and call running a vacuum cleaner over carpeted floors 'housework' has an enormous advantage over the mother who must push the pram daily to distant shops, queue in a launderette, and wash linoleum. Somehow these simple facts are too often ignored in research into child-rearing.

Emotional circumstances may be even more important. A mother who is overwhelmed by her responsibilities, or who feels guilty at dropping out of her former profession, or resents losing the economic freedom and company of her previous job can easily become depressed during these months. If such a mother is too turned in upon herself to react to the infant's social advances, to spot his cues and to respond to him, he will get little from her. When this happens the infant will often add to her misery by appearing to reject her on the few occasions when she forces herself to make social advances to him. He may seem to prefer his father or some other regular visitor. Another vicious circle is set up, with the mother feeling that she is giving more than she has got to spare and is getting nothing back. Where this happens, the best facilities, the highest income, will not make these easy months.

Unfortunately, while depression immediately after a birth is now widely accepted in our society, with nobody expressing surprise if the mother weeps ceaselessly a week after delivery, this later depression, when the drama of the newborn period is over, is little recognized. It can ruin these months for both mother and child. Drugs from a sympathetic G.P. can help, husbands can help, friends can help – if only they realize that help is needed.

Just as vicious circles can be set up between mother and infant during these months, so can beneficial ones. The more a mother does enjoy interacting with her infant, the more the baby will respond and therefore the more she will feel inclined to give him time and attention. This was made very clear in the pilot study reported by David and Appell.[74]

They made detailed observations of the minute-to-minute interaction, at home, of 25 infants with their mothers in Paris. They found a very wide variation in the amount and the nature of the interaction between different mother–baby pairs. But they also found that almost all that variation was due to differences in the behaviour of the *mothers*, not of the babies. Whenever a mother made a social advance to her infant, by smiling at him, talking to him or picking him up, the baby reacted with pleasure and affection, smiling back, stroking her, babbling and generally rewarding her. No baby was ever seen to ignore a maternal advance unless he was fast asleep. But many mothers, on many occasions, failed to respond to advances made by their infants. Sometimes they directly ignored the infant's social talk; sometimes they simply failed to notice his brightening face as they came within view; sometimes they walked straight past him as he 'greeted' her. It was the same mothers who most often failed to respond to their infants socially, who told the interviewers that they were bored with baby-care.

Child developmentalists all pay at least lip-service to the idea that a child's experiences in his earliest months and years are important to his later development as a person. This proposition is notoriously difficult to prove, scientifically, because such a host of other relationships and experiences interpose themselves between the baby in his mother's care and the child he later becomes. It is impossible to prove that a 5-year-old is as he is because of the way he was handled as a baby. It is even impossible to demonstrate a relationship between specific aspects of infant rearing, and later characteristics. It may seem logical that the 7-year-old who sucks his thumb was one who was severely weaned as a baby, but it cannot be proved. Many eminent research workers have tried and failed to show this kind of relationship.

Many people have now reached the conclusion that this whole question of the general atmosphere which prevails between mother and child is probably more important than any specific practice. It looks as though what the mother does, in terms of weaning, or toilet training, or methods of discipline, matters much less than how she does it, in terms of how much she enjoys the child. Of course these nebulous variables of 'enjoying a child' or 'being comfortable in the role of mother' are very difficult to define and therefore to measure, but some research data, excellently reviewed by Ainsworth,[81] suggest that the effort of definition and measurement is worthwhile. The atmospheric variables affect and describe the immediate happiness of mother and baby. But they also appear to have far-reaching effects in terms of the child's later development.

Schaffer and Emerson[46, 66] closely studied and assessed the development of babies of 18 months. There was wide variation between one baby and another on all aspects of development and in degree of attachment to the mother. But there was no relationship at all between the current development and attachment of any one baby and anything which his mother had done in earlier months about feeding or weaning or toilet training. On the other hand, they found a very clear relationship between the babies' current development and attachment and the readiness with which the mothers responded, and always had responded, to their crying. There was an equally clear relationship between the current development and how often the mother did start, and always had started, social interchanges with their infants. The highly attentive, responsive, socializing mothers were the ones who had the infants who were well advanced in all fields and strongly attached to them.

The importance to infants' happiness and optimum development of sensitive responses and social initiative from their mothers has even been demonstrated in Israeli kibbutzim, where infants see very little of their parents, being principally cared for by professional nurses. Gewirtz and Gewirtz[82] found that in this situation infants did not become particularly attached to the nurses who fed and cared for them all day. They reserved their principal attachment for their parents. The nurses were too busy with groups of infants to be able to give much individual attention to any one child. The parents had only a short daily period with their infants, but devoted it to social interaction with them. The concentrated social attention seemed to mean more to the infants than the continuous physical care.

So perhaps mothers should be encouraged to see their infants as interesting, to discover that they are fun to talk to and to play with, that if their social needs are fulfilled they are rewarding companions. It looks as if the mother who can discover all this will be laying good foundations for her baby's later development, as well as having fun giving him fun here and now.

SIX MONTHS' SUMMARY

By 6 months the infant is not only increasingly complex and individual, he is also so emotionally bound up with people, especially the mother, that his actual behaviour is intimately tied up with hers. His crying may be almost non-existent or it may be frequent – depending on his rapport with the mother. His motor play will be optimal only if she gives him opportunities and help. His dexterity in getting and handling objects will partly depend on what she offers him, while his 'talking' will be more frequent and more varied the more she talks directly to him.

But by no means all the variation between the stages reached by 6-month babies is under the mother's control. Even at this age those differences between the premature or slow-starting babies, and others, may remain. If a baby gets off to a slow start, he still has to go through all the stages of all aspects of development. While, once his newborn troubles are over, he may go through some of them faster than most, he is still likely to show a lag at least in some areas. Once again, then, these pointers to the behaviours which are likely at 6 months are only useful in the light of detailed knowledge of which earlier stages the baby has already passed through.

BEHAVIOUR	LIKELY STAGE REACHED AT 6 MONTHS	COMMENTS
Feeding	3 meals and a fourth bottle or breast-feed per 24 hours.	The most usual pattern is for the fourth milk feed to be a late-night one. The fifth milk feed, early in the

BEHAVIOUR	LIKELY STAGE REACHED AT 6 MONTHS	COMMENTS
Feeding		morning, may not have been given up until 4–5 months. Some mothers may prefer to continue this feed and drop the late-night one. Either way the three remaining meals will approximate to ordinary family meal times.
Food	Puréed solids at all 3 meals. Some finger foods such as rusks, apple quarters or cut-up vegetables.	Balance of quantity between milk and solids still very variable, depending on when solids were introduced, and the infant's preferences. Milk intake should not drop below about 1 pint (570ml) per day.
Feeding method	Most infants will be taking some milk from a cup. The few who were breast-fed will mostly be weaned from the breast by now: some to a bottle, some direct to a cup.	Infants who are not offered breast or bottle will tend to take less milk.
	Solid food given in high chair or baby-chair rather than on mother's lap.	Infants will wish to wield spoon, albeit inaccurately. Will like to pick up and self-feed pieces of food.

BEHAVIOUR	LIKELY STAGE REACHED AT 6 MONTHS	COMMENTS
Food preferences	Often marked. May prefer liquid or crisp textures, reject thick purées.	Infant will not starve himself. Brief sucking at beginning of meal may lead to acceptance of solids which would otherwise be rejected.
Weight	Gains very roughly 5 oz. (145g) per week from 3–6 months, i.e. baby born weighing 7 lb. (3·2kg) will now weigh roughly 15½ lb. (7kg).	Consistent gain far more important than high gain. May gain extremely rapidly following illness. High gains are no virtue under other circumstances. Fat babies tend to become fat adults.
Sleep	Roughly a 12-hour night, barely interrupted by a late feed, and either 2 or 3 separate naps of varying length.	Sleep needs are as variable now as earlier, but likely to be consistent with earlier ages, sleepy babies continuing to need more than wakeful ones.
Crying	Discomfort usually causes grizzling before actual crying begins. Full-throated *sudden* crying only usual following fright or pain. Night crying may be due to nightmares. Daytime crying often due to boredom or	Amount of crying largely depends on sensitivity of baby (to noise, etc.) and on sensitivity of mother to his cues. Crying is no longer a normal part of the infant's day as it still was at 3 months. He now has other

BEHAVIOUR	LIKELY STAGE REACHED AT 6 MONTHS	COMMENTS
Crying	loneliness. Unless really upset by long neglect or frank illness, always stops crying when picked up by mother.	signalling mechanisms at his disposal if his caretakers are alert to them.
Teething	Lower central incisor is cut, on average, at 6 months.	Normal children can be born with a tooth, or cut no teeth in the first year. Teething is not an indication of overall development. Teething may cause a sore gum, dribbling, occasional fretfulness. It does not cause changes in stools, fevers, rashes or other signs of illness. Cutting of teeth is not an indication for weaning from breast or bottle.
Motor activities	Rolls from stomach on to back. 1–4 weeks later rolls from back on to stomach. On back, raises head from flat surface. Strains forward if propped sitting. Uses all four limbs in rhythmic smooth kicking.	Ages are variable, the order is not. Takes obvious pleasure in gross physical exercise.

BEHAVIOUR	LIKELY STAGE REACHED AT 6 MONTHS	COMMENTS
Motor Activities	Lying on stomach alternates head-up position, with chest lifted by forearms or hands, with bottom-up position, with legs bent under him. May momentarily manage to keep both head and bottom up, thus being in crawling position. True crawling is unusual at this age, but some progress on floor may be made by slithering and/or rolling.	Safety precautions are needed, as progress across the floor is unpredictable.
Sitting	Lying on back, pulls himself to sitting using adult's hands as handles only. Can sit with minimal support to lower back. May sit alone, leaning forward to use own hands for support.	Likes to sit, where he can see the world, most of the time he is awake. Needs pillows around him, as still topples unexpectedly.
Standing	Tries to pull self to standing when on adult's lap. Held standing, takes full weight; typically 'bounces' as alternately straightens and relaxes knees.	May virtually refuse to *sit* on lap. Many infants regard laps as trampolines at this age.

BEHAVIOUR	LIKELY STAGE REACHED AT 6 MONTHS	COMMENTS
Grasping and manual play	Concentrated play with own hands is dying down; may be partly replaced by discovery of own feet, which are handled and put in mouth.	Objects are always explored by mouth as well as by hand.
	Reaches swiftly and accurately for objects, usually using two-handed approach. Objects usually picked up using palmar grasp; cannot yet take small objects between finger and thumb.	
	Drops first object if given another. Cannot voluntarily let go of objects.	Little use yet made of objects apart from exploration.
Social responses	Very marked. Infant prefers people to any other object, and his mother to any other person.	
	Smiles often, laughs, responds to talk with talk. Often tries to instigate social inter-action, by smiling or talking or waving towards mother.	Heavily reliant on mother for play and entertainment as well as for physical care.
	May object when left, especially by mother. Anticipates normal	

BEHAVIOUR	LIKELY STAGE REACHED AT 6 MONTHS	COMMENTS
Social responses	happenings, 'greeting' mother when she comes in, expressing excitement at meal or outing preparations.	
Hearing and speech	Turns his head and body towards source of sound. Clear pattern of answering with sound when someone talks to him. Babble now contains distinct consonants, and may begin to be intonated.	Even deaf babies babble. Infant's *reaction* to sound is only indication of normal hearing.
	Talks most either when being talked to, or when happily alone, often when he wakes in the morning.	Infants who are talked to a great deal will be more vocal than others. Girls may be more vocal than boys.

SECTION IV

FROM SIX TO TWELVE MONTHS: BROADENING HIS WORLD

CHAPTER NINETEEN

THE INFANT WITHIN THE FAMILY

During the second half of the first year, the relationship which mother and child have made tends to be put to the test. The infant does not develop as rapidly during this period as he did in the first half year, but the developments that take place have a dramatic impact on his mother and the rest of his family. If the mother's relationship with the infant is basically positive, each of them enjoying the other's company, the drama is exciting even if exhausting. But if her relationship with the infant is already to some extent unsatisfactory – perhaps due to her fear of him becoming over-demanding and spoiled – it can seem horrific.

During these months, the infant becomes mobile. His achievement of mobility is the logical extension of the motor abilities he acquired earlier. But the handling of a mobile infant in Western society is *not* a logical extension of the patterns of care the mother arrived at earlier. Non-mobile infants in our society can be, and are, put down out of harm's way and left for varying periods while their mothers do other things than care for them. We expect to have both our hands free and our backs unburdened. And we expect to be able to move freely around our houses. But as the infant learns to roll, to slither, to crawl, to pull himself to standing, and to climb, these expectations have to be revised. Ordinary domestic settings become death traps for the infant, for he acquires his mobility in fits and unpredictable starts, without a vestige of extra good sense to go with it. His mother has to have sense and foresight for both of them, with new abilities and therefore new dangers arising literally from one day to the next.

Previously the infant may have fitted quite smoothly into the domestic setting established before his birth. Room had to be found for his various 'holding devices' – his pram, cot, chair and so on – but otherwise things could be as before. In these months safety devices like fireguards, dummy electric plugs, stairgates and cooker guards have to be installed. And once installed they are a continual inconvenience to other members of the household, who must step over or reach round them as they go about their daily lives. Unless there is a special play area, set apart for the baby when he starts to rove, the whole family's convenience must suffer in other ways. Ornaments, gramophone records, books, must be banished on high or be chewed and broken. Coffee tables can no longer be used for hot cups of coffee; tablecloths can only safely cover empty tables.

The infant spent earlier weeks painstakingly learning to pick things up. Now he can, and he will. Anything he can reach he will take, and anything he takes, he will chew. Two cigarettes might kill him. A cup of tea will scald his soft skin where it would barely redden his mother's. Even where real dangers are anticipated and avoided, there are continual minor annoyances. Wastepaper baskets are up-ended, cushions are pulled off chairs, stray letters are chewed to illegible pulp and the sleeping cat's tail pulled.

Earlier on the infant often got bored, but could be harmlessly entertained if his mother would give her time and thought to occupations for him. Increasingly in these months he thinks of his own. And somehow they are seldom the ones his mother considers suitable. He wants to play with the coal in the bucket and finds his mother's scoldings and bodily removals funny. Again and again he crawls towards that bucket looking at his mother from time to time over his shoulder. In the end either the coal or his mother's temper must go.

He becomes increasingly able to anticipate and to remember. His brightening and his rapid crawl towards the door when he hears his father's key in the lock may entrance both his parents. But the clamour he sets up for ice-cream whenever he is taken to the shops is another matter. His mother used to buy him an ice-cream as an occasional treat, and enjoy his pleasure in it. She may not at all enjoy his demanding it as of right.

Along with all this, the infant's vocal range is rapidly increasing and being put to good use. He no longer divides his sounds between crying, grumbling and pleasant cooing. He learns to shout for attention, to scream his anger or frustration, to clamour at his mother to stop talking on the telephone, or to his father, or to his sister, and talk to *him*.

So the infant increases his impact on his immediate surroundings, and demands increasing, continuous, watchful care from his mother. At the same time he is likely to demand increasing social interaction with her, and to push their whole relationship on to a more and more emotional plane.

By 6 months, the infant who has been making it clear for weeks that he knows his mother from other people, begins to single her out for more and more special attention. Yarrow[47] has shown that where at 4–5 months an infant may treat his mother and a strange woman to equal shares of smiles and talk, by 6 months he will probably ignore the stranger altogether, or give her a sombre stare. All his smiles are now reserved for the known and loved person. Ainsworth[48] found that at around 6 months there were a whole range of behaviours, both gross and subtle, which infants began to reserve exclusively for their mothers. Infants who were in a room with several familiar adults and the mother would always strive to follow if the mother left, but would never try to follow anyone else. If the infant was worried, he would bury his face in his mother's skirt – but not in anyone else's. Playing with the mother, the infant would pat her face, play with her hair and explore her body; such intimacies were granted to no one else. Even certain facial expressions and sounds seemed to be reserved for the mother alone.

Most mothers regard such special behaviours as positive signs of the infant's affection for them. They are gratifying, flattering to the mother. But other emotional changes which are less easy to tolerate tend to arise soon after them. The negative side of the infant's passionate attachment to his mother often begins to show itself in the two separate but related phenomena usually known as '*separation anxiety*' and '*stranger anxiety*'. The baby not only shows his mother special signs of favour, he also objects increasingly strongly whenever she leaves him, and he often objects also to contact with anyone whom he does not know and love.

Separation anxiety and stranger anxiety have been the subject of much argument and some research. Spitz[83] sees them as the same thing, and as both arising directly out of the infant's new ability to differentiate his mother from other people. He argues that as soon as the child 'knows' his own mother, he objects to her going out of his sight, and that the reason he appears to fear strangers is that in some way the presence of a stranger suggests to the infant that his mother has gone.

This argument is misleading in several important ways. Firstly, stranger anxiety seldom manifests itself before 8 months. Indeed Spitz names both these anxieties "8 months' anxiety". He therefore argues that 8 months must be the earliest age at which most infants can differentiate their mother from other people. This is in direct contradiction to the large body of work already mentioned, showing that differentiation begins months earlier.

Secondly, Spitz rests his argument against stranger anxiety being different from separation anxiety on the statement that the infant cannot be actually afraid of strangers, since he has no cause for fear – no stranger has ever hurt him. Again such an argument runs counter to the large body of work, both with human and animal infants, which shows that strangeness is, in itself, enough to cause fear. If it were not, we should all be able to cuddle newborn lambs and calves. Thirdly, infants often demonstrate their fear of strangers while in actual physical contact with their mothers. Spitz disputes this, maintaining that for a child to show fear of a stranger while he can see or feel his mother's presence is highly unusual. But it has been carefully demonstrated by Morgan and Ricciuti.[84]

The opposing point of view, which sees separation anxiety and stranger anxiety as two separate but related phenomena, is well discussed in detail by Bowlby.[12]

In terms of handling an individual child in a particular set of circumstances, it may be vital for a mother to be able to decide whether it is anxiety over separation from her which is upsetting her baby, or anxiety over contact with strangers, or both. A baby who is in hospital, with his mother rooming in, will have to be left by her for a few minutes at a time while she goes to the lavatory or the telephone. If his main horror is separation from her in this strange setting, he may be upset when she leaves him, and somewhat comforted if a nurse will chat to him until she returns. But if stranger anxiety is more of a problem to him than separation, he may stay calm for those few minutes *unless* a well-meaning nurse stops to chat. Similarly if a mother must leave her baby and go out to work, there is little she can do to save him heartbreak if the separation is what is making him miserable. But if the fact that his caretaker is a stranger lies at the root of his misery, there may be a great deal that she can do, in terms of finding a known person to look after him, or taking some weeks to accustom him to the mother substitute.

Unfortunately present research findings can be of little help to such a mother. Few issues in emotional development are simple, and these are more complex than most. There is little unanimity among research workers as to how separation anxiety and stranger anxiety should be defined; there is no unanimity about the ages at which the feelings are likely to show themselves for the first time, reach a peak of intensity or die away. It is even difficult to state the proportion of children who are likely to show either kind of anxiety at any stage of their lives.

Taking a very rough consensus among various workers, mixed with a large dash of observation, it seems that where a close attachment to the mother has been fostered by continual care by her, with little care by other people, separation anxiety will show itself before stranger anxiety. Some degree of worry when the mother goes out of sight is more usual than not by around 7 months. Once it has begun, it may well continue for a long time, certainly into the second year.

Anxiety over contact with strangers is probably less general than anxiety over being left by the mother. Some infants never seem worried by strangers. Those who are going to manifest anxiety usually start to do so around 9 months. And the anxiety may be less long-lasting than separation anxiety, with the infant described as 'thoroughly sociable' by the time he is 18 months.

The problems of precision in describing these phenomena are immense. The reactions of an individual baby on a particular day depend on a vast complex of variables, including those which are themselves difficult to assess, such as his mood or his fatigue. But they also depend on practical variables so peculiar to one baby in one setting that it is almost impossible to make generalizations. The research worker can only record the behaviour of the baby, and use that behaviour to 'place' him on some scale of separation anxiety. He can arrange that the separation experience should be the same for all the research subjects, but he cannot arrange that all the infants should be in a similar mood, nor that the controlled experience should be just as novel for all. Some everyday situations make these difficulties clear:

At 6–8 months, when separation anxiety may be expected to be building up, an infant may be an efficient crawler, or still totally immobile. If he is mobile, he will be accustomed to dealing with his mother going out of sight by attempting to crawl after her. If, at home, he is accustomed to being able to follow her about, he may be confident and secure, and therefore not very anxious. At the same time, a physical barrier, such as being in a playpen, or behind a closed door, may shock him, frustrate him, more than the same barrier would shock an immobile child who has not yet known the joy of being able to follow.

Similarly some fortunate infants are accustomed to a daily life situation where they are seldom left by the mother when they are awake. Domestic arrangements may be such that kitchen, play-space, garden, telephone and front door all adjoin, so that the mother seldom needs to go further out of sight than round the corner. Such an infant may not manifest much separation anxiety. The mother may believe that he is not anxious in this way. But if she had to move to a house where the infant spent most of his time in a room quite separate from her work-space, she might discover that he instantly became very anxious indeed.

Again, some infants have been accustomed since birth to accepting a variety of substitutes as well as the mother. In an experimental situation, the mother's prearranged departure from the room may seem to him similar to her daily departure for work. His reaction may be to look around for her substitute, rather than to yearn after her.

Clearly then, the experimenter, however carefully he sets up a controlled situation of temporary separation from the mother, and however carefully he records the infant's reactions to it, cannot fully understand his results. The baby's reactions are dependent not only on his mood, but also on minutiae of his normal daily life which even the most skilful retrospective interviewing cannot hope to elicit.

For practical purposes it is probably safest to assume that at some ages, on some days, and in some circumstances, all infants will be made anxious by separation from the mother. Safest in the sense that attempts to override the infant's objections, ignore his tears and detach his clinging arms will almost always make him worse. Sometimes such experiences of being made acutely anxious lead to lasting problems which are extremely inconvenient for the mother, as well as unpleasant for the child. If a playpen is always used to keep the baby safe while the mother goes upstairs, and the baby begins to object to this separation, he can quickly reach a point where he begins to panic whenever he is lifted in. Similarly if the mother gets tired of the baby's clinging and following as she moves around the house, and puts him in his cot, alone, he may come to associate his cot with lonely separation, and start sleeping problems which bedevil the whole family for months.

Most infants only react extremely to vanishing mothers when they actually see them depart. The infant may be entirely content to wake alone in his cot, and talk and play until his mother comes to him. Equally if he was absorbed in play when she left the room, he may be unalarmed when he realizes he is alone, and only begin to search and worry for her

after several minutes. Often sound is a reassurance. The infant can hear his mother moving around in the next room, or
hear her speaking on the telephone. He knows where she is,
knows that she has not vanished out of his familiar world, and
therefore he does not demand her until he needs her for something. On the other hand, the mother of a highly anxious
child who makes a practice of slipping away while he is busy
may make matters worse. Often one can see this happening
when the child is left to sleep in his cot or in his pram. The
mother settles him, spends some moments fiddling, just
within his view, perhaps with the toys that hang on his pram.
Then, at a moment when the child is looking at the trees overhead, or getting his fist to his mouth, she slips away. A yell of
betrayed fury follows. And if the pattern is repeated often
enough, the infant may come to anticipate this kind of sur-
reptitious departure, so that he begins to fuss at the mere
sight of pram or cot, knowing that they spell desertion. On the
whole, with most infants, anxiety is less if the infant is told,
by word, intonation and gesture, when the mother is going
to leave him. She may adopt a ritual of departure, such that
she puts the baby down, tucks him in, adjusts the pram hood,
hands him his teddy bear, says, 'See you soon,' and leaves.
There may still be tears, but they are tears at being left, not
tears at being betrayed.

Separation when the infant is awake and up is usually best
handled by avoidance whenever that is possible, and by calling the infant's attention to it when it is inevitable. The
anxious infant who never knows whether he is going to look
up and find his mother gone, can become the infant who keeps
so constant an eye on his mother that he cannot play. If she
must leave the room, and cannot take the baby with her, the
mother can say she is going, and use whatever phrase the
infant is accustomed to – 'Shan't be a minute' or 'Back soon'
– and then continue to talk to the infant as she carries the
laundry downstairs, or whatever. Again the infant may cry,
but his confidence is rebuilt a little each time his mother
reappears as promised.

Separations lasting hours or days rather than minutes

raise different problems. The infant at the height of his attachment to his mother, and anxiety over separation from
her, will not easily tolerate such separations. His understanding of time and of space is negligible. He cannot hold in
his mind a picture of his mother, nor of where she is. He cannot grasp the landmarks so useful with older children, such
as, 'Mummy will come by dinner time.' If she is gone, out of
his sight, for longer than his short memory-span then, as far as
we know, she is gone entirely from the infant's point of view.
She is not where she usually is. She does not do for him what
she usually does. And he has no way of understanding that the
change is temporary. Some people scoffingly refuse to accept
this. They may say, 'You surely cannot believe that the baby
whose mother goes out for the afternoon believes that she will
never come back?' Of course the infant does not *think* this.
He does not have the concepts with which to put such an idea
together. But equally he does not have the concepts with
which to put together the idea that she is sure to come back
soon, that she loves him and would not desert him. All he can
know is that she is gone. And it seems likely that since he is
not yet an autonomous person, who can function without the
adult care he is used to getting from his mother, he is left
with an empty aching void, and a confused sense of loss of
his own identity. His other half, his support, his control, his
interpreter of the world is missing.

Infants should not be expected to span hours or days without a completing adult half. On the other hand, they cannot,
in our culture at least, have their mothers constantly with
them. Mothers often want, and are usually expected, to fill
other roles as well as the mothering one. Fortunately infants
can be provided with substitute attachment figures, to whom
they can turn in the mother's absence. These secondary
people can usually hold them in equilibrium during brief
periods of separation. Fathers, grandparents, nannies and
close friends often fill this role. Even day nurseries and
children's hospitals can, by taking sufficient trouble over
their staffing arrangements, go some way towards providing
babies with mother-substitutes rather than simply caretakers.

For ordinary families there is a great deal to be said for arranging that the baby has the opportunity to become attached to some available person. Without this second string to his emotional bow, the infant whose mother has to go to hospital or on some other urgent trip can be left in a truly desperate plight. Even with a known mother-substitute, he will not feel quite safe, quite 'himself' until his mother returns. But his boat has sunk, leaving him on a life-raft, not struggling in the sea of complete despair.[85]

Clearly stranger anxiety, even if it is not the *same* as separation anxiety, is closely related to it. In ordinary daily life, association with strangers is often part of a separation experience. If a child is left with a strange babysitter, and objects, it is impossible to know whether he is objecting to his mother's absence or the stranger's presence. Mothers' reports about their children's anxiety with strangers are often similarly confused. The baby may object to the clinic nurse undressing him. The mother thinks it is because she is strange, but it may be because he dislikes being held still for undressing, or even because he anticipates an injection such as he had at his last visit.

Morgan and Ricciuti[84] carried out a complex series of experiments with 80 children between 4 and 13 months. These studies have produced some hard facts out of the confusion.

They found that, overall, fear of strangers was less frequent (when the factor of separation from the mother had been excluded) than is usually thought. Furthermore anxiety became more frequent with increasing age, being almost absent in the 6-month babies, and reaching a peak at 1 year. It would certainly, from this sample, have been inappropriate to label it '8 months' anxiety'.

At 6 months there was only one mildly negative reaction to the stranger. All the other babies of this age not only accepted the strangers, but became increasingly sociable as they approached and talked to them. And they were happy to respond to the strangers' advances whether they were seated on their mothers' laps, or in a baby chair some feet away from her.

Slightly increasing numbers of 8-, 10- and 12-month babies evinced some degree of distress at the presence of a stranger. This distress was increased both in the number of babies it affected, and in intensity, both by distance from the mother, and by closeness to the stranger. By 12 months, babies could only tolerate the stranger if there was distance between them, and physical contact between baby and mother. Even so, more than half the 12-month babies were clearly uneasy. Any attempt by the stranger actually to touch the older babies evoked anxiety. On the other hand, smiling and nodding to the baby from a distance, playing a sort of 'peek-a-boo', evoked a pleased response from almost all of them.

Taking this study, together with the existing literature, it does seem that we may overestimate the tendency of infants to fear strangers in *themselves*, and underestimate the importance of what those strangers do. Some adults are shyer than others. But even the least shy would be disconcerted if a total stranger strode up in the street and hugged them. Similarly infants are often labelled as 'shy of strangers' because they object when their mothers hand them over to admiring friends to be dandled, or weep piteously when a passing stranger tickles them in their prams. Mothers who try to force their infants to accept physical advances from people they do not know probably increase their tendency to shy away. Just as detaching the arms of a clinging child only makes him more inclined to cling, so forcibly handing him to someone he does not want to go to can only increase his determination to keep away. If the child is allowed to go voluntarily from his mother's side to examine a strange visitor, not fearing physical capture on to her lap; if he is allowed to play 'peek-a-boo' with strangers in shops, safely perched on his mother's shoulder, and not anticipating being handed over by her, he is far more likely to feel secure about exploring people. It even seems likely that he will eventually go more willingly to playgroup or nursery school or the houses of his friends.

Some mothers do not see the emotional demands which infants make during these months as 'demands' at all. They

are so attuned to the infant, so well-rewarded for their sensitive mothering by his flattering attachment, that they meet
the needs without thinking about them. Such mothers tend to
talk constantly to their babies, to interact with them a great
deal, to be always on the alert, noticing the infant's smiling
gesture as they pass, and pausing to share what he is showing
them even as they go about their own affairs. Many such
women would feel it downright rude to walk down the street
with the baby sitting facing them in a pushchair, and *not*
chat. They would find it impossible to sit and read a book
while the baby watched them. But other mothers feel more
detached from the infant. They do not see him as a person, a
companion – albeit a young one. And therefore they have to
make a deliberate effort to meet the high emotional needs
of this age period. In extreme cases the mother may consciously resent the infant's dependence and his refusal to
accept other people. If a mother once begins to feel sucked dry
by the demands of the infant, his behaviour can fuel her
resentment almost hour by hour. She goes to answer the door
and he cries; she returns and calms him and tries to do the
ironing while listening to the radio – he shouts for attention.
A friend comes for coffee and the baby refuses to get off her
lap or to keep quiet while she chats. When the friend leaves
the mother goes to the lavatory. The baby screams and, if he
is mobile, probably thunders piteously on the door. The
mother becomes more and more convinced that she is being
destroyed as a person in her own right. She is increasingly impatient of the infant's emotional demands; and the more she
rejects them, the stronger they become.

We do not know why some mothers find it easy and some
find it difficult. The reasons must be as diverse as the experiences and personalities of all mothers and all babies put
together, so there will never be generalized answers. But
ironically it does seem that the pattern repeats itself over the
generations, so that mothers who have been closely and
sensitively mothered themselves find it easier to give this
sensitive mothering to their infants, who will, in their turn,
find parenthood rewarding. The converse – insensitive

mothering following insensitive mothering – emerged clearly in a study of battered babies carried out in America.[86] Parents who physically damaged their children, through 'punishment' or 'rough' handling, and who were unable to control their tempers (much though they usually wished to be 'good parents') seemed to lack in their own lives what Erikson[87] called 'basic trust'. They had no sense of their own worth, and could not make their children feel worthy. They did not feel valued themselves and could not make their children feel valued. They did not believe that other people could understand them or meet their needs, and they could not understand nor meet the needs of their children. Perhaps 'basic trust' is the prime benefit of the baby who, hour after hour, day after day, finds himself adequately cared for, adequately understood, sensitively responded to and enjoyed by the mother.

Happily not many parents batter their babies, producing physical injury which requires medical attention. The actual numbers cannot be assessed, since doctors vary in their alertness to the possibility of battering when they see an injured child, parents vary in their readiness to seek medical aid, and hospitals vary in their readiness to report or record such incidents.

But a surprisingly large number of mothers not only physically punish children of this age group, but are prepared to say so to an interviewer. In the Newsons' study,[18] for example, 62 per cent of mothers reported that they had smacked their babies before they were 1 year old. Of course the smacks ranged from a reminding pat on the hand, through a stinging slap on the legs, to a few real blows. But the *concept* of physical punishment for babies was clearly present. And it is a peculiar one.

A baby of this age who is punished cannot, realistically, be being punished for anything other than being a baby, or having a momentarily neglectful or forgetful mother. His behaviour is under *her* control; his 'goodness' is *her* business: it is an essential part of her mothering job to keep him safe and acceptable within his home setting. When he breaks an ornament he does so because his vital curiosity tells him to examine it, his neurophysiological control is too immature for him to examine it gently and his memory span is too short for him to remember that his mother told him not to. His mother forgot to put it out of his reach. Punishment seems irrelevant. Many mothers would accept this, but still say, 'He ought to know better than to tip his dinner out of the dish all over my nice clean floor!' But why should he? A few minutes before, the mother herself was helping him tip bricks out on the floor. Is he supposed to share his mother's ideas about play materials versus eating materials? And as to that clean floor, the mother spent half the morning swooshing bubbly water over it; is the baby supposed to *understand* that soapy water cleans things and gravy dirties them?

Often the stresses which lead a mother actually to punish her baby arise out of his effect on other family members. Sometimes fathers are appalled by the asocial behaviour of infants whom they see very little, and do not understand. Grandmothers may imply that babies in their day were not allowed to behave like this or like that. The mere presence of an irritated father or disapproving grandmother can make the mother far less tolerant than she would be if she were alone with the baby. Feeling that his behaviour is reflecting badly on her, she may be more than usually inclined to slap him and dump him weeping in his cot. Again, older children may complain bitterly (and with reason) when handfuls of their hair are pulled out. The mother has learned to avoid this hazard for herself, but she may feel that justice demands that the older child should see the younger punished. All mothers have to work out the delicate tightrope of their family relationships for themselves. But punishments, at this age, are almost always pointless. The baby will mind the smack, but he will not understand the reasoning behind it. And because he does not understand it, the punishments are liable to escalate. If he is smacked for playing with an electric plug, he will forget in a few minutes. When he returns to the plug his mother is liable to smack him harder. The third time he does it she may lose her temper. It is far easier to avoid starting to punish than it is to stop in the face of what appears to be defiance.

And some punishments are dangerous. A smack that was intended to be gentle can catch a child off balance so that he bangs his head. Shaking him can produce a whiplash effect. His head is still heavy relative to his neck, and actual brain haemorrhages have been reported as a result of the brain banging inside the skull.[88] The mother may also pay dearly for less violent punishments. Being isolated from the mother as a punishment can suddenly increase a child's separation anxiety to fever pitch, so that for weeks he can barely be persuaded to let go of her skirt; being put to bed as a punishment can start sleeping problems.

Somehow the mother has to find ways of staying on the infant's side; of refusing to allow herself to feel against him; of nipping her own resentment in the bud and finding other ways of venting her stresses. Unfortunately our society's ideal is of the mother who mothers sensitively and likes it. To admit that you cannot or do not enjoy this stage of mothering is to admit to a kind of failure. Yet the various units which have been set up to *prevent* baby-battering, and the research groups which have studied mother–child relationships within this age group have all found that mothers were relieved simply to be allowed to admit to being irritated, without feeling censured. It is not easy being the other half of a developing person who is not yet a social being. If welfare authorities, husbands and friends knew this, and could admire mothers for managing it, rather than taking it for granted as 'natural', that in itself would make the job seem a little easier. After all, any difficult job seems more bearable if one is encouraged to be proud of oneself for doing it well.

CHAPTER TWENTY

MORE PHYSICAL FUNDAMENTALS

Feeding, sleep and toileting are the three main areas within which the physiological needs of infants are met. As such they are obviously important. A child who is not reasonably cared for in physical terms cannot develop fully in other areas. Yet in Western societies the importance of these physical-care issues tends to be over-stressed, especially once the newborn period, during which they are vital, is over. Eavesdropping on mothers chatting together at a welfare clinic, a baby's meals, his sleeping habits, his 'progress' in toilet training are continual subjects for riveting discussion. But a mother's attempt to discuss her baby's motor progress, his language development or his social understanding tends to receive only cursory attention. Hospitals, even those which pride themselves on their forward-looking arrangements for play and emotional care for sick children, put these a long way down the list of budget priorities. Excellent physical care always comes first. Even day nurseries – with some honourable exceptions – tend to show off their tiny toilets, their airy cots and their attractive menus. The visitor must ask if he wants to know how the children's other needs are catered for.

There is no doubt that any infant who can be persuaded to follow his mother's wishes in these areas makes her daily life comparatively easy. If he will eat what she puts before him, sleep when she puts him to bed and accept her toileting programme, her child care will be smooth. This is probably why success in any of these areas is such a subject for congratulation between mothers. A baby who will do these things is a 'good' baby. His mother is, by definition, a 'good' mother: she has not spoiled him or let him get away with anything. If such a good baby is also happy, active, alert and intelligent, well and good. But if he is not, he is still a good baby. On the other hand if he is alert, active and happy, but a fussy feeder who sleeps little and soils much, he is definitely *not* good.

A concern with issues which make the job of rearing an infant easier is obviously fair enough. But it is important that all those who are even marginally concerned with infant care should realize to whom these things are important. They matter to the mother, her convenience and her pride, far more than they matter to the baby. Just *because* eating and sleeping and eliminating are basic physiological functions, the infant, given normal care, will look after them for himself. If he is offered a reasonable diet, he will eat enough to keep himself well; he does not care whether his dinner constitutes a 'balanced meal' – it is his mother who cares. As long as he is not subject to acute physical or emotional stress, he will sleep as much as he needs to. He does not care if it is 5 a.m. when he finishes his night, but his mother does. Nothing but frank disease will make him harm himself from constipation; he will pass a motion when he needs to and only his mother cares whether it goes in a pot or his clothes. Very few normal children from ordinary families in Western societies reach school age starving, exhausted from lack of sleep or incontinent. But many well-nourished, rested, continent children reach school verbally incompetent, physically ill-coordinated and pitifully ignorant of the world and how it works.

Perhaps we should readjust our thinking a little, so that we sort out which issues are important to maternal convenience, and which are truly important for the child. The baby who makes good use of his time awake is just as 'good' for himself as the baby who goes to sleep on schedule is 'good' for his mother. From this standpoint mothers are at least as much to be congratulated on finding a new entrancing game for their infants as for finding a new baby cereal they will eat.

FEEDING

Traditionally, weaning is one of the major maternal preoccupations of this half year. It was during these months that infants had to be persuaded gradually to relinquish the breast or their bottles in favour of increasing quantities of solid food, with milk from a cup. But from the kind of information discussed in Chapter 13, and from observation of mother–baby pairs, it is clear that this pattern has changed. Infants are now normally given a wide range of solid foods from a very few weeks of age, so that their diet even at 3 months approximates to the diet of a 9-month baby a generation ago. Very few are breast-fed at all, and only an infinitesimal number are still breast-fed by 6 months. And the bottles are often not withdrawn. They simply stop being receptacles for 'feeds' and become receptacles for comfort drinks. Even where a mother does determinedly wean her infant from the bottle, she is more likely than ever before to provide him with alternatives. Dummies, for example, are widely used in the U.K. by all social classes, while learning to drink from a cup is eased by the use of cups with spouts from which the infant half sucks, half drinks. Present-day grandmothers can probably still remember exactly when they weaned today's mothers. But those mothers find it very difficult to say when they wean *their* babies; it depends what you mean by weaning.

The tendency to allow the infant bottles of milk at bedtime, or even bottles of milk *ad lib.*, while building up his diet towards a full mixed one, leads to some nutritional difficulties. As we saw in Chapter 13, no assessment can be made of any infant's food requirements until his milk intake is known. Once that milk has become a comfort and a beverage, rather than a food, even the mother may not know how much the baby actually drinks. If he drinks a good deal of milk, as we shall see, it is neither sensible nor desirable to expect him much to increase his intake of 'real' food, for he will only get fat. On the other hand if the bottle has been taken from him, or if it has been filled with juice rather than milk, so that his milk intake has dropped drastically, he will genuinely need far more solid food than before.

The food requirements of the infant do not rise in direct proportion to his age. In the early months he grew faster than he does in this second half-year. His requirements were therefore proportionately higher then than now. This is best reflected in the recommended intake of calories per lb. or kg of bodyweight. Table 9 compares the figures already given on page 194, with the figures for this second half-year.

TABLE 9. RECOMMENDED DAILY CALORIES AT 3–6 MONTHS COMPARED WITH 6–12 MONTHS

	Weight lb.	kg	kcal per lb.	per kg	Total kcal per 24 hours
3–6 months	14·4	6·6	52	115	760
6–12 months	19·6	8·9	49	107	955

The needs of any specific infant are, of course, related to his weight. Average birthweight babies who have not been made to put on weight too fast in the early months, will not reach 19 lb. (8·6kg) until around 9–10 months. A weekly gain of around 2–3 oz. (60–90g) is all that is expected. At 6 months, then, such an average baby will need only around 800 kcals per day, going up to around 1,000 when he is a year old.

Apart from very gradually increasing calories, the infant needs no more of any particular nutrient than he did at 3–6 months of age. His desirable protein intake, the quantities of vitamins he needs, the amounts of minerals which he should have all remain the same. He could, therefore, be fed just as he was in the earlier period except for the question of milk. Most babies, by 6 months, will no longer be given an infant milk formula, but will be drinking liquid cow's milk like the rest of the family. As we saw in Table 5 on page 196, liquid cow's milk does not provide the vitamins and minerals the infant needs, without supplementation. Furthermore, the infant's milk consumption may drop due to weaning, or at least to a change in his mother's attitude to his bottle feeds. Table 10 sets out the infant's recommended intake of the

TABLE 10.   DIFFERENCES BETWEEN INFANT'S
QUANTITIES

| | TOTAL CALORIES | PROTEIN | MINERALS | |
	kcal	g	Calcium mg	Iron mg
INFANT'S RECOMMENDED INTAKE:	800	20	600	6
Infant taking 32 oz. (915ml) LACKS	224	0	0	6
Infant taking 20 oz. (1 pt) (about 600ml) LACKS	440	2	0	6
Infant taking 10 oz. (½ pt) (about 300ml) LACKS	620	11	260	6

Note: Cow's milk usually contains a trace of vitamin D, but this
diet. The vitamin C content may be high in summer, but how
diet, heat treatment of milk and exposure to sunlight. For practical

NEEDS AND THE NUTRIENT CONTENTS OF VARIOUS
OF COW'S MILK

		VITAMINS			
A	D	Thiamine	Ribo-flavine	Nicotinic acid	C
µg	µg	mg	mg	mg	mg
450	10	0·3	0·4	5	15
100	10	0	0	0	15
230	10	0·1	0	0	15
340	10	0·2	0	2	15

is too small and too variable to be a reliable contribution to the
much reaches the infant's digestion depends on season, cow's
purposes it is best to treat cow's milk as containing no vitamin C.

various nutrients, and shows where various quantities of unsweetened liquid cow's milk fall short of these.

It is clear from this table that as at younger ages, while the baby continues to drink 32 oz. (915ml) of milk per day, he needs only some calories, his iron, and vitamins A, D and C in drop form. Although appropriate vitamin supplements are available to all U.K. families at a subsidized price, it seems that few mothers actually buy them. The Ministry of Health is, at the time of writing, considering a new advertising campaign to persuade more families to use these vitamin supplements. In the meantime many families may, in fact, be purchasing similar multivitamin preparations directly from chemists at full price, rather than buying more cheaply from welfare food centres.

The use of vitamin-C-containing fruit syrups is extremely widespread in the U.K. A great many babies are given these routinely as an afternoon drink. If this is the case, then vitamin-C deficiency is extremely unlikely. A single teaspoonful of blackcurrant syrup contains enough vitamin C to meet the daily needs. Since such a quantity, diluted with water, makes only about a 2 oz. (60ml) drink, many infants will, in fact, be receiving more.

Vitamin D is a more difficult problem. While a certain amount is vital, enabling calcium and phosphorus to be used in laying down bones and teeth, too much is damaging. The margin between too little and too much is confused by the body's ability to manufacture its own vitamin D when the skin is exposed to sunlight. If there is any sunshine, and if the baby is put in it, even with only his face and arms exposed, he may need no dietary vitamin D at all. On the other hand if he is seldom outside, his need for the vitamin may be urgent. Although hypercalcaemia – the end result of prolonged overdosage with vitamin D – is sometimes reported, and the vitamin levels in fortified baby foods have been reduced because of this risk, a lack of vitamin D, leading to rickets, is far more common. The risk is particularly great among children with dark skins; the extra pigmentation protects them, in this particular, too efficiently from the sun's rays, and makes them less efficient at making their own vitamin D. A recent survey of 569 children in the Midlands revealed 17 who were suffering from frank rickets, with deformities of the bones. All these were dark-skinned children. But 40 per cent of the total sample showed biochemical deficiencies which, untreated, could have led to rickets.[89] Unlike most British authorities, one of the contributors to this book also raises the possibility of deficiencies in intake of calcium itself. There is evidence from Japan suggesting an increase in growth within the child population, following increased intake of calcium. While milk-drinking children in the U.K. are certainly not calcium-deprived, those who refuse milk could be.

A lack of vitamin A is said, by the Ministry of Health, to be unknown in Great Britain. Furthermore there is currently some anxiety among pharmacists (expressed at a meeting of the Pharmaceutical Society in February 1972) about the harm which overdosage of vitamin A may do. Nevertheless without those vitamin drops it is hard to see how babies who reject milk can meet their vitamin-A requirements, unless they eat a great deal of cheese, butter, fortified margarine, or a little liver.

Iron needs have to be met from solid foods. The continuation of the use of fortified baby cereals is an easy way of giving iron. Egg yolk, commonly lauded for its iron content, in fact contributes rather little. One average egg yolk contains around 1mg of dietary iron. To meet the needs from this source alone you would have to feed the infant 6 eggs per *day*. Again, liver is an extremely rich source of iron. More useful to the mother of a liver-detesting infant may be the information that drinking chocolate contains more than 3mg of iron for every 2 teaspoons, and chocolate to eat contains about 0·5mg in a small children's bar.

Dropping the milk intake to a mere 1 pint (about 600ml) per day makes a difference to the infant's remaining dietary needs mainly in terms of simple calories. He must now get more than half his total calories from solid food, instead of only a quarter. But in other respects that pint of milk still protects him from deficiencies. His protein intake falls just under the recommended intake, although it is still above the minimum. But in practice such a small protein lack could not fail to be filled by his solid food, whatever items of diet were chosen to fill his calorie gap. His intake of calcium is still adequate and consumption of the B vitamins is almost so. The trace of thiamine which is missing on paper will again certainly be made good by the traces present in almost all ordinary foods. His need for vitamin-A supplementation has gone up, and his position with respect to vitamins D and C remains the same. The infant can still therefore be fed so as to satisfy his calorie and iron needs, just so long as he receives regular vitamin supplementation.

Mothers who buy infants of this age expensive protein foods – choosing 'high-protein' cereals, and trying to persuade the baby to eat meat and fish – do him no harm, but he does not need this added protein. And if they are on a tight budget, they may be giving him protein foods he will simply waste, biochemically, rather than giving them to older children whose bodies actually need them.

Dropping the milk intake to $\frac{1}{2}$ pint (about 300ml) per day does radically alter the nutritional picture. The infant now lacks some of almost everything. Above all, his protein and calcium intakes are now below safe levels, and these vital nutrients are not easily available as supplements. If such a child will not take more milk, then he must be treated as completely 'weaned'. His milk must be regarded only as a valuable extra, and he must be fed a complete diet, just as an older child is fed. Chapter 25 on feeding in the second year may be useful.

In practice a milk intake as low as $\frac{1}{2}$ pint (about 300ml) is unusual at this age. Mothers often report that the child takes this quantity when they mean that he drinks that much in liquid form. A considerable amount of milk goes into ordinary cooking. A further bout of kitchen experimentation showed the quantities of milk needed to prepare some very ordinary foods often fed to infants in this age group.

Using proprietary baby cereals, the amount of milk

absorbed proved variable, but none took less than 2 oz. (60ml) of milk, and most took 3–4 oz. (90–115ml), to produce a serving of four slightly heaped tablespoons.

Scrambling an egg yolk, to the soft consistency preferred by most infants, used 1 oz. (30ml) of milk.

An egg custard, chocolate or plain, to be served as a pudding, took 3–4 oz. (90–115ml) of milk to one egg, while 2 oz. (60ml) of milk were needed to make a more liquid custard (using custard powder or cornflour) to be served with fruit.

Mashing a half potato to a soft texture used ½ oz. (15ml) of milk, while a serving of potato soup, or other creamed vegetable soup, took 2 oz. (60ml).

Rice or semolina puddings, like the baby cereals, used 3–4 oz. (90–115ml) of milk for a four-tablespoon serving, while almost as much went into a milk jelly or a blancmange.

Of course the actual amount of milk *consumed* by the infant, in the form of foods of this kind, will depend on his appetite. Many infants will not eat portions of this size; or a good deal may go on his chin, or the floor. But over a whole day, most mothers who cook for their infants will find that they have *served* him a good deal of 'concealed' milk.

Clearly baby cereals are again an excellent help in feeding the infant who drinks little milk. They take half a feeding bottle to mix one portion; when mixed they provide around 120 calories, 5–6 grams of protein, 150–200mg of calcium, about 3mg of iron and all the missing B vitamins.

As we saw in Chapter 13, almost all mothers studied in recent years have stated that they use ready-prepared infant foods, in cans and jars, almost to the exclusion of home-cooked foods. Where milk is still meeting most of the infant's vital nutritional needs, the exact composition of these canned foods need not concern the mother very much. They will certainly contain adequate calories and she knows that his iron and his vitamins must be supplemented anyway. But where an infant is taking little milk, some thought does need to be given to what he is getting in his canned dinners. They are often criticized for being too starchy and too sweet. The latter charge is a valid one. The infant who is accustomed to strained or junior fruits will probably refuse freshly stewed apples, even with a reasonable addition of sugar. His canned varieties are more like jam than fresh fruit.

But the charge that the canned dinners contain too much carbohydrate is rather different. Often it is an economic rather than a nutritional charge. When you buy a tin of 'Junior Beef Dinner', you buy 7 grams of protein, equivalent to a flat tablespoon of lean minced stewing steak, and yielding 69 calories. The remaining 54 calories in the tin are made up of a little fat and a lot of starch. This does mean that you are buying rather little actual meat for your money. Clearly the exact composition of the meals should be stated on the tin, so that mothers could see exactly what they were buying. If an infant is gaining weight too fast, so that the mother wants to keep his carbohydrate consumption down while still ensuring his other nutrients, she must clearly cook for him herself, rather than buying composite meals which allow of no adjustment. But then if she were slimming herself she would not expect to do it on bought steak and kidney pie. But in other circumstances, the balance is not an unreasonable one in nutritional terms. A return to the kitchen produced the following comparisons between a widely available canned infant dinner, an equally available infant supper and their home-cooked equivalents (see Table 11).

Both the home-cooked dinner and the home-cooked supper would be regarded as 'ideal' by most people. Yet the dinner yielded only a little more protein than the canned variety, and it had a few more calories too. Similarly the home-cooked supper yielded one third more protein than the can, but one third more calories as well.

These findings hardly support the charge that the canned foods are 'all starch' and 'much too fattening' and that they have 'no goodness in them'. A baby would have been more inclined to get fat on these home-cooked dishes than on their canned equivalents, and while he would have got a little more protein as well, it would almost certainly have been protein he did not need. After all the baby on ½ pint (300ml) of

TABLE II. COMPARISON BETWEEN TWO
PROPRIETARY CANNED INFANT MEALS AND THEIR
HOME-COOKED EQUIVALENTS

Canned Meal	Home-cooked Meal
'Beef Dinner'	1 oz. (30g) cooked, lean minced stewing steak.
	69 kcal, 7g protein
	half a medium sized potato, mashed (1 tablespoon)
	45 kcal, 0·8g protein
	One small carrot, boiled and mashed (1 dessertspoon)
	23 kcal, 0·7g protein
	One tablespoon stock, to mix
	Negligible food value
Total 3 tablespoons of food	*Total* 3 tablespoons of food
123 kcal	137 kcal
7g protein	8·5g protein

While the home-cooked meal does yield a little more protein ($1\frac{1}{2}$g) it also yields more calories (14). In real terms the differences between the two meals are nutritionally insignificant. A somewhat fattier meat or smaller carrot would be enough to cancel the difference out.

Canned Meal	Home-cooked Meal
'Cheese and Egg Supper'	$\frac{1}{2}$ an egg
	$\frac{1}{4}$ oz. (7g) of cheddar cheese
	2 oz. (60ml) milk
	Baked together to make a custard
Total 3 tablespoons of food	*Total* 3 tablespoons of food
75 kcal	110 kcal
4g protein	6·5g protein

Here the difference between the protein content of the two meals (2·5g) is almost exactly matched by the difference in calorie value (35 kcal). Each meal yields about 2g of protein for every 35 kcal. The infant who eats the home-cooked meal is therefore simply getting more to eat than is the infant who eats the canned meal. Spoonful for spoonful the home-cooked meal is more concentrated, but the constituent balance is almost identical; only the bulk is different.

milk per day only lacks 11 grams of protein. One such tin of dinner together with one serving of baby cereal amply meets that need. After that he does not require or benefit from more protein; he only needs more fuel-food, more calories.

Some infants prefer home-cooked foods, and some mothers enjoy preparing them. If this is so there are all kinds of benefits, both nutritional and social. Nutritionally they are better in that they are flexible. More potato can be given if the child is extra-hungry; less sugar can be added if he is having diarrhoea; carbohydrates in general can be cut down if he is gaining weight too fast, or the concentrated calories of some extra fats can be added if he is gaining weight slowly and cannot eat much bulk.

Socially, home-cooked meals may be better in that they enable the baby to share (with suitable mincing and manipulating) what the rest of the family is eating. And they enable him, too, to get used to a variety of flavours and of textures at an early age.

While it is not fair to say that canned infant foods all taste the same, they do tend to be extremely bland if they are savoury, or very sweet if they are sweet at all. Perhaps more important, their texture is consistent from meal to meal. Baby cereal mixed runny or stiff is still perfectly smooth. Tinned dinners progress from strained, through junior to toddler, but the minced texture of the junior foods is consistent, and the chopped up quality of the toddler foods is consistent. And there are no contrasts; no crisp toppings of browned cheese on a tinned cheese savoury. An infant who expects all his food to have this sameness may find it very difficult to adapt to that 'good mixed diet' towards the end of his first year.

But if the mother does not want to take the time to prepare babyfoods, and if the infant accepts canned varieties, there is nothing nutritionally wrong with them. And there is no doubt that they do save an enormous amount of time. All the mother needs to do is to make sure that she has some idea what she is feeding to the baby. If she intends to use cans extensively, it might well be worth her writing to the manu-

facturers of her chosen brands, asking for their analysis
sheets of different varieties. The idea is not that she should
make any attempt to balance the contents of a tin against her
baby's nutritional needs, but simply that she should avoid
being fooled by the descriptive names given to these foods.
These names give no clue to the overall food value – in terms
of calories – or to the protein richness of the particular meal.
Similarly named 'main courses' may literally contain half as
many calories or half as much protein as each other. Often
the puddings contain more calories than the main courses,
while the 'breakfast' and 'supper' cans vary even more
unexpectedly. The unwary mother tends to assume that an
'egg-and-bacon breakfast' will be roughly equivalent to a
'scrambled egg breakfast'. But she would be wrong. If
enough people asked to see the manufacturers' analyses, they
might begin to realize that mothers will buy a dinner in a tin,
but not if it is a pig in a poke.

Whether or not a mother uses prepared babyfoods, at
around 6 months the infant must be given the opportunity to
learn to chew food. Often it is assumed that he will not chew
until he has teeth to do it with. Often also it is unthinkingly
assumed that once he has his four front teeth he is ready to
chew. In fact the critical period for learning to chew seems to
pre-date the appearance of any teeth at all, and chewing is
certainly not assisted by those first teeth, which are for biting,
not for grinding.

In the early months the infant sucks his food; then he
learns to let semi-solids slide down his throat. But he still has
to learn to use his jaws to convert genuinely solid foods into
swallowable textures and he is ready to start by 6 months.
Obvious foods for practice chewing are peeled quarters of
raw apple; strips of raw carrot; pieces of toast; rusks or
biscuits. At the same time, even if the infant's main food is
still proprietary babyfood, some vegetables should be given
him diced up rather than mashed, so that he can practise
picking them up with his fingers, putting them in his mouth,
and chewing them. The new experiences of taste and texture
tend to be far more acceptable to the baby if he has them

under the control of his own fingers than if they are dumped in his mouth from his mother's spoon.

Around 6 months is also the time when many babies begin to imitate people around them – and often especially their mothers. So again this is the time when the infant should be given every opportunity to start to feed himself with a spoon, preferably while his mother is eating her food too. Some infants, who *have* been given the chance, can feed themselves completely by 9 months.

As the infant takes over responsibility for feeding himself, both with his fingers and with a spoon, his own appetite, his eager eating, becomes again the reliable guide to the quantities he needs, which it was in the earliest weeks of life when he was given only milk. Once the infant is competent at feeding himself when he is hungry, or when he particularly likes the offered food, or when he is racing his older sister, he should be regarded as competent on *all* occasions. There is no curious quirk of infant development which makes a child able to feed himself chocolate pudding, and unable to feed himself shepherd's pie. Mothers recognize this if it is put to them, but they still tend to say, 'I just help him a bit at the end, you know, when he is getting bored', or 'When he's tired, I feed him.' Feeding him when he can feed himself is asking for later trouble. An infant who is too bored to bother to eat is not hungry enough to need to eat. And if he is too tired to feed himself he is overtired and should sleep first.

Finger foods rapidly progress from being entertainment, practice and education for the baby and become *food*. The slice of toast which at 6 months he mouthed and sucked may be eaten to the last crumb at 9 months – all 72 calories and 2 grams of protein of it, not to mention that butter . . . It is at this point that 'snacks' may begin to amount to a significant proportion of the infant's daily food – and a misleading proportion to the researcher, because mothers often do not count them, when they are asked what the baby has eaten in the past 24 hours. Recent surveys, large and small, all suggest that snacks are now the rule not the exception. Infants commonly have biscuits or rusks on waking in the morning.

A mid-morning snack of biscuits and a drink is universal, and most also have a mid-afternoon snack, perhaps of cake or more biscuits. In addition, a high proportion of infants get some sweets every day – often on a daily trip to the shops – and ice-cream or ice-lollies on most days. Table 12 gives the more important constituents of such foods. They are often thought of as 'impoverished', but this generalization is meaningless. If snack foods are intended to give the infant calories and pleasure, there is nothing the matter with them,

TABLE 12.   IMPORTANT CONSTITUENTS OF SOME
'SNACK' FOODS

	Portion	Calories	Protein g	Other significant constituents
Milk chocolate	Children's bar or half a 2 oz. bar or 16 'buttons'	164	2·5	70mg calcium; 0·5 mg iron
Vanilla ice-cream	Smallest brickette, smallest cornet, half choc. ice	55	1·2	40mg calcium
Plain sweet biscuits	2 biscuits	141	1·6	Some calcium, iron, B vitamins
Chocolate biscuits	2 biscuits	142	2·0	Some calcium, iron, B vitamins
Currant buns	1 bun	190	4·4	0·5mg iron, some vitamin D and B vitamins
Plain cake (Madeira type)	Small slice	122	1·7	Some iron and B vitamins
Banana	Half small banana	22	0·5	
Roast shelled peanuts	Heaped tablespoon	166	8·0	5mg nicotinic acid
Sultanas	Heaped tablespoon	71	0·5	0·5mg iron
Potato crisps	Individual packet of approx. 23g or just under 1 oz.	145	1·8	Trace elements varying according to brand and added flavourings

nutritionally. But, of course, they cannot give pleasure without giving calories. So if they make the infant unenthusiastic about his real meals, they can *lead* to an impoverished diet overall. Similarly if they do *not* make him unenthusiastic about his real meals, they may make him fat.

SLEEP

Sleep tends to be a major preoccupation among mothers of babies in this age period. As we have seen, caring for the infant becomes increasingly demanding, both physically and emotionally, in the second half-year. As the baby gets older, and especially as he begins to be mobile, the mother can accomplish less and less while he is awake. His nap times and the evening when he is asleep may be the only times when she can accomplish jobs which with his 'help' are potentially dangerous. They may also be the only times when she can do anything at maximum speed and with maximum efficiency. The vast majority of babies are therefore given ample opportunity to sleep. Great trouble may be taken to ensure that they are warm, comfortable and undisturbed. One can assume that between 6 and 9 months the hours of sleep the infant takes are the hours he needs. He still cannot keep himself awake voluntarily.

Unfortunately the hours of sleep he needs and takes are often not the hours his mother would like him to take. And many mothers are misled in their expectations by the pattern of sleep suggested as necessary by many widely used handbooks of infant care. An average figure, taken from several handbooks published for mothers by babyfood manufacturers, for example, would be 16 to 17 hours for infants between 6 and 9 months. Even Dr Spock,[90] while accepting individual variation in sleep needs, suggests 14–16 hours' sleep at 1 year, and suggests that mothers should do all they can to encourage infants to sleep this much.

What evidence we have suggests that many babies sleep very much less than this. The Newsons[18] found a range, at

1 year, from 9 to 18 hours per day. The average in their survey was 13½ hours. Kleitman and Engelmann[6] similarly found infants averaging 13½ hours at 6 months, and maintaining this figure, with a drop to around 13 hours at the age of 2.

Most babies from 6 months will normally sleep through the night – at least in terms of the hours of sleep, even if there are brief awakenings. Such a night probably amounts to roughly 12 hours of sleep. Any remaining sleep is in the form of daytime naps. The majority of babies from 6–9 months still need two such naps. But they vary in length from 20 minutes of actual *sleep* to 3 hours.

Provided that the infant does not come to associate his cot or pram with loneliness, or with crossness from his mother, he may well be happy to spend an hour twice a day in it, even if he does not actually sleep for all of this time. Many babies seem to enjoy a period alone, with plenty of interesting things to look at or play with. Often a pram in the garden, where there are trees moving, clouds, shadows, the occasional bird, is popular. Failing that, toys in his cot, mobiles and pictures to look at, may keep him equally happy. If this pattern can be kept to, it serves the double purpose of giving the mother a little peace and privacy, while leaving the baby free to sleep as and when he needs to.

Occasionally, mothers who are rightly anxious not to make the infant feel that they wish to be rid of him are quick to abandon one of the day-time rest periods as soon as it becomes clear that the child barely sleeps during it. A protesting cry as she leaves, and the infant's struggles to sit himself up, may be enough to make her abandon that nap altogether. In fact, a brief protest on being left is so frequent as to be normal at this age. The infant would prefer his mother to stay. And he states this fact. If he settles down happily within a couple of minutes, all is well. Far more important is to go to him swiftly when he wakes up from a nap, or finally decides that he has had enough rest time. If he is left crying at this point, he is very likely to be put off the whole business of being left alone. He must know that when he needs his mother, she will come.

As we have seen in earlier chapters, and as the range of hours of sleep around the research averages shows, infants vary in their sleep requirements. A baby who goes to sleep peacefully, and within a few minutes of being put to bed at night, or at some point during an hour's daytime rest, can be assumed to have had all the sleep he needs if he wakes after an 8-hour night or a 10-minute nap. In these circumstances the mother has the problem, not the baby. He is awaking because he has finished sleeping. He cannot go to sleep again at will because he is not tired. His mother cannot put him back to sleep again. The 'problem' has to be lived with. If the parents try to force the child to sleep more, a wakeful infant is liable to turn into an infant who *does* have sleep problems. A baby who sleeps from 8 p.m. to 5 a.m. every night, and for two periods of 15 minutes during the day is exhausting. Every possible way of helping him remain content, alone, until a later hour in the morning and, perhaps, from a somewhat earlier hour in the evening, should be tried. A sleeping bag – with sleeves, so that there is no way the infant can get down inside it and smother himself – will keep him reasonably warm while he plays in his cot. Carefully chosen toys will go some way towards keeping him occupied. Sharing a room with an early-waking toddler may keep both children occupied first thing in the morning. At the same time the house needs to be organized so that it is as easy as possible for the mother to accomplish what she needs to do during the day, while in the constant company of the wakeful infant. Once the mother can accept that the baby is not going to sleep in the daytime; once she stops feeling that he ought to sleep, and wasting time and emotional energy on settling him and resettling him for naps he does not need, she and the infant can often arrive at a *modus vivendi*. If there simply is no room for the infant to play safely on the kitchen floor, the mother may find herself doing the vegetables in the playroom. If the infant will not stay in his playpen, and she must use a sewing machine, she and the machine can go inside the pen, leaving the infant to roam, safely protected from the needle, outside. Even the typical mode of interaction between infant and mother may be affected by his wakefulness. A baby who sleeps for 2 hours in the morning, waking for one hour before his dinner, may be able to claim his mother's undivided attention for that hour, especially if she knows he will sleep again in the afternoon. So she may play with him, her other commitments already met. But the baby who is awake all morning has to allow her to do other things than play, part of the time. The pair may adopt ways of playing which do not involve the mother abandoning everything else. The mother can talk while she works, smile and make faces, show the infant what she is doing. He, in his turn, because he is so constantly with her, will probably come to accept a situation where he has part of her attention all of the time, where other infants get all of the mother's attention part of the time.

The infant who wakes continually during the night is a different matter. If he wakes before he has had sufficient sleep for the moment, then something is waking him. Babies become increasingly easy to wake from about 6 months onwards. The infant who can be shown, sleeping, to admiring visitors at 4 months, will almost certainly wake if people go into his room when he is 8 months. So the reason for the night waking may be a practical one. Often the baby who is still sleeping in his parents' room is disturbed by their coming to bed, their talk and moving around, or even their coughing and snoring. Sometimes infants who have always shared a sibling's room become disturbed by his sleeping noises. Obviously it is worth trying to see whether the infant sleeps better alone. Where there is no separate room for him, his cot can sometimes be carried into the living room once the parents are ready to go to bed.

But a great deal of night waking at 6–9 months cannot be so simply explained. Moore and Ucko,[91] in one of the few actual studies of this problem, found that it tended to be the infants who received least attention during the day, and whose mothers were afraid to pick them up when they cried for fear of spoiling them, who woke in the night. Most workers are agreed that some form of 'nightmare' is common after 6 months. I put the word in inverted commas because we cannot, in a pre-verbal child, know what form the night-fright takes. All we know is that the child wakes, usually with a sudden scream. No ordinary cause can be found. He appears afraid, is almost immediately reassured when his mother comes to him, and usually goes rapidly back to sleep.

Even if the actual number of minutes the mother or father must spend awake with the child is small, disturbances of sleep, night after night, for weeks or months, are exhausting. Unfortunately, where simple practical measures to ensure that the infant is not disturbed from outside fail, very little can be done to help the parents. The child cannot wake himself up on purpose. There is therefore no possible logic in regarding night waking as a 'bad habit' which can be broken by leaving the child to cry. In the vast majority of cases nothing but the reassurance of seeing the parent will settle the baby. And the parents will only lose more sleep by lying listening to him crying before they go to him. On the other hand it is important also that the *parents* should not get into bad habits. When the child normally wakes several times in each night, it is easy to get out of bed, almost asleep, and go into his room at the very first murmur. He may not be really awake. Left for a few seconds he might have settled again. Visited, he will certainly surface.

After about 9 months, a change seems to take place in that infants become able to inhibit sleep at will. This can, and all too often does, raise all kinds of new problems. The mother can no longer decide that if the baby needs to sleep he will sleep, and conversely that if he does not sleep he does not need to. On the contrary, some infants fight their drowsiness until they are so tense and exhausted that they cannot relax into sleep. Over-excitement, fear of the dark, a quarrel with mother at bedtime, can all make the infant determined not to go to sleep.

Problems over going to sleep, as opposed to length of sleep, or waking during sleep, often start with an obvious upset. Yarrow[92] reviews the evidence for disturbances following brief periods of hospitalization. Sleep disturbances following the return home were very common, especially between 9 months and 1 year. Less traumatic events can start trouble also. A holiday away from home can break the infant's sleep pattern, so that he cannot be returned to his old behaviour when he gets home. A new room may lead to sleep refusal. Even a shift around of the furniture may cause trouble.

But most often, the tired infant who will not allow himself to go to sleep is reacting primarily to separation from his mother. To allow himself to pass into sleep is to relinquish her altogether. Rather than do this, many babies will cry and scream until she returns, be delighted to see her, accept any entertainment she offers, and then start again as soon as she goes. Others will lie quietly as long as she is in the room, but snap fully awake as soon as she creeps out, settling again when she resignedly sits down once more. A few infants, especially those who have been actually smacked for crying after they were settled for the night, will sit silent in their cots, listening for the sounds of the rest of the family moving around in other rooms.

Luckily, this is the age period during which infants find within themselves resources to help them relinquish the mother at night. These are ritual behaviours which give the infant security and comfort which is within his *own* control, which allow him to comfort *himself* after his mother has left him. Thumb sucking and dummy sucking may have been in the child's repertoire since the first weeks of life, but for many children they take on a new significance during these months. At the same time the child may adopt what Winnicott called a 'transitional object' – meaning an object which stood in for the mother in her absence – and use this object, often in combination with sucking, to comfort himself. This adoption of a soft, cuddly object, often a piece of blanket, or a soft toy, or old nappy, has been studied by various workers.[93] But we still do not know what proportion of infants do in fact form such attachments. Those who do, form them in about equal numbers before and after the first birthday, and once the attachment is formed it is invariably extremely strong, so that the child's 'relationship' with the object needs to be taken almost as seriously as his relationship with other people. Whether such a relationship is actually good for a child, or bad for him, we do not know. Like many things the answer will probably turn out to be a matter of degree. To be able to use such an object to comfort yourself when your mother leaves you for the night is useful. It must also tend to increase the infant's feeling that the world as a whole is a comforting place; that all comfort need not stem from the mother herself. On the other hand a continual need for the object during the day might tend to suggest that the child was being asked to depend too much on himself for comfort, and was perhaps not getting what he needed from people. Furthermore in an extreme case daytime finger-sucking, combined with twisting a blanket around the head, would be likely to limit the infant's exploratory and play behaviour.

Much the same can be said about other comfort habits. Many babies relax themselves for sleep by ritualistic rocking, or by twisting their hair or banging their heads against the cot bars. All these habits can be useful self-relaxers, but all can go too far. The infant who chooses to rock by himself in a corner in the daytime is not being offered, or is not accepting, enough stimulation and interest from his environment. The infant who bangs his head hard enough to hurt needs bumpers round his cot. If he then makes it clear that the ritual is no use to him if it does not hurt, one needs to know why he must hurt himself.

Some ritualistic comfort can be quite deliberately provided by the mother for infants who find it difficult to settle at night. A regular and pleasant bedtime routine is often the start of it. The regularity makes sure that the infant knows when bedtime is coming up; the pleasantness makes sure that he reaches his cot as relaxed, as happy, feeling as securely loved as possible. Many mothers find that the deliberate ritualization of their good-nights, their curtain-drawing, the amount they leave the door open and so on helps the infant to release them gradually, rather than feeling that the mother has walked out on them, leaving them emotionally in mid air. The danger is that once a little ritual has begun, the infant builds and builds on it, until it is effectively putting the parting off for an hour or more.

TOILET 'TRAINING'

Toilet training is a human universal. All infants have to learn not to soil in or near the living space. But the extreme interest, the concern, the anxiety which the whole topic arouses is by no means universal in time or in place. In the London of 300 years ago, chamber pots were in use; people did not void on the floor of their houses. But neither did they have our horror of the sight of faeces. Those same chamber pots were happily emptied out of the windows into the open sewers in the streets below. And many a busy man gave audience while enthroned for defaecation. In the rural village cultures of today children are taught to go to a special place outside the compound. But while they are learning, most of their 'accidents' take place outside where they are already rolling in the dirt. And there are few clothes to worry about. Even in the rural parts of Western societies there tends to be a greater tolerance for the actual dirt of excretion. If children are usually muddy, if there are animals always around, if half the farmyard is trampled into the kitchen at every mealtime, there is likely to be far less fuss about a wet or soiled pair of pants.

In sophisticated societies, with their lavatories, their swept streets, their nappies and plastic pants, the whole business of excretion has been as much concealed as a constant human function can be. The child who, because of his youth, will not conform, is under heavy pressure.

Any attempt to persuade a baby to void into a pot rather than a nappy is usually referred to as toilet 'training'. But often this is a misnomer. Toilet training can only correctly refer to the process by which a child is taught to respond to his own need to void, by telling or signalling to his mother, or going himself to the pot or lavatory. This teaching cannot even begin until the infant is old enough, mature enough, to *recognize* his own need to void. Only very rarely can the infant identify the signals from his full bladder or rectum before he is 1 year old. So the potting that goes on in this half-year is not *training* at all.

Older authorities would dispute this. It used to be maintained that infants, almost from birth, could be conditioned to void, in response to the feeling of the rim of the pot round their buttocks. It was thought that 'good habits' could thus be set up, which would last a lifetime. But there is no research evidence to support this view. Indeed it is difficult to see how the rim of the pot could act as a conditioning stimulus, when there was no pleasurable reinforcement for the baby in performing in the pot.

Even though babies under about 1 year cannot be trained to urinate or pass motions into a pot, clever mothers can put the pot in the right place at the right time, and catch the motions and the urine. Many infants have, from the beginning, a fairly regular voiding pattern, being especially likely to pass a motion immediately after feeding. Furthermore their urine-retention time is very short, so that if they wake dry from a nap, or return dry from an outing, it is a reasonable guess that they will urinate shortly afterwards. Mothers take advantage of these patterns, and pride themselves on having few daytime nappies to wash.

Being 'caught' in this way is most unlikely to bother a 6-month baby. He will let go and void when he needs to, wherever he finds himself. If the mother pots him simply to save herself washing, or to protect chafed skin from wet nappies, there is probably no harm in it. But unfortunately few mothers are so cool about this emotional subject. They tend to feel very strongly about 'success', being filled with pride and pleasure when the pot is used, disappointed when it is left empty, and irritated when the infant immediately soils or wets his nappy. Reactions of this kind are likely to communicate themselves to the infant and may store up trouble for the true training period which still lies ahead. Furthermore, the more successfully mothers 'catch' their infants, the more likely they are to decide that they have 'trained' them. The mother puts the baby on the pot after breakfast each morning and he produces a motion; she catches urine at mid morning, at lunchtime and after his afternoon nap. At suppertime he produces another motion.

For weeks on end she may only wash nap-time and night-time nappies. By the time he is 9–10 months, she is quite convinced that the whole toilet-training business is vastly overplayed, and that she has succeeded from the beginning. Other mothers congratulate her and ask the secret. She is almost certainly in for a nasty shock. Far from being trained, her 9-month baby simply had not begun to care where he put his body products. At around a year he begins to become aware of them; aware of the feelings they give him; aware that they come out of his body and belong to him. At the same time he is increasingly involved in crawling and toddling, so that sitting on a pot (or indeed sitting still anywhere) becomes a very undesirable activity. The smooth successful 'catching' pattern becomes totally disrupted, and the mother finds that, just like other mothers, she now has to toilet train her baby. And, as we shall see, the early catching success does not mean that true training will be easier or quicker than it would have been if the infant had been left in his nappies until he was ready to be taught.

Because of the secrecy and emotionality which we attach to elimination, finding out what mothers actually do about potting and training their infants is beset with difficulties. If mothers are asked what is happening at one given point in time, they tend to over-estimate the infant's 'prowess'; if they are asked later on to remember his toilet training, they tend to look back through rose-tinted spectacles. Survey results have, therefore, to be taken with a large pinch of salt. But those which report a *late* start to training, or *late* success, are likely to be more accurate than others. A mother is unlikely to say that her infant was still in nappies at $3\frac{1}{2}$ when he was not. But she is very likely to say that he was out of them at 2 when he was not.

The accuracy with which researchers can report on toilet training is affected also by the changing fashions in infant handling. Overall changes tend to take place consistently throughout a society, so that, for example, the attitudes epitomized by Truby King[94] have given way to those epitomized by Spock.[95]

But within that overall change, taking several generations, change also takes place more quickly in some sub-groups or socio-economic classes than in others. Average figures, given by a survey, may therefore reflect a wide range of practices all current at the same time in different groups. And, since the production of survey results takes a long time, they may fail to reflect the current practice of those who have moved on to new ideas since the survey was made. The studies quoted below have all been made in the last 10 years. They all show very large numbers of mothers starting to pot their babies during this half-year. Yet if it were possible to carry out a swift survey now, there is little doubt that it would show far more mothers leaving out the catching stage altogether, and delaying training well into the second year.

Drillien's study of 518 Scottish babies[68] showed 90 per cent of all mothers starting to pot their babies before one year, with half the middle-class and a quarter of the working-class mothers starting before 6 months.

The Newsons[18] found that 83 per cent of their Nottingham mothers had started potting before 1 year, with 63 per cent starting before 8 months, and 20 per cent beginning in the first days after birth. In contrast, a study in California reported in 1966[96] found very few mothers starting potting in the early months, and more than 50 per cent of them delaying the start of training until 18 months.

Clearly we cannot generalize about how many mothers will pot or train their infants at different ages. It will depend on who they are, where they live, what their friends do, what their mothers and their doctors and their neighbours advise.

But whatever they do, and whenever they do it, the potting/training is aimed at producing a child who will reliably and independently use a pot or lavatory instead of a nappy or pants. Unfortunately there is no controlled study which directly compares the age at which this happy state is reached in children who were potted early or late. But deductions can be drawn from various studies: all suggest that the age at which the mother starts to pot her infant, or truly to train him, has no bearing whatsoever on the age at which he will be 'trained'. Drillien, for example, found no relationship running in either direction. Her early-potting mothers had 2-year-olds who were neither wetter nor dryer, cleaner nor dirtier than the late-training mothers. The Newsons followed up their study of 1-year-olds with a study of the same children when they were 4.[97] Again they could find no relationship between early or late toileting, and reliability or unreliability at 4 years. Dimson[98] studied 165 families who had, between them, 225 enuretic children and 174 dry ones. The wet and the dry children could not be distinguished in terms of the age at which their mothers started to pot or train them. Finally, in a rare experimental manipulation of ordinary daily life, Brazelton[99] actually encouraged the mothers of 1,170 infants seen in private practice *not* to start any form of potting before their children were 2 years old. All were reliable, at least by day, within 4 months of the start of training.

It does seem, therefore, that early potting is most unlikely to lead to early successful training. The majority of infants will be more or less reliable in the daytime by the middle of their third year, whether they are first put on a pot at 6 days, 6 months or 16 months. Simply in practical terms, early potting seems a lot of effort for not much reward. With a little frivolous arithmetic, one can work out that the mother who starts to pot her baby at 6 months and pots him 6 times a day until he is 2 will have potted him 3,276 times. Each time she will have had to undress and redress him. And, since she will often have been unsuccessful, she will have washed a good many nappies as well. On the other hand the mother who leaves out the catching stage, and starts training her baby at 18 months, will have washed more nappies, but she will only have potted her infant about 1,000 times for the same effect. Since changing a nappy is rather quicker than potting an infant, the training mother has probably saved herself a good deal of time over the catching one!

But of course practical considerations are not the only ones. Once infants do become aware of their excreta as coming from themselves, they become extremely interested in them, concerned about them, and intrigued by the sensations which voiding produces. If they detect over-concern in the mother, or feel that they are being pressured by her in this extremely personal area, they are likely to react both with a marked negative response to being put on the pot, and with greater or lesser emotional disturbance (see Chapter 27, page 398).

Once again the available research data are unsatisfactory. Many attempts have been made to relate anxiety in children to too early or too severe toilet training, or to relate a general miserliness and emotional withholding in adulthood with problems over constipation during the toilet-training period. Generally speaking such attempts have failed, because, as we have said before, the *atmosphere* in which the mother pots or trains her child is likely to be far more important to him and his emotional well-being than what she actually does, or the age at which she does it.

Most workers show that a marked resistance to potting or to later training arises in at least 30 per cent of infants, whether the mother starts early or late. The Newsons,[97] in a coda to their 4-year-olds' survey, had the impression – although they attempted no statistics as they did not believe the mothers' reports were necessarily accurate – that resistance arose less often with infants whose training had been delayed well into the second year. But they point out that the mothers who were prepared to delay training their infants for that long were also likely to be mothers who would be sensitive to the infant's feelings about the matter, and would withdraw pressure at the first signs of unhappiness.

If potting is begun in this half-year, it is important to realize how likely it is that voiding will become an angry issue between mother and child, and how impossible it is for the mother to win any pitched battle she may enter.

The infant in this age group is not capable of becoming clean or dry out of virtue. He does not recognize the signs of impending voiding. He does not know he is about to pass a motion or to pass urine. He therefore has to accept his mother's whisking him off to the pot, apparently at her whim.

The infant cannot, of course, begin to understand what

the mother is up to, nor why. Later, when he knows he is about to void, he will realize that that is why he is put on the pot. Later still he will understand that his mother actually prefers him to perform in the pot; later again he will understand why. But at this stage the whole matter is totally incomprehensible.

If, by happy chance, potting can be incomprehensible but fun, the infant may accept it as just another part of his life. But it is difficult to make it fun. Most infants dislike sitting on a pot anyway, as they feel insecure without the solid floor or a supporting chair. Most of them hate being unexpectedly interrupted in the middle of play, most wake from naps in a bad temper and resent anything the mother does at that moment except cuddle them, and a great many dislike being dressed and undressed. If any or all of these factors do irritate the baby, they are the more likely to make him angry because they recur so frequently. If a mother is going to pot her baby at all, she is likely to do so at least 6 times a day, and she may well do it much more often.

If the infant does object to being put on the pot, and his mother tries to insist she will very quickly find that she has joined in a battle which there is no way for her to win. Just as it is physically impossible to make a child eat if he refuses, so there is no way to make him void in a pot if he refuses. If the mother is prepared physically to force him to stay on the pot, she still cannot make him use it. Within a few days of being made conscious of the matter as an issue between them, the infant will have learned simply to withhold his motion until he is allowed up – and then to pass it on the floor or in his clean nappy. If this apparently wilful bad behaviour makes the mother cross, it only strengthens the baulky infant's determination not to give in. The battle can reach such proportions that it dominates the whole relationship. And all before the infant was physiologically mature enough for training. It seems a high price to pay for a lighter laundry load in the earlier months.

CHAPTER TWENTY-ONE

BECOMING A BIPED

The achievement of mobility, first as a quadruped, then as a biped, occupies a very great deal of the infant's time and energy during this half-year. The process of getting moving comprises three distinct, although overlapping, phases. Firstly the infant must learn to sit alone, balancing himself, without aid from chair-back or cushions. Having achieved this, he will develop some form of progression across the floor, which for brevity we will call crawling. Once this is established, the infant will begin to pull himself to standing posture, with furniture, cot bars or human hands for support. Once he can stand on his two feet, he is on the way to walking.

Gesell[40] points out that sitting up alone is not only the obvious mid point between lying down and standing up, it is also the developmental mid point in terms of neuromuscular control. Control starts from the top and moves downwards. The new infant must learn to control his head as it wavers on his weak neck. Once his neck can cope with his head, he becomes able to control and hold up his shoulders and upper back, so that held in sitting posture the rounded sag in his spine is only at waist and hip level. A little later still, he can keep his whole back straight. Only his hips and legs still remain to be disciplined.

Most infants are at just about this stage at 6 months. Many of them are ready to sit in that they have their heads and backs in control, but few of them can yet balance in the sitting posture. Placed carefully on the floor, they can be balanced for a few seconds, but then the outstretched hands of parent or researcher prove their worth.

Griffiths[100] tested 571 normal infants between birth and 2 years, in order to construct a scale of normal development. 150 of those babies were between 4 and 9 months at the time of testing. She found that during the sixth month almost all could sit up with minimal support from a cushion in the small of the back, and protection from sideways falls. At 7–8 months most of the infants could sit on the floor, but could not be left sitting because they still tended to overbalance unexpectedly. In her sample, it was during the ninth month that most babies became able to sit on the floor and play.

Some infants, during the 7–8-month period, solve the problem of balance when sitting by hunching forward and resting their hands on the floor. This gives a stable, but not a useful position. With his hands taken up with balancing him and his head bent forward, the infant has neither a good view of the world, nor freedom to play. So even if the infant can remain in this posture indefinitely, he does not really count as 'able to sit alone'.

Other babies learn to balance themselves without using their hands, but can maintain the balance only until a 'wobble' sets in. As soon as they move their heads, or stretch out for a toy, or lean forward, the balance goes and they topple. The sitting, in such a case, is true sitting, but it is still not very useful sitting.

With constant practice the infant, before he is 10 months old, reaches a point where he can retain his balance while using his head and his hands freely; he can even lean right forward, retrieve a toy and regain the sitting position. At this point he can truly be said to be sitting independently.

Constant practice means constant falls. Clearly as many of these falls as possible should be from the floor to the floor, rather than from a high-chair to the floor. Chairs which have provided a safe support for younger babies – who maintain a comparatively constant pressure on the seat and the chair-back – may become very dangerous during this phase. The infant sits unsupported for a few seconds, with his back and his arms clear of the chair. Then he relaxes, and hits the chair-back or arm with a thump which makes it rock, or even tip. The floor is the safest place for sitting practice. But even the floor can prove discouragingly hard if the infant's head hits it several times in a day. A simple answer, throughout this period, is to surround the child either with cushions, or with rolled eiderdowns. At 6–7 months the cushions provide that minimal support to the small of the back which will allow him to sit for a few seconds; when he rolls on to his back or forward into crawling position, they also make a soft landing. A little later they may encourage him to try sitting without supporting himself on his hands, and catch him when his own triumph at finding himself sitting leads him to wave his arms and overbalance. Later still, they are there to prevent damage when he leans forward too far for his new-found equilibrium or, worse still, tips straight over backwards because something makes him jump. Of course no baby should ever be left alone in the room if he is thus cushioned. If he fell face down into a cushion, he would probably push up with his arms and clear his nose and mouth. But he could fall awkwardly, perhaps with his arms trapped beneath him. He could smother. But provided he is properly supervised (and no baby of this age group should ever be left free alone in a room), cushioning his falls *is* worthwhile. His fontanelles are still partially open; his skull does not provide the protection of an older child's skull; he *could* hurt himself. Furthermore, motor development is partly dependent on confidence; and recurrent bumps can put the timid off for a long time.

Getting into sitting position unassisted is more variable in its timing than the ability actually to sit. By 6 months, most infants will raise their heads and shoulders from the mattress or floor, when lying flat on their backs. Often the infant will do this when he wants his mother to give him her hands so that he can pull himself up to sitting. Since by this time most babies can roll all the way over from their backs to their stomachs and back again, many roll over, find themselves up against the bars of their cots or the side of the pram, raise their heads and shoulders, and discover that they can use the bars or sides to struggle to a holding-on sitting position alone. Many a mother has been amazed to spot her not-yet-sitting infant peering towards the house over the edge of his pram in the garden. Once this trick is discovered, the infant usually goes on with it, but this still does not mean that he can get himself into sitting position without anything to pull up by. Few babies can do this before they are playing freely in the sitting position at around 9 months. Then the constant practice of going from sitting to crawling position, and of leaning over and righting himself while sitting, gradually teaches him. The most usual method, at this age, is to roll on to the stomach, pull the knees right up, and then move the hands closer and closer to the body, with a final heave that tips the child back on to his bottom.

The development of some form of crawling often parallels the development of independent sitting quite closely in individual infants. At 6 months the infant can almost sit alone; he has just the remaining problem of balance. At 6 months he can almost crawl. If a toy is put on the floor, just out of his reach, as he lies on his stomach, he pulls up with his knees, pushes with his hands and often gets his stomach right off the floor so that he is in true crawling posture. He just has the remaining problem of actually moving forward.

During the seventh and eighth months, most babies clearly *want* to crawl; watching them, one can see that they are thinking forwards, see the effort that is being made. But few will actually progress. Often, in the eighth month, the infant is reluctant to lie flat on his stomach at all; he gets into hands-and-knees position as soon as he turns himself over, or collapses from sitting. Often too, he will rock himself on hands and knees. And he may learn to turn around on hands and knees, swivelling to follow his mother as she moves around the room. Some infants develop idiosyncratic modes of getting around by a combination of rocking, swivelling, rolling over, and squirming on their stomachs. It is not at all unusual to find a baby who cannot yet crawl, in quite a different part of the room from the safe corner where he was left moments before.

During the ninth month, at about the same time that he becomes able to sit safely, and play, with his head and hands free and mobile, the infant will begin actually to progress across the room. To the extreme frustration of many infants, first progress is often backwards. The infant pushes harder with his hands and forearms than he does with his feet and knees, so, with gaze fixed on a longed-for toy just in front of him, he shunts backwards away from it. Fortunately this is a short-lived phase. Once he can crawl backwards the baby will soon get his direction right.

So, by the end of the ninth month, the infant is likely to be able to sit on the floor and play, and crawl across the floor to get things or to follow people.

While sitting up and crawling tend to progress together, walking is definitely a later accomplishment. Many 6-month babies very much enjoy the standing position, held under the arms, on an adult's lap. As we have seen in an earlier chapter (see page 215) many use the lap as a sort of trampoline, pushing down with their feet, momentarily straightening their knees, and then sagging again, in a rhythmic 'jumping' movement. During the seventh month, they begin to use alternate feet, instead of both feet together. The infant now seems to 'dance' rather than to jump. Often one foot is placed on top of the other, and then the underneath foot pulled out and put back on top. But at this stage the infant does not bear his full weight, nor does he make any obvious attempt at progress. There is none of the longing to move forward when he is held standing, which is so obvious at the same age when he is in crawling posture.

It is usually at around 9 months that this dancing movement begins to give way to a definite placing of one foot in front of the other. The infant may enjoy being held up while he wobbles his way a few 'steps'. But few babies will support their full weight at this stage; most will be around 10 months before they can be stood squarely on their own feet.

Contrary to Gesell's belief that neuromuscular control moves downwards, the infant usually learns to keep his knees stiff, to support his weight, before he learns similarly to control his hips. Characteristically he still sags forward slightly at the hip joints although his legs are straight.

This stage in the development of standing is similar to that point in sitting, at 6 months, where the infant could sit, but not balance. Now he can stand, square on the floor, taking all his weight, but he cannot balance.

Once he can take his full weight the baby will quickly learn to pull himself up to standing. Griffiths[100] found that the average age for this was 11 months. Many babies pull themselves up earlier; probably it is partly a question of opportunity. Many infants, for example, first pull themselves to standing in their cots – but will not do so if they wear sleeping-bags. Others start with the bars of a playpen, but if no playpen is used they must find some other, perhaps less obvious aid. Often the mother herself is the first object used. She may be sitting on the floor with the baby, who crawls to her, and works his way up her clothing until he stands triumphant and wobbly, holding on to her shoulder if she is lucky, her hair if she is not.

Just as newly crawling babies are often distressed by their inability to crawl forwards, so newly standing ones are often flummoxed by their inability to sit down again. Sometimes there is a period of several weeks during which the infant pulls himself to standing as soon as he is let loose on the floor, and then cries piteously for help because he cannot let go and sit down again. As soon as he is rescued, he repeats the performance. As with crawling backwards this phase does not usually last for long. The infant either learns to let go and sit down with a plop, or he learns to lower himself, more gently, by sliding down his support and not letting go with his hands until he is nearly there. In the meantime there is nothing to be gained by trying to force the issue – by leaving the baby to cry until he finds his own way down. He will, eventually, but he will get down by falling down, and falls at this stage are bad for his confidence. If this phase is tiresome, the solution may be to take the baby out more, in pram or push-chair. He is not yet at the stage where it occurs to him to want to walk when out on an expedition. He will sit, happily, and rest both his muscles and his own and his mother's nerves.

Within 2 to 3 weeks of learning to pull himself up to

standing posture, and usually, therefore, during the twelfth month, the infant learns to 'cruise' round his support. At the start he is likely to pull himself up so that he is facing the sofa-back or other support and holding on to it with both hands. Maintaining the two-handed grip, he inches his hands along, and follows them with a sideways step with the leading foot. Left straddle-legged, he usually then sits down; indeed it may be this crabwise cruising which first teaches him how to sit down from standing. As greater confidence develops, he begins to move, still sideways, but hand over hand along the support, moving one foot and then bringing the other up to it. With more confidence still, the infant stands further back from the support, so that he holds on more or less at arm's length. By this stage he is using the support purely for balance, and is trusting his full weight to his feet, even during the difficult moments when one foot is in the air in mid step.

It is only at this stage – usually between 12 and 13 months – that most babies appreciate walking while holding an adult's two hands. At earlier stages they tend to be alarmed by the empty space all around them, and to prefer to move around solid furniture.

At the first birthday, most babies will be moving around on their own two feet in *some* fashion. A few will be actually walking, at least a few steps from one support to another. Rather more will be walking around furniture, letting go with one hand to reach with the other hand for the next support. These may also stand without support for a few moments. Most will still be cruising only where they can hold on with both hands. And a good many will still only be pulling themselves up.

Learning to walk takes most babies about 9 months, from the time they first pull themselves to standing, to the time when they can be said to toddle freely around. It also takes them a great deal of physical effort, and a good deal of what, in an older person, would be called courage. Which adult would spend his time hauling himself to his feet, wobbling, falling down; getting up again, taking a step and falling again, day after day after day? Most people would send for a wheelchair after a couple of weeks. In geological time, as Anthony Smith[101] colourfully points out, being a biped is a very recent development. Our ancestors were quadrupeds, with horizontal spines. Our assumption of the upright posture freed our hands for tool use, and contributed to our superiority over other animals. But we achieved it by adapting a quadruped's skeleton, not by an entirely new engineering design. Every new human being repeats, in miniature, the difficulties of turning that skeletal structure upright. And to some extent every human being suffers from the inappropriate design of his spine for bipedal life, for the rest of his years.

In the first year, babies are physically much better adapted to quadrupedal than bipedal life. Compared with adults, or older children, their shoulders are hunched, their necks short, their rib cages rounded, and their bone mass very high in relation to their muscle mass. During the second and third years, all this is modified. Muscle has been shown, by X-ray, to increase its width at twice the rate that bone width increases during the same period. The rib cage becomes progressively flatter, and the neck longer. At the same time the infant's legs straighten and lengthen relative to his body and arms, and his feet develop arches.

When a baby first stands, he looks so peculiar that his mother is often concerned. His arms appear very long in relation to his legs. But time will adjust this relationship, and in the meantime it serves the child well by keeping his centre of gravity low, for balance, while leaving his reach comparatively long. Furthermore this appearance is increased by the child's tendency to straddle his legs and flex his hips, also in an attempt to aid balance. Straight legs, at this age, are the exception rather than the rule. Most infants appear either bandy legged (though some are so encumbered with nappies this is hardly surprising) or knock-kneed. All are flat-footed, and start to walk with the whole sole of the foot put directly to the floor. The arched foot with its heel-toe walk comes later. All these characteristics contribute to the gait we know as 'toddling'. Another 2 years or so will change the toddler

into the straight-limbed, slimmed down, beautifully pro-
portioned, freely moving creature we call a child.

While the sequence of developments, and the ages at
which they occur, are as this chapter has described for most
children in Western societies, neither ages nor sequence are
invariable.

A few infants leave out the crawling stage altogether.
Usually such infants learn to sit steadily at a comparatively
early age. They learn to pull themselves to standing, from the
sitting position, and from then on seem to concentrate their
attention on cruising round the furniture. Cruising satisfies
their desire for mobility, and they do not bother to crawl.
Usually such an infant *can* in fact crawl. If, while he is sitting
down, an attractive object, such as a small bright vehicle, is
pushed across the floor in front of him he will not haul himself
up to go after it, he will follow it at ground level. Infants who
leave out crawling are therefore choosing not to crawl, rather
than unable to do so.

Some infants go through the crawling phase, but in
idiosyncratic ways. A few roll over and over to get quickly
across the room, and then squirm the last foot or two to their
objectives. Others, especially those who are somewhat late in
learning to sit up, lie on their backs, raise their buttocks off
the ground supported by heels and shoulders, and progress
by 'humping'. Some seem late in learning to pull their knees
up under them, and get around by squirming forward on
their hands and elbows, dragging their legs behind them, or
pushing with their toes with legs extended. Some never use
hands and knees for crawling, but rather move on hands and
feet, 'walking like a bear'. This last form of progression is also
sometimes adopted by conventionally crawling babies as a
last stage before walking. Finally, babies who learn to sit
steadily at an early age sometimes adopt the 'bottom shuffle',
getting about on one buttock and one hand. This last method
does sometimes seem to delay walking. A real expert at the
bottom shuffle gets little advantage from learning to walk. A
crawling baby cannot look around very well, and has both
his hands occupied. But a bottom-shuffling baby has the

same visual field (somewhat lower down) as a walking one, and has one hand free. Furthermore he is firmly balanced.

In extremely rare cases, an infant may thumb his nose at the accepted sequence of motor development not by simply leaving one stage out, but by reversing the sequence and learning to crawl, or even to walk, before he learns to sit alone. Illingworth[102] reports one such case, where a bright, well-advanced girl reached the age of 19 months, cruising well around furniture, walking with one hand held, but quite unable to sit up. In the absence of any other reason, it was thought that she must have congenital shortening either of the gluteus maximus muscle, or of the hamstrings. There are also cases in the literature of institutionalized infants who crawled before they could sit up. These may be due to neglect. If an infant is put on the floor he can teach himself to crawl. But without adult help he cannot get himself up to try sitting; if he is left lying in a cot whenever he is not on the floor he may not even know what sitting up feels like.

Some infants follow the usual sequence of motor development, but show a marked acceleration, sitting alone as early as 4–5 months, and walking independently before 9 months. Sometimes such acceleration is part of an overall advanced state of development. But often – to the bitter disappointment of parents who have been proud of their child's early achievements – it proves to bear no relation to overall development. Illingworth[102] quotes the example of a boy whom he saw walking alone at 8 months, and who on formal I.Q. testing at the age of 5 had an I.Q. of 88 – well below the average.

Hot controversy has raged, in recent years, around the question of the motor precocity of African as compared with European babies. Geber and Dean[103] studied 113 Ugandan newborns who behaved like European babies of 3–4 weeks. They studied a further 183 children between 1 month and 6 years, and found that sitting alone was usual at 5 months, while the infants tended to pull themselves to standing at 7 months and walk alone at 9 months.

These findings, and many similar ones, were hotly disputed

by Knobloch.[104] But his sample were American Negroes, where Geber's were Bantu East Africans. His lived in urban America, hers in Uganda.

Ainsworth[48] also found motor precocity in the Ugandan infants she studied. She attributed it, at least in part, to the very close physical relationship between infant and mother. She saw it, therefore, as culturally and socially caused, rather than as a racial phenomenon.

Ironically, Pavenstedt[105] has shown that *adverse* social circumstances can produce motor acceleration also. In her study of grossly deprived and neglected infants, she found motor development far in advance of development in any other field. She attributed this, at least in part, to the absence of safety precautions taken for these infants, or holding devices provided for them.

But while there is some evidence accumulating to suggest that social and environmental factors may influence the age at which walking begins, most European longitudinal studies, looking repeatedly at the same infants over time, have shown no social-class or sex differences relating to motor development. The only consistently recurring variable in such studies has been familial: both early and late walking tend to run in families.

While the possibly accelerating effects of extra motor stimulation, of neglect leading to extra motor practice or of genetic variables remain open questions, some workers consider that specific teaching might lead to earlier independent walking. In the newborn period, infants exhibit a reflex reaction to feeling the soles of their feet touching a hard surface. Held in this position they place one foot after another, as if they were 'walking'. Zelazo, Zelazo and Kolb[106] found that infants whose newborn walking reflex was regularly and deliberately exercised, and who were held in walking position for regular practice even after the reflex died away, learned to walk independently some weeks earlier than a control group of infants. It is not yet clear, however, whether it was the specificity of the walking practice, or the more general motor stimulation given to the experimental infants, which led to the earlier walking. Nor is it clear whether the newborn walking reflex was actually maintained, prevented from dying out as it does in most infants, or whether the reflex died out to be replaced by newly learned walking techniques.

There is ample scope for further research into the development of walking. In the meantime, for practical purposes, it is safe to assume that given every opportunity for physical freedom, physical play and physical assistance from his parents, an infant will walk as soon as he is ready. Over-encouragement to an infant who is not steady on his feet – not ready, in his own view, to walk alone – can be actually dangerous. The skull fontanelles are seldom completely closed even by 1 year. The infant's skull provides far less protection than it will do later. It is not a good idea to encourage falls, and the best way to discourage them is to let the infant decide when and how he will walk.

CHAPTER TWENTY-TWO

BECOMING A TOOL-USER

At 6 months, the infant has become adept at getting hold of objects. If a toy which he wants is offered to him, he will reach out and take it. If it is placed on a table within his reach, he will stretch out and pick it up. He no longer needs the continual visual monitoring, the glancing backwards and forwards between his own hand and the object to which he is reaching, which was typical of his behaviour a few weeks earlier. His reaching is now what Burton, Castle, White and Held[26, 27] describe as 'top-level'. The child sees the object he wants, and without needing to look at his hand – which may be in his lap – stretches directly for it. The extent to which the 6-month infant can do without visual monitoring when reaching out and grasping is illustrated by an unusual experiment conducted by Bower.[107] He found that if infants were shown a brightly coloured and lit object, within easy reach of their hands, they could reach out and grasp it when all light had been extinguished. The reaching and grasping were therefore accomplished completely 'blind'.

In this, his most recent book, Bower also describes an interesting change in the relationship between reaching out to an object and actually grasping it. In younger infants, as they become proficient at reaching for objects, the reaching and the grasping become a single movement. The infant reaches, and, as his hand comes to the object, his fist closes. If he has mis-reached, so that the fist closes on nothing, he withdraws the hand and repeats the whole reach–grasp sequence. Furthermore, babies under about 6 months very seldom reach to an object *without* grasping. Hence the pulled noses and hair of normal motherhood.

Bower believes that at around 6 months reaching and grasping become differentiated behaviours which the infant is progressively able to use together or separately. He has, of course, been able to grasp without reaching since the earliest days of life. But he now becomes able to reach without grasping. Bower sees this as developmentally significant in that once an infant can reach and then grasp, as two separate-but-related actions, he can also presumably learn to grasp and then reach. And that is a prerequisite of tool use.

This separation of the two actions of reaching and grasping has not yet been satisfactorily proved, experimentally. Bower himself maintains that in younger infants there is no measurable pause between the end of reach and the beginning of grasp; while in infants over 6 months there is such a pause, when the arm has finished its movement and the hand has not yet begun the grasp. But this pause is measured in milliseconds. The experiments may prove difficult to duplicate.

In the meantime Bower believes that traditional learning theory can provide an adequate explanation for differentiation between reach and grasp. Younger infants reach out and grasp everything they see that is within reach and which they want. But many such 'objects' are not in fact graspable. At one time or another every infant can be seen vainly trying to capture a dancing sunbeam, clutching at a soap bubble, or trying to pick up a bright picture from the page of a book. The child's world is full of such visual illusions: things which look solid and graspable, and are not. Bower believes that the older infant has learned this and has learnt that to ascertain whether or not an object can be grasped, it is safer to rely on tactile than on visual information. If an object feels graspable, then it is. Our environment does not provide tactile illusions in the way it provides visual ones. Things that feel solid, are solid, even though certain materials may provide surprises by being unexpectedly light, or heavy, for their size.

The older infant therefore looks, reaches and touches, before he grasps.

Whether or not Bower's theoretical formulation and preliminary experiments in this area prove correct, they certainly make sense in terms of the changes in manual behaviour which take place during the months immediately after the infant has learned an accurate top-level reach.

Increasingly, at 7, 8 and 9 months, the infant touches things without trying to grasp them. He pats and strokes the table in front of him; his mother may get her hair stroked without it being pulled; the infant can touch a pet rabbit without squashing its ear in his fist. Increasingly, too, he differentiates the use of his individual fingers and thumbs from the use of his whole hand. At 9 months he can reach out and poke an object with his index finger, instead of pushing it with his hand. A little later, when asked to point something out, he will point with that index finger instead of indicating the object with a wave of the whole hand. And in picking things up, he will pre-adjust his hand to the seen size of the object not simply by shaping the hand as he did earlier, but by approaching very small objects only with the thumb and index finger. Before his first birthday he will oppose finger and thumb so accurately that he can pick up a single currant.

Many mammals will use their fore-limbs to get hold of objects. The 6-month infant's ability to reach out and take things is still very primitive. It is only the very beginning of the manual dexterity which will eventually distinguish him from all other animals.

At 6 months, the most characteristic 'use' which an infant makes of an object is still to put it in his mouth. He may, however, transfer it from one hand to the other. And as he holds it, his fingers will curl round it in a grip which is far more secure than the palmar grasp of the 4–5-month infant.

At this stage, if a second object is handed to the infant while he is holding the first, he will drop the first to receive the second, even if he could comfortably hold one in each of his hands. It is as if his attention span is not great enough to take in two things. The first object is not thrown away, or openly and deliberately rejected, in favour of the second. It simply drops from his hand because his attention is on taking the second.

But the infant's reaction to objects matures quickly. By the end of the sixth month, while he may still mouth the object briefly, he is also likely to do something with it, to make some use of it or some attempt at exploring its possibilities. If the object is a simple cube, such as is used in developmental testing, he may bang it on the table. If it should be a bell, or rattle, which sounds as he picks it up, he may deliberately shake it to make it sound again. Once the infant tends to do something with objects, he is also likely to be able to hold two at the same time. But he is still unlikely to use both together to make a more interesting toy than each separately. He may, for example, wave two rattles, one in each hand. But he will seldom bang the two together so that they combine their sounds to make more.

Few infants over 6 months can get more than passing entertainment out of watching and playing with their own hands. The baby may still suck his fingers or his thumb as a comfort habit when he is tired, worried or sleepy. And he may still glance at them as they pass across his field of vision. But he knows all he needs to know about his hands as objects. They have become all too familiar. Infants who are reared in boring, understimulating conditions – perhaps particularly in institutions – tend to continue with hand play for longer than other babies, and to develop other forms of self-stimulating or masturbatory play. Such a baby may learn the pleasures of rhythmical rocking or head banging, or he may discover that he can comfort and amuse himself by combining thumb sucking with rhythmical pressing of his thighs together, or rubbing of his genitals against the cot bars. All these comfort habits are normal, in the sense that many babies use some of them from time to time. But extensive use of any of them during waking hours does suggest that the baby is having to provide most of his own stimulation and play. If nothing else is provided for him, he will play with himself. But offered people and objects he will play mostly with them.

Some families do not understand the exploratory nature of early manual play. The infant is offered toys, but only a stereotyped small collection. He may have a string of beads or plastic balls strung across his pram, two small toys fastened to the bars of his cot, and two rattles and one teething ring which are offered to him when he is awake in his baby chair or playpen. To limit a baby's playthings in this way is like leaving a hospital patient to lie in bed all day with one book which he has already read. For a 6-month baby, the possibilities of such simple toys are extremely limited. Once they have been thoroughly explored they are no longer entertaining. Failing anything else, he may pick up the rattle and wave it once or twice, just as that hospital patient might idly leaf through his book once more. But then he drops it, and cries.

In this age period infants tend to give maximum attention to objects which are just slightly different from those which they have handled before.[108] Objects which are entirely familiar are boring, and merit little attention. Objects which are completely new and unexpected are often ignored; perhaps they evoke anxiety because of their strangeness, or perhaps their possibilities are simply not recognized by the child. Experiments have been done, for example, which clearly showed that 6-month infants paid far more attention to a slight variation on a tune which had been made familiar to them, than they did either to the familiar version or a totally new tune. Similarly, once accustomed to a particular mobile to look at, they were far more interested in that same mobile with a small alteration than they were in the same one unaltered, or a brand new one.

Infants with older brothers and sisters are usually exposed to just the 'right' mixture of familiar and slightly different objects to play with. Bored with his own bricks, the infant may be handed a giant Lego brick belonging to his brother. It is still a brick, but it has interesting nobbles on it, and being plastic rather than wood it makes a different sound when banged on the table. Bored with his woolly ball, the infant tries a rubber one; his tedious old rattles give place to his sister's maraccas or a tin of model animals which he can shake. Above all, such an infant is able to demonstrate his pleasure in slightly new and different objects; his mother can *see* that he likes the contents of the 3-year-old's toy box better than his own baby toys. But the first baby may not be so lucky. His baby toys may be the only real *toys* in the house.

And it may not occur to his mother to share hers with him.

The desire for constant but slight novelty in the objects he plays with does mean that bought toys are often inappropriate for infants of this age group. Mothers can neither afford, nor store, a continual succession of rattles and balls and bricks and cuddly toys. There are some toys which can be bought now, and used, in many different ways, over a long period. But basic day-to-day entertainment can almost always be better provided from within the existing household. Wooden spoons, small saucepans, boxes with lids, scrumply paper, pieces of material, ribbon and string, will all be pleasurably explored. And when the infant tires of one saucepan, another may please him. It is familiar, but its weight, its size, its colour are different. In our consumer society with its ludicrously elaborate packaging, the family's weekly shopping can provide scores of objects which will interest the infant. The stoutest can be stored to make an 'odds-and-ends box' for the infant to turn out and repack when he is a few months older. Obviously such *ad hoc* play materials have to be closely supervised. A rattle from a reputable shop may bore the baby but it will not cut his mouth; a yoghurt carton will if he bites it.

The infant's progress as a tool-user does seem to be closely related to the opportunities he is given. Between 6 and 8 months he learns about objects by handling them, and the more different objects he handles, the more he will learn. By around 8 months, he also begins to learn by watching demonstrations. The difference can be most clearly seen in the infant's reaction to pencils and paper, and to toys which can be pulled along on strings. At 7 months, the infant will pick up a crayon but however much his mother attracts his attention, and scribbles with it, he is unlikely to copy her. He will chew the crayon and scrumple the paper. But around 8 months, if someone *does* demonstrate the action and result of scribbling, he will definitely watch, and may attempt to copy, although he is unlikely to manage to mark the paper for another couple of months. Similarly, at around 7 months, the infant may manage to pick up a piece of string, attached to a little wheeled toy on the other side of the table. By pulling at the string, he may even draw the toy towards him, but he is unlikely to show much sign of understanding what he has done. Six weeks later, a demonstration will be watched closely and eventually copied. There is seldom any doubt when an infant has understood and deliberately repeated such an achievement. The arrival of the toy is usually greeted with enormous pleasure, grins and lengthy excited babbling.

By 9 months the infant's reaction to two simultaneous objects has changed completely. He no longer disregards the first in favour of the second nor uses them both but separately. Typically he now brings the two together, side by side, as if comparing them. And he begins to use the two objects together; banging them against each other; putting them down on the table top, picking them up again. But his skill with objects is still inhibited by the difficulty he experiences with letting *go* of what he has picked up. Releasing an object is exactly opposite, in its neuro-physiological demands, to grasping. And it involves controlling the fingers separately from the whole hand. Normally it begins to develop at around 9 months, or simultaneously with the beginning of a finger–thumb pincer approach to very small objects, and the ability to use the index finger alone for pointing or poking.

At 9 months most infants can only let go of an object by putting object and hand on to a flat, hard surface. It is in this way that the infant frees his hand from one cube in order to pick up another. The idea of release usually comes before the ability. The infant may respond to the mother's request to 'give it to me' by holding the object out to her. But he cannot actually let go of it. Indeed his fingers may remain quite tightly curled around it, so that she has to uncurl them to retrieve the toy. A little later, if she holds her hand flat under his, he may be able to release the toy on to her palm, as he does on to the table top. But he will still be unable to drop it into a container, or on to the floor.

Deliberate releasing of objects usually starts late in the tenth month. It may usher in a phase which the mother does not entirely enjoy. As with other abilities, once the infant can, he will. And that means weeks of toys dropped over the edge of the pram; food dropped over the feeding tray, flannels dropped out of the bath. Many mothers resort to tying objects on to every piece of equipment the infant uses. This may be why, typically, it is in the tenth month that infants get the idea of swinging things on the end of strings, and much enjoy 'fishing' over the edge of cot or pram.

During the eleventh month, all these dawning abilities together with the child's mobility, are put together in his play. He learns to throw objects away from him, neither dropping them, nor pushing them, but genuinely (if wildly) throwing them. He will throw a soft ball, crawl after it, and do it again. Equally he will behave like a small retriever dog if an adult will throw for him. He learns to push away a wheeled toy as well as pulling it back by its string. His new ability to release objects from the hand makes filling and emptying games a top favourite. The various forms of 'posting box' sold commercially are usually too sophisticated for the child at this stage. But a box and some bricks will be combined and recombined endlessly. The infant may, if he is given a demonstration, even attempt to put one brick on another to make a tower, by the time he is a year old. But here the difficulty he still has in accurate releasing usually foils his attempts. He poises the second brick accurately over the first, but cannot let it go in exactly the right place.

The last three months of the first year should be a time when the infant is encouraged to use these play abilities in daily life, too. Where at 6 months he probably grabbed the spoon with which his mother was feeding him, just because he was an object-grabber, at 9 months he is perfectly aware of its use. His attempts at self-feeding will probably still be extremely messy. But there is some evidence that infants who are prevented from feeding themselves during this vital phase may still be having food ladled into their mouths at 18 months or even 2 years. Feeding by the mother at that kind of age can all too easily become forced-feeding (see Chapter 25). Messy or not, he should be allowed to do all the self-feeding he can manage, now.

In the bath he can and should have the flannel to swish over himself, even if he would still suck the soap if allowed that. In dressing, he knows quite well that shoes go on feet, and will have a go at putting them there. If he is not hurried, he will hold out his arms for a coat or his legs for his trousers. Given the chance, he will imitate many of his mother's domestic activities, presaging the passion for housework which is so typical of the second year.

By his first birthday, the baby can get hold of objects, get rid of them again; retrieve them by a variety of means, including the conceptually difficult one of pulling a string. And he begins to know what to do with them, what they are *for*. He has come a very long way in six months.

CHAPTER TWENTY-THREE

BECOMING A TALKER

As we saw in Chapter 17, the study of very early language development is an extremely difficult field, and one in which there is a scarcity of good research. The study of language in this second half-year is little better. There are disputes among research workers about what infants utter, about what their utterances 'mean', about why they make the sounds they do make and indeed about why they make the effortful transition from sound-making to speech at all. Given that infants do eventually begin to speak, there is further argument about whether understanding of a word must come before that word is spoken, or whether the word can be spoken before it is understood. And all this disputation takes place across many disciplines: as well as linguistic specialists, there are neurologists, physiologists, brain biochemists, psychologists, social psychologists and philosophers researching in this area.

If few pieces of our knowledge about language development are agreed, most workers would be unanimous on one point: the importance of language. In many ways language is the most vital function which an infant develops. It is the basic tool of being a human being. If rising on to his hind legs and becoming a tool-using biped gave developing man an advantage over other animals, developing speech gave him an even greater one. By using language we can convey information about things which are not physically present, and about ideas which do not physically exist. We can say anything which we can do; say what we cannot do; say what no man has ever done. We can discuss possibilities, projects, ideas which are truly original, outside the experience of man. The knowledge of one generation can be passed on to the next without the new generation having to undergo the experiences or do the finding out for itself. The saving of time and effort and the creative possibilities which all this opens up are immeasurable. They add up to what we call 'culture'.

For many generations it was assumed that human language was unique not only in its expression in speech, but also in the degree of abstract conceptual thinking which that speech demonstrated. It could be seen that no other animal spoke as humans speak, and it was assumed that no other animal was capable of the thought processes which lie behind speech. Recent work with animals – especially with dolphins and with chimpanzees – has begun to nibble at those assumptions of our total superiority. Animals cannot be taught to *speak* our language because they do not have the appropriate neuromuscular organization for producing speech sounds with the lips and tongue. The natural language of animals contains, among its postures and other physical signals, comparatively few *sounds* used, for example, to signal danger to a group, or to call the young to the mother or the adults to a hunt. But if a means of expression more suitable than sound can be found, chimpanzees, for example, can learn a great deal of human language.

Several now famous chimpanzees have been raised in human families, treated (as far as possible) as if they were human infants, with the express purpose of assessing the difference in their development, and the points at which they ceased to be able to compete with human children. It has been clear for forty years that such chimps could learn to *understand* words, but not to speak them. The chimpanzee Gua, in the 1930s, learned to understand around 100 words. Vicki, in the 1940s, learned even more. But neither animal could ever utter more than three or four effortful word-approximations. In the 1960s a chimp named Washoe was taught to communicate extensively, using the American Sign Language rather than the spoken word.[109]

Now the Premacks[110] have devised an entirely new 'language' for their chimpanzee, whose name is Sarah. The language consists of a variety of coloured plastic shapes. Using these, Sarah has learned the names of many objects and many people. More importantly, she has clearly shown that she can use the plastic symbols to 'talk' about objects which are not actually there. For example, once she had been taught 'brown colour of chocolate', she could later select on command a brown disc from among four discs of different colours. She must therefore have been able to generate some mental picture of chocolate, or of brownness, against which to match the coloured discs.

Similarly, shown an apple, Sarah could pick out appropriate descriptive symbols for it, in terms of it being red and round, rather than green and square, and so on. Later on, given the blue plastic triangle which was her 'word' for apple, she was able again to 'describe' it correctly, just as she had done when the real apple was there for her to look at.

Finally, and perhaps most surprisingly, Sarah has shown that she can understand grammar, so that she interprets complex sentences correctly rather than simply as a string of 'words'. Told, 'Sarah insert apple pail banana dish ('Sarah, put the apple into the pail and the banana into the dish') she performs correctly. To do this she has to understand that 'apple' and 'pail' go together, but 'banana' does not go with 'pail' even though it is also next to it in sequence. She also has to understand that the word 'insert' applies to both the apple and pail, and the banana and dish simultaneously. Without this kind of understanding she would presumably attempt to put the apple, the pail and the banana all into the dish. Sarah's language development is considered to be at least equal to that of a 2-year-old child.

It is not clear to what extent chimpanzees think, or conceptualize, in the wild. But it is clear that they are capable of doing so, to some extent, if they are taught. No doubt we shall find out the limits over the next few generations of research work.

In the meantime, with indications like these that man is not the only mammal capable of using symbols for at least some degree of abstract thought, it is perhaps not surprising that neurophysiologists can find nothing unique about the *structure* of the human brain. There is no obvious difference between the brains of humans and the higher animals, such that one can say, 'This is a brain that can develop language;

that is a brain which cannot.' It seems then that human language ability must arise from the way in which the given brain structure develops, and works, rather than from the way in which it is constructed. As Lenneberg[111] puts it: 'In general it is not possible to assign any specific neuro-anatomic structure to the capacity for language . . . Language is probably due to the peculiar way in which various parts of the brain work together, or, in other words, to its peculiar function.'

One notable peculiarity of human brains is the sheer length of time over which they continue to develop. In an earlier paper[112] Lenneberg cites the evidence for this long maturation period; he quotes anatomical, histological, biochemical and electrophysiological data, all showing that development continues at least until puberty.

With this long period of brain development goes a marked degree of brain plasticity, such that one part of the brain appears to be capable of taking over the function of another part if and when the need arises. This ability is dramatically demonstrated by work such as that of Bassler.[113] He has shown that infants who lose one complete hemisphere of the brain often do better, in terms of speech development and other abilities, than infants who suffer a less severe but more generalized brain damage. He believes that because the brain is still developing, and because it has this plasticity – this ability to compensate itself – the total removal of one major part allows other parts to take over its function. Where, on the contrary, a damaged part of the brain is left *in situ*, it continues to function, so that no other part usurps its role, but it functions aberrantly, so that normal development cannot take place.

While both the slow maturation and the plasticity of human brain function can be taken as proven, their connection with the development of language is not. But there is a good deal of evidence to support the deduction.

Language develops in infants at widely varying rates, and therefore at a range of ages, but it develops in an invariate sequence. The basic learning may, under optimal conditions, be compressed into two or three years, with only extensions of vocabulary, and the means of expressing complex abstract thought still remaining to be learned. Or the basic learning may stretch over the whole of childhood. At either extreme, the sequence is the same. There are, for example, experimental data demonstrating the identical language-learning sequence in first and later-born children, in the children of deaf and hearing parents, in children from widely varying socio-economic and cultural groups, in children from complete and attentive homes compared with those from broken and neglectful homes. Even children in extremely deprived institutional care develop language in the same sequence as family children, albeit far more slowly.

Mentally retarded children usually begin to acquire speech late, and improve slowly. But if they begin to use language at all they, like other deprived children, will continue to improve all through childhood. When they reach puberty language improvement tends to cease, presumably because brain maturation is then complete.

In practical terms it is unfortunate that this long-drawn-out language learning, within a normal, but usually much briefer, sequence, is not more widely recognized. All too often a child of 6 or 7 whose language development is only equivalent to that of an 18-month infant is 'written off' as being incapable of further language improvement. Even under ideal circumstances such a child would probably never catch up with his more fortunate peers. But if only he could continue to be given the kind of verbal help which is automatically offered to an 18-month infant, he would almost certainly continue to improve until he reached adolescence. And that might mean that he ended up with a 'verbal age' equivalent to a normal 8- or 9-year-old, rather than equivalent to that of a toddler.

But even though language learning can continue throughout childhood, it is clear that the first two years comprise the optimum time for its foundation to be laid. It is far more difficult to teach an infant to use language if he is cured of congenital deafness at 2 years old, than it is to help one who heard normally in his first year or two, and *then* had a period of deafness. Similarly, children who become permanently deaf after about the age of 2 respond far better to language training for the deaf than do children who have been deaf from birth.

Normal infants begin to acquire real speech before they actually need it. They begin to use words at an age and stage when crying, sound-making and gesture are still sufficient to ensure the meeting of their needs. Furthermore those first words, as we shall see (cf. also Chapter 30), are very seldom ones which have anything to do with the infant's needs in the physical sense. There is no obvious reason then why infants should bother to start acquiring speech. It seems that there must be an inbuilt propensity to develop language, just as there is an inbuilt propensity to babble.

Many people believe that the infant's basic motivation for making the effortful transition from babble to real language is social, that it is intimately tied up with his attachment to his mother or her surrogate, and with the pleasure and affection the infant gets from her. For example, Mowrer[114] puts forward what he calls the 'autism theory' of language development. The word 'autism' has psychopathological connotations in everyday speech but in Mowrer's terms the implications are simply 'reinforcement of the self by the self'. He believes that it is hearing his own sounds which stimulates a baby to make further sounds, and that the more affectionate the context in which his first sounds (from the outside world) are heard, the more he will make them himself, and be stimulated to make more. Mowrer cites research work on species of birds which are known to have the ability to reproduce human speech sounds. He points out that such birds only learn to 'talk' if they are made into pets. Once they have learned to associate certain human sounds with loving care from their owners they become alert, hopeful, pleased, when they hear similar sounds from *themselves*. He sums up: 'Words are reproduced if, and only if, they are first made to sound good in the context of affectionate care and attention.'

Dorothea McCarthy[115] derives similar ideas from work with human infants. She believes that infants come to associate the gentle speech sounds they hear with pleasure and with the fulfilment of needs. When the infant then hears his *own* sounds, they sound to him like those gentle speech sounds from his mother, and they therefore also make him feel pleased and contented. So he is stimulated to continue sound-making. McCarthy cites the case of one little girl who had a hearing loss sufficient to cut her off from gentle talk, but not sufficient to protect her from the explosive sounds of anger and prohibition. She could hear when her parents spoke roughly to her, but not when they spoke affectionately. She failed to develop any language until her hearing loss had been detected, and a hearing-aid had enabled her to hear gentle, loving sounds as well.

While this point of view cannot be said to be scientifically proved, it is well supported by observation. Early babbling, and the later inflected sound-making usually called 'jargon-ing', almost always occur when an infant is pleased. When he is angry or distressed he does not 'talk', he cries. It certainly seems that the precursors of language are related to pleasant emotions, not to unpleasant ones. Furthermore the idea that the infant talks because his own talk sounds to him like his mother talking is lent support by the fact that infants tend to talk to themselves in exactly the same way that they talk to their mothers. Babbling alone, in his cot, an infant will make a succession of sounds, pause, as if listening to those sounds, and then answer himself. In the same way when his mother talks to him, he listens to her and then talks back.

Infants who are in institutional care from birth often fail to develop the full range and frequency of sound-making which is normal in family infants. But if a baby is put into such care during the second half of his first year, after a pattern of self-reinforcing babble has established itself, then the pattern usually survives. It may be that the first infant has never had the chance to associate talk with loving care, and therefore does not develop it, while the second baby has already discovered the comforting, amusing aspect of talk, and therefore continues to direct it at himself even when he ceases to get much from his caretakers.

Finally, the first words acquired by infants themselves lend support to this idea that language development is a part of experiencing affection. Infants very seldom begin their speech with need-fulfilling words such as 'milk' or 'up' or 'sleep' or 'want'. The first words are almost always the names of deeply loved people or animals or of highly significant objects which give them pleasure.

At 6 months, most infants will carry on long babble conversations with the mother, listening intently to what she says, as long as she talks directly, face to face. A month later the baby will turn to the mother, definitely looking for her, if she calls to him when she is out of his sight. At this 7-month stage, too, his babble becomes enriched by two syllable 'words'. At first these are linked repetitions of his first cooing sounds: 'ala', 'ama', 'oogoo', 'lala' and 'looloo'. A little later, linked repetitions of his later sounds come into play with 'words' like 'mimi', 'ippi', 'aja' and so forth. The syllables are quite distinct; they are not lifted subjectively out of a blur of sound, but can be written down, phonetically, as they are uttered, with a high degree of agreement between one listener and another. This new repertoire of sound will certainly be brought into play when the baby is being talked to; but it is also practised when he is alone. A dawn chorus of babble often becomes the first thing parents hear each morning, rather than the crying which woke them in the earlier months.

By the eighth month most infants have learned to listen to – and try to join – conversations which are *not* directly aimed at them. If mother and father are talking, and the infant is sitting between them, his head will turn from one adult to the other and back again, as if the conversation was a tennis match he was closely following. Soon he learns how to interrupt. He develops a shout for attention. It may be jocular in tone, but it is a definite shout – not a yell, nor a squeal, but a shout. Some infants also learn their first singing tones about the time they learn to shout. Usually the 'singing' is a few notes up or down a scale. It may be set off by the mother or some other adult singing to the infant, or it may be a reaction to music heard on the radio or gramophone, or even to a musical toy. When it happens it is unmistakably singing, quite unlike any of the infant's other sounds.

Towards the end of the eighth month, and in the ninth, the repetitive babbling syllables are strung together into long-drawn-out repetitive phrases of four or more syllables, such as 'loo-loo-loo-loo-loo'. Once this begins, very definite changes of emphasis and shifts of phrasing can be heard. Soon after, the first multi-syllable complex babbles can be heard. The infant no longer repeats the same sound over and over again, he combines different sounds, so that he says, for example, 'ah-dee-dah-boo'. Once this kind of combination is heard, the infant is on the verge of producing his first words. And his inflections become so marked and varied that he sounds as if he is talking, fluently, but in another language. Ruth Griffiths's English sample[100] produced, on average, one clear word during the ninth month, two clear words and a definite shake of the head for 'no' during the tenth month, and three clear words by 1 year.

First words are difficult to identify or even to define. Infants' early vocabularies are often over-estimated because when they reach the age at which parents begin to *expect* them to produce words, they tend to count as words babbling sounds which the infant has been making for months. Few mothers will maintain that her 6-month baby is addressing her when he says 'mum-mum-mum'. But when he repeats this sequence at 11 months she may stoutly maintain that he says 'mummy'.

A word cannot be counted as a true word until it is used consistently and exclusively to refer to one particular thing. 'Mum-mum' becomes 'mummy' when the child only says it to or about his mother. But there is an in-between stage which complicates matters. Some infants pass through a period during which they clearly understand the identity of a particular object and also clearly realize that a word for it will communicate to the mother. But they have not yet fixated one particular word-sound to that object. For a while they use different words for the same thing as if any old word would do. Mura Jun Ichi[116] instances a child who used the word 'bon-bon' when asking for his ball. Later he used the word 'dan-dan' of the same ball. To the infant these were clearly words. He meant his ball; he did not mean anything else. But he had not 'decided' what to call that ball.

Even once an infant uses one and only one word-sound to mean always one and the same thing, it is not easy to say which of his words are true words. At this stage the sound the child uses may be an 'own word' which is barely related to the correct word for the object. One child, for example, referred to the family dog as 'gig'. His name was 'Tiger'. It is possible that the little girl was trying to approximate to the word 'dog'. Certainly she never referred to anything else as 'gig' and would crawl around, looking for the dog, calling him and eventually greeting him by this name. Once such an 'own word' is recognized by the adults around the child, it should certainly be counted as a true word. The very fact of the adults' recognition means that the sound the child makes is *functioning* as a word. The adults understand it. The word is communicating.

People of philosophical bent have often asked whether infants imitate words before they understand their meaning, or whether understanding must come before the child can imitate the word. As we shall see, the relevance of imitation to word-acquisition is often exaggerated. The question itself is off-centre. Anyone who observes infants finds that they understand a great many words months before they attempt to say any words at all, either spontaneously or in imitation. The mother says, 'Listen, Daddy's coming,' and the baby crawls, grinning, to the door. She says, 'Let's put on your shoes,' and he looks instantly at his own feet. Whether or not he *could* imitate a word whose meaning he did not know seems irrelevant when there are so many words he does understand just waiting to be said when he is ready.

Most infants who are approaching their first birthday are very ready to imitate adults: they copy gestures, ape

BECOMING A TALKER

327

together with the very sociable context of the child's language
learning, tends to make parents feel that they 'teach' their
children to talk. The mother discovers that if she engages the
child in conversation, and makes a clear distinct sound, he
will repeat it back to her. Once she has discovered this, she
may spend long periods of time holding objects up for the
child to see, saying their names, accepting or rejecting the
child's response. While this sort of face-to-face conversation
no doubt helps the child in his general language development,
by giving him lengthy and enjoyable conversations with his
mother, there is quite a lot of evidence that the actual teaching involved is so indirect as hardly to merit the name.

Bullowa, Jones and Duckert[117] carried out an elegant
study, using both film and tape recordings, of a mother trying
to teach her infant to say the word 'shoe'. The teaching and
the infant's responses followed the sequence shown in Table 13.

It seems clear from this fascinating case study that the
mother's direct behaviour had very little effect on the child.

TABLE 13. SEQUENCE OF ONE INFANT'S LEARNING OF
THE WORD 'SHOE'

	Mother	Infant	Comment
Stage 1	Said 'shoe' in clear association with child's shoe		
	→		
		Attempted imitation 'tu'	
	←		
	Rejected imitation		Mother's rejection of imitation did not
	→		
		Continued to use 'tu' for all references to own shoes	lead child to adapt or abandon her own word which had clear reference.

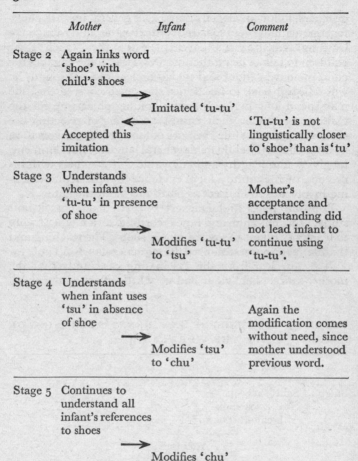

	Mother	*Infant*	*Comment*
Stage 2	Again links word 'shoe' with child's shoes		
		Imitated 'tu-tu'	
	Accepted this imitation		'Tu-tu' is not linguistically closer to 'shoe' than is 'tu'
Stage 3	Understands when infant uses 'tu-tu' in presence of shoe		Mother's acceptance and understanding did not lead infant to continue using 'tu-tu'.
		Modifies 'tu-tu' to 'tsu'	
Stage 4	Understands when infant uses 'tsu' in absence of shoe		Again the modification comes without need, since mother understood previous word.
		Modifies 'tsu' to 'chu'	
Stage 5	Continues to understand all infant's references to shoes		
		Modifies 'chu' to adult 'shu'	

When she rejected the first imitation it nevertheless remained in the child's repertoire, unchanged, for some time. Later, when she accepted and understood, both in the presence and absence of the shoes, a further imitation, her rewarding behaviour did not prevent the child from continuing to adapt the word until she finally arrived at the adult pronunciation. Furthermore the mother's accuracy as a teacher is called into question as well as her effectiveness. The imitation which she did understand and accept was no more accurate than the one she had rejected a few days earlier.

It seems likely, from this and from other evidence, that the infant's eventual production of words comes about more by watching the mother, and listening to her constant use of the word-related-to-the-object, than by her direct teaching. As daily life proceeds, the mother constantly says 'Where are your shoes?' or 'Let's put on your shoes' or 'Oh, what muddy shoes' or 'Off with your shoes.' The mother uses the same noun in a variety of situations, and in combination with a variety of other speech forms. The noun 'shoe' is the one consistent sound amid this complexity, and is always directed at those things that are put on and off feet. The infant may learn more from observing this than he does from having a shoe dangled in front of him while the mother says 'shoe', 'say "shoe"' and so on.

Of course infants eventually learn to speak in the language which they hear spoken around them, even if an American visitor finds himself amazed at the fluency with which Greek 2-year-olds can speak Greek. But at the 9-12 months' stage it appears that infants are learning language in general, rather than any one language in particular. Just like older people, different infants have different voices, and a listener can therefore usually tell which of two infants is 'talking'. But the *nationality* of the infant will not help him to distinguish one from another. Two American babies may sound as similar or as different as do an American and a Japanese. Nakazima[34] made a careful study of speech development in Japanese and American infants. Despite the marked linguistic differences between the two languages, he was able to find no differences whatsoever between the utterances of the two groups of infants, even with the use of spectrographic apparatus. When the infants began to produce their first 'real words', there was still no difference. The first words which Japanese parents accepted as words in Japanese were identical in phonetic composition with those which American parents accepted as real words in American-English. The words were, of course, based on the early universal babbling sounds like 'mama', 'dada', 'nana', 'papa' or 'baba'.

Nationality then made no difference to early sounds or to first words. Even more surprisingly, Nakazima found that nationality was also irrelevant to the trouble which infants experienced in learning the 'difficult' speech sounds. Certain sounds, such as S, Z, TH, R and F, are seldom produced in spontaneous babbling, and are learned only slowly and with difficulty when children are extending their actual vocabularies. Their absence or inaccuracy accounts for much of the lisping and 'babytalk' which is typical of the second and third years. Nakazima found that children whose language employed these sounds extensively learned them no more quickly or easily than children whose languages employed them comparatively little. The sounds were difficult for all children, irrespective of nationality.

It does seem, then, that just as there is 'language' which is basic to all animals, and of which human speech is only a highly developed and sophisticated form, so there are language sounds which are basic to human beings. Differentiation into separate languages is yet another level of sophistication which only comes about when the infant enters the peak phase for individual word and grammatical structure learning, in the second year of life.

ONE-YEAR SUMMARY

The year-old infant has made strides in his development which seem enormous to the adults around him. In fact, he has not changed his behaviour as radically in this second half-year as he did in the first. But now he is mobile (either as a biped or a quadruped); he talks (to some extent) and he uses objects. All these developments make him seem far more like a small human being than he did 6 months earlier.

The particular stage which any individual child will be at when he reaches his first birthday is dependent on the area to which he is devoting most of his time and energy. He is unlikely to forge ahead on all fronts simultaneously. If he is just beginning to acquire words, his motor progress may seem to be at a standstill. If he is concentrating on climbing the stairs and the chairs he may not seem to be learning words at the same time. If he is battling to stay on his own two feet, he may have no time for his toys.

As at 6 months, his relationship with his parents is critical too. If he has already joined some of the typical toddler battles with his mother, over eating, or going to bed, or using a pot, quite a lot of his behaviour may be directed at getting back at her – at venting his frustration and demanding her attention.

While much of the slowness in development which arose from neonatal troubles has now been lost in the passage of time, the sequences of development remain almost invariable. Therefore it is useless to 'expect' a child to pull himself to standing just because he is a year old, unless he sat alone between 7 and 10 months. It is useless to expect him to feed himself with a spoon if he only became adept at reaching out and picking objects up at 9 months. It is useless to expect him to begin to acquire real words, if his private 'jargoning' is not yet heavily inflected and widely varied in content. As

before, the infant's present development, and expectations of
his immediate future development, are only meaningful in
the light of the past.

BEHAVIOUR	LIKELY STAGE REACHED AT 1 YEAR	COMMENTS
Feeding	3 meals at ordinary family times. Snacks at mid morning and afternoon.	Many infants will still be having a bottle, but at *their* bedtime, rather than the mother's. Some will have bottles more or less *ad lib.*, together with frequent snack foods. Their actual food intake may be more than twice as high as their 'meals'.
Food	Many will still be fed almost entirely on proprietary 'convenience' foods. But all should have learned to chew by now, and should be having finger foods.	Infant *could* eat ordinary family diet, with meat minced, and other foods cut up, de-pipped, etc. Few are given the chance.
Feeding method	Infant is perfectly capable of taking all milk from a cup. If he still uses a bottle now, it will be as much a comfort habit as a nutritional tool and he is likely to continue through the second year.	

BEHAVIOUR	LIKELY STAGE REACHED AT 1 YEAR	COMMENTS
Feeding Method	If given the chance earlier, the infant will feed himself from a spoon and with his fingers. He needs only minimal help.	Self-feeding now tends to avert feeding problems later. But it is rare. Most are still fed by the mother at this age.
Food preferences	As at 6 months, infant is likely to prefer soft or crisp foods, gagging on thick or sticky foods or those which, like meat, require lengthy chewing. May like far stronger tastes than mother expects, eating more enthusiastically if allowed some extra salt, grated cheese, salad dressings, etc.	Infant is at height of imitative phase. Will wish to try same foods as mother. None are intrinsically unsuitable; anything he can digest he can have, except alcohol.
Weight	Gains roughly 2–3 oz. (60–90g) per week from 6–12 months. An average birthweight baby (around 7 lb. (3·2kg)) who has gained normally, will now weigh just over 20 lb. (9·1kg).	Both food consumption and weight gain become less consistent around 1 year. If the infant is healthy, there is no point in weekly weighing. Monthly is ample.
Sleep	Average sleep is around $13\frac{1}{2}$ hours with very wide scatter. Most will sleep a 12-hour night. Most will also need 2 'rests' but may sleep	After about 9 months, infant can keep himself awake if he wants to. Upsets may start problems over falling asleep. Cannot wake

BEHAVIOUR	LIKELY STAGE REACHED AT 1 YEAR	COMMENTS
Sleep	for only a few minutes at one or both of these.	himself voluntarily, so night waking which is common can be dealt with only by comfort/reassurance. Comfort habits and the use of comfort objects are common at this age.
Crying	Crying from boredom or loneliness is largely replaced by tears of frustration when fails in self-imposed play task. Crying from anger is frequent. Cries when hurt – frequent when learning to walk – but may also cry from shock of bump which does not hurt. Cries when left by mother, and may cry when faced with strangers.	Infants vary in readiness with which they actually *cry* as opposed to using developing language ability to convey distress. By this age, there should be no crying for which the cause is not clear, even if the cause seems small to an adult.
Teeth	Will have cut two upper front and two lower front teeth. May have cut lower first molar, in which case upper first molar will be on the way.	Cutting of molars often causes some discomfort, relieved by biting hard foods or teething toys. First teeth should be cleaned.
Toilet training	A varying number of infants will have been potted for some	Infants whose bowel movements are regular may become 'clean'.

BEHAVIOUR	LIKELY STAGE REACHED AT 1 YEAR	COMMENTS
Toilet training	months. Many more will start around this time. A few infants begin now to 'tell' – usually after the event.	Few infants will tolerate regular frequent potting because their motor drive is so strong.
Sitting up	Sits independently on a hard surface. Leans forward or sideways and recovers balance. Gets himself unaided to sitting position from any other position.	Inability to sit alone by one year requires investigation.
Crawling	Crawls freely by some method. Usually hands and knees, but may be hands and feet, or, rarely, some version of shuffling on bottom.	Is unlikely to crawl well if sitting steadily has been late in developing. May miss out crawling if advanced in standing and walking.
Standing	Pulls himself to standing by furniture.	May have trouble sitting down from standing.
Walking	May cruise around supporting furniture, or walk a step or two with both hands held. May momentarily stand unsupported.	
Manual play	Touches, strokes and picks up objects accurately. Can separate fingers from	Manual ability and desire to imitate means that infant will readily learn to feed himself

BEHAVIOUR	LIKELY STAGE REACHED AT 1 YEAR	COMMENTS
Manual play	total hand grasp, to pick up tiny objects between finger and thumb. Can throw and push objects away. Uses attached string to retrieve or pull toys. Fills and empties containers with small objects. May attempt to build with bricks, but inaccurate release still causes difficulty. Copies demonstrations: e.g., scribbling with pencil.	with spoon, drink from cup, attempt to put on shoes, etc.
Social responses	Typically highly emotionally attached to mother, to father if he is sufficiently seen, and to other adults who share personal interaction with him. Highly dependent on mother's constant presence, though better able to entertain himself, in her presence, than earlier. May be suspicious or actually fearful of strangers. Reacts to disapproval from mother.	Likely to be highly disturbed by separation from mother at this period. May react badly to any major change, such as house move, holiday, etc.
Language (spoken)	Typically accompanies own play with 'jargoning' – highly inflected complex	Language development is highly variable. Actual words will not be produced before

BEHAVIOUR	LIKELY STAGE REACHED AT I YEAR	COMMENTS
Language (spoken)	babble, with many different syllables strung together, containing exclamation marks, question marks, and paragraphs. Sounds like talk, but has no recognizable words in it. Most have 3 clear words, which may only be loose approximations to actual words, but are used consistently to indicate one particular person or object. Shakes head for 'no'. Shouts for attention. Sings to music. Recognizes mother by voice alone.	expressive jargoning is established. Many normal infants will not say any words until the second year.
Language (understood)	Clearly understands many words and phrases. May obey simple commands to 'bring' or 'give' etc. May point to familiar objects in picture book, hold out foot at mention of 'shoe'.	Absence of expressive jargoning, *together* with failure to understand any words or phrases requires investigation of hearing.

SECTION V

THE SECOND YEAR:
FROM BABY TO TODDLER

CHAPTER TWENTY-FOUR

BEING A TODDLER

Between about 9 months and perhaps 15 months, infants become so diversified as human beings, and so clearly but variously affected by the environment in which they are being reared, that it becomes increasingly difficult to age-categorize their development. Most of the basic 'milestones' are passed. Most of the especial physiological features of early infancy have given way to more mature patterns. One can still give vague 'norms' for both accomplishments and problems, but the range of variation around those norms becomes ever wider. That is why this last section makes no attempt to look at development by quarter- or by half-years. The developments to be discussed now will take place roughly during the second year. Infants who lagged in some or in all respects at the end of their first year will, in most fields, still develop later than others. Infants who were ahead at the end of the first year may stay ahead. Others will unexpectedly spurt forward or drop back in one or several fields. So for some people this section will appear to apply to any infant under $3\frac{1}{2}$; for others it will appear only to apply up to 20 months.

Being a toddler is a little like being an adolescent. The toddler is between babyhood and childhood, just as the adolescent is between childhood and adulthood. The adolescent is often stereotyped as a rebel – as one who fights against the upbringing, the background, the restrictions he has accepted as a child; in the same way the toddler is often stereotyped as likely to be a problem to his parents. He too reaches a stage where he resents and fights the absolute power and control which his mother had over him when he was a baby. He too looks for new fields in which to exercise a new sense of power, a new sense of self. But there the similarity has reached its limits. Many adolescents are ready for self-determination; toddlers are not.

Some families manage to integrate toddlers in such a way that this second year is smooth and easy. When this happens, mothers tend to remember it as a halcyon period; to remember 2 as their 'favourite age'. Looking through case records, and observations, this happy state of affairs seems to come down to both infant and parents being able to stay in step with themselves, and in step with each other. Innumerable chance factors – quite simple, practical ones – seem to play a vital part in this, perhaps a bigger part than many pediatricians or child psychologists allow for. For example, the infant who is concentrating on walking and the play activities associated with it, as summer begins, *and* has a garden, is likely to be happier, and therefore easier to handle, than one who reaches this stage in January, or while living in a cramped flat at the top of a building with neighbours who object to noise.

Mothers who take pleasure in the infant's new mobility, longer waking hours and comparative independence, feeling that there are more and more nice things she can now do with him, are likely to ride through this year easily. Mothers who resent the loss of a comparatively controllable 'baby', or feel that now the toddler has reached this stage he should hurry up and turn into a schoolchild, may enjoy it much less.

Some fathers find that it is only with the advent of toddlerhood that they can really come into their own. They may take great pleasure in doing things with the infant that were not possible before, and may therefore accept easily the concurrent tantrums and bolshiness, seeing them as signs of growing up. Other fathers, often those who have basically resented the demands the infant made on their wives from the beginning, may find a mobile child who even interrupts conversations quite intolerable.

Even the exact 'match' between the toddler and his brothers and sisters can have a major effect on this age period. An older sibling may be thrilled to find that the infant begins to join in games, begins to be company in the garden, begins to laugh at jokes. If a 3-year-old girl spends most of the winter playing versions of 'house', 'mothers and fathers' and 'hospitals', the infant may be her constant companion, happily taking the role of baby or patient, comprehending little, but getting his own fun. But if that same 3-year-old is at the stage where she wants only to draw and paint and try to sew, the infant may be seen as the tiresome creature who grabs the pencils and spoils everything.

The importance of small practical details of daily life are well illustrated by the notes which the sensitive mother of an 18-month girl felt it necessary to make for her own mother, when she took charge of the infant for one whole day and night. They are reproduced verbatim because they give a very warm picture of the life of a toddler, of the issues which the mother felt were important to her, and of the extreme difficulty which any stranger, equipped with less information, or caring for the child in a strange place, would have had in keeping her happy and secure.

NOTES ON ANNE!

Dear Mum,

I know it seems ridiculous, when you know Anne so well, but the more I come to think about your managing with her for a whole day and night, the more I realize what a lot of things there are that you *don't* know, from visits, and which might cause trouble, especially if she is worried anyway because I am not there. So here is a sort of diary.

Before 7 a.m.	If she calls before this, it counts as still the night, and she does not have toys or anything; just resettle her as if it was 3 a.m. (I don't want to lose everything I've gained in getting her to sleep later in the morning!)
About 7.45	She will call. Has the lights on; a drink of diluted orange from her teacher-beaker; two rusks and all her cloth books, in her cot.
About 8 a.m.	She is got up, undressed, and cleaned with baby lotion. She likes to wipe her own face.
	Will insist on wearing a nappy and plastic pants, even though she will probably use the pot all day. I cannot persuade her that pants

are more comfortable and I don't mind the odd
puddle. *She* minds.

About 8.30   Goes in high chair and has slice of toast while
her scrambled egg cooks. Then has both baby
cereal and fruit. Will probably eat the lot and
will not accept *any* help. Has milk from her
teacher-beaker. If she tries to take the lid off,
let her. She is just beginning to like to drink
without the spout, and she is very cross if anyone implies that she can't manage.

Morning: Plays around very self-containedly while housework etc. is done. But is always allowed to hide
in our unmade bed before I make it, so don't
imply that it's tiresome (it is!). Hates hoover
noise. Must be told when it's going on; will then
go out of the room voluntarily until it is
switched off.

If she fetches her shoes, it means she wants to go
in the garden.

If she fetches her teapot she wants her teaset
and the dolls.

Keep her out of our bedroom, as my desk is a
constant temptation to her.

Around 11 a.m.   Has diluted rosehip syrup in her teacher-
beaker, and this is a signal that housework is
over; expects more attention after this. Likes
something like finger paints, or sand, or bricks,
but expects to be helped or played *with* at this
time.

Don't shut the door on her if you go to the loo;
being the wrong side of shut doors panics her.
If she needs her pot she will probably announce,
'Oh dear!'

It doesn't mean you're too late, but only that
she thinks you will be.

12.15 ish   Lunch in high chair. Prefers it if I eat mine at
the same time. Has sieved meat or liver (*not* fish
which she loathes) with mashed potato in with
it, and carrots or peas left to be picked up in her
fingers. Then custard with a tin of baby fruit.
May not eat much; it is her worst meal, always.

Don't try to help her or she will get furious and bat the whole dish on to the floor.

About 1 p.m.

Nap. Has a dry nappy if she needs it, her sleeping-bag, the curtains left open but the door shut. Must have white cat, small teddy, red bear and mohair jersey. Will go to sleep at once, and may wake again at 1.30 or not till 3 p.m. Never goes off again once she is awake.

On waking:

Always miserable and needs cuddling for at least 15 minutes. If you hurry her she will be grizzly for the rest of the day. Likes to go out. Top treat is to push baby-walker around in the park, but if you must shop will accept push-chair if you let her push it some of the way. Very frightened at the moment if running dogs come near. Always visits the next-door cat on the way out and on the way home again.

If it is cold, put her pom-pom hat on; she hates having the hood of her anorak up as it blocks her side vision. May try to tell you about the squirrel we saw in the big oak tree just across the fence. It seems to be called 'Cil'. Don't take her to the playground; all the equipment is too big and fierce for her. She insists on going on the see-saw and then hates it.

About 3.30

Has fresh orange juice and squares of bread and butter with honey. Likes to have it standing up at coffee table. If you put her in her high-chair she'll think it is supper time.

Afterwards usually has stories or records. Will never play on her own at this time. Will resent you even telephoning. It is her most clingy period of the day.

Around 5 p.m.

Is ready for bath. Undress in nursery and take to bath in a towel. Likes to 'dance' and gener-ally scruff while she is naked. Adores the bath but is very scared if you try to lie her down, or splash her. Is always allowed to play for at least 20 minutes, with the plastic mugs and the duck and the blue boat.

Take back to nursery in towel to get ready for

bed. Wears nappy padded with disposables, but no plastic pants. Pyjamas, and sleeping bag, but with her legs left out so that she can stand up in her cot until she is ready to sleep.

Supper   Likes baby cereal with *cheese*, not sugar. Or yoghurt with fruit stirred in. A cut-up apple or pear. All this in her high-chair, but then she has a full bottle, warm, which she will drink on your lap.

6.15 ish   Into bed, with same animals as at nap time. May talk and play for 30 minutes, but any crying is unusual and needs investigation. Loud shouting means she wants her sleeping-bag zipped up and to be tucked up to go to sleep. But sometimes she drops off without demanding this, so I just do it when I go to bed.

Once asleep nothing will wake her except a bad dream. If she does dream and cry, don't get her out of her cot, just pat her and talk and she will go off again.

Leave the landing light on and the door ajar.

Large and small factors are peculiarly heightened during the toddler phase because of the toddler's particular stage of understanding. The toddler begins to move around as fast as an older child, but without the older child's sense or memory. He does, of course, learn by experience, but his learning seems slow, because he does not remember for more than a minute. He cannot 'bear in mind' that he always trips over that step, or bangs his head on that table, nor can he remember prohibitions at least until they have been repeated endlessly over weeks and months. The fascination of the electric plug strikes him afresh several times a day. If the last time he was removed from it and scolded was an hour ago, he has probably genuinely forgotten – though he may remember, and stop if he is reminded before he gets there.

If memory is lacking, so too is forethought. If the infant finds he can climb up on to a chair, he is not going to be stopped from doing so by considerations of how he is going to get down again. If he can shut himself in a cupboard, he will not be stopped by thinking about how dark and frightening it will be in there. However much he dislikes his mother being cross, he will not think about her displeasure before he embarks on a forbidden exploit.

Because he cannot think ahead, the toddler typically cannot defer gratification for a minute, nor calmly accept its being deferred by anyone else. What he wants, he wants *now*. If his mother said she would take him for a walk, and then she is held up by the telephone, the wait is intolerable to him. 'In a minute' is a minute too late.

If the toddler cannot wait a minute for what he wants, neither can he put up with brief discomfort for the sake of subsequent comfort. He may be desperately uncomfortable because his face and hands are sticky with ice-cream. He may weep and wail his misery, but he still cannot accept the face flannel without fuss, for the sake of the eventual comfort it will bring.

The toddler is completely incapable of putting himself in anyone else's shoes, however obvious and clear-cut the situation. He knows he hates having his hair pulled, but that does not mean that he can understand that other children hate having *their* hair pulled too. To understand that, he would have to imagine himself to be the other person; and this he cannot do. Two toddlers together often illustrate this. One pushes the other over, and watches while he cries and is comforted. The injured party then takes identical revenge, and *both* are amazed when the second child falls over, cries and is comforted. The parallel between their experiences is completely lost on them. Mothers who retaliate in kind against their toddler's hitting or biting them often discover that it is useless for this reason. As one ruefully put it: 'He was smacking me quite hard, it really hurt, so finally when he wouldn't stop I smacked him back. He was amazed; really he was. You'd have thought he didn't know what smacking was he was so taken aback.'

Decisions, promises and truth are all beyond the toddler too, however apparently sophisticated his verbal understanding of them. Offered a simple choice, such as 'Would you like to come and have dinner now?' most toddlers will say, or indicate 'No!' Coming to have dinner involves a change of activity; recognizing a desire for dinner means looking forward to the satisfaction of hunger. Put like that, the toddler will elect to go dinnerless, even if he has been grizzly with hunger for the past half hour. The simple statement, 'Dinnertime,' will probably bring him straight to his chair. Offered a choice between a red lollipop and a green one, he will want both. In fact so much will he want both that his enjoyment of the one he is finally given will probably be spoiled. Offered the chance to stay with Mummy, or go with Daddy to buy a newspaper, he will either go with Daddy and whine for Mummy all the way, or stay with Mummy and cry for Daddy as soon as the door closes behind him. Again, choice-making involves foresight and memory. Which will I enjoy most? Which did I like last time?

The toddler cannot understand promises for another year or two. He fusses at leaving the playground, clamouring for one more swing. Mother says: 'If I give you one more will you come home right away afterwards?' The child nods eagerly, but his mind is only on that swing. After one swing, he clamours for another, and is surprised at his mother's moralistic displeasure. Released from a sit on his pot, his mother says: 'Will you come and tell me when you do need to go?' Interested only in being allowed up, the child nods. He may or may not tell when he does need to go, but if he does it will not be because he understood and remembered his promise. There is a very definite place for bargaining in handling small children. Later on, in the third and fourth years, the straightforward logic of 'If I do this, will you do that?' appeals, and is appropriate. At the toddler stage it has no meaning.

Much the same applies to truth. By the end of the second year many toddlers talk fluently enough to issue frequent inaccurate denials of wrongdoing and accusations against other children. The fact that what is said is untrue still has no meaning for them. It might have been true. It might have been the dog who broke the vase or made the puddle on the floor; the child wishes it had been, so he says it was. There may even be a psychological truth for him which happens to be quite different from adult truth. He says his sister knocked him over, when in fact he fell. But if he fell in the course of a squabble, he may well *feel* that she knocked him over.

What this adds up to is the *appearance* of a human being, in a creature who rushes about, talks, understands what is said to him, and generally partakes of family life. But this appearance is superficial; inside the toddler there are not yet the controls and the socially inculcated beliefs and behaviours which we expect of people. As a full human being, the toddler is still an impostor.

In babyhood, the mother's role was to *be* the child, in the subtle sense of lending him identity and interpreting the world to him, and in the more obvious sense of using her brain and muscles to do for him what he could not do for himself. In toddlerhood she has to release him to be himself, allow him to be a separate, definite person: to want different things from her, to like different things, to like different people, to disagree with her, to pursue his own ends even when they conflict with hers. At the same time she has to continue to be the socialized bit of him, the righter of his inadvertent wrongs, the one who clears up his messes, rescues him from dilemmas, comforts the children he has hurt. She has to remain his safe haven, the platform from which he can set off on all his adventures, and to which he can always return.

While the mother's role as interpreter of the world is less continuous than it was – the toddler wanting and needing to explore it for himself – she is still the channel through which his experiences come. It is up to her to simplify what the child must discover, to make things manageable for him. For example, taken to an adventure playground intended for school-age children, the toddler will almost certainly get hurt, and is unlikely to get anything out of the experience to compensate. The other children are too big, the equipment is too complex; the whole setting is wrong for him. It is not explorable. At a toddlers' group or club for under-fives, the adventure becomes manageable. The scale, both physical and psychological, is right for the toddler. This is a sea he can chart. Similarly, taken to tea with a child of the same age, the toddler may enjoy himself, provided his own mother is there to keep his security, and to control for him the impulses to snatch, grab and push which he cannot control for himself. Taken and left there alone, it will, unless the other mother is infinitely skilful, be an afternoon of misery. Within the home this kind of arrangement of experiences applies too. The infant's potential – for destruction in adult terms, exploration in his – has to be recognized and allowed for. If he may not touch this, and this, and this, there must be many things he *can* touch. If he must not climb up on the sofa, what can he climb on? If he must not empty the wastepaper basket, what can he empty?

Some mothers find it difficult to decide what they *really* mind the toddler doing, what they would rather he did not do, and what they mind him doing under certain circumstances and not under others. If one dare assume the toddler's skin – always a risky thing to do – one can see the fearful injustices to which this gives rise. It occurs vaguely to the mother that the child should not turn out the magazine rack. So she takes it from its usual place and puts it in the corner behind the armchair. The roving toddler finds it and empties it. This time mother puts it out of the way on the table. Using a chair the toddler gets to it again. By now, the mother feels he is doing it on purpose. But from the child's point of view if it is in reach at all it is fair game. If she had definitely decided, from the beginning, that he was not to have it, she would have removed it truly out of reach and the issue would never have arisen.

On another day, the rain pours down, the mother feels gay, the toddler is playful, and so she permits, even encourages, a long game with the sofa cushions on the floor. While the child is in his high-chair having tea she restores the room to order. Released from his chair the toddler starts the game all over again, and this time the mother is cross. Her irritation is instantly understandable to any adult, but quite incomprehensible to the toddler.

Next morning the mother starts the child off playing with sand just outside the back door. Gleefully he squidges his hands in it, spreads it around, fills and empties his bucket. His mother is pleased. Brought into lunch he does the same with his chocolate pudding and his mother is most *dis*pleased. Her temper does not improve when the toddler joins in the 'game' with a bucket of soapy water, made necessary by the pudding on the floor.

The point, of course, is simply that in daily life we tend to attribute, unthinkingly, to toddlers far more understanding than they really have. The child does not *know* that mother put the magazines on the table so that he should not get them. He cannot understand that a messy room at 3 p.m. is all right, but that it must be tidy when Daddy comes home at 6 p.m. Far less can he see why squidging sand is to be encouraged and squidging chocolate pudding is not, nor why it is legitimate for his mother to play with water on the kitchen floor and not for him to do so. Most mothers recognize these things in conversation, but they are far more difficult to bear in mind throughout the day.

Toddlerhood can therefore be a time of almost continuous scolding and nagging from the adult world. Unfortunately, the more nagging there is, the more contra-suggestive and uncooperative the infant is likely to become. He cannot be 'good'. He cannot do what is wanted of him, or refrain from doing the opposite because that is what his mother wants. As we have seen, it is not developmentally his role to think yet about what anyone else wants or feels. He can only be 'good' because he feels like doing what his mother happens to want, and because he does not happen to feel like doing what she would dislike. It is up to the mother, therefore, to organize life so that both of them want the same thing, as far as possible, most of the time.

Often the first step is to decide what objects or actions are truly outside the pale. They will vary from one family and situation to the next. Some of them may be to do with safety, the mother perhaps feeling that the toddler cannot be allowed on the stairs alone, or in the kitchen when the stove is in use. Some of them may be to prevent damage. Perhaps there are books that must not be bent and crumpled, records which must not be scratched, or ornaments that must not be broken. Once a mother has decided which particular issues are important to her, she can make it impossible for the child to go wrong. Removing him off the stairs time and again will make nothing but trouble; if the stairs are to be banned, a stair-gate will ban them once and for all, and all fusses with them. Likewise the kitchen: a gate or 'stable-type' door gives the toddler a view without access. Books and records may have to be concentrated in a room where the toddler does not play, or the precious books put on high shelves and his own left at the bottom. If ornaments are not to be broken, they will have to be completely out of reach, and furthermore *never* handed to the child 'just for a treat'. Somehow there has to be space where the child can do *most* of what he likes without being in danger of doing real wrong, or real damage.

Within that space there are lower-level decisions to make. There are drawers of cutlery, table-napkins, mats. He will empty them, and play with the contents. Does it really matter? Can he hurt them? Does it take any longer to put them away at the end of the day than to put away more conventional toys?

The more the mother can remain positive with the toddler, the more positive – and therefore manageable – he will be with her. He is no more capable of driving her round the bend on purpose than he is capable of being nice to her on purpose. Difficult he may be, but not, at this kind of age, deliberately.

Being positive is easy in theory and often impossible at the end of a long hard day. It is worth considerable effort not just because it keeps the toddler happy, but because if he is happy following the mother's positive suggestions, she will not be driven mad. If she does not want him to turn out that drawer, can he be offered another one to turn out? If so, he will never notice that he has been manipulated, where if he is simply forbidden the first drawer there will be trouble. If he feels clingy, can the mother possibly leave the ironing, sit down and positively cuddle him? If she can, the ironing will not get done right away, but at least the toddler will do his clinging with smiles and coos rather than tears and whines. And the ironing would not have been very well or quickly done anyway, with small hands pulling at the mother's infuriated knees. If neither food nor faeces is to be smeared around, can he have paint and plasticine? If he can, he will certainly make a mess, but it will be an acceptable kind of mess and in a place chosen by the mother. Finally, where the toddler must do something that he does not want to do, almost anything tends to work better than a direct order. 'Pick up your bricks' is usually hopeless, where 'I bet you can't pick all those up before I've finished this' may actually get the bricks off the floor.

Some mothers feel that taking this sort of trouble to walk around conflict is a kind of spoiling. The infant ought to do what he is told, and desist when he is told not to, never mind why, nor whether he understands why. The trouble is that he won't. And, worse, the mother will have such a very unpleasant time trying to make him. Furthermore, if the mother does join in direct conflict with him, the infant can almost always win just because he has nothing else to do than play the fight-game. Suppose the mother gets into a quarrel over picking up those bricks. She has not a single chance of victory unless the infant decides to oblige. *She* is the one who wants the floor cleared; the infant does not care if the bricks stay there for ever. So if it comes to waiting each other out, he will win. His memory, his forethought are not sufficiently developed for bribery to be very effective – if he is offered a bribe for when he has picked them up he will want it right now, and that will only complicate matters. The same applies to threats: 'No ice-cream for tea' means nothing until he can actually see the ice-cream dish. Of course the mother can make him desperately unhappy. She can shout at him, smack him, put him out of the room, reduce him to a jelly, but none of that will get the bricks picked up.

Toddlers are not mature enough to be directly taught the

kind of social responsibility, fairness and consideration for others that is so essential to family life. At this stage the mother has to conduct the child's social behaviour for him: not letting him have the bricks if she cannot bear to help him pick them up, avoiding the conflict of wills that arises from absolute orders resolutely refused, leading and guiding the infant into behaving nicely because nothing has made him want to behave otherwise.

There is a pay-off, even for the most discipline-minded parents. If a child reaches the stage where he can begin to understand the feelings of others and the justice of their wants as well as his own, still feeling that his mother is basically well-meaning and on his side, then the chances are that most of the time he will want to please her. At this stage he *will* be able to behave well, or badly, on purpose. He *will* foresee the results of his actions, remember prohibitions, understand restrictions. And so, if he wants to please, he will, with lapses. On the other hand, if this second year has been characterized by trouble and rows, so that the infant feels that his mother is unpredictable, overwhelming, unfair, there is a good chance that the more he sees how she wants him to behave, the more he will be tempted to do the opposite. After all, once you are capable of being good on purpose, you are equally capable of being naughty on purpose . . .

This is why this last section of the book is so largely about the problems that can arise, and what is known about avoiding them. Troubles that arise inadvertently in the second year can, if they are wrongly handled from the child's point of view, become problems that continue throughout early childhood. This is the prime year for socialization; for making that toddler into the beginnings of a real person, rather than an impostor. If he finishes the year a-social, not wanting approval, not caring whether people are cross or not, at odds with himself and his world, he will be infinitely more difficult to handle later. As for being spoiled, there is time later for making sure he is not that. At this age a happy child is an easy child, and a child who can be kept easy through this year will stay comparatively easy later on. He may clamour for his mother's attention at 18 months. Given it in full measure, he will understand, by 2½ or 3, that mother likes to talk to other people sometimes. He will begin to be able to withhold his demands for brief periods. But refused that attention at 18 months, he is likely to become more and more demanding; he will always be testing the mother's love and availability, playing with her irritation like an adult constantly testing a sore tooth with his tongue.

CHAPTER TWENTY-FIVE

FEEDING IN THE SECOND YEAR

This chapter is principally about feeding *problems*. An infant who accepts the diet of his family, in a family where that diet is adequate, needs no more special attention to his food than does any other member of his family. A few foods may be known to upset him, and these will obviously be avoided. Occasionally he may be offered an egg or some cheese in place of a main dish he is known to dislike. He will need help in cutting foods up, removing the bones from fish, knowing when foods are cool enough. But all this applies to older children too. If the infant is eating a good mixed diet, this chapter is irrelevant.

The point of the 'good mixed diet' is that it is *mixed*. As Chapters 13 and 20 should have made clear, working out the food values and the food needs for any individual is an extremely complex business, and one on which there remains considerable controversy among the experts. The simple way of ensuring, in a rich society, that every individual gets what he needs, is to feed him some of a wide range of foods. In this way, incomplete proteins complete each other; vitamin-deficient foods are made good by vitamin-rich ones; varying traces of minerals add up to a sufficiency, and natural hunger ensures that calorie needs are met. Such a mixed diet usually gives us *more* of many nutrients than we actually require. But where food is not scarce, this does not matter, provided the individual does not get too fat.

The pattern of our 'meals' is culture-bound. There is no dietetic law which says that people require three square meals a day, or two main meals and two subsidiary ones. From the nutritional point of view the day's food intake could equally well be divided into 6 or 8 parts, and a good sandwich is often more nourishing than a 'real meal'. But our food preparation is so elaborate – compared with many other parts of the world – that we have made our meals into ceremonies; gathering the family together at certain times of the day so that whoever is cooking can feed them all together.

Authorities differ on the need for regular spacing of food throughout the day. They differ, for example, on the need for a good breakfast. It is known that we do not eat to prepare for energy expenditure, but to make good energy which has been expended. An individual will not feel more energetic because he has eaten a good meal, but he may be hungry for his next meal because he has been energetic. It is also known that the balance between an individual's energy expenditure and his calorie intake is accurate over several days, but not at all accurate day by day. He may eat more on a lazy day, and less on an active one. But all other things being equal, by the end of the week the two measures will balance.

All in all, it seems that just as the good mixed diet covers all possibilities of nutritional need, so regular meals several times a day cover all possible needs for stocking up on nutrients of which the body may have insufficient stores. Some of the combinations of foods which are traditional in Western societies make very good sense here. Fish and chips, eaten together, make quite sure that the protein in the fish can be conserved for tissue building and repair, because the carbohydrates and fats in the chips will cover immediate energy needs. Eaten alone, the fish might be wastefully used by the body for energy. The same applies to hamburger in a bun, to eggs with toast, to roast beef with yorkshire pudding. Combinations of this kind ensure that the protein is 'spared'. But where protein consumption is more than adequate – as it is in most Western families – the pattern of breakfast, lunch and supper is not necessary, merely convenient and socially acceptable.

Unfortunately, a very great many infants between 1 and 2 refuse to eat what their mothers consider to be an adequate diet. Their mothers, anxious to give them every chance of optimal growth and development, and knowing that food is important, get worried. The toddlers, already searching for fields in which to assert their individuality and try out their independence (Chapter 24), soon discover the meal table as an excellent place to attract attention and get the mothers running round them in circles. For many mothers, their young children's eating is a constant haunting worry, often for several years. The whole relationship between mother and child may be distorted by the food battle; the whole family may be disrupted by it. I have talked with mothers who regularly spent 4 or 5 hours every day trying to get a toddler to eat, mothers whose families were not allowed to accept invitations out to meals because the toddler would only eat at home, families where all mealtime conversation had to consist of nursery rhymes and stories to distract the toddler into eating. Not one of these toddlers showed the least signs of being undernourished; often they were fat.

Sadly, when mothers go for advice to infant-welfare clinics or general practitioners, the advice they are given often strengthens their anxiety. While being assured that the child is adequately nourished, they are often told that the child is 'playing them up', that they should ignore him, offer him his meals, remove the uneaten food, say no more about it, and allow no snacks. If advice of this kind is not backed with hard nutritional information, few anxious mothers can possibly take it. If they try, the child may eat nothing for a whole day. That is the limit of most mothers' tolerance. Behind the advice, implicit in it, is a confirmation of the need, the rightness of the good mixed diet. The whole aim is to get the child back to eating 'proper' meals at the 'proper' times.

NUTRITIONAL NEEDS

I think it may be useful to turn this kind of advice upside down, and consider what the infant *needs* to eat, and some of the ways he can get it. I am not advocating the abandonment of 'proper' meals and regular mealtimes. These are social considerations. I want, rather, to lay the basic anxieties about the child's *nutrition*, so that mothers can separate out, for themselves, their nutritional concern from their disciplinary one.

The infant whose birthweight was average, and who has gained weight at the average rate, will weigh around 25 lb. (11·4kg) by the middle of his second year. But just as his food requirements, relative to his weight, dropped during the second half of the first year, so they drop even further during this year.

TABLE 14. RECOMMENDED DAILY CALORIES AT THREE AGE LEVELS

| Age | Weight | | kcal | | Total kcal |
	lb.	kg	per lb.	per kg	per 24 hours
3–6 months	14·4	6·6	52	115	760
6–12 months	19·6	8·9	49	107	955
12–24 months Average at 18 months	25·0	11·4	48	105	1,200

For a mother anxious about feeding, the first point to note is that the total food recommendation for the second year is just about half the recommendation for a boy of 10 years, both in terms of calories and of protein. All too often infants are offered portions of food which are quite unrealistic.

The detailed dietary recommendations for this average-weight 18-month child are given below. They may be compared directly with Table 10 (page 270).

Infants who drink 1 pint (about 600ml) of milk in the day already have an excellent start. The milk gives them more than half the recommended protein (18g). It gives them enough of all the B vitamins except thiamine. Their need for calcium is actually lower than it was in the first year, and the milk gives them all they need (680mg). The need for vitamin A has dropped too, and the milk gives them almost three quarters of it (220μg). The mother who worries about the infant's diet when he *is* drinking this much milk is almost certain to be worrying unnecessarily. The child will see to his

TABLE 15. RECOMMENDED DAILY INTAKE OF
NUTRIENTS FOR INFANTS AGED 18 MONTHS

TOTAL CALORIES	PROTEIN	MINERALS Calcium	Iron	A	D	VITAMINS Thia-mine	Ribo-flavine	Nico-tinic acid	C
kcal	g	mg	mg	μg	μg	mg	mg	mg	mg
1,200	30	500	7	300	10	0·5	0·6	7	20

Note: The recommended daily protein intake during the first year was 20 grams. In the second year that figure represents the minimum which is regarded as being certain to prevent protein deficiency. The recommended level has now gone up to around 30 grams.

total calorie intake, because he will get hungry. Almost whatever he eats to satisfy that hunger will fill the gap between his needs and that pint of milk.

If one considers the foods, or the groups of foods, which children refuse, and which therefore cause their mothers' anxiety, one is struck by the consistency from child to child, and also by the misconceived ideas of 'necessary' foods. I have met no toddler who refused biscuits and cakes, and remarkably few who refused bread and potatoes. If they did refuse them, their mothers would not worry. On the other hand I have met many who refused meat and greens, and their mothers regard these as vital to a good diet.

Protein Foods

As we have seen in earlier chapters, the first-class or animal proteins contain all the amino-acids human beings need. They are therefore a convenient, if expensive, way of ensuring adequate protein intake. They also tend to be useful sources of fat-soluble vitamins and of minerals. But they are by no means the only proteins available to us. A tablespoon of cooked minced stewing steak will yield about 8 grams of protein. Table 16 gives some examples of other, and less expected, foods which will provide the same amount.

TABLE 16.   EXAMPLES OF FOODS WHICH WILL
PROVIDE THE PROTEIN EQUIVALENT OF 1 OZ. (30G)
COOKED MINCED BEEF

Food	Quantity required to yield 8g protein	Comment
White bread	3 slices	Not complete (first-class) protein. But wheat protein has been shown to be excellent for children, maintaining good growth either in the presence of other second-class proteins, or limited first-class.
Brown bread	2½ slices	
Potatoes	4 medium size 8 small new	Experiments have shown that potatoes can support life as the sole article of diet. Very small quantities of first-class protein render them complete.
Biscuits (sweet or chocolate)	8 biscuits on average, according to brand	Will often amount to first-class protein, if milk or egg constituents are included in the recipe.
Plain madeira cake	4 small slices	First-class combination
Baked beans in tomato sauce	6 level tablespoons	Not complete protein
Tinned processed peas	4 level tablespoons	Not complete protein
Roast peanuts	1 heaped tablespoon	Contains all necessary amino-acids but not complete, in sense that relative proportions of amino-acids are at variance with body's needs.

Food	Quantity required to yield 8g protein	Comment
Luncheon meat or 'spam'	2 medium slices	Present food regulations in the U.K. are such that all these can be regarded as first-class protein sources, not inferior to butcher's meat.
Pork sausages	2½ chipolatas	
Fish fingers	2	
Bacon	2 normal rashers	
Cooked ham	2 slices from vacuum pack	

From the above, it is clear that our ideas of which foods are protein sources and which are impoverished are often misguided. Of course protein is most *concentrated* in such foods as lean butcher's meat and cheese, but these are foods of which we eat comparatively little at one time. The concentration of protein in bread and potatoes is low, but we eat a lot of them, so that the protein they contain makes a useful contribution to the diet.

The Vexed Question of Vegetables

Vegetables are often regarded as essential to a good mixed diet. People seldom stop to ask themselves what makes them so valuable. If asked, they answer, 'Vitamin C.'

While many vegetables contain a high concentration of vitamin C when they leave the ground, very few of them contain much by the time they reach the plate. Vitamin C is lost rapidly during storage, especially if there is exposure to sunlight. A green vegetable on display in front of the greengrocer's shop has probably lost half its vitamin-C content even before it is purchased.

Since the vitamin is both water-soluble and destroyed by heat, a great deal of what is left will vanish when it is cooked. At the worst, cabbage cooked for canteen meals and kept hot in a steam table has been shown to contain no vitamin C whatsoever. At best, bought fresh, cooked quickly in very little water and served immediately, it may contain as much as 6mg in a serving.

If people enjoy green vegetables, fine. They will get a variable amount of vitamin C and some vitamin A and calcium. But if they do not – and most toddlers do not – they can hardly be regarded as essential dietary items.

Vitamin C is not a difficult essential to provide. Although the vitamin content of potatoes is variable, children will get some from this source. The juice of a single orange will provide three times the recommended daily intake. A single glass of diluted rosehip, or blackcurrant, juice will do the same. Or the child can be given the correct dose of a multi-vitamin preparation.

Root vegetables, particularly carrots, are usually preferred to green ones. One very small carrot provides the toddler with all the vitamin A he needs for the day, and a little calcium. But that is virtually all. Again, with the multi-vitamins available, and recommended, is the carotene content of the carrot worth a fuss?

In later life, of course, vegetables are valuable as roughage; but at this age the roughage content of cereal products, especially less refined ones, is usually sufficient.

Fresh Fruit

The citrus fruits are the most consistent of all dietary sources of vitamin C because they come in their own packaging, protected from light, and because they are almost always eaten raw, and thus the vitamin is protected from heat.

But the vitamin C in other fruits – highest in summer fruits such as blackcurrants and gooseberries – survives better than the vitamin C in vegetables even when the fruits are eaten cooked. This is because vitamin C is not broken down so rapidly by heat when it is in an acid solution, and most fruits are acid. It is also because the vitamin C which dissolves into the cooking water is commonly eaten as 'juice', where the vegetable water is usually drained away. Tinned fruits normally contain about half the amount of vitamin C which is found in the same fruit when fresh. But it may contain more than the 'fresh' fruit which has been at the greengrocer's for several days. Dried fruits, such as prunes and sultanas, contain no vitamin C.

The protein content of dried fruits – apricots, prunes and even sultanas – looks high on a nutritional table. And it *is* high if the infant likes, and can digest, these fruits in dried form. But soaked back to the natural state, the protein is diluted. Where an ounce of dried apricots contains nearly 5 grams of protein, an ounce of soaked and stewed dried apricots will only contain about ½ gram.

Useful amounts of all the vitamins and minerals are available in a variety of fresh fruits but, apart from vitamin C, the quantities are not sufficient to make fruit the most important source.

Fats

As far as we know, there is no dietary *requirement* for fat, except that the body needs minute quantities of three essential fatty acids, found both in animal and in vegetable fats.

The chances of an infant in the Western world lacking any of these three are minute. Even if the child appears to *eat* no fat, preferring his bread without butter or margarine, his ham, bacon and other meat lean, his salad without dressing, sufficient fat will be used in food *preparation* to meet this biochemical need. And even where a mother is deliberately keeping her use of fats in the kitchen to a minimum – perhaps for the benefit of some other member of the family – there will be fats, animal or vegetable, in any commercially prepared cakes or biscuits, and in other foods cooked outside the home.

The fat-soluble vitamins A and D are present in both butter and in margarine – which is fortified so as to contain more vitamin D than occurs naturally in butter. Since these 'table fats' are also concentrated forms of calories, they are useful foods for the toddler who likes them. But the quantity of vitamins present is not enough to make these items *necessary* to the diet because even if the child eats a great deal of butter or margarine, he is still going to need supplementary vitamins. To meet his daily requirement of vitamin A from butter, he would need to eat only 4 slices of bread, spread to normal thickness. But to meet his vitamin D needs from this source, he would need the quantity one would spread on 60 slices. Using fortified margarine, 12 slices would meet his needs. Of course this is a frivolous calculation, and table fats are used in cooking as well as on bread. The point is that the concentration of vitamins is so low that sufficient to provide the vitamins from table fats alone would also provide a very high calorie intake. The toddler on a mixed diet will get some of his fat-soluble vitamins from table fats, some from meat, cheese and eggs. The toddler who refuses a mixed diet needs vitamin supplementation.

The Egg Battle

Eggs are misunderstood. They, more than any other food except green vegetables, are drawn into moralistic (as opposed to nutritional) arguments at mealtimes. One egg contains just about the same amount of first-class complete protein as the tablespoonful of lean minced beef we postulated earlier. And each egg yolk provides about 1mg of iron – one seventh of the infant's daily requirements. So mothers tend, rightly, to regard them as an extremely valuable food; but they also tend, wrongly, to feel that the child is not 'properly eating *eggs*' if he hates the sight of them.

Many toddlers intensely dislike boiled, poached or fried eggs. Many more will eat them if they are made a little less recognizable in omelettes or scrambled egg dishes. Almost all eat them unknowingly in batter puddings, pancakes, cakes and custards. A boiled egg is not better for the child than 'apple snow' made with beaten egg white, or cheese pudding made with egg yolks and milk.

THE MYTHICAL 'PROBLEM EATER'

It should by now be clear that while a mixed diet, with plenty of milk, eggs, cheese, meat, vegetables and fruit, and ample bread and other carbohydrates to fill up with and provide energy, is an ideal, it is not a nutritional necessity. Much maternal anxiety about toddlers' eating is disciplinary and prejudiced. Two rashers of bacon with bread and butter and an apple may not strike the mother as a 'proper dinner'. Perhaps socially it is not. But it is not a bad meal nutritionally. The toddler who refuses all meat and vegetables, and nibbles cakes and fruit all day may be *behaving badly* but that does not necessarily mean that he is eating badly.

By way of illustration and light relief, Tables 17–20 analyse some of the socially peculiar ways in which a 'difficult eater' might meet his nutritional needs if not his mother's expectations.

These tables require some explanation. The nutrient values ascribed to the different foods named are all derived from the *Manual of Nutrition*.[69] In this sense they are accurate values – the fruit of extremely painstaking research work. Nevertheless they cannot be treated as exact. The accurate nutrient content of 'a piece of bread and butter' depends on the thickness of the slice, whether the crusts are removed, how thickly the butter is spread. Similarly, while the values given for 'one sweet biscuit' are average values for average plain sweet biscuits, the exact content of any one biscuit will, of course, depend on the manufacturer's recipe. In tables such as these one is therefore imposing a spurious appearance of accuracy on data which can really only be approximate.

For this reason, the figures are given only to two significant figures (except in the rare cases where three figures are justifiable). It is quite spurious enough to say that a biscuit contains 70 calories; to state that it contains 68·72 calories is patently absurd. Some of the very small values, such as those for the B vitamins, may seem even more ridiculous. How can we be sure that a small banana contains 0·04mg of riboflavine? The answer is that we cannot be sure, but we do know that it will contain more than 0·03mg and less than 0·05. Furthermore, *if* it contains this amount of riboflavine, it will contain 0·02 of thiamine, or half the quantity. And the relationship between one nutrient and the next is vital.

The tables can therefore be used as a rough guide to the actual nutrient contents of the foods mentioned, and as a rather more accurate guide to the proportions of one nutrient to another. Other than that they are intended merely to illustrate the variety of ways in which widely differing food intakes can add up to a sufficiency of everything, or leave specific lacks which are easily filled. Nobody should be fooled by their apparent accuracy into searching for a food which provides 0·01mg of a particular vitamin, or into criticizing a day's diet because it leaves a child 3 grams short on his protein requirements.

In each table, the day's total intake is compared with the recommended intake given in Table 15, to yield the difference between intake and needs.

Table 17 describes a self-selected high carbohydrate diet. No tricks have been played with it. No portions of cheese have been slipped in; no passion for cooked ham has been postulated. The child has taken only one food in the entire day which would be conventionally regarded as 'good' for him – half a fish finger.

Yet there is remarkably little wrong with the diet, and what is wrong can easily be put right without altering the *kind* of food served, and therefore without risking putting the child off eating altogether.

The most striking point is that the child is having one quarter more calories than the average toddler would be thought to require. If he is a thin, active, tall child, or if he is catching up after illness, this may not matter. But most toddlers eating this diet regularly would become fat. We therefore must find ways of making good the lacks in his diet without adding calories. And we must find ways of reducing his calorie intake without him feeling deprived of his normal food.

TABLE 17. TYPICAL DAY'S FOOD FOR A TODDLER 'HOOKED' ON CARBOHYDRATES

	TOTAL CALORIES	PROTEIN	MINERALS		VITAMINS					
			Cal-cium	Iron	A	D	Thiamine	Ribo-flavine	Nico-tinic acid	C
	kcal	g	mg	mg	μg	μg	mg	mg	mg	mg
On Waking										
2 sweet biscuits	140	1·5	26	0·4	0	0	0·03	0·01	0·4	0
Drink Ribena	65	0	4	0	0	0	0	0·01	0	58
Breakfast										
2 slices white bread and butter	250	4·8	60	1·0	280	0·36	0·1	0	1·4	0
During morning										
2 more biscuits	140	1·5	26	0·4	0	0	0·03	0·01	0·4	0
Dinner										
1 medium potato in chips	270	4·4	16	1·6	0	0	0·12	0·04	2·4	4–16
½ fish finger	25	2	7	0·2	0	0	0·02	0·02	0·6	0
Slice cake	120	1·7	19	0·4	23	0·34	0·02	0·03	0·5	0

During afternoon Children's 1 oz. bar chocolate	165	2·5	70	0·5	2	0	0·01	0·1	0·7	0
Tea/Supper 2 more slices bread and butter	250	4·8	60	1·0	280	0·36	0·1	0	1·4	0
Banana (small)	44	0·6	4	0·2	18	0	0·02	0·04	0·4	6
Cup (4 oz.–120ml) milk	70	4	130	0	44	0	0·04	0·16	1·2	0
Total intake rounded to 2 significant figures	1500	28	420	5·7	650	1·1	0·49	0·42	9·4	68–80†
Difference between intake and needs (to 2 significant figures)	+300	−2*	−80	−1·3	−350	−8·9	−0·01	−0·18	+2·4	+48–60
Comments	Too much: 1/4 in excess of needs	Negligible: lacks 1/15 of needs	Too little: lacks 1/6 of needs	Too little: lacks 1/7 of needs	Ample	Too little: lacks 9/10 of needs	Negligible: lacks 1/50 of needs	Too little: lacks 1/3 of needs	Ample	Ample

* This protein intake is well above the minimum thought to be necessary to protect against protein deficiency, even though it is just below the 'recommended intake' level.

† As we have seen, the vitamin-C content of potatoes varies, especially with length of storage.

TABLE 18. TYPICAL DAY'S FOOD FOR A TODDLER WHO 'EATS LIKE A BIRD'

	TOTAL CALORIES	PROTEIN	MINERALS Calcium	Iron	VITAMINS A	D	Thiamine	Riboflavine	Nicotinic acid	C
	kcal	g	mg	mg	µg	µg	mg	mg	mg	mg
Breakfast										
½ portion (2 tablespoons) baby cereal	60	3	100	2	16	2	0·1	0·2	1·5	0
½ egg	25	1·7	8	0·4	45	0·2	0·1	0·05	0·5	0
Mug (8 oz. – 250ml) milk	140	8	260	0	88	0	0·08	0·32	2·4	0
During morning										
Drink Ribena	65	0	4	0	0	0	0	0·01	0	58
1 sweet biscuit	70	0·75	13	0·2	0	0	0·01	0·005	0·2	0
Dinner										
2 teaspoons minced beef	30	4	1	0·7	0	0	0·005	0·03	1·5	0
¼ medium boiled potato	23	0·4	1	0·1	0	0	0·02	0·01	0·3	1–4
2 teaspoons frozen peas	7	0·7	2	0·15	7	0	0·03	0·01	0·3	2

During afternoon Vanilla ice cream (small)	55	1·2	39	0·1	0	0	0·01	0·06	0·3	0
Tea/Supper ½ tin toddler cheese savoury	110	6	110	0·1	60	0	0·1	0·01	1·5	0
Mug (8 oz. – 250ml) milk	140	8	260	0	88	0	0·08	0·32	2·4	0
Total intake*	730	33	800	3·8	300	2·2	0·54	1	11	61–64 †
Difference between intake and needs*	−470	+3	+300	−3·2	0	−7·8	+0·04	+0·04	+4	41–44 †
Comments	Too little: lacks 1/3 of needs	Ample	Ample	Too little: lacks 1/2 of needs	Ample	Too little: lacks 4/5 of needs	Ample	Ample	Ample	Ample

* Rounded to 2 significant figures.
† Vitamin-C content of potatoes is variable.

The child is urgently in need of extra vitamin D. This should certainly be supplemented. A multi-vitamin preparation will do no harm, even though his vitamin A and C intakes are adequate. But vitamin D alone can be given. Such a large lack of the vitamin would be difficult to make up in any other way since he does not eat fatty fish or eggs. The use of a fortified margarine instead of butter would probably be the only other practical way of meeting his need.

The child also lacks some calcium, some iron and some riboflavine. These needs can be met in a variety of ways. For example, if the juice of a fresh orange were substituted for the blackcurrant syrup, this would serve the dual purpose of increasing his iron intake while reducing his calories. Similarly the substitution of ice-cream for cake at dinnertime would increase his calcium intake, leave his protein untouched and reduce his calories a little. Substitution of crispbread for ordinary bread at one meal would increase his iron intake and cut down his calories. A thin spreading of Marmite or some other yeast extract would ensure his riboflavine intake.

Finally, if his calorie intake is still too high and he is obviously getting fat, manipulation of the table fats he eats can reduce the calories without him noticing the change. One ounce of butter contains 211 calories and only 0·1 gram of protein. He needs some – this is the main source of his abundant vitamin A – but his intake could be cut by half without damaging the diet in any way.

To contrast with this diet, which contains quite a large quantity of carbohydrate relative to protein, Table 18 gives a diet which does not contain very much of *anything*. This is the child whose mother worries because he 'eats like a bird'.

This diet is basically excellent. But just as the first example was high in calories, so this one is very low. The child is having only two thirds of the calories that an 'average' toddler is thought to need. Again, this may not matter. If he has always been small, is gaining weight steadily (even if slowly), is healthy, energetic, and wants no more of *any* kind of food, then it can be assumed that his appetite is correctly controlling his food intake. But if he is gaining weight more slowly than hitherto, seems listless or tired, or would like more of certain kinds of food though not of what his mother offers, then he should have it.

The child's only specific lacks – apart from calories – are vitamin D and iron. The first should be supplemented. His iron needs could be met by substituting fresh orange juice for blackcurrant syrup, and perhaps by offering crispbread or bread and butter instead of his morning biscuit. He might also accept a mixture of half-beef half-liver at dinner time.

If the child wants, or will happily accept, some extra food, the mother does not have to worry about what it is. He needs the food only for fuel as he is getting plenty of all the vital nutrients. He can therefore have whatever he prefers that his mother is prepared to buy and serve. However 'fattening' the additional food, he will not get fat because he has an actual gap between his energy expenditure and his food intake. Indeed, on this diet, he may be burning some of his protein foods for fuel, so that the addition of extra carbohydrates would actually improve the quality of the diet by sparing those proteins for tissue building and growth.

Perhaps he would like a sweet course at lunch and supper time. Perhaps he would eat a greater quantity of sausages or spam or bacon than he eats of pure minced beef. Perhaps he is bored with boiled potatoes, and would eat more if they were sautéed or baked. Any addition of cereal products, potatoes or chocolate would, of course, give him extra iron.

Failing all this, if he does seem to need more food, but will not eagerly eat a bulkier diet, the answer lies in additional sugar and fats. An ounce of butter could be used on his vegetables during the day, even if he will not eat it on bread. Sugar could go on his cereal, some on fruit; and he could be allowed some sweets.

Even further from the 'good mixed diet' ideal are the really barmy diets, (Tables 19 and 20) adopted by two healthy toddlers. Neither is recommended, but very little is needed to make the diets at least adequate, and they may therefore be comforting to desperate mothers!

TABLE 19. DAY'S FOOD TAKEN BY A TODDLER ACCEPTING ONLY MILK AND BREAD AND BUTTER

	TOTAL CALORIES	PROTEIN	MINERALS		VITAMINS					
			Cal-cium	Iron	A	D	Thiamine	Ribo-flavine	Nico-tinic acid	C
	kcal	g	mg	mg	μg	μg	mg	mg	mg	mg
During the day infant eats:										
8 slices of bread spread with butter	1,000	19	240	4	1,100	1·4	0·4	0	5·6	0
1 pint (about 600ml) milk	360	20	680	0	240	0·2	0·2	0·4	0	0
Total intake*	1,300	39	920	4	1,300	1·6	0·6	0·4	5·6	0

Difference between intake and needs*	+100	+9	+430	-3	+1,000	-8.4	+0.1	-0.2	-1.4	-20
Comments	Ample	Ample	Ample	Too little: lacks almost 1/2 of needs	Ample	Too little: lacks 4/5 of needs	Ample	Too little: lacks 1/3 of needs	Too little: lacks 1/5 of needs	Too little: lacks total need

* Rounded to 2 significant figures.

TABLE 20. DAY'S FOOD TAKEN BY A TODDLER ACCEPTING ONLY PEANUTS, CHIPPED POTATOES AND APPLES

	TOTAL CALORIES	PROTEIN	MINERALS		VITAMINS					
			Cal-cium	Iron	A	D	thiamine	ribo-flavine	nico-tinic acid	C
	kcal	g	mg	mg	µg	µg	mg	mg	mg	mg
During the day infant consumes:										
2 oz. (60g) roast shelled peanuts	330	16	17	0·6	0	0	0·07	0·03	5·9	0
12 oz. chips (3 medium potatoes)	800	13	36	4·8	0	0	0·36	0·12	7·2	24
3 apples, net weight 8 oz. (250g)	100	0·8	8	0·8	8	0	0·08	0·08	0	8
Total intake*	1,200	30	61	6·2	8	0	0·51	0·23	13	32

Difference between intake and needs*									
0	0	−440	−0·8	−290	−10	+0·01	−0·37	+6	+12

Comments									
Ample	Ample	Too little: lacks 9/10 of needs	Negligible: lacks 1/9 of needs	Too little: lacks almost total need	Too little: lacks total need	Ample	Too little: lacks almost 2/3 of needs	Ample	Ample

* Rounded to 2 significant figures.

Clearly the diet shown in Table 19 is not as 'barmy' or as 'impoverished' as most people would assume. The toddler lacks only iron and vitamins D and C. He is not getting the full recommendation for riboflavine and nicotinic acid, but in practice the deficiency is so small it would be unlikely to matter unless the child ate literally *nothing* else for a long period.

Obviously he, like most toddlers, should have a correct daily dosage of multi-vitamins. Apart from these, he needs more iron. Brown bread tends to contain more than white bread, so substitution of some brown for white would help. Other than this, if he will accept some of his milk flavoured with drinking chocolate, two heaped teaspoonfuls will meet his deficiency completely. If he will not, every two-ounce (60g) bar of milk chocolate which he eats will give him 1 missing mg of iron. But if he has many, he will get fat – his calories are already on the high side.

This method of analysis is somewhat misleading when we come to the diet in Table 20. The toddler appears, from the figures, to be getting ample protein. But he is getting it entirely from peanuts and potatoes, with no 'first-class' animal protein at all. While the amino-acid composition of peanuts is such that they are an excellent source of vegetable protein, containing *some* of all the essential amino-acids (see page 176), the balance between these constituents is not ideal. And unfortunately the balance is not corrected by the amino-acid composition of potatoes. The infant could maintain good health and growth on this protein mixture for some time. But he would be much better off if some form of animal protein could be added.

Since the diet is extremely low in calcium, the obvious addition to aim for would be milk. Even two thirds of a pint of milk would render the proteins complete, as well as giving adequate calcium intake. If he will not drink milk as milk, he might drink cocoa or milkshakes. If even these are refused, a good deal of milk can be slipped in by way of ice-cream or even milk chocolate.

FEEDING IN THE SECOND YEAR

The toddler also lacks vitamins A and D. On such a restricted diet he can only certainly get enough if he regularly receives a multi-vitamin preparation.

SUMMING UP

The lesson these examples teach is not that a good mixed diet is to be scorned. It is still the safe way to feed an infant. The way that ensures that he misses nothing, either among the food elements we recognize and can set recommendations for, or among the vitamins and minerals which year by year are being shown to be important, though levels cannot yet be set. The mixed diet is also, in our culture, the easy way to feed an infant. He can share in what is being prepared for everybody else. It is very tiresome to cook chips three times every day. Again, it is psychologically the best way to feed him. Idiosyncratic diets mean that the child has become aware of what he eats as a focus of maternal attention. It has ceased to be a simple and pleasurable matter of satisfying hunger, and become an emotional issue. Later on, his social life will be affected – much of our social intercourse focuses round the meal table.

But the examples do demonstrate how easy it is to meet a toddler's nutritional needs, how many enormously divergent diets will do this, and what comparatively tiny quantities are needed. After all, the packet of peanuts and the pint of milk which the children in our last examples are living on might well serve their fathers as an afternoon snack and a late night drink barely counted into their assessment of their daily diet.

The example of the child who is hooked on carbohydrates should allay the fears of those whose charges dislike meat, cheese and eggs. There is a lot of protein in 'carbohydrate' foods. The toddler who eats like a bird might teach us a little about the size of portion we serve to young children. Many would eat more, if they were not continually faced with three times the amount they actually want.

The Child Who is Fat

The fat toddler, or the one who is gaining weight too fast and is clearly therefore going to get fat, is almost certainly eating a high carbohydrate diet. But this does not mean that the only way to give him fewer calories is to try putting him on a high protein diet – such as his slimming mother might adopt.

The first place to look for help is in the child's consumption of snacks (see page 281). If he is a constant consumer of potato crisps, sweets, ice-creams and biscuits, he may be getting more calories in his snacks than in his meals.

If so, some good can often be done by offering him his treat snack foods as part of his *meals*, and offering the meal-time foods he is less keen on as snacks. If he has ice-cream at dinner time, instead of rice pudding, that pudding can be available when he demands an afternoon snack. Of course he is then less likely to eat the rice pudding. Similarly, why not crisps for tea, and then bread and butter if he demands more food before bedtime?

The easiest way to cut down an infant's calorie intake, without making him conscious of any change in his diet, is to limit his intake of fats. These are the most concentrated form of calories, and they add the fewest valuable nutrients to the diet. To deprive the child of bread and potatoes is to deprive him of extremely nutritious food. To deprive him of butter is to take away only calories and vitamin A, and the vitamins should be supplemented anyway. Most people spread butter or margarine on bread at the rate of about 1 oz. (30g) to 3 slices – more than 200 calories. It would take about the same amount to make fried bread, or sauté potatoes. Chipped potatoes have three times the calorie value of boiled ones, and twice the calorie value of roast.

If the child's milk intake is drastically cut, the balance of the rest of his diet may be upset – his protein and calcium intake may drop too far. But it is worth remembering that the food value of milk is in the *milk* not in the cream, which is almost entirely fat. Skim milk yields just as much protein and calcium for many fewer calories. If the child is drinking more than about 1½ pints (860ml) of milk per day, as well as eating too much in total, it is worth trying to cut him back to somewhere nearer a pint (about 600ml) – although not below this. Unfortunately many mothers do this by offering the infant a proprietary vitamin-C fruit syrup, suitably diluted, instead of the milk. This will not help the fat child. A glass of black-currant juice made with 1 oz. (30ml) of the syrup to 4 oz. (115ml) of water will give him exactly the same calories as the same size glass of milk. If the child's feelings are hurt by being offered plain water, a low-calorie fruit squash – provided he gets his ration of vitamin C in other ways – is a better alternative. Two birds can be killed with the one stone if fresh orange juice is used – half the calories and plenty of vitamin C.

Feeding Problems

The easy way to deal with feeding problems is to avoid them. Perhaps the easiest way to avoid them is not only to read, but also to believe the kind of information contained earlier in this chapter. If mothers really *believe* that the packet of pea-nuts the infant consumed in his pushchair on the way to the shops, together with the milk he drank at breakfast, and the apple he is eating now, will nourish him adequately for much of the day, they are far less likely to convey anxiety to that child when he does not eat his next proper 'meal'.

Accepting, indeed encouraging, the infant's dawning desire for independence will usually help in avoiding feeding problems too. The child who feels that his mother is over-bearing and smothering is more likely than most to be on the lookout for battlegrounds. And he may choose the meal table. Even if he does not feel generally oppressed, he may well come to resent being fed by his mother. Being fed with a spoon is an uncomfortable business. Perhaps parents should feed each other a few spoonsful and discover this for themselves. The food does not come at the right rate; the feeder does not select exactly the right combination on each spoonful, and it all makes one feel very helpless. Of course infants have to be fed during the months when they cannot feed themselves. But usually these months are over by the first birthday, yet very few babies are allowed to feed themselves at this age. Perhaps the mother wants to avoid the mess of self-feeding, or speed the child's meal up, or give him sloppy tinned foods which are difficult to manage. As long as she ladles in the food, the child does not eat, he is fed. Eating is not something active which he does but something which he must passively accept. If he can be allowed to feed himself, his eating can become his business, and can be kept separate from the vagaries of his relationship with his mother.

Toddlers will not, of course, feed themselves to adult standards. The child will use his fingers most of the time, a spoon some of the time. He will eat in idiosyncratic orders and combinations, alternating peas with stewed fruit and dipping cheese in his custard. But if he is allowed this degree of self-determination, he is likely to eat the amount he needs of what he likes and his nutrition is unlikely to become bedevilled with discipline. If he cannot have his pudding until he has finished his first course it will not take him long to realize that his mother minds more about him eating the savoury foods. By the laws of toddler contra-suggestiveness such a realization may quickly make him want the meat less and the pudding more. If he cannot have his food at all unless he eats it 'nicely' he may well decide that he does not want it that much anyway.

If the infant is to be allowed to eat what he wants from what is available on the table, and to eat it in the way he finds easiest, the corollary is that if he does *not* want to eat, that is his business too. The whole idea is ruined if the mother lets him feed himself the amount he wants and then tries to push a bit more in, or if she lets him eat the bits he likes and then tries to give him the bits he has rejected.

Sometimes it is weaning from the bottle which makes meal-time trouble at around a year. If the infant has been allowed a bottle for this long, he has usually built it into his bedtime routine and made it part of his comfort rituals. Mothers who in conversation express horror at the idea of allowing a baby to suck himself to sleep with a bottle, find themselves doing so. The infant *might* choke. His teeth will certainly suffer, but peaceful naptimes and evenings are so desirable that the infant gets his bottle all the same. If it is taken away from him at this sort of age, he may refuse adamantly to touch milk from a cup. Water and fruit juice he will drink competently, but if he cannot have milk in a bottle he will not have it at all. Those rejected cups of milk can start a cycle of pressure from the mother and refusal from the child which rapidly spreads to include other foods too. It seems that this may be the most difficult stage for weaning from the bottle. If the mother does not want to allow the infant to have his bottle through most of the second year at least, she would probably do better to wean him much earlier – at 8–9 months. Weaned at a year, both his nutrition and his eating patterns are likely to suffer.

Often it is not the food itself which starts feeding problems, but the social conventions of the family dining table. Sitting up to table and being reasonably still and quiet go against the infant's every instinct at this age. His attention span is still very limited. When he plays freely he wanders from position to position, from object to object. He never voluntarily sits still for the length of time a family meal is likely to take. Furthermore he cannot join in general conversation, nor easily keep quiet while other people talk to each other and ignore him. He likes conversation, but he likes it to be directed exclusively at him! So if he is forced to join in social eating, forced to sit still, he will probably make the mealtime extremely uncomfortable for everyone else and end up by being scolded or banished. Over many days, such an atmosphere at mealtimes does not make for enthusiastic eating. Parents who feel they must demand conventional table manners from anyone who eats at their table may do better to feed the infant on his own for a few more months. After all he *is* still an impostor in human shape. Parents who feel that it is good for the infant to feel himself part of a family group round the dinner table might try sitting him up with them, but allowing him to get down as soon as he has finished what he wants to eat. Gradually he can be taught that once he has elected to leave the table his meal is over, that he cannot return every two minutes for another mouthful. He can later learn not to bother the others who are enjoying their leisurely meal. At 3 or 4 he will regard it as a privilege to sit up with the adults and be able to join their talk. At 1 or 2 he regards it as torment and will make it torment for all.

Once feeding problems form they are difficult to deal with. But they are usually best handled by exactly the same methods which hopefully avoid their formation.

The mother who finds herself trying to feed a toddler food which he refuses needs to ask herself, honestly, whether he appears in any way malnourished. If he is healthy, growing, energetic and cheerful (except at mealtimes!) she has to try and accept that her worry is not rational, or at least that it is not really about the child's nutrition. Possibly a few days of actually making a note of what the child eats, and comparing it with the information earlier in this chapter may help. If, having worked out exactly what the child is eating and having compared it with what he needs, she still finds herself worried, a check-up of the infant's general health by his doctor may reassure her. Somehow or other she has got to become convinced that the child will not starve himself into illness. Without that conviction the mother is bound to go on worrying. And if she goes on worrying she will have to be superhuman to conceal the anxiety from the already sensitized child.

If the mother can reduce her own anxiety, the next step is to consider how much effect her present policy is actually having on what the child eats. How much extra food does he take because of those hours of persuasion and scolding? Usually the answer is very little. Making a person eat is impossible. So trying is doomed to failure and bound to make the situation worse.

It is not easy to stop trying to make a bolshy child eat good food, expensively bought and lovingly prepared. The more one tries to find things the child will like, and make them delicious and attractive, the more hurtful and maddening it is when he rejects them. So it often helps to simplify the whole performance. There is no point in cooking minced liver and three vegetables if he is not going to eat them, so what is he likely to eat? If sandwiches are a possibility he can be given those instead. If he eats them, well and good. If he does not, at least the mother has not wasted so much money or time.

Even when mothers make the effort to get themselves into this new, less emotional state of mind over the infant's eating, he is often very slow to respond. If he has come to regard meals as horrible or as a challenge to his independence, or as a battleground with his mother, or indeed as anything except opportunities to satisfy his hunger with food, it will take him quite a long time to come to regard them differently. Some-times a radical change of scene speeds things up. If the rows have always been associated with a high-chair at the living room table, a low table–chair combination (which can probably be borrowed) in the kitchen may strike him as quite different. If he has always wanted to get down from his chair, to get away from the meal, then giving it to him on a stool while he sits on the floor may work. He is not confined or tied down, so he may stay voluntarily. However it is done, the infant has somehow got to be made to feel that things have changed. He has to be helped to see practical evidence of his mother's determined change of attitude.

But it will not happen very quickly. And all too often a mother starts out with the explicit intention of adopting this kind of line, and then finds that she has ruined it all for herself because her nerve or her patience failed her at a critical moment. She gives him what he likes and leaves him to get on with it, but then she cannot resist the temptation to feed him the last few bits 'because he really seemed to be enjoying it'. Or she brings him in from a long walk and finds herself ladling in his tea 'because he is so tired'. She puts him in the borrowed low-chair, with much emphasis on how nice and different it all is, and he gets out again without eating anything. Before she can stop herself his mother has swooped him up and dumped him in the hated high-chair after all. Hardest to bear of all is the day when, unforced, the child goes from waking to bedtime without eating anything. Probably there were really some snacks that the mother has forgotten, but it is not easy to hang on to the fact that the infant will just be hungry tomorrow; that letting him not eat is good mothering, not bad; and that he will not starve himself.

The infant who has really got his mother and the rest of his family involved in his non-eating may have come to feel that food is his principal means of getting attention. When his mother decides not to fuss about it any more, he may actually miss the attention that used to centre on him at mealtimes, even though most of it was cross attention. If this is the case, the child may adamantly refuse to feed himself.

Such a refusal does not mean that the resolving-eating-problems policy needs changing. The child will feed himself when he is both really hungry and really sure that his mother will not change her mind and revert to the old ways. But it does make it even more difficult for the mother to stick to her chosen guns. If he positively asks the mother to feed him it seems brutal to refuse, and difficult to remember that if she consents he will at once reject her attempts.

If the infant has to be faced out in this way the mother needs to make it very clear to him that she has not stopped bothering about what he eats because she does not *care* about him any more. He has to be helped towards feeling that the fuss has only stopped because his mother now flatteringly regards him as old enough to decide for himself about food. At mealtimes she may be able to emphasize this by eating her own food with the child, saying, and conveying, that eating is something they do together, she enjoying her food, he enjoying his. But outside mealtimes the infant will probably need to have made up to him the amount of attention and fuss he used to get over food. If he is to be left to get on with eating in his own way, he needs to feel that his mother is just as involved (or temporarily even more involved) as she ever was in all other aspects of his life. She will not feed him, but she will play with him. She will not interest herself in the state of his plate, but she will look at his toy car.

If the mother manages to remain adamant in her refusal to fuss over food any longer, some infants will do their best to get a fuss started in some other area of life. Often, having ceased to be able to involve the mother in a food fuss the infant will try a pot fuss. Mothers who want to stay sane will keep an eye out for this manoeuvre and resolutely refuse to be trapped into it. The months when one is dealing with an eating problem are not the months for toilet training. One emotionally charged issue at a time is quite enough.

CHAPTER TWENTY-SIX

SLEEP AND ITS PROBLEMS

A majority of infants will adopt sleep patterns in their second year that are consistent with their first. Very wakeful children will probably continue to need little sleep, while the sleepy ones may go on needing plenty. But in other ways sleep in the second year is a different issue from in the first, because infants can now keep themselves awake. They can therefore have sleeping problems themselves, where in earlier months the problem really belonged to the parents.

Somewhere between 1 and 2 most babies go through a phase over daytime naps which is awkward for them and for their mothers. They reach a point where one nap in the day is not enough, and two naps is too many. The infant who used to rest between 10 a.m. and 11.30, and between 2 p.m. and 3.30, and sleep for some of both those periods, is now not ready to be put to bed in the morning, but if allowed to stay up cannot last until after lunch. By midday, just when his meal is cooking, he is exhausted, whiny, and may even drop off to sleep on the floor. If the mother, trying to avoid this, puts him to bed at 11.30 a.m. and gives him a late lunch, the same thing happens in the afternoon. He does not want to go to bed after lunch, but cannot stay awake happily until bedtime. By the end of the second year, this awkwardness usually resolves itself into a single nap, taken either before a late lunch, or after an early one. But in the meantime the mother may find herself giving the infant his midday meal at 11.30 a.m. or putting him to bed for the night at 5 p.m.

By soon after a year, most infants bitterly resent being woken up from their naps. Many are quite unable to eat or play or do anything but moan for as much as an hour after such an awakening. The timing of naps therefore has to be calculated carefully around the mother's other commitments. If she wakes him just in time for lunch, he is unlikely to eat any. If she leaves him to sleep during the afternoon, and then has to wake him to go and meet other children from school, he is likely to make it impossible for her to give the older ones proper attention. But if she lets him sleep as long as he likes during the afternoon, he may not wake himself until 5 p.m. and will not then be ready to go to bed at his usual time.

Physical exhaustion often plays a part in this sort of minor difficulty. The infant is likely to be pushing himself to the limits of his strength in learning to walk and climb. He is also likely to be hurting and surprising himself several times a day with the falls that go with this physical activity. As with an older child, the more tired he gets, the less well he manages his body: coordination becomes increasingly effortful. The more his coordination fails him, the more physical effort he has to put into everything he does, and the more times he will fail and fall. He may therefore need ways of resting physically, which are different from actual naps. Being taken out in his pushchair in the second half of the morning or afternoon may rest him sufficiently to last without a sleep until after lunch or until bedtime. A period of sitting-down play, with the mother showing him books or helping him build, or teaching him nursery rhymes, may have the same effect.

Getting overtired is a common problem in the second year, and one which mothers sometimes unwittingly encourage. If the infant is difficult to put to bed at night, mothers sometimes feel that the more energetic he is during the day, the more likely he is to sleep well. Often the exact reverse is the truth. The newly mobile infant is bombarded with stimuli. Much of this he provides for himself, as he crawls, and walks; much more is provided by other people and other children, and all the places he is taken to. A public sandpit may be an idyllic place for him to play if it is comparatively empty. But that same sandpit in high summer, seething with bigger children, noisy, alarming and incomprehensible, may well be too much for him to take in. He may be far too tired, too excited, too strung up to sleep when bedtime comes.

Trouble in settling children down for the night in the

second year is so general we ought almost to consider it normal. Unfortunately many advice handbooks are misleading. They tend to imply that the infant should be affectionately but firmly put to bed at the time decided by the mother, and that that should be that. Mothers, reading this sort of advice, often believe that this is what happens in every house but their own, and that it is only their own mishandling of the situation which has led their infant to cause such trouble every evening. In fact when survey workers give mothers the chance to say, in an uncritical atmosphere, what actually happens when they put their toddlers to bed, it becomes clear that somewhere around 50 per cent of all infants between 1 and 2 years regularly make a major fuss about bedtime.[18,68] The Newson survey gives detailed accounts, in the mothers' own words, of the lengths to which families went, every night, to get 1-year-olds settled. It is clear that every practice scorned by the advice books is in fact *common* practice. Infants are sat with, rocked, sung to, cuddled, taken back downstairs, allowed to stay up until all hours, cuddled to sleep on the parents' bed, walked up and down, fed and re-fed.

Such extreme nightly measures seem absurd to the fortunate families whose toddlers settle happily. But nightly settling problems are very disrupting, so much so that parents will do virtually anything to avoid or cut them short. The mother wants to get the infant settled so that she can give her attention to older children, to her husband and to supper – which may well be the main meal for husbands who eat sandwiches on the job, or children who dislike their school dinners. Furthermore many women cannot properly relax and enjoy adult company until they know that the infant is settled. And they are very conscious that they *are* bad company until they stop listening to their husbands with one ear – with the other ear halfway up the stairs.

Many (43 per cent in the Newson survey) solve the problem by giving the infant a bottle to take to bed with him. In discussion, they know full well that the infant could choke if he goes to sleep with milk dripping into his mouth; they know that nothing could be worse for his new teeth. But getting the infant settled seems worth almost anything.

Much the same applies to bringing the baby back downstairs again. Mothers realize that they are inviting bad habits when they do this; that the infant cannot be expected to regard bedtime as final if he can get another hour of sociability by crying. But if the infant will not let the mother out of his bedroom, and the potatoes are burning, the older child has news and the husband is hungry, the situation tends to resolve into 'I'll break the bad habit tomorrow, if I can just get through tonight.'

Many authorities, including Illingworth,[73] believe that these problems would not arise if mothers would be firm from the very first time the child cries on being left for the night. They believe that while the mother should peep in from time to time to make sure that the howling child has not cried himself sick, he should not see the mother once he has been settled. It is difficult to see the feasibility or the logic of this view. Its possibility is limited by the fact that infants at this age can keep themselves awake, and cry if they feel like it, literally for hours. Few people's housing is so isolated that they could leave the child for long without complaints from neighbours. And even if neighbours do not complain, older children will certainly be kept awake as well as the parents' nerves shattered.

Logically, if the infant is crying because he cannot, for the moment, bear to see his mother go, it is difficult to see why her refusal to return should make him feel more able to relinquish her. Indeed, leaving him to cry alone is only likely to make him feel more sure that letting her go in the first place is dangerous. One is working, after all, towards the child being *content* to be left to sleep, not towards him going to sleep in abandoned despair.

There is, however, a 'testing cry'. Almost every infant in this age group will begin to cry when he is left for the night – and often when he is left for a nap too. If his cry is a test, a simple statement that he would prefer the mother to stay with him, and an attempt to see whether she will, then it will only last for a couple of minutes. If the infant does not really feel abandoned, or unable to be alone, he will then stop crying; fall asleep if he is ready, or start to play or talk if he is not. But if it was not a testing cry, the crying will build up. If the mother then stays away, what message is she conveying? 'Don't bother to cry, because I shall not come back, however sad you are.' It hardly seems a message likely to lead to easier bedtimes on subsequent nights.

There is a middle road between leaving the child desperately alone, and allowing him victory in terms of getting him up again, or sitting with him. The sort of message this middle road is supposed to convey is, 'There is no need to cry. You are not deserted, we will always come if you need us, but it is the end of today and time to go to sleep.' Such a message seems most likely to get through to the child if one of his parents goes back, every five minutes or so, for as long as he continues to fuss, but stays on each visit only long enough to smile, tuck him up, repeat his usual goodnight, and leave again. If the house happens to be so arranged that the infant's sleeping room is close to the family quarters, the mother may be able to have the same effect by calling to the infant. Or he may never begin to fuss if he can hear her moving around, tidying up, bathing the next child and so on. The point is that the infant should feel that there is no *need* to cry, because his mother is available, and that there is no *point* in crying, because she will not let him start his day again.

Sometimes this kind of policy can be made easier on the parents and the child if a mild sedative is prescribed by a doctor for the infant. Many people are shocked at this idea. They are convinced that the problem is due to the mother's mishandling; convinced that it could be put right with a little firmness, and revolted at the idea of 'sleeping pills for babies'. In fact such sedation can act as a much kinder version of the 'leaving the baby to cry' policy, and a much briefer and less exhausting version of the 'visit him for two minutes every five minutes' policy. The whole point is that if such a drug is prescribed, it is given well before bedtime, so that the infant makes no connection between the medicine and sleep, and so that he reaches his bed already relaxed and sleepy. Left alone, he cries and his mother visits him. A few minutes later, he finds himself too sleepy and comfortable to be bothered to grumble any more; he finds himself asleep. Over a few nights, the infant ceases to connect being put to bed with crying and misery, and a cross, harassed mother. He begins to expect to go to sleep. In this way a problem pattern can be reversed.

Many doctors will not prescribe such sedation. And it does not always work. Sedative drugs are notoriously difficult to prescribe for the very young, because they can excite rather than calm a child, and so have the reverse of the desired effect. But they are certainly worth considering before the parents reach screaming (or slapping) point.

By the middle of the second year, a new reason for visiting the crying child, rather than leaving him alone, often emerges. Infants who are left, often start to learn to get out of their cots. If mother will not come to them, they go to find her. This is a development which has to be avoided at almost any cost, because once it has begun it is extraordinarily difficult to deal with. While he is learning to climb out, the infant may hurt himself – cot sides are high for a child who is only just learning to climb. Once he has succeeded in getting out, he may find himself on dangerous stairs in search of his mother. But above all, once it has occurred to him that he *can* get out of bed at will, only the most medieval methods will actually stop him. Of course he can be physically imprisoned, by stretching netting over the top of his cot, strapping him in, or locking his door. But once being put to bed does literally mean being put into prison, all hope of peaceful bedtimes and peaceful nights is gone. Very few mothers actually go to these lengths. But thousands are driven wild by their toddlers appearing downstairs or in the parents' bedroom, several times during the evening and night.

If the infant is always visited when he cries and is never got out of his cot or taken downstairs, he is unlikely to think of getting out for himself. He is even less likely to think of it if he has always been accustomed to wearing a sleeping-bag.

Once the child has begun to wander at night it is too late for this solution. He will either climb out despite the bag, and fall and hurt himself, or he will regard the bag as a trap and refuse to wear it. But if he has always worn one, he will know he cannot get out and walk until his mother comes and takes it off. A simple piece of mother upwomanship, but very effective.

Waking in the night, as at younger ages, must have a cause. The child cannot wake himself on purpose. A few small-scale observational studies have shown that most infants do, in fact, wake several times during the night, but without their parents even being aware of it. They wake themselves turning over, and go back to sleep again without demanding attention. For this reason, the alert mother who hears a small sound from the child's room, should not be too quick to go in. Drillien[68] found that night waking was associated with over-anxiety in the mother. It seemed clear, in her study, that some of the waking had been caused by mothers not giving unalarmed babies the chance to resettle themselves. And no sensible, attached infant is going to ignore the mother if she actually walks in, unsummoned.

On the other hand, a sudden scream or sudden crying almost always means fear or discomfort. And there is never any purpose in leaving the child. Indeed the longer he is left, the longer it will probably take to resettle him. Macfarlane, Allen and Honzik,[118] in a careful statistical study of behaviour problems in normal children, found that nearly 30 per cent of girls and nearly 40 per cent of boys woke frequently in the night at 21 months. Often the cause was bad dreams; often it was unknown. In the Newson study[18] 35 per cent of mothers of 1-year-old babies had had to get up to them at least once during the night immediately preceding the interview.

In the majority of night-waking incidents, all the child needs is a reassuring glimpse of a parent. Whatever fear has beset him in his sleep is dispelled by this reassurance. But if the comforting is not quickly forthcoming, the distress can build up to panic proportions, and the child may be shaky and tense for a long time after the parent finally arrives. As far as we know there is little that can be done to cure night waking. The drugs which sometimes prove useful in helping the child relax into sleep will not keep him there all night. Indeed one of their unfortunate effects can be to make any nightmare very much worse. Sedated, the child may be confused and difficult to reassure if he wakes later in the night. Obvious practical aids help some families. Many children under 2 go to sleep in a muddle of blankets, and wake because they are cold in the small hours. Covering them when the mother goes to bed may help; a sleeping-bag may help even more. Nightlights are far more general than most handbooks imply. I have come across very few small children who are left to sleep in total darkness. But a light will not prevent the child waking; its only effect on night waking may be to prevent him being frightened when he does wake. A few children who are deeply attached to their dummies, or to transitional comfort objects, may cry because when they wake, momentarily, they cannot find them. Tying them to the cot bars may enable the infant to resettle himself.

Otherwise the phase has to be lived through. Mothers, partly in order to feel they are doing *something* about it, will probably try every solution they can find in books or the experiences of friends. But what helps one child sleep through the night may make another worse. Cutting out the daytime nap may make one sleep longer at night; but another will simply be too tired to settle, and then too tense to sleep soundly. A larger supper will help one, and give another indigestion. Gleaning through the sparse available evidence, only one factor seems at all general, and that is the whole emotional tenor of the infant's daily life. It does seem clear that *both* settling to sleep, and sleeping through the night, are associated with overall calm and happiness. These problems are seen at their worst when an infant has suffered obvious trauma: a new baby has arrived, his mother has started work outside the house, his father has gone away. Mothers report that they are easiest to manage when the child is particularly relaxed and pleased with life.

Early waking in the morning is very general during this year. The infant is tired enough to begin his sleep at 6 p.m., but by 5.30 a.m. he has had plenty of night. He is awake, hungry and usually very cheerful. How much this matters to the parents depends on many practical factors. Some families get up by 6 a.m. anyway. Others go to bed late and would like to sleep until 8 a.m. There may be an older child who also wakes early, and is delighted with the toddler's company. Or there may be a younger baby whom the mother does not want awakened.

Between 1 and 2 early waking is not usually as difficult to live with as it is in earlier months. The infant is at his best first thing in the morning, and can usually be persuaded to occupy himself very happily if toys, books, and perhaps a rusk or two are left within his reach. At worst his mother may have to come to him, change his nappy and open his curtains or switch on his light. But after that he will probably give her another hour or two of peace and song. Often, too, this is the time of day when the 3- or 4-year-old most likes the infant. They may amuse each other, talk to each other, in a way they do at no other time. There are no adults around so the two of them are not vying for adult attention. The infant is in his cot, so the older child can escape his attentions if they move in a hair-pulling direction; the infant has no one else to pass him toys or help him with things, so he is likely to give the older one the benefit of the kind of charm he usually reserves for his mother.

Towards 2 years, many infants will accept the mother's desire for morning peace to a point where they will wait for a given signal before shouting for attention. They may learn to wait until they hear her alarm clock go off, or until the radio is switched on. In the winter, early waking is an excellent argument for providing infants with low wattage nightlights. No child can be expected to occupy itself for an hour or more in total darkness.

Common sleep problems in the second year do add up to a very great deal of fatigue for parents. With bedtime problems, night waking, and early morning waking, the parents may never get a peaceful evening and a solid 8-hour night. If there is also a new baby needing night feeds, or an older child having occasional nightmares, sleep may become the parents' chief treat in life. Yet the exhaustion which comes from months of broken nights is often overlooked, by husbands who cannot understand why their wives are so grumpy, or doctors who prescribe tranquillizers for the 'bored housewives' syndrome'.

CHAPTER TWENTY-SEVEN

TOILET TRAINING

At one year, many babies will be thoroughly experienced in sitting on pots, while others will never have met a pot in their lives. As we saw in Chapter 20, it does not seem to make any difference to the child's eventual acquisition of control. True toilet *training*, as opposed to conditioning or catching, starts in this second year.

For reasons already discussed, it is extremely difficult to find out how mothers actually go about toilet training. We know much more about the ages at which success is, or is not, achieved than we do about training methods. Our 'knowledge' of the process of toilet training must come more from the informal observations of doctors and welfare nurses, who see infants while training is in progress, than from formal statistical surveys, where the mother's lack of memory and her desire to show up well may seriously distort the results.

Toilet training is unique among infant-socialization processes in that it offers only intellectual satisfaction to the child. When we set out to socialize a child's eating, or even his sleeping patterns, we are only attempting to steer or deflect things he positively wants to do anyway. Hunger is a positive feeling, and eating satisfies it. However overlaid with emotional problems the eating process may become, that physiological need–fulfilment pattern remains, working on the parents' side. The same is true of sleep. However great a fight the child may put up, eventually he wants to sleep; at the end of the battle letting go into sleep fulfils a need.

Elimination is a physiological need, too, but when we toilet train a child we are not trying to persuade him to void (as we try to persuade him to eat or to sleep), we are trying to persuade him *not* to void in his pants or on the floor, but to save it for a pot or lavatory. There is nothing in this for the child except eventually, and if all goes smoothly, a satisfaction in being grown up, in being like the parents, and in pleasing them. The strength of adults' early training is shown by the difficulty which they often have in believing that wet pants are not uncomfortable for an infant, that bowel motions do not smell disgusting to them. Many adults cannot understand why an infant does not prefer to be clean. Eventually he will so prefer, but only when he has absorbed the message, however gently it is conveyed, that wet pants are babyish; that soiled ones are 'dirty'.

True toilet training cannot even begin until the infant shows, by word or gesture, that he is aware when he has wet or soiled himself. At around a year, everyone in the house may know when the infant passes a motion – except him. He may turn scarlet, strain as if constipated although he is not, grunt and generally make his performance clear. But he may still appear quite unconscious of having produced anything. When he urinates the child may become motionless on the floor, then pull himself to his feet leaving a puddle behind him. But he does not even glance back at it; he still does not connect the bodily sensations with the product.

Most infants begin to make this vital connection somewhere between 1 year and 15 months. When the child urinates, he will point out the puddle to his mother, or clutch his wet nappies with an exclamation. Placed on a pot when a bowel action is obviously imminent, he may look in the pot to see what came out.

Once the child connects his bodily sensations with a product, things become both easier and more difficult for the training mother. They are easier in that the infant is on the way towards learning to tell her *before* the event rather than after. But they are more difficult in that the child becomes aware that what he produces is his, comes out of his body, is part of him and therefore does not belong to the mother, should not necessarily be in her power.

This is the basic toilet-training conflict. The infant is being asked to treat what he rightly regards as part of himself as if it belonged to the mother. He is being asked to give it to her, where she says, when she says. It is his gift to bestow, yet he is not allowed to decide not to give it.

The more capable of being trained the child becomes, the less he may wish to be trained. The more able he is to withhold his urine or faeces, the more he may decide to withhold them from the mother, not from the nappy. The more valuable she makes the gift seem, the more may he decide that today she shall not have it.

Against that, the mother can set only the child's desire to grow up, together with any flattering acknowledgements of being grown up that she can think of for a particular child – like wearing ordinary pants instead of nappies, or being allowed to take his own toilet paper.

Bowel training almost always precedes bladder training. Indeed bowel training may, in infants who have been potted well before a year, simply progress from catching. Bowel control is far easier for infants. Most only move their bowels once or at most twice a day by this age and many not that often. Many are naturally quite regular in their timing, the motion almost always occurring at the same time in the day. The signs of an impending motion are often clear for the mother to see, but the urgency is not nearly as great as it is for urination. The mother therefore has time calmly to take the child to the lavatory or pot when she knows a motion is coming, and the infant is not bored by frequent unsuccessful visits. Gradually, at around 15 months, he becomes interested in what he produces. Very shortly after that, he may attract his mother's attention when he is about to perform, although he would still carry on in his pants if she ignored him. By 18 months he may actually ask for the pot, and by 20 months – the average in Ruth Griffiths's sample[100] – his bowel training may be complete so that he only soils his pants during rare episodes of diarrhoea, and is horrified if he does so.

But that smooth and easy picture is an ideal, and it is entirely dependent on the infant remaining happy to be taken to the lavatory when he is going to have a motion. Often the 18-month baby is at just the stage of emotional development when he least wishes to fall in with any urgent suggestion of the mother. If she tries to rush him in to dinner or hurry him into his clothes, he fusses. So he is equally likely to refuse if she tries to hustle him to the lavatory.

When he realizes how important it is to her that they get there in time, his negativism is likely to increase. He is contra-suggestive. At least when she hurries him to dinner, he knows he is going to get the dinner. When she hurries him to the lavatory he is only going to have a motion, and he was going to have that anyway – only she cares where. If mild negativism is met with increased pressure, accidents with scoldings, successes with real triumph, the infant often begins to see his motions as an area of real power over the mother. He can really make her care. If this stage is reached, the infant may actually refuse to sit on the pot at all; or, even more cleverly, may sit there quite goodly, but use his new power to withhold the motion until he is allowed to get up. The mother *knows* he needs to go, but she cannot make him. In extreme instances, the infant will perform anywhere but in the lavatory or pot, and any time except when his mother suggests it. Worse still, he may learn to withhold until his motions have become so dry and hard and his colon so distended that it loses sensation, and he becomes actually unable to go; truly constipated.

Most families experience something in between these two extremes. The infant remains reasonably cooperative, but has days when he will not use the pot or indeed pass a motion at all; on other days he will have accidents, or refuse to go when his mother first pots him and then relent a little later on but rather too late. Most mothers manage to avoid extremes of concern, though few fail to get irritated once soiling is obviously calculated. The hope, in bowel training, is to prevent the infant seeing it as a weapon in the power game, by keeping the emotional temperature of the whole process down. Macfarlane, Allen and Honzik[118] found that by 21 months only 32 per cent of boys and 20 per cent of girls in their sample still regularly soiled.

Urine training is a far more difficult problem for the infant – and therefore for the mother. The physiological difficulty is well explained by Muellner.[119] He points out that the infant's first method of holding up the passing of urine comes through learning to prevent the destrusor muscle from contracting, and simultaneously holding in the levator ani muscle. As an older child would put it, he 'clenches his bottom' and, as the older child would certainly explain, you cannot do that for long. The intra-abdominal pressure has already reached a high level, and the urgency to urinate is extreme. Only later does the child learn to take charge of matters at an earlier stage, by using the diaphragm and the abdominal muscles to control intra-abdominal pressure. Once he can do this, he can delay much longer. But it is later still before he can void voluntarily when the bladder is not full. Furthermore, his bladder capacity at the age of 2 years is normally only half that of a 4-year-old.

Urine training is practically difficult too. In this second year of life the infant may need to urinate 8 or more times during the day, depending on how much he drinks, the temperature, whether he has any fever and so on. The problem is therefore not one which can be dealt with for the day in one successful potting. The mother has to be alert all day to help the infant. The infant has to be alert, or at least prepared to have his activities interrupted, all day, too. Obviously discouraging accidents are far more likely than they are with bowel training. Obviously too the infant is the more likely to get fed up with the whole business. Less obviously, the mother may find herself being very inconsistent in her handling of the infant's urination. At home she may keep an eye on the child or the clock or both, and pot him consistently, congratulating him on being a big boy who does not need nappies in the daytime any more. But as soon as she takes him out she may find herself having to put those nappies back on. She knows she will not get him to a public lavatory in a busy high street in time.

Time is of the essence early in urine training. At around 15 months, the infant may tell his mother he has wet himself. At 16 months he may announce, often with a loud scream, that he is about to do so. A month or so later, he learns the first bottom-clenching control, but it is momentary only, and furthermore it roots him to the spot. He cannot run for his pot because if he moves he will urinate. Only if the mother gets to him like greased lightning can she help him to be in time. At 18–20 months, that more timely intra-abdominal control may have begun, so that the infant does have time to tell and then go. But his waiting time is still not very long, and he cannot yet urinate in advance of needing to. It is no use, at this age, asking him to go to the lavatory now, so that he will not need to go later, at the shops. He cannot go until he does need to, and then it must still be quickly. Hardly surprisingly, then, far more children still regularly wet themselves by day at 21 months than soil themselves. In Macfarlane's sample[118] 62 per cent of boys and 43 per cent of girls still did so at this age. Daytime control for the whole sample was not certain until the children were $3\frac{1}{2}$.

Clearly there is a delicate balance to be struck in toilet training. It has to be made clear to infants that their parents would prefer them to use a lavatory or a pot, and that older people always do so. Very occasionally mothers are so concerned not to put pressure on a child, but to 'leave him to train himself', that they forget to communicate this preference. Illingworth[73] quotes one such mother of a 4-year-old girl, who had attempted no training of any kind because she 'did not mind washing nappies'. Many children, neglected in this way, would in fact copy other members of the family and train themselves before 4 years. But it is no kindness to leave them to do so. By 3, most children will experience some scorn from other children if they are still in nappies. There are no severer critics of toilet-training deficiencies than those who have only just completed their own.

At the same time, there must be no temptation to the child to use toileting as a battleground. The mother's apparent emotions about the matter have to be kept at low key. Wet or soiled pants are not wicked; clean or dry ones are not superb accomplishments. It is just a nuisance or a pity when they are wet or dirty, clever and grown up when they are dry or clean.

The constant interference of daily activities which urine

training involves needs to be kept to a minimum. Unless the infant prefers to use the lavatory, a pot is useful because it is portable; it can be brought to the playing child rather than his needing to be taken out of the room and away from what he was doing. Clothes also need to be easy. It is seldom any use trying to urine train a child who wears nappies in the day. He may fail to notice a small urination. And the pins and general difficulty of getting him undressed will certainly be too much for his precarious early control. The boredom of being laid on his back for redressing will also irritate him. Once the mother decides she is seriously trying to help him stay dry, it has got to be pants and puddles.

Once any trouble starts over toileting, no authority any longer suggests that the mother should join battle. Trouble usually starts with the infant not wanting to sit on the pot. Often in the first instance this is only because he was busy with something else. But if the mother tries to insist, it becomes a physical battle. Unless she holds him down, he gets off. If she holds him down she is overpowering him in just the way he finds most objectionable. It is as if she tried to force feed him, or tied him in his cot in a lying down position. She cannot win – she cannot force him to void any more than she can force him to eat or sleep – but she can very easily turn what started as an objection of the moment into a real problem.

Some infants do become toilet-training problems, how- ever sensitively they appear to have been handled. A study of the very many theories put forward by different workers, both theoreticians and research workers, does not produce any one reason or even any convincing group of reasons.

Immaturity is probably often a factor. The infant may be less physiologically ready for training than he appears, and attempts to train him make him anxious and resentful. He is socially mature enough to realize what the mother wants, and even – with part of him – to want to do what she wants, but he cannot manage.

Sometimes small practical considerations have a dis- proportionate effect. The child may feel insecure and wobbly sitting on a pot instead of a supporting chair, or the solid floor. Or he may feel afraid sitting high up on the hollow lavatory. Occasionally he may pass a hard motion which hurts, or which even makes a tiny anal tear which is sore for several days. A girl may be sore from fingering herself, so that urine stings. Mishaps of this kind can put the infant off for a day or two. Then if the objections are tactlessly handled by the mother, the whole business may become an issue between them.

The real issue probably centres around the new sense of independent self which is a vital part of being a toddler; of growing away from babyhood towards childhood. The child sees his motions as a part of himself. Passing them is physically pleasurable and the mother receives them with pleasure, as if they were a gift. Yet they are not a gift which the child is allowed to bestow as he pleases. Nor are they a part of himself which he is easily permitted to play with nor to keep. They are quickly flushed down the lavatory.

Sometimes objections to toilet training become confused with the child's feelings about genital play. As far as we know all children eventually discover the particular pleasure of genital play as opposed to play with other parts of the body. The casual clutching of earlier months gives way to a more deliberate, obviously pleasurable rhythmical handling. And this discovery of masturbation often takes place during the toilet-training months. If the parents have made it clear to the baby that they disapprove of genital play this new pleasure will already be a guilty one. The parents angrily remove the child's hands from his own body just as they remove his faeces if he tries to play with them. They try to control his giving of genital pleasure to himself just as they try to control his passing of his own motions. The toddler tends to see such control as intrusive and overpowering. He is at a developmental stage when he must assert himself by taking issue with the mother on anything that comes up. And, as we have seen, toileting comes up more frequently than most issues; counting in urination, more frequently even than those other prime areas for conflict, meals and sleep.

As with feeding problems, the two most useful pieces of avoiding action do seem to be for the mother to be prepared to leave things alone at the very first sign of trouble, never allowing herself to be trapped into insisting that the child use the pot when he cannot be persuaded to want to. And to hand the responsibility primarily to him at the very first possible moment. If the pot is on the floor in the room where the child plays, and he has pants he can pull down (or even none if it is warm enough) he is far more likely to go and do it for himself than he is to submit to being done to. And if he empties the pot himself and pulls the chain, he may actually feel that disposing of his waste products is fun – rather than mother hurtfully rejecting a gift.

CHAPTER TWENTY-EIGHT

MOBILITY

Learning to walk alone is regarded as a major landmark in an infant's development. But often, what he *does* with his ability to walk is ignored. Once he can walk alone, mothers and other observers lose interest in his mobility. This is a pity. Just as the infant learns to get hold of objects first, and then only gradually learns what to do with them, how to use them, so he learns to walk first, and then only gradually learns to use his walking in such a way as to approximate to mature patterns of mobility.

As we saw in Chapter 21, the majority of infants can make some form of progress on their own two feet by the first birthday. Some will only pull themselves to standing by furniture, cot or playpen bars, and then cruise round the support. Others will hand themselves from one support to another, thus getting around a conveniently arranged room; others will actually relinquish their hold on one support to cross a gap to the next. A few will walk without any support at all.

Almost all infants will pass through these stages on their way to independent walking. There is little purpose in trying to persuade the child who does not yet hand himself from one support to another, to toddle two steps across the room towards his mother. This is asking him to leave out two stages. And he will not. If he did he would almost certainly fall; and as we have seen, falls at this age are to be discouraged. They can do damage to both skull and confidence.

This kind of premature 'encouragement' from parents and caretakers is very common. It often arises because the infant's mobility does not increase at a consistent pace. He passes from one stage to the next, but often there is a long period between two specific stages, during which he appears to have got stuck. He has learned a certain degree of walking competence, and progresses no further, often for several months. Illingworth[102] points out that once the child has become a biped to *any degree* a delay in actual independent walking is very seldom a cause for concern. Any spasticity, or other disease affecting neuromuscular control, will already have manifested itself during the first stages of learning to walk.

Such delay, after reaching a certain level of competence, is usually a simple reflection of the fact that the infant does not have enough hours of waking time, enough energy and concentration available, to progress at an equal rate in all developmental fields. As early as 1946, Gesell[120] put it thus: 'The course of development turns upon itself in a manner to suggest a spiral kind of neuromotor organization, characteristic of reciprocal interweaving . . .'

Having reached a certain point in his walking development, the child turns his developmental attention to other matters. His bipedal achievements have given him some added mobility, an interesting new view of the world, and extra height so that he can reach more objects. He may be happy to rest upon that, and *use* the new view, the new interest and the new objects. He may enter a phase where he concentrates for the moment on play with toys, or on learning to talk, or on a high level of social interaction with adults.

Getting stuck in this way in walking development may also reflect a lack of confidence. In such a child, the point where development stops is usually the point between walking competently with any form of support, even one finger from an adult, and actually taking off across the room alone. A particular fall may shake his confidence, so that he decides to abandon independent walking for the moment. Slippery floors or shoes may make independent walking feel impossibly difficult. The rowdy presence of older pre-school children may make the middle of the floor on his own two feet feel a very vulnerable place to be. Such children continue to develop their ability to walk even while they continue to insist on token support. When they do finally gain the confidence to set out alone, they usually do so with great competence, as if they had been practising for weeks.

A child who stops progressing in his walking is therefore seldom a cause for concern. Regression is a different matter. If an infant's balance and muscular control appear to slip back, so that he is actually less competent at, say, 18 months than he was at 15 months, there has to be a reason. If the reason is not obvious, advice should be sought.

But usually the reason is obvious, and the prognosis excellent. Severe illness, even of quite unimportant aetiology, such as an acute infection of any kind, with high fever and some days of comparative immobility, will reduce both the infant's energy and his muscle tone to a point where he has to regress a little and then catch himself up. He may revert to crawling, and then repeat all the stages of learning to walk, all over again. Only this time he 're-learns' them in a few days instead of over months. Parents whose children suffer an illness known to be serious, and known to be occasionally followed by brain damage, such as meningitis or encephalitis, often go through days of needless agony because this natural regression is not recognized. The doctors may assure them that the infant has come through his experience undamaged, but they watch the child who could walk three steps alone before he was ill, crawl uncertainly around the room, barely able to pull himself up to stand at the cot bars, and they cannot believe he is not permanently damaged. They fail to allow for the effects of confinement, drugs, trauma, and little food. And they panic.

Any severe emotional upset may have much the same effect. Separation from the mother often leads to a general regression to more babyish ways, and this will include more babyish locomotion. Just as recovery from illness will start the infant back to progressing again, so the end of the emotional upset will give him the confidence, the heart, to catch himself up again.

Griffiths[100] had 150 infants between 10 and 15 months of age in her sample. At 12 months, most of them could side-step confidently around the furniture and could walk at least one or two steps with their hands held. At 13 months most could stand alone for at least a few seconds: they would release their grasp on the furniture before sitting down, for example, or remain erect for a few moments if the mother gently disengaged her hands. Once this stage was reached, the babies tended to progress rapidly to independent walking, so that most were taking one or two steps between supports, quite alone, by the end of the 14th month. By 16 months most of the infants were toddling competently, and had largely abandoned crawling as their ordinary means of getting around.

Infants tend to remain partly dependent on supporting furniture or adult hands for some weeks after they can first walk alone because they cannot yet get up alone. Few infants learn to get to their feet without support until 15–16 months. Just as the baby who can sit on the floor and play, still, for some weeks, has to be put in sitting position by his mother, so the baby who can toddle has to have help in getting into toddling position in the first place. The infant's actual mobility can therefore often be pleasurably increased by giving him what is commonly known, in England, as a baby-walker. This is simply a small truck, or cart, so designed that its handle can be used by the baby to pull himself upright, without it tipping, and so that as he walks with it it does not run away from him. Obviously the design is vital. A doll's pram or other push-cart designed for older children can be disastrous. It tips backwards when the child pulls himself up, and once he starts it rolling it goes too fast for him. Given a baby-walker, the child can use a garden or park, taking his pull-up support and his toddling support with him across the grass. With years of use ahead as a brick truck or doll's pram, such a walker is an excellent investment.

The first competent toddling, around the sixteenth month, has many limitations. The two most unnerving are that the infant can neither stop suddenly, nor change direction. Collisions, painful meetings with doorposts, and falls down garden steps are the frequent result. Such accidents are most common out of doors. It is usually there that the infant has space to get up the speed which leads to disaster due to absence of brakes and steering.

By the seventeenth month, most infants are so steady on their feet that the mere process of walking need not take up all their energy and attention; they can do other things at the same time. The infant will probably be able to stoop from standing posture and pick a toy up off the floor, rather than sitting down to get the toy, and then having to get up again. Having got the toy he will be able to walk and carry it at the same time. He can look over his shoulder as he walks, and will therefore probably enjoy pulling a toy along behind him on a string. Very shortly afterwards he learns to retreat by walking backwards.

By 20 months he will probably be able to run, rather than merely toddling fast; and he may be able to jump so that both his feet leave the ground together. Few infants will be able to balance on one leg, however, until the third year, even though by 2 they will be able to kick a football after a shuffling fashion.

The actual use the infant makes of his increasing mobility does not depend only on his ability; it also depends very largely on his attachment to his mother, and therefore on her behaviour.

Infants are most mobile and most exploratory when their mothers are present in a familiar setting. In these circumstances the infant walks about, exploring, playing, conscious always of his mother's presence, using her as a secure base. Some of the earliest observations and thought upon mother as an explorer's base were made by William Blatz.[121] Since then many studies have demonstrated that the infant's willingness to move around and to explore are largely dependent on his mother's presence. The human child and the infant rhesus monkey need the mother to give them the courage to face the insecurity of the wider world, to refer to for reassurance as they explore it and to return to in haste if it proves alarming. The kind of behaviour which demonstrates this need has been well shown in a study of 1-year-olds placed in a strange playroom environment and observed with their mothers, with mother plus a stranger, with just a stranger and quite alone.[122]

All the infants played most actively and covered most ground when they were alone with their mothers. The addition of a stranger slightly diminished their activity, but most were prepared to accept the stranger's advances. Left alone with the stranger, the infants became immobilized. If they had failed to notice the mother leaving, their play tailed off as soon as they did notice. Those who became actually distressed could often be somewhat comforted by the stranger, but none could regain their former mobility and activity with only her presence for support. Left quite alone most of the infants did not move at all.

The disruptive effect on play of being left by the mother seemed also to be cumulative. Where the mother's first reappearance usually cued active pleased greeting-behaviour by the infant, her second departure and return evoked miserable clinging. Had the research design demanded a third departure, few of the mothers would have been able to interest the child in a toy sufficiently to escape yet again.

The parallel with a normal situation with the mother and child together at home is not perfect, of course, because the experimental playroom was strange to the infants. Nevertheless it remains generally true, from observations made in homes, that the more sure the infant is that the mother is there, and will remain there, the more independent activity he will indulge in. Sometimes mothers will say, in frustration, 'This morning I was busy, trying to clean round the house and so on, and he wouldn't let me alone for a minute, whining and clinging round my legs. Now I sit down to play with him and he doesn't want to know – he's all over the place and busy as a bee.'

The independent locomotion of slightly older children, from around 15 months to 2 years, has been beautifully observed by Anderson.[123] He studied 35 children whose mothers were sitting peacefully in the sunshine in a secluded corner of a familiar park.

Of the 35 children, 24 remained within 200 feet of the mother in any direction, without her taking any action whatsoever to retain contact with the child. 8 infants set off to go farther afield, attracted by seeing swings in the distance. All the mothers of these infants got up to follow as escorts, with the infants still remaining within their self-prescribed distance limit. Only 3 children had to be retrieved by the mothers because they wandered too far or got out of immediate sight.

The behaviour of the infants was highly consistent. All tended to move away from the mother in a direct line, and in short bursts punctuated by brief stops on the way. Their original foray was not caused by seeing something interesting. It was simply a moving away for its own sake. When the infants started to return, they often did so without ever looking at the mother, as if they were so aware of her exact position that a visual check on how far away they had got was unnecessary. The return journey was never instigated by an alarming external event, simply by it being 'time to return to base' by the infant's own internal clock. Once the infants had started back towards their mothers, they tended to progress in longer stretches, stopping less often than on the outward journey. But as they got closer to the mother, so the halts became longer, until finally that journey was over altogether.

Half of the children finished the journey still out of physical reach of the mother. They made their next outward sortie without physical, verbal or eye-to-eye contact having been made. It was as if it was enough for these children to have been briefly in the mother's orbit. Another quarter of the children rested close to the mother before setting out again; the remaining quarter made actual contact, leaning against the mother or climbing on to her lap. Mothers and infants spoke to each other only when they were in close contact. Very few mothers attempted to keep in contact with their exploring infants by calling to them. Those who did were totally unsuccessful – the infants behaved as if they were outside the maternal aura, and therefore not reachable by voice alone.

If the mother got up from her seat, and moved to retrieve something, or into a new patch of sunlight, without first signalling her intention to the infant, he at once became rooted to the spot. His natural coming and going pattern was broken by her shift, and usually no amount of patient calling would induce him to join her in her new position. The mother had first to retrieve the infant, and then let him start going and coming again from the new base.

We regard walking as a means of moving along, and getting from one place to another. But toddlers do not. Not only do they naturally tend to go and come to a seated mother, they are quite incapable of following, or moving along with, a *moving* mother. The infants observed by Anderson tended to ask for transport as soon as the mother signalled her intention of moving on. If a pushchair was offered, they climbed willingly into it. If there was no pushchair, they at once held up their arms to be carried. When mothers tried to make the toddlers walk along with them, there was invariably trouble. Holding the mother's hand, and with her walking extremely slowly, the infant might manage for a few yards. But after that either the mother would lose her patience and drag the child by the arm, or he would move deliberately and directly in front of her, and stand holding up his arms, demanding to be carried.

Bowlby[12] calls on data from a further 12 children studied by Anderson, to confirm their complete inefficiency in remaining oriented to a moving figure. The mothers of these 12 children were each moving very slowly through the park with their infants following them. Each child stopped repeatedly at varying distances from the mother, so that each mother spent more time waiting for the child than walking. Frequently the children wandered off course, and were then distressed because the mother was not where they had expected her to be, even although she was still in close, full view.

Bowlby believes, on the basis of these and other data, that following behaviour does not develop in human infants before about 3 years. Until that time it is instinctive for the child to seek transport whenever the mother moves, even though he is fully capable of covering great distances when she is still. After 3 years the infant can use newly developed goal-corrected systems to keep with a moving object, but for a further year or two most will prefer to be attached to that object, by holding hands, clutching clothes, or holding on to the pram handle.

Observations of animals tend to confirm this view. Many herd-animal young run and frolic while their mothers graze; orienting their excursions around the herd. But as soon as the herd begins to move off, the young return to their mothers, to move close against their sides, or under their bellies. Similar behaviour can be seen among apes even by casual observation in a zoo. As long as the mother ape sits grooming herself on a branch, her infant will play and explore all over the available cage space. But if the mother moves to another branch, the baby will freeze and cry until she fetches it. If the mother indicates that she is moving across to the eating place, the infant at once clings to her belly fur for transport, even though he had made eight independent journeys across the intervening space in the previous ten minutes.

An understanding of these peculiarities of early walking helps mother-child harmony. All too often mothers are highly irritated by their infant's refusal to walk home, when they are clearly not tired, having been toddling all over the place two minutes before. All too often the infant's refusal to hold the mother's hand and walk nicely beside her is seen as a wilful desire to escape and play, rather than an actual inability to stay oriented to her moving thigh. And all too often those constant stops and wanderings off in the wrong direction are seen as a desire to explore, a refusal to come home, rather than an inability to follow.

Handbooks of advice on child rearing commonly advise mothers to deal with this kind of lagging behaviour in the second year by keeping moving slowly ahead, on the grounds that the child will catch up when he sees mother getting further away. He may, but he may not. Mother's self-removal may leave him totally disoriented. If the following ability of toddlers was as good as these books suggest, there would not be so many lost and terrified infants in parks,

streets and shops. Using a pushchair should not be seen as a
sour reflection on the child's ability to walk, but as a means
of keeping him where he wants to be while his mother is in
motion – close.

CHAPTER TWENTY-NINE

LEARNING TO THINK

By his first birthday the infant's perceptions, through his five senses, have largely become organized into meaningful wholes. He recognizes objects, even when their lighting or their position or their context is unusual. He will know that his bottle is his bottle, even if it is presented endways on. He will know that his big beachball is itself, even if it is so far away across the grass that it looks small. He will recognize his mother's voice even when he cannot see her, and the ice-cream van's chimes even if ice-cream has not been mentioned.

But the infant has still got a good deal of perceptual sophistication to acquire by experience. He tends to see wholes, rather than the component parts of wholes, so that he will not notice the flowers that make up the pattern on the wallpaper unless they are pointed out to him; he will not be the one to notice the blood on the family dog's cut leg. He is still more readily fooled than an older person by tricks of environmental lighting, exclaiming at the 'pretty brick' when a piece of coal is turned into gleaming glass by a shaft of sunlight. Even more than an adult, he may be amazed at the lightness of a large parcel, of the heaviness of a small piece of lead. And much of his perceptual recognition is dependent on context. He may still greet his mother with a blank stare when she returns from the hairdresser with a new style, fail to recognize his father if he arrives home in a strange car, be unable to realize that it is his mother speaking if she talks to him on the telephone.

But all in all, the 1-year-old's perceptions are ready for the very beginning of the fresh and more complex organization we call concept formation.

If a perception is the organization of simple sense impressions into meaningful wholes, concepts are the groupings and categories into which such perceptions fall. Before he can form a concept, the infant must discover and define for himself the critical features common to a group of objects or a group of events.

Concepts therefore depend crucially on the development of language. Indeed whether they can exist at all without language being at least understood, if not spoken, is a subject of hot philosophical dispute. The nature of a child's concepts also depends on his culture. A Western infant may have, say, three different impressions which he must learn to recognize as 'rice': dry rice in the packet or jar, rice pudding, and the boiled rice that sometimes accompanies meat dishes. An Indonesian infant may have as many as a dozen 'rice' impressions of far greater variability and subtlety – for instance, rice growing in the paddy, which is dramatically different from rice prepared for eating, and refined rice, which is only a little different from rice left with the outer husk.

The infant begins the developments which will lead to concept formation through play. He has learned to see and hear and feel things more or less as adults do, and he has learned to get hold of things and manipulate them. By seeing, getting and manipulating, he finds out more and more about the nature of things: how they work, what they do, how they resemble each other and differ. During this year he will learn about up and down, about few and many, about in and out, about big and small, heavy and light, loud and soft. He will learn that what is round rolls, that what is square does not; that paper scrumples where thin wood will not; that water is wet and will wet him.

We know that infants learn all these things. As we shall see, we can watch them doing it, and by the end of the year, we shall be able to hear their growing understanding in their early speech. But how these cognitive processes take place remains largely a mystery.

The most systematic and comprehensive theory of cognitive development throughout childhood is probably that of Jean Piaget, the Swiss psychologist who began to study his own children, and others, during the 1930s and who wrote copious, brilliant, difficult papers, an unfamiliar mixture of research and theory, without making much impact on the English-speaking world until the 1950s. Flavell's book *The Developmental Psychology of Jean Piaget*[124] is generally regarded as giving a fair and accurate picture of Piaget's work. A complete picture cannot be given here, but some of Piaget's ideas are basic to our understanding of the growth of intellectual functioning.

Piaget regards intelligence as a form of adaptive behaviour, a means of coping with the environment, and organizing and reorganizing thought and action – adapting these to changes in the outside world. He believes that this process of adaptation starts with the random, diffuse, instinctive behaviour of the newborn baby and progresses, by definable stages, to the formal abstract logical reasoning of the adult. The child passes from one stage in this development to the next through his own continuous creative activity and his continuous interaction with his environment. At each stage, the child's knowledge and understanding of the world (his 'schemata' as Piaget's words are best translated) expand. New information coming in from the environment makes the old schemata gradually inappropriate. Accommodation takes place, letting in the new stimuli, and causing each particular schema to be restructured.

Piaget labels the first stage of intellectual development the 'sensori-motor' stage and sees it as lasting from birth until about 2 years, moving in this period through six phases. In the first month of life the infant's only schemata are his instincts. These he exercises (the first phase). Through exercising them, he gradually learns to coordinate them with appropriate responses, so that by the fourth month, or thereabouts, hand and eye, ear and eye are operating together (the second phase). In the third phase the infant, between roughly 4 and 8 months, begins to anticipate the results of his own actions, and to repeat, intentionally, those that are pleasurable in their results. He begins to be interested in the world of objects, and to know objects as separate from himself, and as existing even when they are not seen. In the fourth phase, he begins to differentiate means from ends, repeating actions which make others laugh, searching for toys which he has dropped. At around 1 year, he enters the fifth phase, a phase of extreme curiosity, experimentation and varied behaviour. Through this phase, he reaches the vital sixth phase, during which, at about 18 months, he becomes able to respond to or to think about objects and happenings which are not presently in view, and to invent for himself new mental combinations of objects or ideas. At this stage the infant becomes capable of imagination, of originality, of primitive symbolism.

Once this stage is reached, one can clearly see problem solving, planning, remembering and pretending going on in the child's activities. Although he has years of speech development, of experience and of maturation ahead of him, the foundations of his human intelligence are clearly seen.

The infant's very first concepts are broad, vague, over-generalized and always attached to concrete objects. As we shall see in the next chapter, the *child's* ability to make the concepts in the first place, and the *observer's* ability to know that he has done so, are both intimately tied up with language. The child may learn the word 'dog' among his first labels. But his use of the word, as a label for the family pet, will not suggest that he has yet formed a concept of animals, let alone a concept of dogs. To form such a concept, he must learn to put all furry animals, both real and pictured, into one category in his mind. We shall probably only realize that he has done this when he begins to refer to all of them as 'dogs'.

The idea of all furry creatures as 'dogs' is both over-generalized, and concrete. The child is applying one very broad concept to a large variety of specific objects. The concept will, during the second year, become less vague, while still remaining concrete. By the time he reaches 2 years, the infant may have 'dogs' and 'horses' as mutually exclusive concepts, clearly knowing the differences between the two, and able to sort equines and canines into suitable groupings. But his concepts will remain concrete for some further time. He will at this stage find his mother all the dogs on a sheet of pictures, but he will not find her all the 'nice things' or all the 'heavy things'.

Some people would maintain that these very early, general, concrete concepts are not true concepts at all – that they do not become so until the child can do more with them than attach them to concrete realities. But here again language is critical. When an infant makes it clear that he differentiates dogs and horses, we cannot know, until he can use language to tell us, whether he merely *perceives* them visually as different, accepting that the different appearances of different dogs are less various than the difference between any dog and any horse, or whether he can in fact compare and describe them in terms of other characteristics. Eventually he may say, 'Doggie bow-wow, horsie neieieigh!' Then we shall know that he is demonstrating true concepts. He has abstracted characteristics (the sounds the animals make), generalized them (all dogs bark, all horses neigh) and compared them (dogs do not neigh, horses do not bark). But he may have known all this before he could say it.

The infant's concepts of numbers remain extremely primitive throughout the second year. By the time he is 2 he may understand more and less and bigger and smaller, but any number of objects more than one is likely to be regarded as two or many.

Time concepts remain very simple too. In so far as they exist at all, they usually relate – because at this stage concepts are concrete – to the infant's own daily pattern. For example, the infant learns that when he wakes up it is morning, and that the meal he then receives is called breakfast. But he may then go right through toddlerhood believing that there are 2 days in every 24 hours, because when he wakes up from his afternoon nap it must be morning, and tea must therefore be breakfast.

Perhaps the most vital aspects of concept formation during this second year are concerned with the new ways in which the infant's new thinking allows him to deal with objects – to play. In the 12–18 month period, he is a scientist and an explorer. He deliberately sets out to separate means from ends, and causes from effects. Where at 9 months he might manage to put cubes in a box, and at 1 year enjoyed putting them in and out, now he decides that he wants the cubes and can hold that end in view while he fetches a stool and clambers on to it in order to reach them. His behaviour is purposive. He did not climb on the stool just for the sake of climbing, but in order to get those cubes.

By around 18 months, his behaviour is not only purposive, goal-directed, he has also reached the vital stage of being able to think about and respond to objects and events that are not immediately, concretely present. He can have a goal in his mind, and make a long-term plan for getting there. For example, released from his high-chair after lunch, he may go straight to the closed garden door, struggle to open it, return to the garden where he was playing before lunch, and retrieve his ball from where he left it. He had that ball clearly in his mind, could remember where it was, could plan to play with it some more, and could execute that plan through obstacles and time-elapse. This dawning ability to think about what is not there enables him also to anticipate events better than before. A few months ago, he might cover his face with his hands when he saw his mother coming towards him with the face flannel. Now he may cover his face as soon as his mother leads him towards the bathroom. He has a mental image of that flannel, a concept of face-washing.

Once the infant has reached this stage, he becomes capable of making new 'mental combinations'. He does not have to see two things together before he can think about combining them. Out of the blue, without ever having seen anyone do it before, he may fetch his toy walking stick, and use it to hook towards him a toy that has rolled under the fence out of reach. Imagination blossoms in other ways too. Familiar toys begin to be used in truly original ways. His saucepan is put on his teddy bear's head for a hat. This may not look very original to his mother, who has often seen children use saucepans for hats. But it is original for the infant, who has not seen it done, but simply 'thought of it'. Symbolic play begins to come into its own at this stage. Again the importance of symbolic play is often missed by mothers, because they do not recognize the difference between an infant doing 'housework' in direct imitation of his mother, and the child doing 'housework' at his own instigation in an area he has mentally designated as his own 'house'. A 15-month infant may want to be given a cloth, and allowed to help Daddy clean the car. But a 2-year-old infant who takes a pair of pants off the clothes horse, dips it in the dog's water bowl, and cleans his pedal car with it, is involved in play that is conceptually far more advanced.

Sensori-motor development is the principal criterion, in the Western world, for infant intelligence. Developmental tests for pre-verbal infants are based upon sensori-motor achievements, on what the infant will do with objects, the nature of his exploration, his persistence in solving tasks with objects, his understanding of the relationship between what he does and how the object behaves. Unfortunately a confusion of long standing exists about the use of such tests. It is a confusion based upon our difficulty in deciding what we mean by 'intelligence' either in the infant or in the older person, and upon our desire to predict later intelligence from earlier performance.

Psychologists used to believe that however difficult it might be to find the exact words with which to define intelligence, it was, in the end, an entity: a separate factor from specific abilities, a factor not open to influence from the environment, not modified by teaching or opportunity, nor by the drive or motivation of the person being studied. Such external influences might affect what the individual *did* with his intelligence, but not that intelligence itself. Sir Cyril Burt, for example, wrote in 1934:[125] 'Of all our mental qualities it is the most far reaching; fortunately it can be measured with accuracy and ease ... It is inherited, or at least innate, not due to teaching or training; it is intellectual, not emotional or moral, and remains uninfluenced by industry or zeal.'

If such a view of intelligence were correct, it should be possible to devise intelligence tests which could be repeated, over and over again, on the same individual, over a period of years, and yield similar results each time. And it should be possible to devise tests for children, and from their results predict accurately the adult level of intelligence to be expected for each child.

Fortunately the stated scope of this book is sufficiently limited that I do not have to enter the fearsome labyrinth of argument between those psychologists who still maintain that intelligence testing can measure up to this, and those who maintain that it cannot. It must suffice to say that it has not proved easy to be sure what we measure in an 'intelligence test'. Many people do well on some types of test and badly on others. The roles of teaching, training, industry and zeal in actual *intelligence* remain dubious, but it has been shown again and again that all these, and many other emotional factors, play a large part in determining how well an individual performs on an intelligence *test*.

With young children under about 5 years, and even more so under 3 years, countless careful follow-up studies have shown that developmental testing is almost useless in predicting an individual child's later intelligence, however that intelligence is defined. Bayley,[126] who devised one of the most widely used infant development tests, known as the 'Bayley Mental-Development Index', wrote in 1970: 'The findings of these early studies of mental growth of infants have been repeated sufficiently often so that it is now well established that test scores earned in the first year or two have relatively little predictive validity.' Most of the tests in current use in the Western world have been exhaustively reviewed and critically evaluated by Stott and Ball,[127] who reached much the same conclusion.

The nature of infant development does not lend itself to formal testing designed to relate an individual child at a given moment in time to others of the same age. Nor does it lend itself to testing designed to predict his future position relative to others. The tests tend to be based on the measurement of the infant's current capabilities relative to his age, within each of several areas, such as his motor abilities, his verbal achievements and his sensori-motor development. A score is assigned to each of these, and some kind of composite developmental quotient arrived at by combining them. That quotient is then used at a later date to compare the infant's new development with what he achieved at the first testing.

But, as we have seen, infants do not forge ahead steadily in all fields. They may spurt for a while in motor progress, leaving sensori-motor activities almost abandoned. Having reached a given point in, say, learning to walk, they may then rest on their motor laurels, and put all their energies into learning words. So at any given point in time there is little logical relationship between the infant's measured abilities in one area and another. The fact that his motor score is high tells us nothing about his verbal score.

In order to arrive at a quotient of any kind, these natural peaks and lags, the differences between the infant's advanced and retarded areas, must be smoothed out and forgotten in favour of an average or weighted score. A particular score could therefore be arrived at in a number of different ways. In one child a given score may indicate high verbal ability, average motor ability and low sensori-motor ability. In another child of the same age, the identical score may represent low verbal ability, average sensori-motor ability and high motor ability. To call the two children 'the same' in any sense is patently unreal.

Again, attempts to relate the child's profile and quotient at one age to those at a later age are also doomed. His advancement in motor abilities at 1 year does not predict a similar advancement a year later. Nor does an above average overall quotient predict overall superiority a year later. The natural spikes and valleys of his development see to that.

Lewis and McGurk[128] carried out a small-scale but intensive study of 20 infants which nicely proves these points. At 3, 6, 9, 12, 18 and 24 months they gave the infants the Object-Permanence Scale from a test of sensori-motor development,[129] and the Mental Index from the Bayley Scales of Infant Development.[130] At 24 months they added an adaptation of the Peabody Picture Vocabulary Test. They found no positive correlations whatsoever between the scores, for an individual infant, on any of the tests at the earlier ages, and his scores on any of the tests at 24 months. Looking only at the results achieved at the 24-month testing, there was no relationship between an infant's sensori-motor scores and his verbal scores. There was, on the other hand, a positive relationship between his Mental-Development Index score at 24 months and his Peabody verbal test, reflecting the fact that at this age the Mental-Development Index is heavily verbally loaded, and was therefore measuring much the same achievement as the Peabody test.

If we can get away from our desire to predict later performance from developmental tests carried out in infancy, they become an extremely useful descriptive tool. If we can stop trying to see what the infant *will* be like, they are an excellent way of describing what he *is* like. If we can escape from the tendency to wrap all his abilities up together into one developmental 'score', we can use the profile of his different abilities, at any one point in time, to see how those abilities relate to each other, how widely different they are, whether this is an infant who *does* tend to develop steadily over all fields, or an infant with marked spurts and lags.

The value of this kind of profile picture can clearly be seen in the case material from her pilot work which Griffiths[100] describes. The profiles give the reader a 'feel' for the child they describe which cannot easily be obtained from an ordinary written description. Her relating of the peaks and valleys of a given profile to 'norms' or 'averages' adds depth too. It seems a pity that with all her first-hand evidence of the value of the profile procedure, and the invalidity of using it to assign an overall 'quotient', Griffiths devotes the remainder of her book to recommending and describing the derivation of 'general quotients' from her test items.

Developmental testing of large and representative groups of infants has gone a long way towards showing us the usual sequences in infant development, and the ages (and the range of ages) at which most infants become able to do a variety of things. Without this kind of research work, books like this one could not be written. And there is a continuing need for research of this kind, because fashions in child-rearing change, society changes, children change. The British 2-year-old of today is capable of things his mother could not have done at the same age, because she would not have been given the chance to try. But this is developmental testing for research purposes. The observers are not attempting to say anything about the individual children they study, simply to study them and count them.

Developmental testing of individual children for the purpose of advising their parents is a very different and far more difficult matter. Often it is useful. For example, testing can help to identify the child with a mental or physical defect.[131] Where parents are worried about a child, and no obvious handicap can be found, testing may help to pin-point areas where the child is experiencing difficulty and may benefit from special help. Where a foster mother accepts a child after months of inadequate institutional care, developmental testing may enable the pediatrician to advise her of the ways in which the infant's development appears to have suffered so far. Careful, informed handling by that foster mother now may prevent that child being assessed as 'backward' a year later. Again, where a child seems backward in some particular respect, developmental testing may enable the parents to be assured that he is within the normal range, or advised to have him tested at a later date to check that he is progressing.

Finally, developmental testing can be a useful tool in the hands of those who seek social improvement for deprived groups of children. Suppose, for example, that an organization wants to set up playgroups for children confined to high apartment blocks, or slum streets, with little opportunity for exploratory play. Developmental testing can both lend credence to the need – by demonstrating that the children are generally behind the norms – and can identify the optimum nature of the help to be offered – by showing the areas of development in which the deprivation is taking the greatest toll. Later testing can then serve as part of an evaluation of the programme's success. But even here, a lack of understanding of the nature of development and developmental testing sometimes leads to unfortunate errors. Suppose that there is evidence that the children lack opportunities for sensori-motor play, and are behind the norms for their ages in such achievements as the understanding of object-permanence and cause and effect. Having carried out the programme, the testing which is intended to evaluate that programme must use the same criteria. To give a general test, such as the mental development index, for such a purpose would be as foolish as to give 10-year-olds an intelligence test to evaluate a course in history. The 10-year-olds need a history test; the infants a test of sensori-motor development.

As Lewis and McGurk put it:[128]

It cannot be emphasized too strongly that the success of specific intervention programs must be assessed according to specific criteria related to the content of the program. By focusing attention upon the criteria for evaluating programs, the necessity for careful specification of the program's goals will be emphasized ... the failure to specify goals has been a contributing factor in the confusion over means of evaluating intervention programs.

Even used within these limits, developmental testing is not easy nor objective. Even in the here-and-now, faced with an individual child, we cannot say, from available tests alone, that this child *is* behind for his age, highly gifted, mentally retarded or anything else. To yield useful information, the tests have to be administered as part of a clinical and history-taking situation. They are merely a tool for the examiner to use in assessing the child; their results alone are meaningless.

The subjectivity of such tests arises out of the fact that *how* the infant approaches the task items is at least as important as what he manages to accomplish. His general interest, his alertness, his ability to concentrate are all vitally important – especially in sensori-motor tests. But important though these things are, they are not measurable, although they can be seen and felt by the examiner. Furthermore they are dependent in their turn on other immeasurable variables such as the infant's mood, his physiological state, and the extent to which the set task is similar to or different from games he is used to at home. As a frivolous but nonetheless telling example, I was disconcerted by the total inability of a very bright 18-month girl to come to grips with the simplest type of form-board. Offered the board, with its big round holes, its square and its triangular holes, she appeared quite uninterested in the matching blocks; quite incapable of grasping the *idea* of fitting them in, much less of actually doing so. If I had been attempting to use the test completely objectively, I should have scored a failure, and should not have progressed with this girl to the more difficult items later in the test. But it turned out that she had an older sister whose current passion was jigsaw puzzles. This infant was accustomed to doing lift-out board puzzles of up to ten pieces. The task I set her was as unchallenging as it would be to ask a 10-year-old to write his name. The task was simply beneath her notice.

Even in apparently simpler motor items, an objective pass-or-fail scoring system can be very misleading. It sounds simple to assess whether or not an infant can sit alone for up to one minute. But at 7 months the infant may be unable to sit alone, and, from the state of his head and neck control, be clearly some weeks or months away from independent sitting. Or he may be on the verge of sitting, but not quite able to manage a full minute today, in this strange setting. Or he may be able to sit, not only for a minute but all afternoon, playing freely. Subjective assessment of the infant must therefore play some part in helping the examiner to decide at what age level he should begin to test the infant, how far forward, beyond the infant's chronological age, he should continue, and how much belief he should put in the mother's statements that 'he can usually do that . . .'. At the same time, the examiner has to decide how much allowance to make for the almost right, the nearly-there performances. The infant is usually being tested in a strange setting, and always by a strange examiner. Could he sit alone, if intelligent interest in the strange room did not make him crane his head around so? Does he know the little cubes are in that closed box, and merely refuse to look because he is worried by the stranger? Does the way he *looks* at the pictures suggest that his mother is correct in saying he can name six objects, even though he chooses to be silent here, today?

Background information is needed too, if developmental-test results are to be useful – or if they are to avoid being downright misleading.[102] Gesell's tests,[40, 132] which form the basis of most of those in use today, were originally designed to be used in conjunction with a home visit by a trained social worker, a complete physical examination of the child, a careful history from the mother and a full staff conference of all those involved with the family. Today few can work under such ideal and leisured conditions. But any attempt to use developmental tests without *some* background data can be disastrous. That 18-month child who 'could not do' the first formboard managed all the sensori-motor items up to the age-norm for 3-year-olds. If I had not chatted to her mother about her preferred activities at home, and thus found out about the jigsaw puzzles, I should have stopped the test after two attempts at the formboard, and scored her somewhat below average for her age. Similarly, if a child is brought for testing because of lateness in walking, only patient inquiry can discover that late walking runs in the infant's family. With that information the examiner, if all other aspects of development are normal, can safely reassure the parents; without it he might instigate all kinds of medical tests designed to exclude motor handicaps. Finally, if the examiner does not find out, in detail, about the child's recent experiences, he may totally misread the developmental level. One mother, for example, was given an appointment for her infant to be tested some weeks ahead. In the interim he had measles, badly. Not realizing this could make any difference, she kept the appointment, and was horrified to be told that her baby was 'lagging behind rather badly at present'. She worried for three months, and then brought her bright, cheerful, forward infant to another clinic. Once the misunderstanding was cleared up she could not understand how *she* had been so silly as not to mention the illness: 'But he seemed so grim and certain; he said, "The tests show . . ."!'

People who accept all these limitations and shortcomings

of developmental testing in infancy still tend to believe that at the extremes of intelligence such tests must be more accurate than not. Yet it is at the extremes that a misinterpretation by parents, nursery-school teachers or even doctors can be most tragic.

An infant whose development is accelerated in all fields, and remains so over a year or more, may be highly gifted. Certainly highly gifted adults often turn out to have been rapid developers in infancy. But he may not be highly gifted. Plenty of 'average' adults were also rapid developers. Such a child may simply go through many stages of development more rapidly than most infants, and then settle on a plateau, to consolidate everything he has learned. He is most unlikely to be of below average intelligence when he grows up, but average he may well be. And it is a tragedy if his perfectly normal abilities, by the time he reaches school, seem disappointing to parents who were convinced they had a prodigy. At best, very early signs of rapid development should be taken only to mean that the child is not retarded, and that he is receiving care of a kind which is excellent for him. Parents can take such results as a good report for them in a parenthood examination, but not as a prediction that they have reared the new Einstein.

The infant whose actual development is not particularly accelerated, but who *seems* very bright, very alive, interested and intense, is somewhat more likely than the first infant to turn out to be highly intelligent. Gesell[132] said that it was not excellent performance in one or all fields which indicated a highly gifted child, but the *manner* of his performance: '... intensification and diversification of behaviour rather than conspicuous acceleration. The maturity level is less affected than the vividness and vitality of reaction ... the infant with superior equipment exploits his physical surroundings in a more varied manner, and is more sensitive and responsive to his social environment.' Nothing we have learned since upsets Gesell's judgement, which he summarized thus: 'The scorable end-products may not be far in advance, but the manner of performance is superior.'

The infant whose development lags behind in all fields certainly needs investigation, because there are numerous handicaps from which he may suffer. But he may not. Once careful examination and testing has excluded obvious problems, such a child may well simply be a 'slow starter'. Such infants often get off to a bad start, being premature, or excessively jumpy or sleepy babies. Others seem perfectly normal in early infancy, but go through the normal phases of development more slowly than most. Some workers believe this to be due to a delay in maturation of the nervous system. Some believe it to be due to minor damage during birth, to a brain which was normal *in utero*, and which gradually heals and adapts itself. Yet others, notably Prechtl,[133] believe that many such children have actual minimal brain damage, which increasing maturity enables them to overcome.

Whatever the causes – and no doubt they are various, and variously combined – if there is no discernible handicap, by 1 year, either a slow but steady improvement, or a sudden acceleration in development is highly likely. Just as it is tragic if early advancement leads parents to expect too much of their eventually average infants, so it is tragic if early slowness leads parents to label a child as 'retarded', or at least to decide that his intellectual potential is low. Where some parents might be spurred to offer all the extra help, stimulation and affection they could muster to such a child, many would give up. As we have seen in earlier chapters, it is the alert, highly responsive, and therefore highly rewarding and enjoyable babies who tend to get the most attention from the adult world. Yet it may be the slower, less responsive, less rewarding ones who need and will benefit from that attention most.

CHAPTER THIRTY

LANGUAGE

The higher the level of an individual's intelligence, the better one expects his language ability to be. And vice versa. In very young children, language development is probably the best single indicator of later intelligence; though that is saying little as all infant abilities are unreliable predictors. But the relationship between intelligence and language is not one-way. We need intelligence to learn to understand and to use language, fluently and richly; we also need fluent rich language for our intelligence to work with. If high intelligence helps us to find the words to say what we think, so the words we know help us to decide what to think.

What do we, of a temperate climate, think about snow? Probably not very much. There is deep snow and powdery snow and wet snow; snow is fun for the kids, inconvenient for the adults – clean, dirty, frozen, mushy. That is about all. But the Eskimo language is rich in snow concepts, it has snow words which are not only difficult for us to understand, but are uncommonly difficult for us to learn. We cannot translate them into words we use about snow. While the differences between them are too subtle for us, all those words mean something to the Eskimo. For him 'snow' is hardly a unitary concept. He does not think about snow as we do.

More surprisingly, some languages handle relative concepts, such as size, in ways which materially affect the thinking of those who speak them. The African language Kpelle *has* words which translate as 'big' and 'small', but the word for 'big' is *used* very much more frequently. A group of children reared speaking Kpelle was compared with a group of American children on a test of size discrimination.[139] During a preliminary phase, the children were asked to guess whether the experimenter was 'thinking about' the larger block or the smaller one. American children guessed equally between the two, but the Kpelle children almost always guessed that he was thinking about the larger. Later in the experiment, it was shown that they could be *taught* to discriminate accurately between the two blocks – they could *perceive* that one was larger than the other – but even after this, on a return to the guessing game, they returned to their bias towards the concept that came naturally to them from their language: 'big' not 'small'.

Peculiarities of environment may therefore affect language and through it, thought. And peculiarities of language may affect concept formation and spontaneous thought.

An experiment by O'Connor and Hermelin[134] shows that the mere presence, or absence, of verbal labelling ability may affect ability on a 'practical task'. They found that while mentally retarded children can be taught to discriminate one shape from another with a fair degree of accuracy, those who do not spontaneously *label* the different shapes with words perform less well than those who do, and furthermore the non-labellers do not remember their own classification system. On each trial they have to rediscover the classification principles all over again. If such children are directly taught appropriate verbal labels, so that they can think 'This is the *square* one, that is the *round* one', their performance improves, and they remember it, so that the shape discrimination remains intact over time. It is as if they are, from the beginning, capable of *seeing* the difference between a square and a circle, but can only make these differences into meaningful, consistent, lasting concepts with the help of words.

This vital quality of language affecting what is thought, and how intelligence is used, as well as representing the individual's ability to think at all, has been cogently put forward, in its wider social context, by Bernstein.[135] His argument that the 'restricted verbal code', typical of the language of the lower socio-economic classes in Britain, actually restricts certain kinds of thought, and the ability to learn through kinds of communication typical of the middle or professional classes, has received a good deal of attention. It deserves a great deal more.

In Chapter 23 we suggested that while much is known about the order and rate of language acquisition by children, very little is known about why and how language is acquired at all.

Two principal theories have been put forward. Language acquisition as a straightforward learning process has been described by Skinner.[136] He, and his many followers, believe that the child learns to *understand* language by a classical conditioning process, such that by endless repetition he comes to associate the sound of the word 'dog' with the sight of a pictured or real dog, until eventually the word–sound comes to evoke the same behaviour as the sight–impression. He believes that the child comes to *use* language by operant conditioning, his attempts at saying 'dog' being reinforced by the mother or some other adult, and the strength of the reinforcement lending him the motivation to try.

Proponents of the other main theory, laid down by Chomsky[137, 138] and much elaborated by Lenneberg[111] and others, find the learning model naive and untenable. They argue for the existence of some kind of inherent 'language-acquisition device'. They do not claim that they have identified such a device, or that they can describe it, but that without it, language could not develop. Imitation and reinforcement could not, alone, account for the extraordinary rapidity with which a child learns his own language once he has begun. They could not alone account for his beginning to learn it – because you cannot reinforce behaviour which has not begun to appear. Nor could they conceivably account for the child's learning not only of words but of grammar and syntax, which alone enable him both to understand and to speak sentences he has never heard before: to generate 'new language' for himself.

The specialist literature in the development of language is extremely complex. A brief and lucid account is to be found in one chapter of an excellent book by Mittler.[131] A comprehensive but still readable account was published by Menyuk in 1971.[139]

Children, at almost all ages, and especially in the second year, invariably understand more language than they can use. Infants may demonstrate that they understand a good deal that is said to them well before their first birthday. By the middle of the second year, the mother may report 'He understands everything you say to him,' even though he may still only have a few words that he uses himself. But the actual degree of the child's *verbal*, as opposed to his general *social* understanding, is very difficult to assess. The infant may understand the *sense* of a given command, by combining verbal understanding with the context, the situation, and gestures so minute that the mother does not even realize she is making them. Perhaps the table is laid for lunch, and the mother has been cooking. She turns to the child (who can also smell food, and is probably hungry) and says, 'Dinner-time now.' The infant goes at once to the table, and holds up his arms to be lifted into his high-chair. How much did he understand the words? I put this point to a mother, who scoffed. Experimentally, in exactly the situation I have described, she turned to the child and said, 'Dinner not ready yet.' The infant looked at her, looked at the table, looked back at her, and went on with his play. The mother was triumphant. But as she spoke to the child, she had shaken her head slightly; her whole demeanour had suggested a negative statement: she had not begun to move towards the child; she had not taken off her apron. All sorts of cues had been different. Interested, now, she came and played briefly with the child, and after a few minutes, being careful *not* to indicate the table, she said, 'Now shall we have dinner?' The infant looked at her. He clearly knew she had asked him something; equally clearly he did not know what. He waited for her to cue him, and as she rose, holding out her hand to him and moving towards the table, he went, happily.

Of course at this level of understanding the mother is communicating with the infant, but she is doing it through a combination of his perceptions, not simply through his speech perception. A little later, he will understand one key word of her communication, but still need gestures to explain what has been said about it. If the mother says 'Give me the ball' the infant will pick up the ball, and he will wait. When she holds out her hand and says again 'Give me the ball' he will bring it to her. Clearly this level of communication between parent and child is extremely personal and subtle. It sheds some light on the language retardation which is so general among infants in inadequate institutional care, or those who are hospitalized or otherwise left among strangers. A stranger's cues are different from the mother's. Put those cues in a strange environment, and the world must suddenly appear utterly incomprehensible to a child who, in his own home, was just beginning to 'understand'. Often toddlers will not speak to strangers, and become extremely shy if the stranger tries to speak directly to them. This kind of perceptual difficulty may be a contributing factor. The stranger gets the context, the intonations, the facial expressions and the gestures 'wrong'. It is comic to hear the mother acting as interpreter for the stranger in such a situation. The visitor says, 'What a pretty dress!' beaming down at the toddler. The toddler looks worriedly blank and puts a finger in her mouth. 'She likes your pretty dress,' says mother. Toddler beams, holds out her skirt, and smiles shyly.

Most infants begin to speak their first words at around a year – although, as we have seen, there is a very wide range in language acquisition. These first words are almost invariably labels. They are the names for people, animals, or other highly significant objects in the child's immediate environment.

An unusual study, in which mothers with psychological training kept journals of their children's verbal development over several years,[140] found that single words were produced in the following order of frequency: first, people's names, then animals' names, then names for food and drink. Once some of these names were in the children's repertoire, parts of the body, clothes and everyday articles used in the home were named with equal frequency. The names for toys, furnishings and any objects outside the home appeared much less often, and later than any of these. No abstract nouns, those describing groups or concepts, such as size, weight or measure, appeared before 2 years in this sample. For all these children adjectives – whether as single words or as parts of two-word phrases – appeared after nouns, and the first adjectives were always those conveying a value judgement such as 'nice', 'naughty' or 'pretty'. The next category of adjectives to appear were those conveying sense impressions, such as 'hot' or 'cold'.

The first words are sometimes standard ones, correct copies of the adult name. More often they are approximations of the adult word. Sometimes they are self-words – invented by the child. With such a variety of possible sounds, it is sometimes difficult to recognize a word for a word. It is probably safe to call a sound a word when the infant uses it consistently and exclusively, for a single object or class of objects. A 'gaw' is a ball if it is always a ball, and never anything other than a ball.

Some authorities would say that 'gaw' was a self-word for ball; others would say it was a word approximation, because it contains one sound in common with the standard word. Winitz and Irwin,[141] using this last, generous, definition of word approximation, found the following shift between the three classes of utterance, between children who were studied at 13 months and again at 18 months.

TABLE 21.   SHIFT TOWARDS STANDARD SPEECH FORMS
EARLY IN THE SECOND YEAR

Speech classified as	13 months	18 months
Approximations	83%	56%
Standard	16%	38%
Self-language	1%	6%

First words, which are labels for things, are usually regarded, in a Skinnerian way, as nothing *more* than labels.

The child is seen as simply learning that the name of this is 'dog', the name of that is 'John' and so forth. But observation of infants suggests that these first words have a more complex communicative purpose. The infant does not simply state, 'Dog,' as if to say, 'That is a dog.' Sometimes he states it in the way the linguists would call 'declarative'. But sometimes he uses the word as an emphatic. 'Dog!' he says, expressing surprise, annoyance, delight at the dog's arrival. And he uses the word as a question too. 'Dog?' he asks, perhaps looking at an animal, perhaps hearing a noise at the door.

Some people have denied that there is any communicative meaning to the varied intonations attached to early labelling words. They have maintained that the child learns the labels, but is also practising the adult intonations and inflections of speech, just as he did when he jargoned at an earlier stage. The juxtaposition of intonation and label is, they argue, a chance one. Menyuk[139] believes, on the basis of her experiments, that the variation in intonation and inflection is both meaningful and deliberate on the infant's part. She makes the often neglected point that it is more effortful for the child to exclaim or to question than to declare. Why should he make the effort to say 'Dog?' if he only wished to declare the presence and recognizability of 'Dog'?

We all so readily accept that speech begins with single words that we seldom stop to ask ourselves why the infant should choose to begin in this way. Why does his speech not begin with phrases that he often hears repeated, such as 'Night night darling' or 'Upsadaisy baby'? If he is going to begin with single words, why does he choose the particular words he selects? We do not know. Menyuk speculates that the infant may only be able to store in his memory a single word, at this stage, not a word sequence. Certainly we know from experiments with the repetition of strings of numbers by older children that the capacity to store an increasing number in short-term memory increases with age. Certainly, too, the infant tends to select either a single-syllable word, or one syllable of a multi-syllable word, or a multi-syllable word that is repetitious (such as 'dad-dad' or 'ba-ba'). It may be that he also hears (or more correctly, auditorily perceives, which is to say *meaningfully* hears) only the isolated words, or the first or last or most stressed words of a sentence. These words may stand out for him from what is otherwise still a blur of talk.

Menyuk makes the point that the actual word the child selects is usually a 'topic' word – the subject of conversation rather than what is said about that subject. He learns the word 'dog' both because the dog is important to him, and because whatever we say about the dog, that word is the one consistent sound in a vast complexity of other sounds involved in: 'I must put the dog out', 'Where's the dog?' 'Let's find the dog' and so on. In adult speech, we do not always stress, verbally, the topic word of a sentence. We may say: 'Oh, for heaven's *sake* close that door.' But when we speak to very young children most of us tend to stress the topic word without necessarily realizing we are doing it. We say: 'Close the *door*, darling.' And if we get no response we repeat: 'The *door*, close the *door*.'

According to Griffiths's[100] norms for British babies, most infants will say 3 words by the end of the twelfth month – whether these are standard, approximations or self-words. Four or 5 words will be clear by the fifteenth month and 6 or 7 by the seventeenth month. In her sample progress was rather steady, giving 9 words by the nineteenth month, 12 by the twentieth and 20 by the end of the second year. While no doubt these were accurate norms for the words *observed* in her studies of infants, the actual numbers of words are very much lower than those suggested by others. Most agree that new words come very slowly at the beginning, so that the child may only acquire 1 new word a month between, say, 11 months and 15 months. But most also agree that there is a tremendous spurt in word acquisition around the middle of the year, so that the infant's spoken vocabulary may grow from say, 20 words at 18 months to more than 200 words at 21 months.[112]

It is interesting to note, by comparing studies of the 1920s with those of the present day, that children of *all* ages appear to have larger vocabularies now than then. Perhaps this is a genuine gain from the advent of television; perhaps it is an artefact reflecting our greater interest in very young children, our greater readiness to listen to them with care. But between the difficulties of defining what we *mean* by a word, the difficulties of *evoking* those words in a test situation, the unreliability of mothers' reports of their children's words, and the enormous range of age at which language develops, the actual number of words spoken by a child in the second year is probably among the least valid and interesting measures of his language ability.

Somewhere around the middle of the second year, and almost invariably *after* he has learned at least a small number of single-word name–labels, the infant begins to put two words together; to speak in 'phrases' rather than in single words. Just as we accept, without much thought, the fact that speech begins with single-word labels, so we accept this progression to two-word phrases. Yet they are not an obvious development. There is no *a priori* reason why these typical phrases *should* be the next stage in speech. Why not sentences?

The easy answer is that the infant begins to feel the need to communicate both more accurately and more economically. Certainly a two-word phrase allows him to do this. Suppose he has just finished a biscuit, and he wants another one, of a particular kind out of the variety in the tin. In one-word communication he may have to say, as separate communication items: 'bikkit!', 'more?', 'gimme!'. He may be misunderstood at the first stage, his mother taking his first 'bikkit' to be a comment on the one he has just consumed, rather than a demand for more. Clearly he is likely to get his biscuit more quickly and efficiently if he can start out by demanding 'more bikkit'.

But we have no reason to assume that the infant wants economy in communication. The desire to say things in the fewest and most telling number of words is a peculiarly adult one. The infant is in no hurry. Furthermore we have no

reason to suppose that he feels the need for greater explicit-
ness. Few of his early words are need-fulfilling ones, and he
has managed to get what he wanted up to now with single
words linked with gesture and context. Why should he
suddenly find this combination unsatisfactory? Perhaps he
does. Perhaps mothers who are consciously trying to make
their infants speak become deliberately dense at this stage.
Perhaps a greater contact with people from the outside
world makes it incumbent on the infant to speak more
explicitly. Certainly this sometimes happens. One small boy
had reached the one-word stage when he had to be hospitalized with meningitis. His mother was with him all the time
except during the most unpleasant procedure of a spinal tap.
During the ten minutes of her exclusion from the room, the
following development of communication took place, for the
very first time:—

'Mummy!'
'Want Mummy.'
'Mummy *come*.'
'Want my mummy.'
'Oh, mummy come!'

There seemed little doubt, in this case, that the infant was
experiencing, for the first important time, an apparent failure
by the adult world to understand what he wanted. Under the
extreme stress of a painful and frightening procedure, he
produced more and more explicit speech. But most infant
speech, as we have seen, is not need-fulfilling. Most two-word
phrases are not produced under unpleasant stress, but in
interest or excitement. It does seem that the development
from single words to two-word phrases must be part of the
inherent language-acquisition device, or inbuilt propensity
for language development, postulated by the Chomsky
school of thought.

By this argument, the lengthening of the child's utterances
probably occurs as the result of the maturing of the vocal
mechanisms, and the auditory memory span. The infant
becomes able to notice and to retain not only the single

'topic' words of sentences he often hears, but the words he hears used to describe them, or what they do.

The content of the two-word phrase is almost always of this kind. The child does not learn the word adjacent to the topic word in adult speech. He does not progress from 'ball' to '*the* ball'. He rather moves from 'ball' to 'nice ball' or 'go ball' or 'John ball'. He puts together the nouns with which he started his naming, with main verbs and principal adjectives. He uses his new 'second word' to amplify what he used to communicate via intonation and inflection only. Earlier he might watch the family dog depart rapidly through the park and say 'Dog!' in tones of shocked/delighted surprise. Now he says 'Dog gone!'

The importance of this two-word stage is twofold. Firstly it demonstrates the infant's ability, already stressed in Chapter 29, to think about objects when they are not immediately present. A child who wanders round the room saying 'Ted? Ted?' may be deduced to be thinking about finding his teddy bear; but no deduction is needed once he says 'Ted gone?' or 'Where ted?' His planning can be seen more clearly too. Seeing a forbidden ashtray on the table he proposes to climb on, he may at an earlier stage announce 'Tray!', to which his mother is likely to reply, 'Yes, ashtray, darling, don't touch.' Now he can say 'Tray up!' making it quite clear that he wants his mother to pick the ashtray up out of harm's way. His beginning conceptualization becomes clearer too. Perhaps he is still at the stage where all animals are referred to as 'pussy'. But now he can make it clear that while he still does not have another *word* for non-cat animals, he sees, he perceives, that they are not all the same. '*Big* pussy!' he may announce when he meets an alsatian dog in the park. His two-word phrases allow us to see something of his developing thinking. Probably they also help his thinking to develop. If he perceives the differences and similarities among things – which, as we have seen, is the basis of concept formation – those perceptions will be both sharpened, made consistent, and more easily remembered as he finds the words to label those differences and similarities.

The second vitally important thing about the two-word phrase stage is that it demonstrates the fact that the infant has already learned the basic rules of grammar and syntax in his language before he could do more than attach a few labels. He invariably gets the *sequence* of words right in the context of what he is trying to say. Talking directly to his brother, he says 'naughty boy', not 'boy naughty'; reporting that brother's wrongdoing to his mother, he says 'boy naughty', not 'naughty boy'. Telling his mother that he has seen a lorry through the window, he says 'see lorry'. But trying to make her come and see it, he pulls her skirt saying, 'Lorry, see!' His language is not a meaningless jumble but a telegraphese, leaving out auxiliary verbs, articles, prepositions, and many word-endings. Only in certain consistent ways does he string words together wrongly.

The grammatical mistakes that he does make are both logical (in the sense that they are wrong but logical deductions) and consistent from child to child. For example, the infant tends to make all nouns plural by adding an 'S' or 'Z' to them, as in 'shop/shops'. He talks of 'mans' and 'childs' and 'sheeps' and 'shoeses'. Similarly he puts all verbs into the past tense by adding a 'D' sound, so that he says 'goed' and 'comed' as well as 'jumped' and 'laughed'. Some word orders are consistently confused, too, usually where they involve inserting an extra word between two words which customarily come together. Most infants, for example, will request mother to 'put on it' or to 'pick up it'. The passive of verbs is usually ignored. The '-ing' endings are simply left out, so that the child announces 'I go', 'I come', 'Daddy run' and so on.

As we saw in Chapter 23, the role of the adult as a direct teacher of new words is extremely dubious. While there is no doubt that imitation plays a part in language learning, by giving the child often-repeated models to pick up, it does not seem that direct imitation, at the time, plays a very large part.

This seems to hold true for more complex speech learning. The infant's two-word and later three-word telegraphese is singularly resistant both to the models offered by the ordinary

adult speech he hears around him, and to direct attempts to
teach him to expand it. Ervin-Tripp[142] set out to see whether,
if they were given a model to copy, young children at this
telegraphese stage of speech development would produce
sentences that were more complex than their spontaneous
speech. Had the infants been willing and able to repeat the
more complex sentences offered to them, it would have
demonstrated that imitation was at least one of the mechanisms by which new speech forms could be acquired. A few
of the infants did imitate speech forms and structures which
they only produced in their spontaneous speech some weeks
or months later. But equally, some infants refused to imitate
speech forms which they *were* already producing in their
spontaneous speech. Most of the time the infants reproduced,
out of the model given them, exactly that complexity of
sentence structure which they were already using in spontaneous speech.

These results should not be surprising. The infant's telegraphese is his very own. His two-word and three-word
phrases are not imitations of what he has heard adults say.
What adult has said to a child, 'See lots mans!' when
watching a football match? The adult is likely to say, 'See
what a lot of men!' Compared in terms of sounds, the two
sentences have very little in common.

It seems that the adults' role at this stage is not that of
teacher or even model, but of provider of innumerable consistent examples of the rules of the grammar and syntax of
the child's language. The child reproduces the sense of the
sentence he hears, obeying the rules in so far as he has understood and generalized them, and reducing the complexity to
the level he can manage to express. When mother wants to
help father avoid yet another rough-and-tumble game, she
says, 'Daddy's having a little rest now.' Hearing this, over
and over again enables the child to produce 'Daddy have
rest', rather than 'have Daddy rest' or 'rest have Daddy' or
'Daddy rest have'. But it does not enable him to reproduce
the mother's sentence.

Mothers spend a good deal of time, at this stage of speech

development, expanding their children's telegraphese into sentences. In one study[143] two mothers were observed with their infants, and it was found that they thus expanded no less than 30 per cent of the utterances their children made. If, for example the mother said something such as, 'Now let's get your shoes on,' the child would answer with part of her sentence, such as 'shoes on', and the mother would expand the child's communication by repeating what she had said at the beginning. Or the infant would volunteer something like 'out now' and the mother would reply, 'You want to go out into the garden now.'

In this experiment, the mother's expansions had little effect on the child's immediate responses. Only 1 per cent of the time did the child answer with *any* elaboration of his original utterance, and even on those occasions it was usually only a different way of saying the same thing, still within the child's own telegraphese. For example he might say 'gar-gar now' in response to the mother's expansion of his request to go into the garden.

But even while such expansions do not lead infants to copy more complex speech forms, they may still play a vital role in offering models for the child to add to his general linguistic thinking. Furthermore they often help the *mother* in her communication with the child. She expands or repeats what he has said in order to recode his telegraphese into her own language, and make sure she has understood him correctly. If she has not, he will correct her.

With somewhat older children, newly admitted to nursery groups at the age of 2½–3, experiments have shown that deliberate expansions of everything the child says are less effective in increasing his verbal competence than a comparable period of talking and play with an adult. Once again such results tend to indicate that the adult's vital role in infant speech learnings is not that of teacher but that of stimulus-provider. The more language the child hears, especially language which is directed at him, with appropriate facial and gesturing cues, the more language-models he has to use in his own language development. Seen from this point of view, the more direct attempts to teach him language, by correcting what he says, are, for him, boring. He has already grasped whatever he can say in telegraphese. He is not ready to say thé same thing more correctly. He wants to say new things, different things. The expanded sentence and the corrected grammar will come, in their own good time, with his maturing.

In the meantime, those who need to understand the language of very young children can learn it just as they would learn a foreign tongue. Mothers pick it up by constantly interacting with the infant from the time he begins to babble to the time when he talks as she does, but many people whose professions bring them into close communication with infants have had no such experience. The dentist who must fill a milk tooth, the doctor who must give an injection, or find out what hurts, the nurse who must make sure the child knows mother will come soon, the stranger who finds a lost toddler and wants to know where he last saw his mother, all need to know how this early language works, and could all do their jobs more effectively if they could communicate with those who speak it. Parental interpreters are not always present when they are needed most.

CHAPTER THIRTY-ONE

FEARS AND PHOBIAS;
TEARS AND TANTRUMS

Nobody can be sure that he understands what a toddler is thinking or feeling. It is difficult enough to know what a fully communicating adult thinks and feels, as opposed to what he wants us to believe he thinks or feels. Therefore when one writes about the emotions of toddlers, one lays oneself open to a charge of trying to get inside their skins, trying to pretend an insight which is really only guesswork.

The attempt is valid nevertheless, if it is based upon the *behaviour* of infants. We cannot know exactly what they think, nor what they feel, but we can see how they behave. Where there is a high degree of consistency between one child and the next, it is reasonable to try and see what circumstances and what handling contribute to that behaviour. This has been superbly done by Bowlby.[144] His book should be read, ideally, by all who deal with young children. Above all it should be read by those who cannot accept the idea of infants having, and suffering from, the kinds of emotion described in this brief chapter.

In the second year of life, as we hinted in Chapter 24, two related issues seem to dominate the toddler's relationship with his adult world. On the one hand he seeks ever-increasing personal independence and autonomy, resenting the power adults have over him, reacting negatively to coercion, wanting to go his own way, in his own time, for his own reasons. On the other hand he actively seeks more and more protection and support from his mother, fearing separation from her above all things, shying away from strangers, resenting any other people who take her time and attention from him. If he were capable of conceptualizing his relationship with his mother, an infant of this age would probably describe the ideal mother as one who had nothing to do all day but follow him around, never interfering, never coercing, but always there when he glanced up, always on tap when the adventurer decided to be a baby again.

Life being what it is, both prongs of this situation get the toddler into emotional and practical trouble. The thwarting of his drive for independence, his developing ego, expose him to frustration, to anger, to hate. The thwarting of his desire for dependence, his need to cling to his mother, expose him to anxiety and fear. To complicate matters further, feeling angry makes him anxious and afraid, while feeling anxious and afraid makes him angry. His own emotions are his worst enemy. They are, as far as one can see, as strong at this age as they will ever be in his life. But he has not had the time to grow a protective skin over them. He has not enough experience to know how to deal with them; he cannot control himself.

Within this simplified framework one can see most of the fears and the furies of young children as revolving around twin poles: anxiety round separation, anger round the desire for autonomy. Too little care and protection and the infant's separation anxieties are touched off; too much and his desire for autonomy breaks out in anger. The exact balance which keeps him both unafraid and unfrustrated differs for every infant at every stage of his development. For many, it varies day by day and hour by hour. It is the sensing and acting out of this balance which describes sensitive mothering of a toddler. And it is the individuality of each infant's needs which makes continuous mothering, by one person, so much more likely to be smooth and easy than care that is shifted along many, or changed from one caretaker to another in mid infancy.

Every human being carries within himself a sort of reservoir of anxiety. Nobody is secure and happy, self-confident and self-approving, right through the layers of his personality. But as we grow up we learn all kinds of ways of dealing with our anxiety. We seek certain kinds of security, perhaps in relationships with other people, perhaps in our jobs, or our children. We learn to avoid situations which make us feel anxious, or to recognize specific anxieties so that they become known devils. We manipulate our environments and the people around us in all sorts of ways to keep ourselves comfortable. And when we fail, the drug industry provides the pills that tide millions of us over crises.

Toddlers are anxious however securely, lovingly and sensitively they are reared. They have not developed many defences against anxiety. The defences which they do have are not in their own power; they are in the power of the adult world. As we have seen, many infants are anxious over separation from their mothers at night. By a year, most have developed specific defences against that anxiety, such as sucking a dummy, and cuddling a special piece of blanket. With those aids, the toddler's night-time anxiety stays down at a tolerable level. But whether he gets those aids or not is in the hands of others. His mother may wash his blanket and not get it dry by bedtime. His father may decide he is too old for a dummy and throw it away. The babysitter may not realize the importance of the precious objects; the jealous older child may hide them to make the baby cry.

The infant is vulnerable to anxiety when he is separated from his mother in the daytime, too. His own defence against this is simple. He stays close to her. As we have seen, very few toddlers will voluntarily put themselves more than a certain distance away from the mother at any time, unless they are with another close person, who temporarily stands in for her. But once again this simple mechanism for staying anxiety-free is not in the toddler's own control. His mother goes out for the day leaving him with a neighbour, or she goes into the lavatory and locks the door between them. He can never be quite sure of being allowed to feel safe.

The infant begins to get anxious whenever his own emotions begin to get out of control. His mother can usually damp down his feelings before they reach explosion point, but once again he cannot make her; he cannot usually even convey his need. All too often her response is the very opposite of what he needs. The more hysterical his laughter becomes, the more she tickles him. The angrier he gets, the crosser she becomes; the more demanding and clinging he gets, the more she pushes him away.

In some families, even the child's own anxious feelings are not allowed to be his own. Not only is he not able to arrange his own solutions to his anxieties, he is not even allowed to experience them. In one single hour spent in a children's public playground, I noted 38 instances of parents *telling* their toddlers what they did and did not feel, against all the evidence of the child's behaviour and attempted words: 'You don't mind him', 'That's not too high for you', 'You don't want to go home' . . . Perhaps it was just a 'manner of speaking'. Perhaps the parents did not *mean* to imply that they knew better than the child what he felt. But how is the toddler supposed to know that? Is he supposed to be a mind-reader? It must surely seem to him that his parents refuse outright to understand his feelings.

Some infants are clearly more anxious, overall, than others. They may function with anxiety always close beneath the surface, and many small fears always operative. Other children seem generally more phlegmatic. But all infants vary markedly in their anxiety levels from time to time. Anxiety tends to show itself in a general clinginess – apprehension about new things, new places, new people, a reluctance to explore and adventure – and in physiological tensions, with sleep difficulties, lack of appetite and so forth. But it also manifests itself in actual specific fears.

Unfortunately where fears are concerned we tend to treat toddlers as if they were miniature versions of adults. When a child is afraid of something which many adults fear, he is usually sympathetically handled. Few parents will scoff at the toddler who wakes pale, trembling and sweat-soaked from a nightmare. We all have nightmares. We know what they feel like. But when the toddler expresses a fear that seems to the adult to be simply silly, it is often treated with bossiness, irritation or even shame. We forget that the toddler has an intrinsic fear of the strange; we forget that he does not have our experience or our knowlegde to call on. Meeting his first tortoise, an 18-month boy reacted immediately with pure horror: "'Way, 'way,' he said, scarlet-faced. 'It's a tortoise, darling,' said his mother, picking it up and moving towards him. 'Notty,' wailed the toddler, exploding into tears and backing up against the wall. 'Don't be silly, darling, it's a nice tortoise,' said his mother, and she carried it right up to him, took his desperate flailing hand and forced him to touch it. 'Ho'bble,' screamed the child. The mother could not see that the child *could* be afraid of a tortoise. He had never met one before; had had no nasty experiences with tortoises; it made no noise . . . Yet she herself disliked spiders. I wonder how many spiders had bitten or roared at her? And how she would have felt about somebody who forced one into her protesting hand to prove its harmlessness?

We are always out to *prove* something to our infants, when it comes to fear. Out to prove that fears are illogical (although we pander to our own, and accept politely those of other adults), out to prove that 'you'll like it when you get used to it' as we plunge the screaming child into the swimming bath, or push him higher on the swing. Perhaps we need to re-think our attitudes to two separate issues: fearlessness and bravery. Fearlessness is simply not being afraid. It comes from not feeling fear. Logically, then, the less we frighten children, the more fearless they will be. Bravery is doing, or putting up with, what *does* frighten or hurt you. If that is what we are asking of our toddlers, then we should not pretend that we want them not to be afraid. Rather than 'It's a nice tortoise, darling', we should be saying: 'I know it is a horrible tortoise and you would like it to go away, but I want you to touch it to show what a brave boy you are.' Written out like that it looks silly. But logically it is the message that particular mother must have been conveying.

All toddlers have transient fears which arise unexpectedly, and may pass as quickly. But a great many acquire the focused fears which are usually called phobias. Sometimes the mother can date the beginning of a phobia, recounting the incident which touched it off. With hindsight, she says that the child must have been really terrified when that big dog knocked him down in the park, because he has been increasingly afraid of dogs ever since. But the degree of the child's disturbance may be quite out of proportion to that original incident. The child may have weathered far worse frights without any sequel. The phobia arises from his own inner state far more than from outward happenings. When his inner anxiety builds up a psychological pressure, it seeks an outlet; the child is vulnerable to fear. He will focus that fear on whatever frightening stimulus presents itself.

The frequency of actual phobias in the toddler population is difficult to assess because it is difficult to define. A child may be afraid of swinging on swings, without being made afraid by *seeing* swings. He may be afraid of dogs when they run or bark at him, without being afraid of dogs in the distance. Perhaps a phobia is most usefully discriminated from an ordinary fear if it is considered in terms of the effect which it has on the infant's ordinary life. An ordinary real fear will only affect his life when circumstances require him to meet the feared object. As long as he is not faced with the thing he fears, he does not think about it. As long as he can avoid or reject it, the rest of his life is unaffected. But a phobia works on the child through his new imagination. He is not only afraid when he meets a dog, he is afraid when he sees one, when he thinks about one, when he sees a picture of one. He not only avoids dogs when they are there, he constantly seeks to avoid going where they *may* be. In an extreme case, his whole life may be permeated with dogs, so that he must ride in his pushchair in case there should be a dog in the street; cannot go in the park in case dogs should be there, cannot enjoy his picture book because there is a dog on the third page, cannot cuddle his toy monkey because it is suddenly a dog.

Among the 100 infants of 21 months studied by Macfarlane, Allen and Honzik,[118] around 30 per cent had acute specific fears. At 3 years old nearly 70 per cent of the infants were affected. The most frequent fear was of dogs. After dogs came darkness and the bogeys associated with it. Less frequent were snakes, and such specific alarming noises as fire-engine sirens or ambulance alarms. In Drillien's sample[68] of nearly 450 infants, the numbers experiencing acute specific fears for at least 6 months were assessed by social class and also by whether the care they were receiving was considered generally 'good' or not. On that basis the range was enormous, with only 7 per cent of children receiving good care in homes of social class I or II being reported to have fears, while 53 per cent of those receiving unsatisfactory care in social-class-IV homes were thus reported. Interestingly, Drillien's middle-class range – social class III – reported acute fears in about 37 per cent of infants irrespective of the judgement on standard of care – and that is close to Macfarlane's overall figure.

The distinction between fear and phobia is important, because while fear can be realistic, and therefore open to rational explanation and demonstration, phobias are not realistic, and to try and prove their irrationality to the victim is often cruel and always useless.

Behavioural psychologists have developed methods of handling phobias in adults which are often highly effective. The adult, whose life is being ruined by a specific phobia, is very gradually 'de-sensitized'. First he is shown the feared object at a distance which allows him to stay calm and un-afraid. Very gradually, day by day, the feared object is brought closer to him, always staying within his own limits of calm, never making him afraid, until eventually he can look at it and even touch it, without panic. Parents often try to do this kind of thing with their phobic toddlers. They argue that if they could just persuade the child to *touch* a nice warm cuddly dog, he would find out how silly it was to be afraid. Unfortunately such attempts are usually made from an adult's point of view rather than with a real understanding of the child's. An adult *knows* that fear of dogs is largely irrational. He knows that other people can live with dogs and that his own life would be much easier if he could stop being so afraid of them. A very young child knows none of these things. Such children can be de-sensitized, but the process needs to be far more gradual than most people realize. If he sees a dog in the distance today and does not panic, he has made a step forward. But this step will not make him able to pass within six feet of a dog tomorrow, and touch one next week. Attempts to force toddlers out of phobias or to force the pace when de-sensitizing them, invariably make matters worse. So if the problem is so acute that it is interfering with daily life, most parents would be well advised to ask for psychiatric help and advice in dealing with it. In less extreme cases most phobic toddlers will respond, slowly, to a general lessening of their overall level of anxiety, the level of anxiety which led to the phobia forming in the first place. Sometimes the infant is under a particular and identifiable stress. Perhaps a new babysitter has been introduced, or his mother has started to go out to work, or there is a new baby present or imminent, or a row going on about toilet training or giving up a bottle.

Often no obvious cause of this kind can be found. The infant has simply reached a stage where his development has got out of step with itself. He feels as we feel when we say: 'I just don't seem to be able to cope at the moment.' When we say that, we want somebody to take off us some of our responsibilities and problems, so that we can have the time and the energy to cope with the remaining ones and thus catch ourselves up. The same is true of the toddler. Perhaps he is trying to forge ahead on too many fronts at once. Perhaps he is at that stage of learning to walk where he falls down just *too* many times, has too many bumps and bruises. Perhaps he is fighting his mother for independence rather harder than his dependent-baby bit really likes – telling her to 'let me!' when a bit of him would like her to do it for him. This kind of situation usually resolves if, for a while, the child is treated either as if he were a little younger than he is, or (which is really the same thing) as if he were slightly unwell. If the mother alters her handling in this direction, she need not know exactly what the trouble is. The infant has the opportunity to retrench on any one or on all fronts. And he will be quick to reassert himself when he has caught himself up again.

What will not help him become unafraid is fear. What will not reduce his anxiety level is making him anxious. The children whose lives are most beset and disordered by fears and phobias tend to be those whose parents decide that they are clingy because they are 'spoiled' or that they are fearful because they are 'sissy'. Such a decision, followed by a toughening-up policy, can only leave the toddler more exposed to the anxiety he could not manage in the first place. The usual vicious circle is set up, with the child demanding more and more support, and the parents offering less and less, so that he demands even more and they offer even less. Things can reach such a pitch that the infant has hardly any time and energy left for exploring, for growing, for asserting himself. He cannot be the tough adventurous child his parents want, because they keep him too busy filling his dependency needs.

With his anxiety running at a manageable level, and his fears tactfully handled, the toddler's other big problem area can come to the fore. Just as all toddlers, whatever their up-bringing, must be at least a little anxious, so all must be at least a little frustrated. Just as the warmest parents cannot prevent their child feeling the anxious loneliness of independent life from time to time, so the most imaginative and permissive parents cannot prevent him feeling frustration. If they do not directly frustrate him, he will frustrate himself; objects will frustrate him; the world will frustrate him. Frustration is implicit in the very drives which ensure his development.

As we have seen, the infant has strong drives to practise each new ability as it comes within his developmental scope. When he can get on to his two legs, he must, however many times he falls down. When he can get the screw-top off the jar, he must, however much the process maddens him. The difficulties of what he must accomplish are so great that without a powerful self-perpetuating drive towards attainment he would give up. So when people stop him doing what he wants to do, he is frustrated; when he cannot manage what he sets himself to do he is frustrated; when objects will not behave as he intends them to, he is frustrated.

Just as individual children vary in their vulnerability to anxiety and to fears, so they vary in their vulnerability to frustration. Some infants seem always able to cope with it better than others. They vary, of course, from stage to stage and day to day, but they seem always basically philosophical, patient, ready to try again. Others seem to set themselves unattainable standards and to be thrown into despair by small setbacks.

The kind of frustration which causes most trouble between parents and child is the frustration of his basic autonomy as a person which is implicit in the socialization of his physiological functions during this year. The infant begins to feel himself to be a separate individual. He no longer accepts, unquestioningly, his mother's right of total control. He is liable to resent her insistence on his using a pot; on his eating certain foods, wearing certain clothes, going to bed at certain times; coming when he is called, going out when it suits her, coming home when she thinks it is time. Any situation involving control by an adult can become an autonomy issue at this stage in development. As soon as the infant feels himself harried, bullied, pressured, he reacts negatively. Yet as long as he feels that he is being allowed to control his own life, he will use that pot, eat the food, stay in bed, come, go and love it.[145] Mothers need not only the usual virtues of tact and patience and humour, but also talent as actresses. The mother in a rush to get home must appear anything but hurried. Swoop the toddler into his pushchair when he meant to walk and all hell will be let loose; but offer to be his horse and *pull* him home and he will probably ride with glee.

Frustrating objects are often educational. The child may get furious because he cannot fit a round peg into a square hole. Nevertheless it is a fact of solid geometry that such pegs will *not* fit square holes, and it is a fact which, if he is ready to fit any kind of peg into any kind of hole, the infant is ready to learn. But he need not be left to wrestle unaided. Just as the 6-year-old will fight her knitting until her temper is completely gone, if mother does not tactfully lure her away into a romp in the garden, so the infant who is getting very frustrated with such a task needs help in concluding it, and then something easier to do for a while. Perhaps he even needs an easier version of the same toy, a big cardboard box with *big* holes for tennis balls and blocks, for example. There is frustration with objects which has a positive effect – spurring the child on to success and pleasure in his own achievement; and there is the negative kind which is self-defeating, making him angrier and angrier and less and less competent, until there is no hope of him succeeding and pleasing himself.

Often the behaviour of objects is understood, but the child is frustrated by his own small size or unsteady gait. He may long to push the doll's pram, but be unable to reach the handle; long to throw the football but be too unbalanced to manage its weight. There is little virtue and much grief in this kind of situation. As we have said before, children do not need, for their development or for their happiness, rooms full of expensive toys. But any equipment they are to have must fit them. To be shown a push-toy which is too high is as maddening for a child as a six-foot cooker would be to his mother. To try and play ball with a real football is as sad as to try and play tennis with a cricket ball. If he cannot have a little pram, or a baby-walker or small push-cart, and an inflatable beach ball or plastic 'football' he is better off with none at all, until he is bigger.

Very few families manage to strike the balance between the amount of frustration which is reasonable and even developmentally useful, and the amount which is too much, all the time. The child is as liable to degrees of anger which are, to an adult, incomprehensible, as he is to puzzling degrees of fear. Even more infants have temper tantrums than have phobias. Hardly surprisingly, temper tantrums are most usual in active, energetic, determined children. Such children are very clear what they want to do, and they want to do a lot. They mind correspondingly much when they cannot, or are not allowed, to do it. In Macfarlane's sample[118] 60 per cent of boys and 45 per cent of girls had frequent tantrums at 21 months, while they were frequent in nearly 70 per cent of the 3-year-olds. In Drillien's sample[68] a range over social class was reported similar to that for acute fears, with about 37 per cent of the infants of the social-class-III families reporting frequent tantrums, while around 60 per cent of the social-class-IV families experienced them. In the Newson survey[18] 14 per cent of the study infants were already having very frequent tantrums at 1 year of age, while nearly half the sample were already having quite a few.

Temper tantrum is an unfortunate term. 'Temper', in common parlance, is a derogatory word. We apologize for losing our tempers; speak scoffingly of people 'getting in a real temper'; express our dislike of people by dismissing them as 'thoroughly bad-tempered'. Accordingly, an infant having a temper tantrum tends to be regarded as naughty, as giving way to something he should control. Yet in infants of this age group a temper tantrum is very close to an emotional blown fuse. It is what happens when the load of frustration within the child builds up to such a tension that only an explosive discharge can release it. A true tantrum is not within the toddler's control at all, and it is an event that is far more unpleasant for him than for his embarrassed or infuriated mother.

Tantrums take many forms. Some infants rush frantically about, banging into furniture, hitting themselves against walls. Others throw themselves on the floor, and roll and kick, as if struggling with an unseen devil. Yet others, the most alarming of all, scream themselves to a point where after one long breath out, they cannot for the moment breathe in again. They may turn greyish blue in the face. A very few even have convulsions. These last extremes, which are well discussed in a paper by Livingston,[146] are very unusual. They are mentioned here only to emphasize the extremity of the situation in which the toddler having a tantrum finds himself. He is lost to the world. He is not open to exhortation, to scolding, to shouts, to smacks. He is overwhelmed by his own internal anger. Probably he is also terrified by it. He seems to

feel that he would like to kill everyone and destroy everything. Can he know that he cannot? Over the years he has
got to learn that it is safe to be angry, that feelings and words
cannot physically injure people or things. But at this stage he
cannot know these things. His anger must feel hideously all-
powerful.

The mother's job is to prevent him hurting himself or any-
body or anything else. The child must not, at all costs, recover himself to discover proof that he is dangerous. A
smashed vase, a lump on his head, a scratch down his
mother's face are all likely to be seen as proof of his horrible
power, and evidence that even his mother cannot control
him. So it may be best for his mother to hold him, on the
floor, secure in her arms. As he calms down, he finds himself
close to her. He finds, often with touching amazement, that
everything is quite unchanged by the storm. Slowly he relaxes;
the screams subside into sobs; the furious monster reverts to a
pathetic baby who has frightened himself silly.

Unfortunately toddlers often do not find the world unchanged by the storm. Anger tends to provoke anger, and
many mothers lose their tempers to match the child, giving
shout for shout. Fifty per cent of the mothers in the Newson
survey got angry and punished their year-old babies for
having tantrums. While the storm is on, punishment and
anger are totally ineffective. When it is over, they will only
increase the child's feeling that the world is an aggressive and
dangerous place, with himself one of its angriest and most
dangerous occupants.

Many mothers find tantrums both alarming and socially
embarrassing. I have known mothers reach a point where
they would not take their child into a shop in case he threw a
tantrum for sweets; I have known others treat their child
with saccharine sweetness whenever there were visitors
present, hoping to avert trouble.

Such attitudes are disastrous. A child who finds that the
horrific experience of a genuine, uncontrollable tantrum
actually serves as a way of controlling his mother, and getting
what he wants, would not be human if he did not move

towards the semi-voluntary tantrums typical of mishandled 4-year-olds. Such a child 'works himself up' on purpose, to a point where he genuinely loses control.

The child must see, from the very first outburst, that tantrums are horrible for him, and absolutely nothing to do with getting what he wants. He needs comfort and love afterwards, but he should never get sweets or anything else he might see as a reward. His behaviour must have changed nothing, either in his favour, or against him.

Along with making sure that the child achieves nothing by his outburst, the mother needs also to be very sure that he had to be driven into such a fury of frustration in the first place. Handling toddlers takes infinite patience and tact. Mothers cannot be patient and tactful all the time, but the frequency of tantrums will at this stage very directly reflect how much of the time they do manage it. Very few issues are worth a direct clash. Safety, cruelty and reasonable peace for everybody are obvious issues, but even these can usually be dealt with by diversion and friendly talk. The child need seldom be backed into a corner from which he can only explode in rage. The mother needs to ask herself, 'Why can't he? Do I really mind if he does?' The mother's mouth may be open to say 'No' when, just in time, she realizes that the issue does not really matter.

Yesterday I watched an 18-month boy ask his mother to open his sandpit. She said, 'No; nearly bathtime.' The child tried to pull the cover off himself. She removed him. He fought away, tried again, could not manage, and exploded. When he would accept comfort again, the mother said to me, 'I didn't realize he wanted to *that* much,' and opened the sandpit. If she was going to give in, eventually, she would have done much better to have accepted the child's first request.

Tantrums teach a child nothing good or useful. They are essentially unconstructive, as well as unpleasant for all concerned. Yet just as some parents feel that frightened children must be 'toughened up' (thus making them more liable to fear), so some parents feel that angry children must be 'shown they can't have it all their own way' (thus making them more liable to frustration). The child's own increasing competence deals with both his dependence and anxiety and his independence and frustration, in time. When he is big enough, and brave enough, and can manage his own body and emotions and everyday objects easily enough, he will not need so much reassurance, and he will not meet such continual frustration. When he can talk freely, about what he is thinking and imagining as well as what is there in front of him, he will be able to accept reassuring *words* in lieu of some of his mother's continual physical closeness, and remonstrating words instead of physical restrictions. Once he can understand a little more about how the world works, distinguish a little more clearly between fantasy and reality, he will be able to see the illogic of his fears, the logic of the restrictions imposed upon him.

The calmer, the smoother, the happier he is kept, while he does this vital growing up, the more inclined he will be, at 3 or 4, to use his new abilities in what we regard as a socialized manner. He has already come an extraordinarily long way since we first opened the parcel two years ago.

BIBLIOGRAPHY

1. Gairdner, D.: 'The Fate of the Foreskin', *British Medical Journal*, 1, 1949.
2. McCarthy, D., Douglas, J. and Mogford, C.: 'Circumcision in a National Sample of Four-Year-Old Children', *British Medical Journal*, 2, 1952.
3. Joint Committee of the Royal College of Obstetricians and Gynaecologists and the Population Investigation Committee: *Maternity in Great Britain*, Oxford University Press, 1948.
4. Shukla, A., Forsyth, H. A., Anderson, C. and Marway, S. M.: 'Some Aspects of Infant Nutrition in the First Year of Life: A Field Study in Dudley, Worcs, England', *British Medical Journal*, 4, 1972.
5. Taitz, L. S.: 'Infantile Overnutrition among Artificially Fed Infants in the Sheffield Region', *British Medical Journal*, 1, 1972.
6. Kleitman, N. and Engelmann, T. G.: 'Sleep Characteristics of Infants', *Journal of Applied Physiology*, 6, 1953.
7. Moore, T. and Ucko, L. E.: 'Nightwaking in Early Infancy', *Archives of Diseases in Childhood*, 32, 1957.
8. Scopes, J. W.: 'Metabolic Rate and Temperature Control in the Newborn Baby', *British Medical Bulletin*, 22 January 1966.
9. Wolff, P. H.: 'The Natural History of Crying and Other Vocalisations in Early Infancy', in *Determinants of Infant Behaviour*, vol. IV, ed. Foss, B., Methuen, 1969.
10. Scott, J. P.: 'Critical Periods in Behavioural Development', *Science*, vol. 138, 1962.
11. Harlow, H. F.: 'The Nature of Love', *American Psychologist*, 13, 673, 1958.
12. Bowlby, J.: *Attachment*, Penguin Books, 1971.
13. Prechtl, H. F. R.: 'Problems of Behavioural Studies in the Newborn Infant', in *Advances in the Study of Behaviour*, vol. I, ed. Lehrman, D. S. and Hinde, R. A., Academic Press, 1965.
14. Fantz, R. L.: 'Pattern Discrimination and Selective Atten-

tion as Determinants of Perceptual Development from Birth', in *Perceptual Development in Children*, ed. Aline, J., Kidd, J. and Rivoire, J. L., University of London Press, 1966.

15. Wolff, P. H.: 'Observations on the Early Development of Smiling', in *Determinants of Infant Behaviour*, vol. II, ed. Foss, B., Methuen, 1963.

16. Formby, D.: 'Maternal Recognition of the Infant's Cry', *Developmental Medicine and Child Neurology*, 9, 1967.

17. Eid, E. E.: 'Follow Up Study of the Physical Growth of Children Who Had Excessive Weight Gain in the First Six Months', *British Medical Journal*, 2, 1970.

18. Newson, J. and Newson, E.: *Infant Care in an Urban Community*, Allen & Unwin, 1963.

19. Illingworth, R. S.: 'Three-months Colic', *Archives of Diseases in Childhood*, 29, 1954.

20. Lakin, M.: 'Personality Factors in Mothers of Excessively Crying (Colicky) Babies', *Monograph of the Society for Research in Child Development*, 22, 1957.

21. Paradise, J. L.: 'Maternal and Other Factors in the Etiology of Infantile Colic', *Journal of the American Medical Association*, 197, 1966.

22. Jorup, S.: 'Colonic Hyperperistalsis in Neurolabile Infants', *Acta paediatrica*, Uppsala, 41, supplement 85, 1952.

23. Illingworth, R. S.: 'Evening Colic in Infants. A Double Blind Trial of Dicyclomine Hydrochloride', *Lancet*, 2, 1959.

24. Halverson, H. M.: 'An Experimental Study of Prehension in Infants by Means of Systematic Cinema Records', *Genetic Psychology Monograph*, 10, 1932.

25. Bower, T.: 'Object Perception in Infants', *Perception*, 1, 1972.

26. White, B., Castle, P. and Held, R.: 'Observations on the Development of Visually-Directed Reaching', *Child Development*, 35, 1964.

27. Burton, L., White, B. and Held, R.: 'Plasticity of Sensorimotor Development in the Human Infant', in *The Causes of Behaviour: Readings in child development and educational psychology*, ed. Rosenblith, J. R. and Allinsmith, W., Allyn & Bacon, Boston, 1966.

28. Von Békésy, G. and Rosenblith, W.: 'The Mechanical Properties of the Ear', in *Handbook of Experimental Psychology*, ed. Stevens, S. S., John Wiley, 1951.

29. Eisenberg, R. B.: 'Auditory Behaviour in the Human

Neonate. A Preliminary Report', *Journal of Speech and Hearing Research*, 7, 1964.

30. Eisenberg, R. B.: 'Auditory Behaviour in the Human Neonate; Methodological Problems and the Logical Design of Research Procedures', *Journal of Auditory Research*, 5, 1965.

31. Eisenberg, R. B.: 'Habituation to an Acoustic Pattern as an Index of Differences among Human Neonates', *Journal of Auditory Research*, 6, 1966.

32. Eisenberg, R. B.: 'Stimulus Significance as a Determinant of Newborn Responses to Sound', *Paper to Society for Research in Child Development*, New York, 1967.

33. Simner, M.: 'Response of the Newborn Infant to the Cry of Another Infant', *Paper to Society for Research in Child Development*, New York, 1969.

34. Nakazima, S.: 'A Comparative Study of the Speech Developments of Japanese and American–English in Childhood', *Studia Phonologica*, 2, 1962.

35. Rheingold, H. L.: 'The Development of Social Behaviour in the Human Infant', *Monograph of the Society for Research in Child Development*, 31, 1966.

36. Weisberg, P.: 'Social and Nonsocial Conditioning of Infant Vocalisations', *Child Development*, 34, 1963.

37. Bowlby, J.: *Maternal Care and Mental Health*, World Health Organization, 1951. Available as *Child Care and the Growth of Love*, Penguin Books, 1965.

38. Watson, J. B.: *Psychological Care of Infant and Child*, W. Norton, New York, 1928.

39. Gesell, A.: *Infancy and Human Growth*, Macmillan, 1928.

40. Gesell, A.: *The First Five Years of Life*, Methuen, latest edition 1959.

41. Gewirtz, J. L.: 'Mechanisms of Social Learning; Some Roles of Stimulation and Behaviour in Early Development', in *Handbook of Socialisation Theory and Research*, ed. Goslin, D. A., Rand McNally, 1968.

42. Piaget, J.: *The Origins of Intelligence in the Child*, Routledge & Kegan Paul, 1953.

43. Piaget, J.: *The Child's Construction of Reality*, Routledge & Kegan Paul, 1955.

44. Frank, L. K.: *On the Importance of Infancy*, Random House, 1966.

45. Dollard, J. and Miller, N. E.: *Personality and Psychotherapy*, McGraw Hill, 1950.

46. Schaffer, H. R. and Emerson, P. E.: 'The Development of Social Attachments in Infancy', *Monograph of the Society for Research in Child Development*, 29, 1964.

47. Yarrow, L. J.: 'The Development of Focused Relationships during Infancy', in *Exceptional Infant*, vol. I, ed. Hellmuth, J., Special Child Publications, 1967.

48. Ainsworth, M. D. S.: *Infancy in Uganda. Infant Care and the Growth of Attachment*, Johns Hopkins Press, 1967.

49. Kagan, J.: 'On the Need for Relativism', *American Psychologist*, 22, 1967.

50. Escalona, S. K.: *The Roots of Individuality*, Tavistock Publications, 1969.

51. Lipsitt, L. P.: 'The Development of Human Behaviour: Theoretical Considerations for Future Research', in *The Biopsychology of Development*, ed. Tobach, E., Aronson, L. and Shaw, E., Academic Press, 1971.

52. Kessen, W., Williams, E. J. and Williams, J. P.: 'Selection and Test Response Measures in the Study of the Human Newborn', *Child Development*, 32, 1961.

53. Chess, T. A., Birch, H. G. and Hertzig, M. E.: *Behavioral Individuality in Early Childhood*, New York University Press, 1964.

54. Schaefer, E. S. and Bayley, N.: 'Maternal Behaviour, Child Behaviour and Their Intercorrelations from Infancy through Adolescence', *Monograph of the Society for Research in Child Development*, 28, 1963.

55. Schaffer, H. R.: 'Activity Level as a Constitutional Determinant of Infantile Reaction to Deprivation', *Child Development*, 37, 1966.

56. Bell, R. Q.: 'Detection of Cross-Stage Relations between Transition Periods in Which the Form of Behaviour Differs Markedly: A Longitudinal Study of the Newborn and Preschool Periods', *Monograph of the Society for Research in Child Development*, 36, 1971.

57. Moss, H. A.: 'Sex, Age and State as Determinants of Mother–Infant Interaction', *Merrill-Palmer Quarterly*, 13, 1967.

58. Moss, H. A. and Robson, K. S.: 'Maternal Influence on Social/Visual Behaviour', *Child Development*, 39, 1968.

59. Moss, H. A., Robson, K. S. and Pedersen, F.: 'Determinants of Maternal Stimulation of Infants and Consequences of Treatment for Later Reactions to Strangers', *Developmental Psychology*, 1, 1969.

60. Moss, H. A. and Robson, K. S.: 'The Relation between the Amount of Time Infants Spend in Various States, and the Development of Visual Behaviour', *Child Development*, 41, 1970.

61. Caudill, W. and Weinstein, H.: 'Childcare and Infant Behaviour in Japanese and American Urban Middle Class Families', in *Yearbook of the International Sociological Association*, ed. Konig, R. and Hill, R., 1966.

62. Kimura, D.: 'Functional Assymmetry of the Brain in Dichotic Listening', *Cortex*, III, 1967.

63. Knox, C.: 'Cerebral Processing of Nonverbal Sounds in Boys and Girls', *Neuropsychologia*, 8, 1970.

64. Rosenzweig, M.: 'Effects of Environment on the Development of Brain and Behaviour', in *The Biopsychology of Behaviour*, ed. Tobach, E., Academic Press, 1971.

65. Rosenzweig, M., Bennett, E. and Diamond, M.: 'Brain Changes in Response to Experience', *Scientific American*, February 1972.

66. Schaffer, H. R. and Emerson, P. E.: 'Patterns of Response to Physical Contact in Early Human Development', *Journal of Child Psychology and Psychiatry*, 5, 1964.

67. Tanner, J. M., Whitehouse, R. H. and Takaishi, H.: 'Standards from Birth to Maturity for Height, Weight, Height Velocity and Weight Velocity: British Children', *Archives of Diseases in Childhood*, 41, 613, 1966.

68. Drillien, C. M.: *The Growth and Development of the Prematurely Born Infant*, E. and S. Livingstone, 1964.

69. Ministry of Agriculture, Fisheries and Food: *Manual of Nutrition*, H.M.S.O., 1970.

70. Department of Health and Social Security: *Recommended Intakes of Nutrients for the U.K.*, H.M.S.O., 1970.

71. Brook, C., Lloyd, J. and Wolf, H.: 'Relation between Age of Onset of Obesity and Size and Number of Adipose Cells', *British Medical Journal*, 2, 1972.

72. Guthrie, L.: 'Teething', *British Medical Journal*, 2, 1908.

73. Illingworth, R. S.: *The Normal Child*, Churchill Livingstone, 1972.

74. David, M. and Appell, G.: 'Mother–Child Relations', in *Modern Perspectives in International Child Psychiatry*, ed. Howells, J. G., Oliver & Boyd, 1969.

75. Bruner, J. S. and Koslowski, B.: 'Visually Adapted Constituents of Manipulatory Action', *Perception*, 1, 1972.

76. Bower, T.: 'The Object in the World of the Infant', *Scientific American*, October 1971.

77. Lenneberg, E. H.: 'Speech as a Motor Skill with Special Reference to Non-Aphasic Disorders', in *The Acquisition of Language*, ed. Bellugi, U. and Brown, R. W., *Monograph of the Society for Research in Child Development*, 29, 1964.

78. Irwin, O. C.: 'Language and Communication', in *Handbook of Research Methods in Child Development*, ed. Mussen, P. H., John Wiley, 1960.

79. Kagan, J.: *Change and Continuity in Infancy*, John Wiley, 1971.

80. Kagan, J. and Lewis, M.: 'Studies of Attention', *Merrill–Palmer Quarterly*, vol. II, 1965.

81. Ainsworth, M. D. S.: 'The Development of Infant–Mother Attachment', in *Review of Child Development Research*, vol. III, ed. Caldwell, B. M. and Ricciuti, H. N., Russell Sage Foundation, 1967.

82. Gewirtz, H. B. and Gewirtz, J. L.: 'Visiting and Caretaking Patterns for Kibbutz Infants: Age and Sex Trends', *American Journal of Orthopsychiatry*, 39, 1968.

83. Spitz, R.: *The First Year of Life*, International University Press, New York, 1965.

84. Morgan, G. A. and Ricciuti, H. N.: 'Infants' Response to Strangers during the First Year of Life', in *Determinants of Infant Behaviour*, ed. Foss, B., vol. IV, Methuen, 1969.

85. Robertson, J. and Robertson, J.: *A Series of Films, and Written Guides, on the Response of Young Children of Previous Good Experience to Separation from the Mother, When the Substitute Care Meets, or Fails to Meet, Their Emotional Needs*, Tavistock Institute of Human Relations, London; New York University Film Library, 1967, 1968, 1969.

86. Helfer, R. E. and Kempe, H. C.: *The Battered Child*, University of Chicago Press, 1968.

87. Erikson, E.: *Childhood and Society*, W. Norton, New York, 1950.

88. Caffey, J.: 'On the Theory and Practice of Shaking Infants; Its Potential Residual Effects of Permanent Brain Damage and Mental Retardation', *American Journal of Diseases of Children*, vol. 124, August 1972.

89. Howard, A. N. and McLean Baird, I., ed: *Nutritional Deficiencies in Modern Society* (based on a symposium held by the Food Education Society in 1972), Newman Books, 1973.

90. Spock, B.: *Dr. Spock Talks with Mothers,* Pan Books, 1962.
91. Moore, T. and Ucko, L. E.: 'Nightwaking in Early Infancy', *Archives of Diseases in Childhood,* 32, 1957.
92. Yarrow, L. J.: 'Separation from Parents during Early Childhood', in *Review of Child Development Research,* vol. I, ed. Hoffman, M. L. and Hoffman, L. W., Russell Sage Foundation, 1964.
93. Stevenson, O.: 'The First Treasured Possession', *Psychoanalytic Study of the Child,* 9, 1954.
94. Liddiard, M.: *The Mothercraft Manual; An Outline of the Work of Sir Truby King,* Churchill, 1928.
95. Spock, B.: *Baby and Child Care,* New English Library, 1969.
96. Heinstein, M.: *Child Rearing in California,* Bureau of Maternal and Child Health: State of California Department of Public Health, 1966.
97. Newson, J. and Newson, E.: *Four Years Old in an Urban Community,* Allen & Unwin, 1968.
98. Dimson, S. B.: 'Toilet Training and Enuresis', *British Medical Journal,* 2, 1959.
99. Brazelton, T. B.: 'A Child-Oriented Approach to Toilet Training', *Pediatrics,* 29, 1962.
100. Griffiths, R.: *The Abilities of Babies,* University of London Press, 1964.
101. Smith A.: *The Body,* Allen & Unwin, 1968, Penguin Books, revised edition 1974.
102. Illingworth, R. S.: *The Development of the Infant and Young Child,* E. & S. Livingstone, 1970.
103. Geber, M. and Dean, R. F. A.: 'Gesell Tests in African Children', *Pediatrics,* 20, 1957.
104. Knobloch, H.: 'Precocity of African Children', *Pediatrics,* 22, 1958.
105. Pavenstedt, E.: *The Drifters. Children of Disorganised Lower Class Families,* Churchill, 1967.
106. Zelazo, P., Zelazo, N. and Kolb, S.: '"Walking" in the Newborn', *Science,* vol. 176, April 1972.
107. Bower, T.: *Development in Infancy,* W. H. Freeman, San Francisco, 1974.
108. Kagan, J.: 'Do Infants Think?', *Scientific American,* March 1972.
109. Gardner, R. A. and Gardner, B. C.: 'Teaching Sign Language to a Chimpanzee', *Science,* vol. 165, 1969.

110. Premack, A. and Premack, D.: 'Teaching Language to an Ape', *Scientific American*, October 1972.

111. Lenneberg, E. H.: *Biological Foundations of Language*, John Wiley, 1967.

112. Lenneberg, E. H.: 'The Natural History of Language', in *Genesis of Language*, ed. Smith, F. and Miller, G. A., M.I.T. Press, Cambridge, Mass., 1966.

113. Bassler, L. S.: 'Hemiplegia of Early Onset and the Faculty of Speech, with Special Reference to the Effects of Hemipherectomy', *Brain*, 85, 1962.

114. Mowrer, O. H.: 'Hearing and Speaking: An Analysis of Language Learning', *Journal of Speech and Hearing Disorders*, vol. 23, 1960.

115. McCarthy, D.: 'Affective Aspects of Language Learning', in *Perceptual Development in Children*, ed. Kidd, A. H. and Rivoire, J. L., University of London Press, 1966.

116. Mura Jun Ichi: 'The Sounds of Infants', *Studia Phonologica*, vol. 3, 1963–4.

117. Bullowa, M., Jones, L. G. and Duckert, A.: 'The Acquisition of a Word', *Language and Speech*, vol. 7, 1964.

118. Macfarlane, J. W., Allen, L. and Honzik, M. P.: *Behaviour Problems of Normal Children*, University of California Press, 1954.

119. Muellner, S. R.: 'Obstacles to the Treatment of Primary Enuresis', *Journal of the American Medical Association*, 178, 1961.

120. Gesell, A.: 'The Ontogenesis of Infant Behaviour', in *Manual of Child Psychology*, ed. Carmichael, L., John Wiley, 1946.

121. Blatz, W. E.: *Human Security. Some Reflections*, University of Toronto Press, 1966.

122. Ainsworth, M. and Wittig, B. A.: 'Attachment and Exploratory Behaviour of One Year Olds in a Strange Situation', in *Determinants of Infant Behaviour*, vol. IV, ed. Foss, B., Methuen, 1969.

123. Anderson, J. W.: 'Attachment Behaviour Out of Doors', in *Ethological Studies of Human Behaviour*, ed. Burton Jones, N., Cambridge University Press, 1971.

124. Flavell, J. H.: *The Developmental Psychology of Jean Piaget*, Van Nostrand, 1963.

125. Burt, C., Miller, E. and Moodie, W.: *How the Mind Works*, Appleton-Century-Crofts, 1934.

126. Bayley, N.: 'Mental Development Index', in *Manual of*

Child Psychology, ed. Mussen, P. H., John Wiley, 1970.

127. Stott, L. S. and Ball, R. S.: 'Infant and Pre-School Mental Tests: Review and Evaluation', *Monograph of the Society for Research in Child Development*, 30, 1965.

128. Lewis, M. and McGurk, H.: 'Evaluation of Infant Intelligence Scales', *Science*, vol. 178, 1972.

129. Escalona, S. and Corman, H.: 'The Evaluation of Piaget's Hypothesis Concerning the Development of Sensori-Motor Intelligence: Methodological Issues', *Paper to Society for Research in Child Development*, New York, 1967.

130. Bayley, N.: 'Mental Growth during the First Three Years. A Developmental Study of Sixty-One Children by Repeated Tests', *Genetic Psychology Monograph*, 14, 1933.

131. Mittler, P.: *The Psychological Assessment of Mental and Physical Handicaps*, Methuen, 1970.

132. Gesell, A.: *Developmental Diagnosis*, Hoeber, New York, 1947.

133. Prechtl, H. F. R. and Stemmer, C. J., 'The Choreiform Syndrome in Children', *Developmental Medicine and Child Neurology*, 4, 119, 1962.

134. O'Connor, N. and Hermelin, B.: 'Cognitive Deficits in Children', *British Medical Bulletin*, 27, no. 3, 1971.

135. Bernstein, B.: 'A Public Language: Some Sociological Implications of a Linguistic Form', *British Journal of Sociology*, vol. 10, 1959.

136. Skinner, B. F.: *Verbal Behaviour*, Appleton-Century-Crofts, 1957.

137. Chomsky, N.: *Syntactic Structure*, Mouton, The Hague, 1957.

138. Chomsky, N.: *Aspects of the Theory of Syntax*, M.I.T. Press, Cambridge, Mass., 1965.

139. Menyuk, P.: *The Acquisition and Development of Language*, Prentice-Hall, 1971.

140. Przetacznikowa, M.: 'Study in the Use of the Longitudinal Method for Investigating the Verbal Behaviour of Children of Pre-School Age', in *Determinants of Behavioural Development*, ed. Monks, F. J., Academic Press, 1972.

141. Winitz, H. and Irwin, O. C.: 'Syllabic and Phonetic Structure of Infants' Early Words', *Journal of Speech and Hearing Research*, I, 1958.

142. Ervin-Tripp, S. M.: 'Imitations and Structural Changes in Children's Language', in *New Directions in the Study of Language*, ed. Lenneberg, E., M.I.T. Press, Cambridge, Mass., 1964.

143. Slobin, D. I.: 'Some Thoughts on the Relation of Comprehension to Speech', *Paper to American Speech and Hearing Association*, San Francisco, 1964.

144. Bowlby, J.: *Separation, Anxiety and Anger*, Hogarth Press, 1973.

145. Leach, P. J.: 'A Critical Study of the Literature Concerning Rigidity', in *Thought and Personality*, ed. Warr, P. B., Penguin Education, 1970.

146. Livingston, S.: 'Breath-Holding Spells in Children', *Journal of the American Medical Association*, 212, 1970.

INDEX OF AUTHORS

INDEX

MORE ABOUT PENGUINS
AND PELICANS

Penguinews, which appears every month, contains details of all the new books issued by Penguins as they are published. From time to time it is supplemented by *Penguins in Print*, which is a complete list of all titles available. (There are some five thousand of these.)

A specimen copy of *Penguinews* will be sent to your free on request. For a year's issues (including the complete lists) please send 50p if you live in the British Isles, or 75p if you live elsewhere. Just write to Dept EP, Penguin Books Ltd, Harmondsworth, Middlesex, enclosing a cheque or postal order, and your name will be added to the mailing list.

In the U.S.A.: For a complete list of books available from Penguin in the United States write to Dept CS, Penguin Books Inc., 7110 Ambassador Road, Baltimore, Maryland 21207.

In Canada: For a complete list of books available from Penguin in Canada write to Penguin Books Canada Ltd, 41 Steelcase Road West, Markham, Ontario.

THE PSYCHOLOGY OF CHILDHOOD
AND ADOLESCENCE

C. I. Sandström

In this concise study of the processes of growing up Professor Sandström has produced a book which, although it is perfectly suited to the initial needs of university students and teachers in training, will appeal almost as much to parents and ordinary readers. His text covers the whole story of human physical and mental growth from conception to puberty.

Outlining the scope and history of developmental psychology, Professor Sandström goes on to detail the stages of growth in the womb, during the months after birth, and (year by year) up to the age of ten. There follows chapters on physical development, learning and perception, motivation. language and thought, intelligence, the emotions, social adjustment, and personality. The special conditions of puberty and of schooling are handled in the final chapters.

Throughout this masterly study the author necessarily refers to norms of developement; these neatly represent the average stages of growing up, but (as Professor Mace comments in his introduction) they must only be applied to individual children with caution.

CONTRARY IMAGINATIONS
A Psychological Study of the English Schoolboy

Liam Hudson

Why does one boy become an arts specialist and his neighbour a scientist? Why do some pupils use their brains effectively and others not? Do we pay enough attention to personality in assessing ability?

In this controversial study Dr Liam Hudson, Director of the Research Unit on Intellectual Development at King's College, Cambridge, argues that personality counts for as much as ability in the student's choice of subject. He distinguishes between two types of personality, the scientific 'converger' and the artistic, imaginative 'diverger', and examines examples of each in depth. He then speculates on the nature of original thought, and the ways in which intellectual and personal qualities interact. His argument combines the disciplines of intelligence testing and psychoanalysis in a highly original way, and his clear and jargon-free presentation will appeal to all those interested in intelligent children, in psychology, or in both.

(Not for sale in the U.S.A.)

THE PSYCHOLOGY OF PLAY

Susanna Millar

The term 'play' has long been a linguistic waste-paper basket for behaviour which look voluntary but seems to have no biological or social use. What counts as 'play'? What explanations have been given for it, and how far are they adequate Why do children and the young of many animal species play? To answer such questions Susanna Millar here discusses psychological theories about play and reviews observational and experimental studies of the play of animals of different evolutionary development, of children at different ages, in cultures, and in therapy. She relates different forms of play to a number of underlying behavioural mechanisms which modern methods of experimental psychology are beginning to uncover. Susanna Millar argues that play is behaviour which looks paradoxical, but has a variety of biological functions related to childhood development and other specific conditions.

PATTERNS OF INFANT CARE

John and Elizabeth Newson

Mother, doctor, health visitor, midwife – Spiock, Gibbens de Kok, Truby King ... the amount of theory and advice, both professional and amateur, that showers on the young mother is equalled only by its astonishing contradictions. And indeed, as the authors quietly point out, 'very few theories of child rearing have been subjected to the inconvenience of being reconciled with the empirical evidence.'

What then is that evidence? Armed with common sense and a tape recorder, the authors interviewed in their Nottingham homes over 700 mothers of one-year-old children to find out, quite simply, how babies are brought up in England today. The result is a landmark in our knowledge of childhood The answers parents gave on subjects ranging from breast- and bottle-feeding, sleeping, eating, and punishment, to father's place in the home and class differences in infant rearing make a fascinating and, on occasions, hilarious kaleidoscope of life with young children.

'Wonderfully human piece of sociological research' – *Yorkshire Post*